Beth,

Thanks for all your help
with my book! Hope you
enjoy reading this final
version,

    Your Peace Corps friend,

       Don

Mukho Memories

A Peace Corps / Korea Memoir

Don Haffner

D1521134

MUKHO

MEMORIES

묵호 추억

DON HAFFNER

On this page, the title of the book and the author's name are written in a lettering style designed by the author. The book's title is repeated in archaic Hangeul – the Korean alphabet. The oval chop (seal) is the author's Korean name in Chinese characters. The round chop is the author's Korean name in Hangeul.

First published by Dog Ear Publishing
4011 Vincennes Rd
Indianapolis, IN 46268
www.dogearpublishing.net

ISBN: 978-1-4575-5384-4

This book is printed on acid-free paper.

Printed in the United States of America

Dedication

This book is dedicated to:

My parents, Don and Betty Haffner; my son, Otto Haffner; and my wife and proofreader, Carol Benson, who proved to me that "love is lovelier the second time around." Sing it along with me! ("The Second Time" words by Sammy Cohen, music by Jimmy Van Heusen, performed by Bing Crosby, Frank Sinatra and many others)

Acknowledgments

Gamsahamnida (thank you) to my Returned Peace Corps Volunteer (RPCV) friends, Beth Gamburd, Ed Haugh, and Katherine M. Forcey, who were kind enough to read the first draft of *Mukho Memories*. I've incorporated most of their suggestions and corrections into this final version, especially their advice about which superfluous parts to remove from the very rough abstract that I had sent them. There are still a few superfluous parts that I have left in just because I decided I liked them too much, but this final version is greatly improved thanks to them.

I'd also like to thank my School for International Training grad school friend and fellow writer T. Lee Mitchell for reading a later and shorter rendition of *Mukho Memories*. His reading with non-Peace Corps/Korea eyes gave further suggestions that hopefully will make the story more understandable to those without Peace Corps experience and/or the experience of having lived and worked in Korea. He also found many errors, which I duly corrected.

Most of all, my heartfelt thanks to my wife, Carol Benson, whose Catholic parochial school English grammar and spelling training was so much better than my Downriver Detroit public school education. Also, English was always my worst academic subject in school. When I get to words with more than four letters my spelling gets a little hazardous. My cognizance of which two-word combos are actually one word and which for some unknown reason stay as two words is also very shaky. Carol made hundreds of thousands, if not millions, of corrections that I have incorporated into this greatly improved, almost ready for prime time (Is "prime time" one word or two?) published narrative.

The aforementioned people all helped to make this book much more interesting and readable than it otherwise would have been. Trust me when I say that the mistakes you might find herein are all mine, all homegrown, even though a huge number were corrected thanks to the aid of those mentioned above.

I want to also give a special thank you to Fred B. Fred is an Albion College friend, who saved and returned the letters that I had sent to him throughout my Peace Corps/Korea experience. In addition, I thank him for taking a photograph of the copy of the "Dying Gaul' statue at Jasmine Hill Gardens, Wetumpka, Alabama. (The original is in Rome, Italy.)

Thanks also to you, dear reader, for glancing at (if you got this far you must at least be glancing), reading, or actually perusing this book about my mental and physical journey during my three years of volunteering in the Peace Corps.

Note on Romanization

The McCune-Reischauer system of Romanization was used exclusively in Korea until near the end of my three years in the Peace Corps (1972–1975). Then the Korean Government began using a newer Revised Romanization system. Most maps produced since the mid-1970s use this newer system. Mukho did not change spelling with the new system, but Taegu became Daegu, Pusan became Busan, etc. Shortly after I finished my Peace Corps service the town of Mukho disappeared from the Korean map. It merged with the smaller town just to its south, Bupyeong, and was given the new name of Donghae City.

For the Korean place names, words, and phrases mentioned in the book I have for the most part tried to use the Revised Romanization system. (In a few cases I actually use the Don Haffner unofficial method.) In other words, I am not completely consistent. I agree with Ralph Waldo Emerson in that, "A foolish consistency is the hobgoblin of little minds, adored by little statesmen and philosophers and divines."

Although the new revised system tends to use more letters, it doesn't use the accent marks that were used in many words with McCune-Reischauer, which makes the new system a little simpler. There are a couple of cases where I use the McCune-Reischauer spelling at the beginning of the book on purpose; one is the spelling of a city (Kangnung), and the other of a monument (Tongnip-mun). I use these McCune-Reischauer spellings in order to give examples in the book of the changes in spelling with the new Revised Romanization system and my personal reaction to them at the time. These changes become obvious when the newer spellings are given in the book.

Map of South Korea

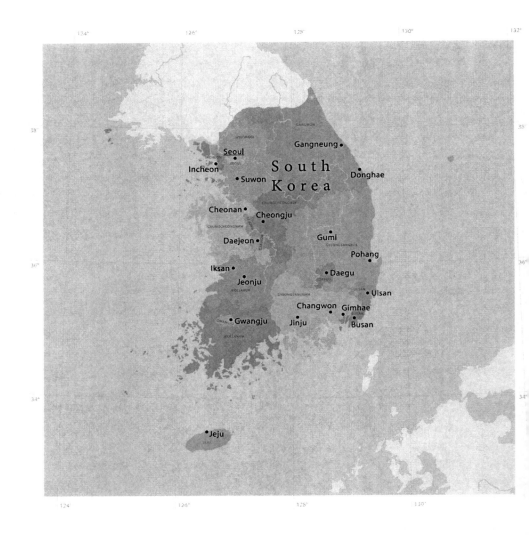

Preface

This is it!
This is me!
Warts and all,
For all to see.
No more rewriting, reworking the parts,
I know each paragraph by heart.
(Sung to the tune of "This Is It" written by Mack David and Jerry Livingston, as performed by Bugs Bunny and Daffy Duck)

It was in 1990 during the absolute worst period of my life that I started writing this book. I had the beginning of it all figured out and the ending too, just about as you'll read them here now. It was to encompass my three years in the Peace Corps for the most part. I figured I just had to fill in the middle and I'd be done. After typing about five pages in 1990, I quit. Life was too hectic, and I just wasn't ready to write it all down. I printed out what little I'd completed, stuck those five pages in a file, and got busy with other things like raising my son as a single parent (but with a lot of help from my mother and father), writing songs, recording a CD, and working for a living. Twenty-two years later, at the end of the summer of 2012, I dug out the file and decided it was time to fill in the middle. Filling in the middle has ended up being a lot harder and taking a lot longer than I thought it would, but here is the finished product.

Oddly enough, I always thought I'd be famous one way or another: for my singing, my songwriting, or both (go to Youtube and enter "Haffhere"); for my poetry; for my playwriting (I wrote one short play in college); or maybe now for my nonfiction writing. If not, I also have a great idea for a TV reality show— *Skinny Dipping with the Stars*. Maybe I'll be famous for that.

I was semi-famous during my years of working as the *chibujang* (Resident Director) for the Korea Branch of the Pearl S. Buck Foundation (PSBF), where I worked from 1979 to 1988. I have a big, thick binder called "Don's Fifteen Minutes of Fame," mostly filled with articles from Korean and American publications mentioning me—some with photographs of me in which I'm surrounded by several of the Amerasians (children fathered by Americans, usually U.S. military personnel, and abandoned in Asia) that PSBF was helping. Those were the days.

But this is my story as I remember it of my Peace Corps experience in the town of Mukho, Korea, now known as Donghae-shi (East Sea City). I did not keep a diary or write little notes on calendars. There are some quotes in these pages from a few letters and documents that I managed to save, but most of the stories are taken from my memory bank. (Or is it a credit union? I'm not sure; forty years later, parts of my story are a little foggy.) The conversations and events herein all happened, but I might not always have the right people at the right event or the right words coming out of the right mouth. Also, the sequence of events may not be quite correct. The events all happened, but they might be a bit jumbled in the telling due to my faulty memory.

Some of the stories to follow I've told over and over throughout the years, and those who have known me will recognize them. But many of the stories included herein I've never told to anyone. Being old now, I trust enough years have gone by that I can tell these experiences. Hopefully, the people I've had the pleasure to know throughout my life will not mind my revealing these conversations, occurrences, and events. But just in case, I have changed most of the names of those mentioned in the following pages, in the event that I've said anything they'd rather I hadn't.

Don Haffner
15 August 2016
Greater Detroit, Michigan

A Note from the Head Proofreader

I am so proud of my husband, the author of this book, for all of his accomplishments and contributions. He has dedicated his life to doing good through education and nonprofit organizations, and I believe all of this work had its roots in his Peace Corps experience in Korea in the 1970s. I've been hearing some of these stories over the years, but some are new to me. Anyone who has met Don knows that his time in Korea had a great effect on him. In fact, I think he is part Korean now. In 2011 I finally had the opportunity to travel to Korea with Don, to see it for the first time, and what an amazing experience that was! I now know firsthand why he loves Korea and its people so much.

The writing of this book was a labor of love. Thanks to all who helped. Long live the Peace Corps!

Carol Benson
September 2016

Table of Contents

CHAPTER 1

Day of Destiny

Unbeknownst to me, this day was to be my day of destiny. This day was to be the day that changed my life, the first day of the rest of my life. But it started as a typical day.

The bells of the Albion College chapel rang eleven times as I lay half asleep in my dorm room. I heard a few of the guys on my corridor out in the hall returning from their ten o'clock classes as I sat up in bed to look out the window. It was a typical late-winter-moving-into-early-spring Thursday in Michigan, cloudy and gray. There were breaks in the clouds here and there, and the sun was trying to shine through but just wasn't quite succeeding. I rubbed the sleepy fuzziness from my eyes and looked around the room.

It was the last semester of my senior year, and unlike most students at Albion College, I had a room to myself because I was an RA (Resident Assistant), a dorm counselor, or maybe more accurately a dorm advisor. I really didn't counsel much or advise either but mostly was an upperclassman buddy for the freshman guys on my corridor, all twenty-four of them. I lived three out of my four years in college in a freshman dorm, one year when I myself was a freshman, obviously, and the last two years as a freshman dorm RA. (My sophomore year I lived in the Sigma Nu fraternity house.) Since college I have often told people the reason I am not normal is because I spent three out of four years in freshman dorms while in college—some truth to that!

My room faced toward the west, and my corridor was Second West of Suzy Hall. You might ask why a guys' dorm would be called Suzy Hall, and I wouldn't blame you for asking. It had been an all-female dorm until my senior year and was known as Suzanna Wesley Hall, "Suzy" for short. Between my junior and senior years, the administration in their esteemed wisdom decided to make it the freshman dorm for both male and female students. The center portion and the first small sections on the east and west wings were now set up for freshman guys, and the longer east and west sections extending back from this guys' part were for the first-year gals. The official name was changed to Wesley Hall, but it was and will always be Suzy to me.

I slowly glanced around my room this fateful morning. The walls and the built-in desks were covered with an eclectic bunch of stuff that I had collected over the past four years of college. In the corner, sitting on the desk on the left side of the room, was a battered, four-foot-high torpedo-shaped brass and beveled glass chandelier from the old Parker Inn. The Parker Inn had been abandoned for years. Earlier in the semester two of the guys on my corridor and I had reconnoitered the place and noticed that there were three of these chandeliers in the lobby. On another night, we went back in and took them down, lugged them into a car I'd borrowed from one of my Sigma Nu fraternity brothers, and drove back to the dorm. We each kept one. Mine was propped up on the desk on the left side of my room and leaning against the walls in the corner. I planned to have it repaired and installed over the front door of my southern plantation-style mansion, which I was sure I would get when I became rich and famous someday. Decades later, still far from famous and very poor, I sold it "as-is" at a garage sale.

In between the two desks was a window. The desk on the right side of my room I kept clear in case I ever needed to do some studying. I rarely worked in my room, though, because I went to the library most nights Sunday through Thursday and did any studying I had to do there. Above this desk was a "KEEP OUT: positively no admittance" sign. It was printed on heavy poster board and mounted to an old-looking piece of ¾ inch plywood. During our freshman year, this sign had been nailed to a tree in front of the new science center, which was under construction just across the street from Seaton Hall, the freshman boys' dorm at the time. I liked the antique look of it, so late one evening I extricated it from the tree it was nailed to and hung it in my dorm room.

Next to the "KEEP OUT" sign but on the side wall was a plaque that stated:

MIAA CHAMPS
1969 SOCCER
Presented to
DON HAFFNER
IN RECOGNITION OF YOUR
OUTSTANDING CONTRIBUTION
TO THIS CHAMPIONSHIP TEAM

I had never played soccer in my life before going to college. I'm not sure I had ever even seen a soccer match. But I noticed a sign in the gym during orientation week which said that soccer was to be a league sport for the first time in 1968, and players (or at least warm bodies) were needed. It sounded interesting, exotic, foreign, so I tried out. Having a fairly warm body, I made the team.

I can tell you it was a joy to have been on the 1969 Albion College championship soccer team, as it was the only championship team of any kind I have ever played on, and so far (up to 2015) it is the only championship soccer team Albion has ever had. Hopefully that will change one of these years.

Next to the plaque was a photo of the 1969 soccer team. I'm standing next to the coach and look so young. I am clean-shaven and have short hair—more on this later.

On the same wall to the right of the soccer team photograph was a sign that said on the top half in French:

TEST
DE GROSSESSE
RÉSULTAT
APRÉS 2 HEURES

As shown, the Es in RESULTAT and APRES had an accent mark over them. Don't ask me why, I flunked French in high school. (More on that later too.) Under this French part it read in English:

PREGNANCY
TESTS
RESULTS
IN 2 HOURS

No accent marks on the English part. Shouldn't we have fun accents like the French? I don't get it. This sign was a souvenir from the summer of 1968's International Key Club (High School Junior Kiwanis Club) Convention in Montréal, Canada. I appropriated it from a wall in downtown Montréal.

By this point you are probably thinking that I was quite the kleptomaniac in my youth and should have been locked up. For one thing, I never got caught, which was lucky. I also ceased and desisted from my life of crime after I'd turned twenty-one, and I have tried to be a fine and upstanding citizen since then.

Attached to the top of the "Pregnancy Test" sign was a small button that read, "Stop at two," a motto of Zero Population Growth (ZPG). I had been a charter member of Albion College's ZPG group. ZPG was an organization based on the Malthusian ideas of Dr. Paul R. Ehrlich as presented in his famous book *The Population Bomb* published in 1968. My original copy is still sitting somewhere on our bookshelves. It stated that, at some point in the future, the population "shit" would hit the planet's ecosystem "fan." That made sense to me, and in the second semester of my freshman year, I and a handful of other concerned students formed the Albion College Chapter of Zero Population Growth.

Next to the "Pregnancy Tests" sign with the "Stop at two" button on top was a framed poster of the singer/songwriter Harry Nilsson. The poster came with his *Nilsson Schmilsson* album. It is a somewhat fuzzy replica of the album cover. I've always admired Harry, who had an amazing voice and was also a talented songwriter. (My favorite song on the jukebox at the Sigma Nu fraternity house at Albion was "Rainmaker" by Harry.) The photo shows him standing in front of a refrigerator in a wide-whale corduroy robe with his right hand in his robe pocket and his left hand crossed in front of him holding a pipe. He had hair down nearly to his shoulders, a mustache, and a beard. He also had the misfortune of having a face that looked a god-awful lot like mine. In addition, during much of my junior and senior years in college, I too had hair nearly down to my shoulders, a mustache, and a beard. All the guys on my corridor assumed it was a photo of me. Some would ask where the picture was taken and how I had gotten it enlarged. I told them that one year at the Michigan State Fair they'd had a booth where you could go in and get your picture taken with different clothing and backgrounds. I told my corridor mates, "I thought it was fun to wear a robe in front of the fridge while holding my dad's pipe." They all said it was great, and this little white lie of mine went on for quite a while until one of the guys on the corridor saw Nilsson's album somewhere and ratted me out.

Next to Harry's photo was a picture of a Playboy bunny named Maikin. Back in the spring of 1968, a high school friend and I went to the Detroit Autorama. Maikin, a cute, petite, blonde, blue-eyed Danish gal, was there signing photos of herself (fully dressed, both her and the photo), and we got in line to get her picture and autograph.

"Hi, Maikin," I said when I got up to the table.

"What's your name?"

"My name's Don. Could you write 'To Don, Love, Maikin?'"

"Sure," she said while writing with felt pen across her picture.

"Wow, thanks," I brilliantly articulated. Maikin's picture with "To Don, Love, Maikin" written on it had hung on my dorm room wall for all four years of college. Of course, when guys each year asked where I got the picture, I told them that Maikin and I had dated because my Uncle Hugh invited me to the Playboy Mansion in Chicago upon occasion, and on one such visit Maikin and I hit it off. Many would believe me until they later figured out that though his family name and mine sound almost alike when said fast, mine is H-A-F-F-N-E-R while

Hugh's is H-E-F-N-E-R. Oh, how as a youth in downriver Detroit I had wished that Hugh Hefner really was my uncle. Come to think of it, almost fifty years later, I still wish Hugh Hefner was my uncle.

On the opposite wall in my dorm room was a collage that I had thrown together one night at home at my parents' house during the summer between my freshman and sophomore years. Besides pictures of the Beatles and Cream, there are many cutesy sayings cut out of magazines like, "I just washed my hair and *can* do a thing with it."

Most of these wall hangings from my senior year dorm room are still around our house. Today the "Keep Out: positively no admittance" sign is attached to the door of the storeroom in our basement as a warning to all trespassers. The Harry Nilsson poster, the "Test De Grossese Résultat Aprés 2 Heures—Pregnancy Tests Results in 2 Hours" sign with the "Stop at two" button, and the collage are also in the basement hanging above my workbench. The photo of the 1969 Albion Soccer Team and the MIAA Champs plaque are on another wall in the finished part of our basement. The chandelier was sold in a garage sale as earlier noted, while the picture of Maikin must have been thrown away after college. Sadly, it's gone.

The last thing I glanced at before getting up that morning was the two-gallon fish tank on the corner of the desk on the right side of the room with a few tiger barbs in it. Especially at night before going to sleep, it was relaxing and mesmerizing to just sit and watch the fish swimming around, sort of like meditating or getting high on nature.

On this late-winter day of my senior year in college, though, I needed to get out of bed. It was getting late, and I had to get down to my job as a dishwasher. This was the seventh out of eight semesters that I had worked as a dishwasher for the food service company, which we lovingly called the "Food Circus." I washed the dishes in the basement dining area of Suzy Hall. In my last semester at Albion, I was now, of course, a highly skilled dishwasher, and it has been comforting all of my life to know that I have this skill to fall back on in hard times.

After an hour and a half of washing dishes, I stopped off at the student mailboxes, which were also in the basement. I opened my mailbox and in it was a large manila envelope. When I pulled it out I saw the return address, "Peace Corps, Washington, D.C." My heart began pounding. Here was what could be the answer to my prayers. I had filled out a Peace Corps application in the fall semester, and here was my answer. Entering the Peace Corps was my life's plan, my one and only plan. If the answer was "NO," I had no backup plan for my life after college. I hurriedly opened the envelope, read the cover letter, and "**YES**," they were offering me a chance to go to the Republic of Korea—South Korea—to teach English as a Second Language (ESL) at the middle-school level. Funny, English had always been my worst academic subject, and now it looked like I might become an English teacher. Even funnier, I had started working toward a teaching certificate, on my father's suggestion, earlier in my college career, but I had quit. I was going to major in history, no problem there, and minor in geology until I took a geology class in sedimentation. Dr. John Penobscot taught this class, and I was one of three students. It is hard to hide in the back when there are only two other students in class with you. But worse than not being able to hide was the boredom I felt. I could hardly stay awake in class and hated the laboratory work. This wasn't Dr. Penobscot's fault; he was a great instructor and had lots of interesting stories about his days working for one of America's largest oil companies. I just wasn't interested in the subject. On top of this, the first education course I took bored me even more than Dr. Penobscot's sedimentation class did. Both classes to me were like watching paint dry, watching grass grow, or more appropriately like watching sediment settling in murky water. I thought, *"Oh Lord! Gag me."* I never took another education class or geology class at Albion after those two disasters. In another irony of my life, about a decade and a half after college, I got a MS degree from the University of Southern California in—drum roll—**EDUCATION!** Years later I found the graduate-level education classes to be very interesting, while the undergrad pedagogy course had proven to be brutally tedious. When I informed my father that I wasn't going to get a teaching certificate at Albion, he was upset. He kept telling me that with the certificate I'd always have a career to fall back on. I should have reminded him of my dishwashing skill, but instead I informed him I didn't think I wanted to be an elementary or secondary-level teacher in America anyway. Now I was being offered a Peace Corps position as an English teacher at the middle-school level in Korea. Poetic justice, or maybe injustice! Besides the cover letter there was a pamphlet with photographs of volunteers together with Korean middle-school boys and girls in their black military-like uniforms and pictures of volunteers' living accommodations—small rooms with little or no furniture and bedroll-like things that they slept on that looked about as thick as a sleeping bag.

I don't know when I first began thinking about joining the Peace Corps. I was only nine years old when John F. Kennedy stood on the steps of the University of Michigan's Union and gave a short speech, first mentioning the idea of the Peace Corps. On the forty-year anniversary of JFK's speech, I stood at that very same spot and read Kennedy's speech to a crowd of fellow Southeast Michigan (SEMI) Returned Peace Corps Volunteers (RPCV), representatives from Peace

Corps Washington and University of Michigan students and staff. Our local SEMI Returned Peace Corps Volunteer group had been involved in the planning of this commemorative event. When we started discussing who should read JFK's speech, one of the other members of our group suggested that I should because my job then was the Studio Director for Recording for the Blind & Dyslexic's (RFB&D) Michigan Unit (RFB&D, now known as Learning Ally, records textbooks for use by blind and dyslexic students). I didn't bother to mention that I didn't actually read the textbooks we recorded, but in fact supervised the volunteer readers who did. At any rate, I got picked, and I had the honor of being John F. Kennedy's stand-in. I began by asking the assembled crowd of "tens of thousands" (actually maybe fifty) to imagine a younger, more handsome man with a lot more hair. Then I read his short speech from forty years earlier that he had given during his campaign for the presidency and which included his first mention that there should be a Peace Corps-like organization. Although I have a vague remembrance of our fifth grade class having had a mock election in the fall of 1960 (and I'm sure Nixon won), I know I had not heard of the Peace Corps at that point.

I do think that *National Geographic* magazine had a lot to do with my desire to go overseas and live in a foreign country. *National Geographic* was sort of like Uncle Hugh's *Playboy* magazine in that lots of people looked at the pictures, but few really read the articles in either of them. I actually did read all the captions under the photographs, even though I rarely read the articles, but I often got the gist of what the articles were about from these captions. Of course, *National Geographic,* like *Playboy,* was also mostly known for its fine photographs. In addition, it was the one place where pre-adolescent boys could openly see bare-breasted women. My parents were quite conservative when it came to nudity or sexual matters. I never got the sex talk that you always hear about between fathers and sons. My parents just didn't talk about such things. Come to think of it, I never gave my son the talk either. My mother did not like nudity, even in fine art. She always dressed very conservatively, and the worst part for her after having a stroke in 2011 was being in the hospital with those god-awful gowns they make people wear. But even though there were never any girlie magazines in our house, occasionally *National Geographic* would have an article about native people in the Amazon or in other places where the women didn't wear anything above the waist. I'd practically wear out the page corners in that section of the magazine checking out the women over and over. Even before getting *National Geographic* each month, my Aunt Ruth had given me a subscription to *Ranger Rick* (no semi-naked women there), the children's version of *National Geographic.* Later, when

I got into my early teens, Aunt Ruth switched to a subscription of the famous yellow-covered real *National Geographic.* I kept every issue until, after a while, half the basement was filled with them. George Carlin once joked that if everyone in the U.S. got rid of their back issues of *National Geographic,* the North American continent would raise by several inches. (It might be a way to offset global warming for us. Florida wouldn't end up underwater that way.) While looking at the pictures in *National Geographic,* I dreamed of visiting and living in various exotic places. When I heard about the Peace Corps, it just seemed like the natural thing to do.

Before my friends and I got our driver's licenses, we used to get on the Allen Road bus, and for fifty cents we could ride it to downtown Detroit. For us, Detroit was an exotic, exciting place to wander around. We would go into the downtown Hudson's department store. There we would wander floor after floor.

On my twelfth birthday, my parents threw me a party and for my present I got a record player, which looked like a suitcase with detachable speakers. (It still works, but I have to let it warm up for five to ten minutes or so before it gets going to the proper speed.) The first album I ever bought with my own money was on one of our trips downtown to Hudson's. They had a large record department, and I went to the classical section. There I looked for the "Haffner Symphony" by Mozart. I found an Angel Stereo record called "Mozart Symphonies: No. 35 in D, 'Haffner,' No. 36 in C, 'Linz' and the Overture to 'The Abduction from the Seraglio'" by Otto Klemperer: Philharmonia Orchestra recorded in 1962. The front cover had a view of the town square of Dresden, Germany, as it looked in the eighteenth century. It said on the back, "There is certainly no better *Haffner* on disc (THE GRAMOPHONE)." That was good enough for me. I bought it with what little money I had at the time, and I still play it on occasion. I had heard about the Haffner Symphony because, in our family lore, we were descended from Sigmund Haffner of Salzburg, Austria, who was Burgermeister (Mayor) during the late 1700s. The Haffner Symphony was written for his daughter's wedding, and the first movement of it was played by a string quartet at my 2003 wedding to Carol. In the 1980s, I did some genealogical research and found that, for one thing, Burgermeister Haffner had no sons who lived to adulthood, so we couldn't be his direct descendents. In addition, our branch of the Haffner family is from Zallenfelde, a small farming community in East Prussia, now called Salkowice, near the city of Gdansk, Poland (Danzig when it was German). So this family legend on my father's side of the family turned out to be erroneous. But even though we're not related to Burgermeister Sigmund Haffner, I still like the Haffner Symphony.

After exploring Hudson's we'd often go over to Cobo Hall and wander all of its hallways. There we'd linger in the area where they had plaques of all the great Detroit sports stars from the Tigers, Lions, and Red Wings teams. The Pistons were still very new to Detroit at that time and were not yet represented.

We'd usually also go to the Metropolitan Building at 33 John R Street and go up to the 9th floor, room 908, where my Uncle Bob had his shop, Haffner Jewelry. (Catchy name, right?) The Neo-Gothic building, which was opened in 1925, was colloquially known as the "Jewelers Building." My grandfather, Otto Haffner, was a jeweler, and Uncle Bob had learned from his father as well as other jewelers in the building, and in 1951 opened his own shop there. In 1978 the owners lost the building in a tax lien foreclosure to the City of Detroit, and the tenants in the building were forced to move out. My uncle moved Haffner Jewelry out to Royal Oak, a suburb north of Detroit. The Metropolitan Building ended up being a hollow shell, owned by the city of Detroit. A few years ago my son, Otto, and I skulked around the abandoned building looking for any possible vestige of my uncle's shop or my grandfather Otto's, which had been on the 8th floor. Unfortunately, nothing much remained intact inside the building, and all the doors had been removed, or at least the glass had been broken out. My son and I were hoping to find a door with "Haffner Jewelry" or my grandfather's "Service Jewelers" sign intact. It did remind me of the Parker Inn salvaging during my college days. Thankfully, the Metroplitan Building was purchased in 2014 and is being refurbished. I can't wait until it is finished and opened again.

After visiting my uncle's shop, we'd usually go for lunch to Broadway Market close by the Metropolitan Building. There we'd always get a deli sandwich and a loganberry juice drink, which was our all-time favorite. On the way back to the bus stop, we'd often visit the Detroit Library's Downtown Branch in a beautiful old building near Hudson's.

On one of these visits to downtown Detroit when coming out of Hudson's and heading across an open park-like area toward the Crowley's Department Store, I saw a kiosk that said "Peace Corps" on it. Inside was a guy, probably in his late twenties, with blond hair and a full beard and mustache. I looked at him while he was talking to some other people, and I thought to myself, *"I want to look like that when I grow up."* The beard and mustache made him look intelligent and sophisticated. With his blond hair and blue eyes, he looked like a Viking, which interested and inspired me. At a time when virtually every adult male in the U.S. was clean-shaven, he stood out like a Greek god on Olympus or a Norse god like Odin or Thor. I started talking to him, and he told me about the Peace Corps, about how after college you could join. You would live and work in a third-world country and help that country to develop during your two-year commitment. He gave me a pamphlet about volunteering, and, if not before, certainly from that moment on, I knew I wanted to join the Peace Corps. I was probably thirteen years old at the time.

The evening of this day of destiny in the spring of my senior year at Albion, I telephoned my parents and let them know that the Peace Corps had offered me a possible teaching position in Korea. They took it very well. I had been talking about wanting to join the Peace Corps since junior high school. In addition, they knew I had applied the previous fall, so it wasn't a huge shock. Although I sensed that they really didn't want me to join, they told me that if this was what I wanted to do, then I should do it and that they were happy for me.

The next day, I sent back the letter of intent to the Peace Corps letting them know that I was very interested in serving in Korea.

CHAPTER 2

PRe-Invitational STaging (PRIST): What Branch of the Service?

On Sunday, May 14, 1972, Albion's graduation day came with all its pomp and circumstance. It was also Mother's Day that year. I was in the choir, and we sang "O All Ye Works of the Lord" to begin the proceedings. Following our singing, Norman Cousins, who was then the editor of *World Review* magazine, gave his commencement address, "What Does It Take to Believe in the Future?" I actually don't remember a word he said, but I'm sure his talk was great. Diplomas were handed out, and my parents and I headed home with my eyes focused firmly on the future and Peace Corps service.

The very next day, I headed down to Florida with a college friend, Jeff Alpena, and camped out for a week on one of the islands in the Keys. At the end of the week I called home from a pay phone (no cell phones in those days), and my mother told me an envelope from Peace Corps had arrived. I asked her to open it. It contained a plane ticket to fly to Denver for the PRe-Invitational STaging (PRIST) in early June. Jeff and I headed up the coast and stopped in St. Augustine to tour the old Spanish fort and church there. I found it interesting that the Catholic gift shop next to the church was bigger than the church itself.

After returning home from Florida, I bided my time until the PRIST. The Sunday before leaving I went with my parents to Allen Park, a downriver suburb of Detroit where I had grown up. My Aunt June, my mother's sister, and her husband, Uncle Dick, still lived there, and we often went to their house to play cards. They asked about my upcoming trip to Denver. I mentioned my fear that I might not make the grade and maybe I wouldn't be asked to join the Peace Corps. Aunt June said emphatically, "If you want to go, you will be invited." Aunt June had no doubt that I was Peace Corps material. I appreciated her conviction and confidence in me and my abilities even though I wasn't so sure.

On June 2, 1972, I flew out to Denver and checked into the downtown hotel with high expectations but also trepidation. While opening my suitcase and putting my toiletries into the bathroom, my roommate walked in. In our conversation, he explained to me that when he first applied to Peace Corps he didn't have a job, but now he did and was no longer interested in joining. I was appalled.

"If you know you're not going to join, then why did you come here?" I inquired.

"Oh, I may want to join at some point in the future."

"Seriously?"

"Sure, why not?"

I thought to myself, *"It sounds more like you wanted a free vacation courtesy of Uncle Sam."* Even so, I didn't let his scam dampen my buzz, and I went downstairs to the convention area where Peace Corps had an office. There I picked up my information packet and looked at all the pictures on the wall. A couple of pictures of Korean toilets puzzled me. There was a porcelain white trough-like thing on the floor surrounded by white tile. I just didn't get how it worked even after staring at the photograph for quite a while. But not wanting anyone to think me simpleminded or unworldly, I tore myself away.

We had a dinner that evening, followed by introductions of the facilitators and short speeches. Dozens of prospective volunteers were there, and this was the second of two three-day PRISTs for Korea. The next day I had breakfast and followed the schedule. There were large group sessions with films about Korea and other sessions where we broke up into smaller groups. It was explained to us that we would be teaching English as a Second Language (ESL) to first-year middle school students together with a Korean co-teacher. One of the things I remember most is being told about all the things we would miss while serving and the things about Korea that we might not like—the political situation, the tension with North Korea, sanitary conditions, lack of central heating, lack of indoor plumbing, and so on.

One small group session the first day was with eight other prospective volunteers. All nine of us were young and fresh out of college for the most part except for one man who walked in after we had started and sat down with us – he looked to be in his fifties. The facilitator asked us to pick a partner to interview. Every one of the young, fresh-out-of-college types paired off, leaving me as the odd person. Then the facilitator asked the fifty-something man if he'd be willing to be my partner. He agreed, and we were given our assignment. We were to interview each other for about five minutes each and then come back and introduce our partner to the group. *"OK,"* I thought, *"a little dorky, but that's fine."* We all went out of the room and found different quiet places to do our interviews. My partner saw a couple of chairs in a corner, and we went there. He interviewed me first, and we went through my youth in Allen Park, Albion College, work experience, and so forth. Then it was my turn to interview him. His name was Jim Wixom, and he too was from Michigan. He'd had a series of jobs with the Michigan state government, including working for the highway commission and helping to route I-75 through Detroit, working with the state's environmental commission, and other impressive-sounding jobs. He also told me that he had just been hired to be the new Peace Corps/Korea Program Director and would be heading to Seoul in a few days. *"Just my luck,"* I thought, *"I have to interview the guy who'll be the head honcho in Korea."*

The facilitator came out, told us time had expired, rounded everyone up, and got us all back into the room. Each one of us got a few minutes to introduce and describe the person we had interviewed. They all went on and on about how wonderful and caring, gentle, kind, and empathetic each partner was, and I was thinking, *"Oh, gag me."* These people had spent five damn minutes interviewing each other and acted like this was a best friend they had known all their life. Jim and I were last, and he described me first. "Don is a wonderful, caring individual who..... blah, blah." Then it was my turn. I said, "This is Jim Wixom. He is from Michigan and has worked for the state government there for a couple of decades in several very interesting and impressive positions." Stop. "Oh, and he's the new Director of Peace Corps/Korea." The facilitator said something like, "Yes, but how do you feel about Jim?" I said, "Yeah, I'm not one to make quick first impressions, and I try not to because they are often wrong, but he seems like a nice guy." I was expecting after that statement to be told that there was no place for an overly logical, rational, non-touchy-feely person like me in the Peace Corps—or at least I expected further questions from the facilitator guy who was really getting on my nerves by this point. Thankfully, we had run out of time, and I slid out of the room as fast as I could.

The second day was more of the same, until at one point they asked who was still interested in being in the next group going to Korea in July to teach English at the middle school level. I raised my hand along with a handful of other people—maybe fifteen or so. Then those of us still interested were asked to stay in the room while the vast majority left.

Each of us had an individual session with one of the Peace Corps people. I remember being asked if I could handle the probable isolation. I was reminded that I might be the only Peace Corps Volunteer in a small town, and I was asked if I thought I would be able to handle being all alone. I mentioned that I might have an advantage being an only child. Where people with siblings grew up always having someone around their age to talk to, I had grown up with no siblings and was used to being alone with my own thoughts. I told the Peace Corps staff person that I felt I'd have no problem being the only American at my Peace Corps site.

Another question was about the physical hardship. Would I be able to deal with the cold in winter with no central heat or live in a house with no running hot water and probably no indoor bathroom facilities? To this question I replied that I was looking forward to this harder and simpler life. I mentioned that I had wanted to be a Peace Corps Volunteer for years now, probably since junior high school. I wanted to get to know another culture as well or almost as well as I know our culture. A large part of my desire to be a Peace Corps Volunteer, I explained to them, was to live the way the majority of the people on the planet lived and not spend my whole life existing in the lap of American luxury. I was also asked if I would be willing to cut my hair short and shave my mustache. I had shaved my beard before graduating from Albion. Korea, I was told, is a very conservative country, and men are not allowed to let their hair grow long. Also, traditionally, only elderly men grew facial hair. No male trainees were permitted to leave the U.S. with long hair or any facial hair. I replied that this would be no problem. I explained that I had cut my hair and shaved in college in order to play soccer in my sophomore year – the very year that Albion's soccer team had won the MIAA championship. After the soccer season ended in my freshman year, I had let my mustache grow out and let my hair grow long over my ears. Just before returning to school for the second year of college I shaved and sheared. Immediately after the season ended in my sophomore year I re-grew my 'stache and let my hair grow long again. By my junior year the college and league had ended the ban on sportsmen looking hippie-like.

After this individual question-and-answer session at the PRIST, we were told that we would be members of the K-23 training group. We would be the twenty-third group of Korea Peace Corps Trainees. We would also be the first group to actually train in Korea. The earlier twenty-two groups had all trained in the US—either in Brattleboro, Vermont, at the School for International Training, or in Hawaii. I couldn't help thinking that I wished we would be training in Hawaii, but then I also thought it was better to be in Korea because it would be less likely that they'd flunk me out after spending the plane fare to send me that much farther away from home. I was worried that I wouldn't do well in learning the Korean language after having flunked French in high school. We filled out forms and were given more information about items to pack, inoculations that were needed, how to get a passport (I already had one), how to get a Korean visa in our passports, and other preparations we should make. Near the end of the day they asked if any of us were interested in getting our inoculations done the next morning before heading out to the airport to catch our flights home. I said I was and was told that just up the street was a military induction center. If I went there the next morning I could get all of my shots and my yellow World Health Organization (WHO) card that I would need to travel to Korea.

So the next morning, June 5, I went into the induction center with a paper given to me by Peace Corps. I walked into a rather large room with a line of young-looking guys, probably just out of high school. I got into line and waited. It moved fairly quickly, and I saw in front of those of us in line a desk with a large man, a U.S. Army sergeant, sitting behind it. As each young man reached the desk, the sergeant said in a very gruff, raspy, and deep voice, "What branch of the service?" The young men would answer Army, Navy, Marines, Air Force, or Coast Guard. The sergeant would then point to his left or right, depending on the answer, and say in the same deep, raspy, rough voice, "Over there." This exact scenario happened each time a new young man got to the desk. Then I got to the desk. In his gruff, rough, gravelly voice, he said to me, "What branch of the service?" I very sheepishly answered, "Uh, I'm joining the Peace Corps." His voice totally changed to a normal, pleasant, soft, very attractive voice, and he said, "Peace Corps? Wait a minute." He yelled, "Hey, George, where do we send Peace Corps people?" George said, "Over there," and pointed to the left of the nice sergeant. In his soft, kind, gentle voice, he said "You can just go over there," and pointed. "Thanks," I said. As I walked away and the next young man stepped up, the sergeant resumed his raspy, deep, grating, gravelly, rough Army voice. "What branch of the service?" I walked away smiling, shaking my head, and thought to myself, *Boy, I sure am glad I'm not joining the military.* It also reminded me of Arlo Guthrie's "Alice's Restaurant" song and movie.

Off to the sergeant's left, there was another line and another wait. As they (whomever "they" are) always say, the military is all about hurry up and wait. So I waited. When I got to the front of this line and showed them my Peace Corps paperwork, they had me fill out a yellow International Certificate of Vaccination card, as approved by The World Health Organization. Then I rolled up my sleeves and walked along following the soon-to-be soldiers in front of me: left arm—wham—a smallpox vaccination, right arm—wham—a cholera vaccination, left arm again—wham—a typhoid vaccination—and after each one a stamp with the Denver Department of Health address, the doctor's signature, batch number, and approved insignia. Afterwards I went back to the hotel, packed, checked out, and left for the airport.

CHAPTER 3

Preparations to Leave for Korea: Remember, You Have to Marry a German Girl!

Back at home in Sterling Heights, Michigan, I now knew that in just over a month I would be leaving for Korea. I sent my passport to the Korean Embassy in Washington, D.C., and it came back with a stamp that said:

> Republic of Korea Entry Visa No.001-2123 Good for multiple journeys to the Republic of Korea within forty-eight months of date here-of if passport remains valid. JUN 21 1972 For the Ambassador (signature) Third Secretary & Vice Consul Washington D. C. Period of stay: (an X) Status: 7-3

I spent the month visiting family and friends; I would not be seeing them again for at least two years. As the day of departure grew near, I began picking out what clothes I would take. I spent the last couple of days before leaving writing down the lyrics to many of my favorite songs. Koreans, we had been told, love to sing and would expect us to sing often at social events. I wanted to have a repertoire of good songs to sing so I wouldn't have to rely on my made-up lyrics. The day before leaving I visited a barber shop. I had not been in a barber shop for years, as I had trimmed my own hair throughout college. On this day I got my hair cut very short, and it made me look like I was still in high school. I hated how young I looked with short hair, but I had to take one for the Corps.

Then, on the morning of the flight, I shaved off my mustache. Now I looked even younger. A funny thing is that after coming back from the PRIST, I had looked at the brochure "Koreagraphy: A day in a two-year dance" again. This brochure was sent by Peace Corps Washington, D.C. along with the invitation letter to join the Peace Corps/Korea program that I had received at Albion back in the late winter/early spring. I noticed right away that one of the male volunteers who appeared on a half dozen or more of the twenty pages in this publication had a full beard and a mustache. Talk about mixed signals! I found this incongruous, but I shaved anyway.

Peace Corps Volunteers always flew US-owned airline carriers, but because Northwest Orient Airline employees were on strike, we were flying on Japan Airlines out of San Francisco. A plane ticket had come for me to fly to San Francisco on June 7, 1972. There we were told to take a taxi to a motel near the airport where we would spend the night, and then on June 8 we would fly to Honolulu, Hawaii, for a two-hour layover and then on to Tokyo, Japan. By the time we got to Tokyo, between the time difference, the length of the flight, and crossing the International Date Line, it was the evening of June 9. After an overnight in Japan at the airport hotel, we would finally land at Kimpo Airport near Seoul, Korea, on June 10, 1972.

On June 7, my parents drove me to Metro Airport just outside Detroit. We picked up my paternal grandmother, Emma, along the way. My grandmother was half German and half Swiss-Deutsch. Her maiden name was Christ. It was pronounced with a short vowel sound, but my father's running joke whenever we visited Grandma or she came over to our house was to say, "Emma Christ, are you here again?" He'd pronounce Christ with a long vowel sound, as in Jesus Christ, and everyone would laugh each time even though we'd all heard it a million times before. (Of course, I have numerous running jokes that I have used over and over just like my father, but I do try to wait until I have a new or at least somewhat new audience before reusing them.)

At any rate, we got to the airport, and in those days everyone could walk all the way to the gate. There was no security to go through. In fact, we used to go to the airport to hang out and sometimes took our dates during high school and college. There was a mezzanine pool hall in the main terminal, and we would often play some pool for a while and then wander around. Sometimes we'd go to different gates and welcome the people getting off the plane. "Welcome back!" we'd yell and pretend like there was someone we knew in the crowd exiting the flight. One night we went into a doorway marked "Employees Only" on the mezzanine level in the back behind where the pool hall was. It led to a stairway, and we went up to the top where there was a door that opened onto the roof of the terminal. After this discovery, whenever we visited we always went up onto the roof and walked around while watching the planes landing and taking off. Can't do that no more (or anymore)!

They were building the airport hotel and the second terminal during our high school days, and we often wandered around, sometimes entering the construction zones when no one was looking. We discovered another door, not visible from the hotel's registration area or from the walkway connecting the hotel to the two terminals, which was also marked "Employees Only." This door led into the maids' elevator. We took it up to the second floor where it led into a maids' closet full of shelves for towels and supplies. Then we went out of the closet and into the hallway where the guest rooms were being completed. Finally, we wandered around the corner where they were still building the hotel's swimming pool. I kept this information in mind for later use.

Fast-forward to the summer after my freshman year in college (the summer of 1969) and one hot and muggy night three buddies and I headed out to the airport. The other three guys were Eli Biddle, Barry Wyandotte, and Ken Saugatuck. Eli was a Melvindale High School buddy who had also been my roommate at Albion during our freshman year. Barry and Ken were older guys from Allen Park High School who both had worked at United Shirt Distributors (USD) in Lincoln Park where I began working when I was only thirteen years old. My father worked for USD all his life, and the president offered me a job to help behind the cash register at Christmas and other busy times during the year. I was paid a dollar an hour under the table until I turned fifteen and got a special working permit. Barry, by the summer of 1969, had graduated from Central Michigan University and was about to start teaching at the high school level in the fall. Ken had graduated from Northern Michigan University (NMU) a couple years earlier. He was drafted into the army right after graduating from NMU, and by the summer of 1969 he was a Vietnam War Veteran. I had talked them all into taking a dip in the airport hotel pool.

Ken drove us out to the airport. He parked his car in the airport garage, and we all left our IDs hidden in the car—just in case. "Follow me," I said. I led the way. We went into the new terminal, which had been designed by a Japanese architect. The ceiling of the terminal was made of rough concrete, and the design of the ceiling looked like several small rowboats suspended above us upside down. We then headed down the walkway towards the hotel. Just before the lobby and registration desk, I turned up a side hallway. After making sure no one was around, I pushed opened the "Employees Only" door and waved my three caballeros in. We went up the elevator to the second floor where we each grabbed a large and luxurious beige bath towel with the hotel name prominently displayed on it. We then headed out the maids' closet door, down the hall, and out to the hotel's outdoor swimming pool. Out in the distance planes were landing and taking off. It was a sunny, hot, and very humid summer's evening and a lovely setting. We four all had worn our swimsuits under our slacks, so we took off our trousers and shirts, threw them over chaise longue chairs, and jumped in the pool. There were a couple of attractive middle-aged ladies lounging on a couple other chaise longue chairs on the other side of the swimming pool. Barry, being the ladies' man that he always was, tried to talk to the women, but they ignored him. We spent the next couple of hours until near dark swimming and hanging out.

After spending some time sitting at the side of the pool waiting for our swimsuits to dry out, we slipped our pants back on and got ready to leave.

When we left, we went down an outdoor spiral staircase that descended into the main hallway and headed back toward the new terminal. We had the towels in our hands as we headed for the main doors of this Japanese-architect designed terminal. Suddenly an airport employee came roaring around the corner on one of those electric cars (maybe not quite roaring, but buzzing). It screeched to a halt, and the employee yelled at a couple of security guards, "These are the guys, grab them!" The guards approached us and said, "Come with us." They took us outside the terminal to a couple of waiting airport police cars, and we got in. The cars sped off to the airport police station. Who knew they even had one? I didn't.

We were taken into the station and escorted into a room with a table about eight feet long that had several chairs around it. "Sit down," we were told. I followed Eli, Barry, and Ken in, and we all threw our stolen towels on the first chair by the door. We then sat in the next four chairs on the door side of the table, and I was in the chair right next to the one holding the towels. One cop walked around the table on the other side, turned on a light that was like a spotlight on a pole, and shined it at us. Barry said, "Oh wow, just like *Dragnet.*" The cop sat down and said, "Don't joke, this is serious. You were trespassing on private property." He went on and on telling us in essence that if we ever got caught again swimming in the airport pool then we would never be allowed to set foot in Detroit's Metropolitan Airport ever again. We'd be banned for life. We all looked at each other like, *"Is this guy crazy?"*

"You mean you'll set up a permanent roadblock just searching for us?" Barry said.

"Don't be a smart-ass."

"Right," Barry replied.

"Let me see your IDs," the cop then said.

"We don't have any ID with us," we all replied.

"How'd you get here?" he questioned.

"I drove," Ken finally answered. The cops then drove Ken back to his car, and they made him retrieve his ID.

"What's your name?" one cop questioned me.

"Tony Dequindre," I replied. Tony was one of my childhood friends. He had moved with his family to Flint years before.

"What's your address?"

"Fifteen-five-fifty-five Keppen Avenue, Allen Park, Michigan." This had actually been Tony's easy-to-remember address before he and his family moved away. The cop asked Eli and Barry their names and addresses, and they also gave false information. Poor Ken, the Vietnam Vet, was brought back in and sat down after having had his real name and address recorded for posterity. The cop then said that we were free to go, but he reminded us never to do this again or we'd never, ever, even in a million years, be allowed to enter the airport grounds. I stood up and stopped with my hand on the top towel. I turned around and motioned to Ken with my eyes toward the towels (clearly marked with the name of the hotel). He smiled and shrugged his shoulders a little. I picked up the top towel and threw it over my shoulder. Ken took the second one, Barry the third, and Eli the last.

We walked out of the interrogation/torture room, past several of the airport's finest security personnel, out the front door, and headed down the sidewalk toward the airport parking structure. After we were out of hearing range of the police station, we all stopped, circled, and doubled over quite literally laughing our asses off.

"The only real crime we are guilty of is stealing these towels!" I blurted out.

"And we stole them right under the noses of a half dozen cops," Ken added.

"Those clowns make Barney Fife look like a genius," Barry said.

"I thought I'd die when the cop turned on that spotlight and you said it was just like *Dragnet*," Eli said to Barry.

"Yeah, that was a great line," Ken and I threw in. All the way back to the car we discussed how these clowns would be cordoning off the airport and looking for Tony Dequindre, Sam Houston, and Harry Houdini, the names we had given them. Well, maybe not exactly the last two, but still whatever fake names Barry and Eli had given. "How dumb can cops get?" Barry asked. But Ken said, "You all laugh, but they have my real name, and I'll never be able to fly out of Metro Airport ever again." Then we all burst out laughing again. I used that fine towel throughout the rest of my college years.

There were lots of great memories affiliated with this airport, and today I would be adding one more. I was leaving for the adventure of a lifetime—the Peace Corps. When the time came to get on the San Francisco-bound flight I hugged my father, hugged and kissed my mother, and then turned to hug and kiss my grandmother, Emma. She blurted out, "Remember, Donnie, you have to marry a German girl." I answered, "OK, Grandma, I'll look for one, but there may not be too many in Korea." I walked through the door, turning and waving goodbye one last time, and then disappeared from their view down the ramp.

I got to San Francisco in the early afternoon, picked up my bags, hired a taxi, and took it to the small motel we were told to go to and which was not too far from the entrance to the airport. After checking in and putting my bags into the room, I came back out and looked around. A little later another taxi pulled up, and a guy got out. I asked if he was also a Peace Corps trainee, and he said he was. We introduced ourselves. His name was Bob Kern, and after he threw his bags into his room, I suggested we take a walk around the vicinity as there didn't seem to be anyone else around yet. We walked down the street and then followed some railroad tracks. Bob was from Pennsylvania, and he told me how he had graduated from college and then joined the U.S. Navy. After serving in the military, he decided that he wanted to be a Peace Corps Volunteer and joined up. I told Bob about my youth in the downriver Detroit suburbs of Allen Park and Melvindale. As we walked by old buildings along the tracks, I told him about how since I was a kid I've always loved to go exploring in dark, old, abandoned buildings like the Parker Inn in Albion or the Metropolitan Building in Detroit.

By the time we returned to the motel there were several other PC trainees who had arrived. I saw a cute gal, and I walked over and introduced myself. Her name was Carrie Anne Tawas. Carrie Anne said she was from Bowling Green, Kentucky. So I broke into song:

> Way down in Bowlin' Green, Prettiest girls I've ever seen…
> ("Bowlin' Green" written by Terry Slater and Jacqueline Ertel, performed by The Everly Brothers)

Carrie Anne laughed. Good sign, I thought. We stood talking for a while, and then a bunch of us decided to head into downtown San Fran to grab dinner and wander around. By the time we finished dinner it was getting dark, and a few of us traversed the streets around San Francisco's famous Chinatown. I was still hanging near Carrie Anne when a woman who was either mentally challenged or, more likely, high on something came up to our small group. She said something about Barbra Streisand being the best female singer in the world. I said, "Oh give me a break, everyone knows that Dionne Warwick is the best female singer in the world." The lady got upset and started speaking more loudly. Carrie Anne pushed me away and said, "Don, that's not nice. Don't agitate her." I just walked away and watched Carrie Anne as she carried on a short conversation with the Streisand-loving lady. Carrie Anne then came back up next to me and mumbled something about the poor lady. I said, "Yeah, too bad, but truthfully I think she's right about Barbra." We all got into a couple of taxis and returned to our motel where I met the guy who was my roommate for the evening. He had already gone to bed but half woke up as I rattled around in the dark.

The next morning some official person from Peace Corps, whom we had met the afternoon before, gave a packet of information to Steve Moross, one of the two married guys in our group of twenty-nine. They had joined along with their wives. Steve was entrusted with herding us through the airports and making sure we all made it safe and sound to Seoul. A bus appeared and took us all to San Fran's airport. We had tickets but didn't have seat assignments yet, so I made sure that I was in line right behind Carrie Anne for the Japan Airlines (JAL) check-in. I told the famous Henny Youngman joke about airline check-in and bags while waiting in line. "Did you hear about the guy who walked up to the airline check-in? The airline employee asked if he had any bags to check, and he said, 'Yes, three: I want this one to go to Cleveland, this one to go to Omaha, and this one to Seattle.' The airline employee replied, 'Sir, we can't do that.' And he said, 'Why not? You did it last week.'" As I was finishing the joke we got up to the check-in counter. We were given our seat assignments, and lo and behold, Carrie Anne and I got seats right next to each other. Fancy that!

Our plane was a Japan Airlines brand-new 747 expanded with an upper deck floor, which JAL had made into a first-class lounge. Once on the plane, we all found our seats, and Carrie Anne and I were in the fifth row in coach in the middle area. I was on the right aisle, and Carrie Anne was next to me on my left. All the other members of our group were in the rows behind us. The pilot got on the intercom and said, "Welcome to Japan Airlines, I hope you will enjoy your fright!" Carrie Anne looked at me with feigned terror, and I said, "Don't worry, I think he meant flight." We ordered drinks and kept up a conversation all the way to Honolulu where we had a layover of a couple of hours for refueling. We had to get off the plane, so we wandered around the airport, looked out the windows, and saw the palm trees swaying in the breeze. Part of me still wished we were having our training program in this tropical paradise.

Back on the plane after takeoff, Carrie Anne and I headed up to the second-floor lounge, which was technically in the first-class section. We had noticed no one going up there on the first leg of our flight, and no one said anything to us as we climbed up the spiral staircase. There was no one else there. Every once in a while, a stewardess would come up and we'd order more drinks. When it was mealtime we'd return to our seats.

At one point, we were sitting and drinking in our assigned seats in coach when we heard the sound of a typewriter being used in the row behind us. I turned around and saw Steve Marquette from Boston with a little portable typewriter in his lap, just typing away.

"What the heck are you doing?" I asked.

"Typing a letter to my mother," was his reply.

"You're kidding, right?"

"No, I'm letting her know of our progress so far." I looked at Carrie Anne, rolled my eyes, and she laughed.

As we got nearer to Tokyo, we started to get tired. Carrie Anne rested her head against my shoulder and held my hand.

"You have good hands for the theater."

"What do you mean?" I asked.

"You have prominent veins. This is good for makeup when they need to make you age during the course of a play. They can draw lines along your veins."

"That's interesting, as I'm a thespian."

"You are? What plays have you been in?"

"Oh, many, but the most recent one was a one-act play called, 'Gallows Humor' by Jack Richardson. I had the lead role of the prison warden."

"I don't know that one."

"It's weird but quite fascinating. Are you a thespian also?" I inquired.

"Yes, I've been in many productions at Western Kentucky University."

"Like what?"

"The last play I was in was *Hedda Gabler* by Henrik Ibsen. I played the aunt, Juliane Tesman."

"Ah, yes, I read *Hedda Gabler* in the Moderm Theater class I took at Albion. Good play. Ibsen is very interesting." We moved on to other topics, thankfully, as I would have been hard-pressed to think up anymore plays and parts as the play "Gallows Humor" during my senior year in college was my one and only actual acting experience.

Finally, we arrived in Tokyo. It was early evening, and the married Steve told us to congregate at the baggage claim for instructions. It was the evening of July 9. Planes did not fly into Kimpo Airport near Seoul at night. Kimpo evidently had no radar, and it would have been dangerous to try to land in the dark. So we got to spend the night in Tokyo, or at least in the hotel at Haneda Airport in Tokyo.

In the baggage claim area, after we all got our bags, Steve Moross told us to go through Customs, where we would get a paper good for a twenty-four-hour stay stapled into our passports, and then we were to walk across the street in front of the terminal to the airport hotel. In the lobby of the hotel Steve told us to pair off and get our room assignments from a young Japanese hotel employee sitting behind a desk over near the registration counter. I could see guys pairing off and gals pairing off, and I just moved to the far back of the group. I did not really know any of the guys other than Bob Kern, whom I had walked with along the railroad tracks in San Francisco, and I could see he was already in line with one of the other guys. I had spent the last day and a half talking only to Carrie Anne for the most part. So, I figured I'd wait until everyone had gotten their room assignments, and whichever guy was left, I'd room with him. Carrie Anne had wandered off, and then she reappeared next to me.

"Karen Gibraltar wants to room with me, but she's weird, and I don't want to room with her. What should I do?" she asked.

"Tell her you're rooming with me," I said with a laugh.

"Good idea."

"I know," I said while laughing. I was kidding. Carrie Anne disappeared. After the majority of our group had gotten their room assignments, were given their keys, and headed up the elevator, there were only a couple of pairs of guys left in front of the desk in the lobby. I joined in the line behind them and alongside Carrie Anne. We were the last two people in the group to register. The nice young Japanese man asked Carrie Anne her name. "Carrie Anne Tawas," she said. He wrote her name down, looked at me and said, "Ah, so! Mr. Tawas." I said, "No, Mr. Haffner." He looked at me like I was the devil incarnate. I pointed at the paper right next to where he had written Carrie Anne's name and I said, "Haffner, H-A-F-F-N-E-R." He wrote my name down, but kept staring up at me in between writing each letter. We grabbed our keys and said, "Thank you."

As we walked away I was thinking that this might be the end of my Peace Corps career. I envisioned the Peace Corps' Washington, D.C. office getting a list of our room assignments and the two of us being thrown on the next flight back to the States for improper fraternization or sororitization, whichever. But, I also figured what's done is done. Besides, obviously we had an odd number of guys and gals. It wasn't my fault that none of the guys picked me to be their roommate in Tokyo. That was to be my line of defense. In addition, we were saving the government money by rooming together rather than demanding two separate rooms. Oh, the altruism! Oh, the sacrifices I was willing to make to help the federal government balance the budget! The Tea Party would have loved me had they been around in those days. So we lugged our bags to our room. Carrie Anne said some people had mentioned meeting up in the bar on the top floor of the hotel. We freshened up and headed to the hotel bar. Up in the bar many people from the group were already ensconced. We found a couple of seats with them and ordered drinks. I listened to the conversations going on around me, but didn't really join in much. After a couple more drinks, I yawned and fairly loudly said, "I'm bushed. Anyone else want to call it a night?" Carrie Anne also yawned and said, "I'll head out with you," and we left.

The next morning after breakfast, all of us K-23s met in the lobby of the hotel, walked back across the street, into the terminal, and boarded our JAL plane for the final leg of our flight to Seoul, Korea. It was July 10, 1972—a fateful day indeed!

CHAPTER 4

K-23 Training Program: If You're Homely and You're Lonely...

A couple of hours later we were landing at Kimpo Airport. We all deplaned, got our bags, and went through Customs where our passports were stamped:

> Admitted 1972 7. 10.
> Port Kimpo
> Ministry of Justice
> Republic of Korea

As we came out of the Customs area, several of the Peace Corps staff and our trainers were waiting for us. Once we had all gathered, we headed to the parking lot outside the terminal where a bus awaited us. I was steering clear of Carrie Anne because I didn't want everyone to know we'd had an affair already. As I entered the bus, I saw Carrie Anne was sitting near the front, so I headed way toward the rear and sat on the right side (door side) of the bus the third row from the back.

We departed from the airport, and in less than an hour we were in Seoul. The bus headed up a hill that we were told was Nam-san (South Mountain). The bus parked, and we got out at a scenic overlook. Below us was the main downtown section of Seoul. Off in the distance were other larger mountains, and the city sat between the mountain we were on and the mountains off to the north. As we got off the bus, we all walked across the parking lot toward an area covered with patio stones. At the edge of a cliff, there was a banister-like stone fence. Between the paved parking lot and the curb at the edge of the patio area was a drainage gutter covered by two-foot-wide cement slabs that had cut outs at each end just wider than and a few inches longer than an average human foot. In front of me was a gal named Patty Olivet who had large breasts, and who I had noticed wasn't wearing a bra. Several Korean men were staring at her bouncy knockers as she pointed with her right index finger off toward downtown Seoul and said, "Oh, look." Not watching where she was going, she proceeded to step right into the gap between the gutter paving stones. Her foot went down into the six-inch-deep gutter and she fell forward. Luckily, the gutter had no water in it. Several of us trainees ran over to make sure she was not hurt. She didn't seem to be hurt physically, though her pride was bruised a little. We helped her up and extracted her foot out of the gutter. She had slightly scraped her shin, but otherwise was OK. We continued to the banister and all said, "Oh, wow." It was a beautiful sight from up here, and in the months and years ahead we would get to know this city like the backs of our hands, but for today it was all a mystery.

Then we got back on the bus and were told that we were headed to the city of Daegu about four hours away by expressway. This expressway, the Gyeongbu Expressway, stretched from Seoul down to Busan (a total of 258 miles) and had just been finished a couple of years earlier in 1970. Seoul was the largest city, Busan the second-largest city and the largest port, while Daegu was the third-largest city in South Korea. Since the expressway was finished, the Republic of Korea's economy had really begun to boom.

As we drove away from Nam-san I started talking with the two guys who sat behind me. I had my seat to myself and sat with my back against the side of the bus to more easily talk with Nick Mack and Jack Fisher. Nick was a trip. He was from New York, and very quickly after leaving Nam-san he began telling off-color, dirty sex jokes. One after another for four hours he told joke after joke never repeating any. I couldn't believe his memory. Jack and I, along with most of the guys in the back of the bus, were doubled over laughing for much of the trip. Once in a while there would be a gap while Nick caught his breath, and Jack or I would say something, but then Nick would start another joke. Again we'd start laughing our heads off.

Jim Wixom, the new Peace Corps/Korea Director, whom I had interviewed and then introduced at our small group session during the PRIST, was sitting about three rows ahead of me alongside his wife. I had not bothered to ask him if he remembered me from Denver and was just as happy if he didn't, but I had shaken his hand and said "Hello" earlier as he greeted all of us getting on the bus at Kimpo. I noticed that, every once in a while, he would turn back and look toward the back of the bus with a somewhat disgusted look on his face. I'm sure he could hear some, and maybe all, of Nick's filthy sex jokes.

A couple of hours into the trip, one of the trainers, Moe Cass, announced that there were three different sized rooms at the New Grand Hotel in Daegu where we would be staying for the next three months during our training program. There were a few single rooms, mostly double rooms, and a few triples. We were told to think about what kind of room we'd like and/or whom we'd like to room with. In a few minutes he'd be working his way toward the back of the bus and writing down our preferences. I immediately noticed Carrie Anne was agitated. She was anxiously talking with a guy and gal sitting together next to her across the aisle. Having the feeling she was trying to set up something that would tie me to her, I turned around and asked Jack and Nick if they wouldn't like to get a triple room so the three of us could stay together. They both agreed that it would be great to get a triple together. Sure enough, I had no sooner gotten their agreement than Carrie Anne came back and sat next to me.

"Don," she whispered, "I'm going to room with Kathy. John Schoolcraft and Kathy Fowlerville have already been living together in college for a couple of years now. If you and John room together, we can switch later, and then you and I will be roommates. Won't that be great?"

"Oh, gee," I said, "Jack and Nick want to be my roommates in a triple, and I wouldn't want to disappoint them."

"OK, I'll get a single, and you can visit whenever," she countered after a moment's thought.

"Great," I said with a bit of skepticism.

"Wow, I dodged a bullet this time," I philosophized to myself. I didn't want to tempt the fates any more than I already had. I hoped that we had gotten away with our one-night tryst in Tokyo, but I was pretty sure we'd get caught if I roomed permanently with Carrie Anne throughout our training.

When Moe got to Carrie Anne she talked with him and then she flashed a "thumb's up" sign my way, so I knew she had gotten a single room. When he got back to Nick, Jack and me, there was still a triple available, and I was pleased as Hawaiian Punch to be rooming with them because they seemed like intelligent and interesting guys. We got to Daegu and checked into the New Grand Hotel, which was fairly new, but it wasn't all that grand. It was air-conditioned, though, and being that Daegu is hot as hell and muggy as the Everglades in the summer, that was important. It also had western-style sitdown toilets, which was an added plus, not the strange squat kind I had seen in the photographs during our PRIST. We got our room assignments, settled in, had dinner, and at a meeting after dinner were told our official training would begin the next morning. All twenty-nine of us K-23s and twenty-three trainers stayed together in the New Grand Hotel.

Every day we studied four to six hours of Korean language and two to four hours of Teaching English to Speakers of Other Languages (TESOL). Although at PRIST English teaching was called English as a Second Language (ESL), in training they usually called it TESOL. (Same thing either way.) In addition, we had cross-cultural instruction on some days and extracurricular cross-cultural activities. The first week of language classes we were just arbitrarily thrown together five in each class. After a week the classes were rearranged, and I'm sure I was in the "Korean for Dummies" level class. I am not a good language learner as my high school flunking of French had already sufficiently proven. In college I took German and got a C the first semester and a measly CD (C– or D+) the second. I still think the professor cut me a lot of slack because our family name is German and/or maybe he really liked Mozart's Haffner symphony because even the CD grade seemed a gift. Obviously, learning foreign languages was not my forte. During the first couple of weeks, more than one of our trainers told me I would probably be really good in Korean because I walked around singing all the time. They thought if my memory for song lyrics was that good then I would easily learn Korean. I assured them that this theory of theirs was very wrong. Only when and if we studied Korean songs might this lyric memorization ability of mine help. Only if words have a tune with them can I remember them easily, and even then I often mangle the lyrics—even when they're in English.

My roommates Jack and Nick on the other hand were geniuses in Korean. After a few days they were already talking to the Korean language teachers in Korean after class, and I couldn't understand a word any of them was saying. It was downright depressing to see how quickly they picked up the language as if they were both sponges and how slowly I learned as if my brain were a sieve. Somehow I must have missed all the important synapses for foreign language learning, while Nick and Jack had multiple-lane freeways for each of these synapses. They, of course, were in the most advanced class out of the six groups.

I was glad that I roomed with these two brilliant guys because even though they made me feel a little dumb, they were also a lot of fun to hang out with and talk to. Jack Fisher especially had interesting stories. He was a few years older than I and was an Ohio State University grad, although I didn't hold that against him. He had been drafted right after college like Ken Saugatuck, my airport hotel swimming pool buddy, also had been. Because of Jack's intelligence, he had been sent by the U.S. Army to their language school in Monterey, California, to learn the Indonesian language. After studying Indonesian for several months, he was told there was no need for a linguist in Indonesia at the time and was sent to the Republic of Korea instead. By the way, the Korean and Indonesian languages are not related at all. All that time and expense was wasted. You'd think the Army would have insured there was a need for an Indonesian language specialist before sending someone for training, but *au contraire*, as my French Canadian ancestors always said (and one of the few things I remembered from my high school French class). I've heard many similar stories like this over the years about waste, repetition, and mismanagement in the military. It just makes me shake my head in disbelief. Tea Party, take note!

Jack told Nick and me that he'd had a Korean girlfriend during his stay here in the Army. Of course, this had given him some knowledge of the Korean language before the Peace Corps, but he claimed it wasn't really all that much. He had even considered marrying this Korean gal but then thought the better of it. He did enjoy Korea so much he decided to join the Peace Corps hoping to return, and he did.

My other roommate, Nick Mack, was also fun to talk to. He was funny for one thing, as evidenced by his dirty joke performance on the bus. A graduate of Columbia University, he claimed to have performed in comedy clubs in New York during his college years. One day he mentioned that he was writing an epic poem. I asked if I could see it, and he pulled out several typewritten pages and handed them to me. I began reading and realized very quickly that it must have been a brilliant piece of writing because it had all these references to Greek gods and other things that I had never heard of and I couldn't understand a word of it. Handing it back later, I told him it was great and asked him to let me read the finished work when he was all done. He said he would. I don't know if he ever actually did finish it, but if so he must have forgotten my request because I've never seen it.

Carrie Anne and I stayed friends, but I mostly steered clear. I needed all my energy for language learning. Also, Carrie Anne turned out to be a huge complainer, and I just don't like complainers. Every Friday afternoon we would have a bitch session. Professor Chae, Jang-gee, the Project Director, would ask if anyone had any complaints. Carrie Anne complained every week. Often, she complained that her toilet wasn't working properly. And like many other members of our group, she was always complaining about the food.

The food was quite bad. They often tried to cook quasi-American food, and that was the worst to me. They did Korean food most of the time, but it wasn't all that good either. The funniest food they made was the one that got the most complaints. It was their famous fish head soup. Korean meals always came with some kind of soup, side dishes like *kimchi*, other vegetables, maybe some fish, and a bowl of rice of course. Often, the soup they'd serve was a broth with a fish head in it, brain included, and some white radish. In high school, some students used to say, "If fish is brain food, you should eat a whale." (The fact that whales aren't fish seemed to elude my fellow high school classmates.) But I couldn't help thinking, *"If fish is brain food, then fish brains must really be brain food."* Besides the brain, another distraction was that the eyes would still be in the head and whichever one was floating above the broth would stare up at you. I'd spoon up the broth, mix it with some rice, eat the white radish and get out with my chopsticks what little fish flesh there might be at the back of the head by the gills. It was tolerable.

At first, using chopsticks every day for every meal was a bit of an ordeal. The muscles in my right hand would hurt and sometimes cramp up during meals for the first few days. Also, although you'd sometimes get the bamboo or wooden chopsticks like we see in Chinese restaurants in the U.S., the New Grand Hotel and many restaurants in Korea used much thinner metal chopsticks, which are even more difficult to get used to using. Naturally after a few days or maybe a couple of weeks we all got used to them and thought nothing of it anymore.

I sat at lunch one day with Bob Kern. We started talking about Asian history courses we had taken in college when he said, "Wait a minute! I have to show you the great textbook that I used for my Asian history classes. I'll be right back." He ran out of the lunch room and returned a couple of minutes later.

"Check this book out. It's the best."

"That book was written by my college's Asian history professor."

"Yeah, right!" he replied. I already had a reputation of being a joker.

"No! Seriously! Check it out! Dr. Quale is from Albion College in Michigan." He opened the book and checked. On the title page it said, "G. Robina Quale, Albion College, *Eastern Civilizations*, Appleton-Century-Crofts, New York."

"You're kidding! You went to Albion, and Dr. Quale was your professor," Bob exclaimed.

"Yes, I took several of her classes." Then I explained to Bob that it was because of Dr. Quale and her Asian history classes that I ended up in Korea. The Peace Corps application in those days asked which country you would like to serve in. There were three lines on which you could write your first, second and third choices. I wrote India as my first choice and anywhere in Asia as my second. The third line I left blank. After Dr. Quale's courses on Asian history, I wanted to serve in Asia. I especially wanted to serve in India because of its long history, exotic culture, and its unique Hindu religion. Unfortunately, Peace Corps Volunteers were not being sent to India in 1972. The American president, Richard Nixon, had sided with Pakistan during the Indo-Pakistani War of 1971, and for internal political reasons Indira Gandhi would not allow any new PCV's to enter India. So Peace Corps offered me the opportunity to come to Korea instead. *"That's somewhere in Asia,"* I thought when I opened that manila envelope from Peace Corps on that fateful spring day my senior year at Albion.

About halfway through our training during one of the Friday bitch sessions, when as usual many of our fellow trainees were complaining to high heaven about the food, I suggested that we tell the New Grand Hotel to serve only Korean food because at least the kitchen staff knew how to cook Korean food. I'm sure all my fellow trainees envisioned fish head soup for breakfast, lunch, and dinner, and they prodeeded to vehemently attack me from all sides of the room. I argued back that we might as well get used to all Korean food as that is what we would get when we were sent to our city, town, or village for our permanent teaching assignments. I was out voted by a huge margin, however, and we continued to be served lousy, quasi-American food part of the time.

Many evenings the trainers and trainees would go out drinking, but I decided not to imbibe. Having so much trouble with learning Korean, I knew if I drank and caroused around at night then I'd be even worse. I began to worry that they might ship me home, not for my tryst with Carrie Anne in Tokyo, but for my poor language ability. Things were not looking so good for me anymore.

One other trainee who became a good buddy of mine during training was Charlie Sarnia. He didn't drink either, and we had very similar views on so many things that in the evenings we would just sit and talk for hours. Charlie was a Notre Dame grad and had played drums in the marching band there. Sometimes he'd bang away with his fingers on a table and would keep up a mean beat.

Charlie and I, along with a couple of other trainees, were sitting in Charlie's room after lunch one afternoon just before our afternoon TESOL class was to start, and Steve Marquette, the typist from the airplane, walked in carrying a pile of his clothes and waving at one of the hotel maids to follow him into the room. Steve and the maid stopped just inside the door.

"How do I tell her I want her to launder my clothes?" Steve asked.

"Just say, 'Washie, washie!'" I immediately replied. The maid got a big smile on her face and repeated, "Washie, washie!" She reached out and grabbed the clothes out of the astonished Steve's hands and left the room. We all looked at each other and laughed.

"Well, that worked," Steve said.

"Yeah, I learned that from Hop Sing on *Bonanza*," I added.

Two days later we were sitting in Charlie's room again, and Steve was with us. The maid walked in with his laundered clothes in her hands, Steve stood up, and as she handed him the clothes she said, "Checkie, checkie!" Steve took his pants and shirts, checked to make sure they were in fact his and paid her. Then she left. We all laughed again, and I said, "Can anyone explain to me why we are spending so much time studying Korean when to communicate all we have to do is take any American word, put 'ie' at the end and say it twice? We could shorten our training by a month and a half to two months by using this simple communication method."

The English teaching classes were easier and more fun for me because I didn't feel as dumb as I did in the Korean classes. I caught on quickly and enjoyed learning teaching methods, how to use visual aids, games, songs, and the teaching tricks of the trade. One trick I remember was backward build-up. If you had the sentence "I went downtown to go shopping," you'd have the students repeat after you starting with the last word of the sentence and then build it up backwards, hence the name backward build-up. "Repeat after me – 'shopping.'" The students would repeat, "shopping." Then you'd say, "go shopping." The students would repeat, "go shopping." And so on. Another trick was substitution drills. Teacher: "This is a book." Students repeat: "This is a book." Teacher says, "pencil." Students say, "This is a pencil." And so on.

We began very quickly in Korean class learning *Hangeul,* the Korean phonetic alphabet. At least with *Hangeul* I could keep up. *Hangeul* is more scientific, simpler, and more exact than our alphabet and consequently easier and faster to learn. It is an alphabet of 24 consonants and vowels, and in a few days we could read pretty much anything in *Hangeul* and pronounce it correctly even if we had no idea what we were saying. We could walk around town and read the store names and signs. Sometimes one of the trainers would say, "You know that one, what's the name of that shop?"

"Ram-bu-ran-tu," we'd pronounce.

"No, don't know that word in Korean," we'd say.

"Read it faster," the trainer would say, and we'd read it over and over.

"Oh, Rembrandt," one of us would suddenly say. Many shop names were actually English words or names of famous western people or places. But because Korean has to be written in syllable clusters, it would sound funny. Usually the syllables have to be consonant then vowel, so that it often takes more syllables in Korean to say an English word than when written in our Latin alphabet.

In language class we sometimes used readings. One day we were reading in Korean about Ernest Hemingway and his story, "The Snows of Kilimanjaro." Suddenly there was a big commotion in the hallway, someone bursting out of a classroom crying loudly and running down the hall. When we broke for lunch we heard about what had happened. In the most advanced class, the one that both of my roommates Nick and Jack were in, they too were reading the story in *Hangeul* about Ernest Hemingway. One of the other students in the class, Karen Gibraltar (the same Karen that Carrie Anne had not wanted to room with in Tokyo) was taking her turn at reading. When she got to Hemingway's story she hesitated. The

Korean word for snow is *nun*, which sounds like "noon." *Nun* also means eye in Korean. Karen translated the sentence with Hemingway's story name as "The Eyes of Kilimanjaro." Nick threw his papers on the floor and said, "You idiot! That's 'The Snows of Kilimanjaro.'" Karen burst into tears, ran out of the classroom crying, and ran up to her own room in the hotel. The Korean teacher gave Nick a dirty look and ran out after her. Evidently, it took a while before Karen could be persuaded to return to class, and everyone was pissed at Nick. Well, almost everyone. I went over and sat with Nick at lunch to give him moral support. He was sorry, he told me.

"But, who the hell wouldn't know that it was 'The Snows of Kilimanjaro' and not 'The Eyes of Kilimanjaro?'"

"Indeed," I said, "but maybe you could have been a little less demonstrative."

"Yeah, I suppose you're right."

"Probably!" I responded.

There was one big problem involved with our learning of the Korean written language. Korean newspapers, as well as most books and magazines in South Korea, also used Chinese characters mixed with the *Hangeul*. Without knowing several hundred Chinese characters in addition to knowing the simple twenty-four-letter Korean alphabet, there were very few publications that could be read. Interestingly enough, in North Korea Chinese characters are not used. But traditions die hard, and in South Korea they continued to use Chinese characters mixed with *Hangeul*. For most of Korean history, Chinese characters were used exclusively, and since they were so difficult to learn, they gave power to the elite (*Yangban*) class. They could afford to spend the time needed to learn hundreds and even thousands of characters. *Hangeul* was created in the fifteenth century during the reign of King Sejong the Great, but after he died it fell into disuse. The *Yangban* suppressed the use of *Hangeul* because, to them, it was an easy alphabet that any lowlife could learn in a few hours, and this was threatening to their honored place in society. It was American missionaries who began using this alphabet again extensively in the late nineteenth century, after Korea opened up to the west, in order to more easily teach Christianity.

One day, we walked into language class and our Korean instructors told us we would be given our Korean names that day. Korean names all come from Chinese characters. When it was my turn, I was told my family name would be Ha. The Chinese character pronounced "ha" that is used as a family name means "wide river," and our instructor wrote the character slowly on the board, so I could copy it. There are many other Chinese characters pronounced "ha," but only the one meaning wide river is used as a family name in Korea. Since Haffner starts with the letters h and a, they selected Ha as the closest sounding Korean name to mine. Then my given name was to be Doe-young. Doe means "moral path." It is the Chinese character pronounced dao or tao in Chinese and is the name of the Chinese religion Taoism. Young means "blossoming" and is the Chinese character that along with the character for country means England. Because I went to Albion (another name for England) College and its teams are called the Britons, this seemed fitting to me. So my name in Korean was, and still is, Ha, Doe-young. In Korean the family name is always said before the given name. I was told by many Koreans that this was a fine name.

European names have meaning, too, of course. My full name is Donald Richard Haffner. Donald in Gaelic means "world ruler." Richard is Germanic in origin and means "powerful leader." Haffner is also German and means "potter" or "pottery maker." So, while in the Orient I'm the wide river, moral path, blossoming guy, in the Occident I am the world ruler, powerfully leading, pottery maker. If that doesn't "bowl" you over, nothing will.

The next trainee to get his Korean name was Bob Saks. I had already been calling him Bobby Socks, which was bad enough, but when he was given his full Korean name that had been chosen for him by the Korean language teachers, there was a huge roar of laughter. There is a Korean family name pronounced Suck. So Bob was told his family name would be Suck. A few snickers were heard. Then our teacher said, "And your full name will be Suck, No-bean." Everyone burst out laughing, and we all nearly fell off our chairs. Our poor language teacher seemed to have no idea why this was so funny. She finally got us all calmed down and was obviously perturbed by our disrespectful outburst. She wrote the Chinese characters on the board and explained their meaning.

From that day on we were called by our Korean names in class. Unfortunately for our instructor, every time she called on Mr. Suck, No-bean, the four of us fellow classmates would again burst out laughing. After a couple of days, our teacher came in and announced that Bob would no longer be Suck, No-bean; he would from this day forward be known as Shin, No-bean. We still laughed a little at the No-bean part, but it wasn't anywhere near as funny as Suck, No-bean was.

The Foreign Minister of Korea from 1982 until his death in 1983 was Lee, Bum-suk. Foreign Minister Lee was murdered by North Korean agents in Rangoon, Burma, in a failed assassination attempt on President Chun, Doo-hwan. The bombing killed seventeen members of Chun's visiting delegation and four Burmese government officials. After Peace Corps I got to know people who had known Foreign Minister Lee, and they told me that he would walk up to Americans, introduce himself with a very serious look on his face, and then smile and say, "It's OK, you can laugh. I know what my name means in English."

Partway through training, we began learning Korean through dialogues. In the afternoons we also learned how to teach using dialogues in our English teacher training classes. The dialogues in Korean class went along with slides that were shown with comic book-like characters in them. The dialogues helped, and I began feeling a little less like a fish out of water and more like a guppy trying to swim up a river rapids. I began to think that at least I might learn enough to be allowed to stay in Korea. Then my throat started to bother me and kept getting worse. I had strep throat and missed almost a week of language class since I could hardly speak. When I got back into class, I was even more lost than before.

The Korean language builds sentences sort of the opposite of the way we do in English. Where we usually start with the subject followed by the verb and then everything else, in Korean the sentence starts with everything else and always ends with the verb. Often there is no subject, especially if the subject is a pronoun and it is implied by context. In addition, Korean has verb endings that tell the tense and the level of speech. Different verb endings are used depending on whether you are speaking to a child, an adult who is of similar status to you, or to someone who is much older and/or in a higher position or status. We were learning the high form in class, the *imnida* verb ending. For example: *ga* means go. To a child you can just say *ga*. To someone your same age or level you can say *gayeo* or, a little more politely, *gasayeo*. To an older or higher level person, it's *gamnida*. It can get confusing, but it was funny when we got outside the New Grand Hotel. Sometimes one or another of us trainees would be talking to little kids on the street and it would come across to them probably sounding like, "Honorable sir/madam please blah blah." It must have been hilarious to the adult Koreans listening to us addressing children this way. But most Koreans seemed to deeply appreciate the fact that we Americans were trying to learn their language at all.

It's hot and humid throughout South Korea in the summer and there is a monsoonal rainy season which just adds to the discomfort. Daegu especially is hot and humid as Hades (Is Hades humid?) in the summer because it is surrounded by mountains and heats up like a metal bowl sitting on a heating coil every day. The summer of '72 was no exception. Thank god the New Grand Hotel was air-conditioned, but outside on the streets we sweated bullets.

I remember one day walking along just after a rainstorm with Jack who was well over six feet tall. A little kid threw a ball, and it got stuck on the roof of a one-story building. The kid looked pained until Jack walked up, stretched his long arm up, and grabbed the ball. We could hear the boy exclaim "Wha!" in surprise. Jack must have seemed like the Jolly Green Giant (or, more accurately, a Jolly White Giant) to this small Korean boy, who had a smile from cheek to cheek as Jack handed him the ball and we continued sweating and dripping on our way.

Jack asked one day if I'd like to go with him to Camp Henry, the American Army Base in Daegu. I knew he was going to buy marijuana. Marijuana was illegal in Korea but always available around U.S. military installations. *"What the heck, why not live dangerously?"* I thought to myself. So we got into a taxi and headed for Camp Henry. When we got near the base, we immediately went to one of the bars by the main gate and ordered beers. I was looking around at the ladies who worked there serving, as well as others who obviously did their work later in the evenings not serving beer. Jack said he'd be back in a few minutes and left me alone. Of course, one of the ladies who was hanging out and did her best work at night, came over and started talking to me in broken English. This was fun, but Jack came back and suggested we drink up and head out. He had bought the stuff and was anxious to get back and smoke some. Jack and the other pot smokers would sometimes head over to a nearby park to sit and smoke. Sometimes I'd head over to the park named *Dalseong-gongwon* (Dalseong Park) with them. I enjoyed their company and talking with them, but I had never smoked pot and wasn't about to start then. I just passed the joint on when it got to me without taking a puff. As my pot smoking friends in college used to say, "Don gets high on nature." I didn't need any drug or chemical help of any kind.

Throughout the course of the training program, we also had cross-cultural training. One of my favorite Peace Corps terms came out of these cross-cultural training sessions, "Culturally In-Sensitive" or "CIS," as in "don't be CIS." We'd say that to each other when we caught someone not being sensitive to the Korean culture. "Don't be CIS!"

One of the first cross-cultural lessons we learned took place in an elevator in a tall building in Daegu. Instead of the number four for the fourth floor there was an F. We, of course, asked why this was so, and one of our cross-cultural instructors told us that the number four in Korean is pronounced *"sa"* as is the Chinese character for death. So rather than have a four on the keypads in the elevators they have an F. That way no one is reminded of death every time they announce that they want to get off on the fourth floor. Instead "F *chusayeo* (please)," they'd say. This was slightly funny as the Korean language doesn't have an "f" sound, and Koreans would actually say, "Eh-poo *chusayeo*."

Another interesting coincidental language/number juxtaposition in Korean is the Korean word for move, which is *"i-sa."* The Korean number two is pronounced like a long E and *sa*, as already mentioned, is four. So moving companies in Korea have cornered all the phone numbers ending with 2, 4, 2, 4. That way, when people read the seven-digit phone numbers for moving companies, they come out sounding in Korean like three numbers and then the words move, move (*i-sa, i-sa*).

For our cross-cultural training, we often had lectures about Korean culture and also field trips. My favorite lecture was given by Richard Rutt, an Anglican bishop who first came to Korea in 1954. He wrote the classic book *Korean Works and Days* about Korean village life in early post-Korean War South Korea while he was working in a village in Gyeonggi province, the province which surrounds Seoul. In 1968 he was appointed the Anglican bishop of Daejeon. He had also just published in early 1972 another book entitled *A Biography of James Scarth Gale and a New Edition of His History of the Korean People.* James Scarth Gale was a Canadian missionary who first came to Korea in 1888. He was a prolific writer, translator, and lexicographer. Gale had originally published his famous book *History of the Korean People* in 1927. Bishop Rutt, who was a commanding presence, held all of us trainees and trainers in awe with his amazing knowledge of Korean culture, history, and language. It was my hope to someday have at least a small percentage of his grasp of Korea, the Korean language, and the Korean people.

Another interesting lecture was given by a female shaman. She spoke through an interpreter about Korean Shamanism. Then she asked if anyone would like to have her tell their fortune. Several of us raised our hands, including me, but she chose my roommate Nick. I found this interesting because he was probably the most brilliant of all of us, and here she chose him. I figured he probably had the strongest vibes coming from his brain. She went on in general terms about his future, although the one thing I seem to remember her saying was that he'd get married soon. He did end up marrying Mary Davisburg, one of our fellow K-23 trainees, but not until after they both had finished their two years of Peace Corps service and had returned to the States.

Although yoga is not of Korean origin, several of us took yoga as a cross-cultural activity each Wednesday in the late afternoon after our TESOL classes were finished. Russ Frankenmuth, our Cross Cultural Training Coordinator, set up this activity and went with us. We would all jump into a couple of taxis and head to downtown Daegu where the yoga studio was located.

Each Wednesday in yoga, we learned many different positions or *asanas*. In one of the early sessions we did the bow pose. In the bow pose, you lie on your stomach, reach back with your hands, grab your ankles, lift your legs and push them and your arms as far toward the ceiling as you can. When I did this, I got a sharp pain in my right lower abdomen. I yelled, "Ouch!" and fell over. I'd had a slight hernia on the right side since my junior year in college and had been told by a doctor in the summer of 1971 that I probably shouldn't play soccer my senior year. I played anyway and had no big problem with it, but this bow pose really hurt. The Korean instructor came over and with Russ translating asked what the problem was. I explained to Russ that I had a slight hernia and that it hurt like hell when I stretched into bow. Russ ran over and grabbed his Korean-English dictionary. Hernia is not a word that one usually knows in a foreign language. Russ found hernia in the dictionary (*talchang*) and explained my plight. The instructor told me through Russ that I should continue to do bow everyday, but gently to the point where I felt only a slight twinge and then stop. Over time, he told me, my hernia would go away. I religiously did bow nearly every day throughout the rest of training and for months after at my Peace Corps site. He was right. Over time, I could stretch farther and farther into bow, and after a few weeks the pain disappeared. I have never had a problem with any pain on my right side since. Yoga cured my hernia.

The instructor also noticed that my right leg is longer than the left by almost a half an inch. He suggested lying on my back and stretching my right arm as far as I could away from my shoulder while stretching my left leg as far as I could away from my hip, so the left leg and right arm were stretching in the opposite directions. If I did this a half dozen times three or more days a week, over time, my left leg would become the same length as my right, he predicted. I tried to do this for several months but finally quit and gave up. My right leg is still longer than my left, and I always have to get at least one leg of new pre-hemmed pants altered (or, as one guy I used to work with at United Shirt Distributors used to say, "alternated").

Nick Mack decided to learn a Korean traditional musical instrument that looked like a simple piccolo. I walked into our room one day, and Nick was playing away on it.

"What the heck is that?" I asked.

"It's a *piri*." (A piri is a double reed instrument, made of bamboo, with eight finger holes.)

"Oh! Did you know that George Harrison wrote a song about the *piri*?"

"Really?"

"Yes," and then I started singing, "Isn't it a *piri*, isn't it a shame." (Actually it is "Isn't It a Pity" written and performed by George Harrison)

"Mother of God, I fell into that one, didn't I?" Nick often said, "Mother of God," and I picked up this affectation. Every once in a while, you'll still hear me say it.

I remember one day heading into downtown Daegu with a couple of other trainees and Tim Metamora. Tim, one of the training program's Peace Corps Volunteer (PCV) Assistants, saw a pretty young Korean gal and stuck his upper torso out the window and began waving and yelling toward her. I was embarrassed and thought how CIS (culturally insensitive) can you get. This was typical Tim behavior, as he was always on the prowl for women, even though we were told that Koreans were very conservative about sexual matters. We were told we should never have an affair with women who lived in our towns. It was better to leave on the weekends and go to a different town or city for amorous activities. Tim also was not that good in language ability either. One day someone mentioned they wanted to get a grape Fanta at the store. Coke and Fanta were available throughout South Korea even then. He said, "Oh, just say '*porto hwanta chusayyeo*.'" The first "a" in *hwanta* he pronounced like the "a" in at. We had learned that grape was *podo* with no "r" sound in it, and Fanta, because there is no "f" sound in Korean was *hwanta,* but the first "a" was not like the "a" in at, but rather like the "a" in ha. He was close, but no cigar for Tim.

Not having an "f" sound made it hard for Koreans to say my family name. When Koreans said it, Haffner came out as a three syllable word—ha-poo-nah. "F"s usually become a "p" sound or sometimes a "hw" sound as in *hwanta.* Also, Koreans can't say the "ner" at the end of Haffner very well and it comes out "nah." This is one good reason why we all were given and used Korean names during our Peace Corps service.

One afternoon several of us went off with one of the trainers to an area of town with traditional Chinese medicine shops. We walked into one and immediately all noticed the interesting aroma in the shop. Behind a counter there was a large built-in wooden cabinet with dozens of small drawers like those in old library card catalogs, each with different Chinese characters written on them. The apothecary shop owner explained, again with the help of our trainer as translator, that depending on the type of malady, he would pull out several different herbs and other items like deer antler, which had been cut off in the spring when engorged with blood and sliced into very thin wafers. These were put into a piece of white paper folded in a very intricate way almost like origami. Then the patient would take this mixture home, open the packet, place the contents into a pot of water, put the pot on a stove or over the charcoal used for heating and render it down until the concoction looked like mush. Then it was extracted from the pot, put into cheesecloth-like fabric which was folded up around it and squeezed using a couple of sticks, one wrapped around each end of the cloth, turned in opposite directions and thus dripping the liquid into a cup. Then the ill person would drink the potion. Often the treatment required several packets with the contents boiled, squeezed and drunk a couple of times a day for several days.

We left the Chinese medicine shop and went down the block to an acupuncturist's shop. Again we met the owner, and he showed us the chart on the wall with all the locations where needles might be placed, depending on the malady. He answered our questions and then asked if any of us would like to experience being stuck by the needles. Carrie Anne Tawas volunteered and stepped forward. The acupuncturist took out one of the needles from a small box. It had a large head on one end and was a couple of inches long. He held the head of the needle with his right hand. Then he stuck his tongue out a little, pinched his tongue with his left thumb and index finger and then ran his thumb and index finger over the length of the needle from the head down to the sharp point in order to (in his mind, I guess) sterilize it completely. I turned to whoever was standing next to me and whispered, "Ain't no way he's sticking one of those in me." He told Carrie Anne to hold out her arm. She didn't seem to be troubled in the least by his sanitation methods. She held out her arm, and he inserted the sharp end into it below her elbow and then twirled it with his thumb and index finger, hence twisting the needle while still in her arm. Carrie Anne said, "Oh, it tingles a little." Then he asked if anyone else would like to try. I saw everyone else sort of cringe and move their arms away from the front of their bodies. They were obviously bothered as I was by his contaminated methods. So, we took our leave and returned to the New Grand Hotel for the evening.

On one of our excursions around Daegu with Russ Frankenmuth and Tim Metamora we were walking along the sidewalk. It had rained earlier in the day, and there were puddles here and there. Patty Olivet and another trainee were walking along in front of us, while I was walking next to Tim with Russ and with several others behind us. A Korean middle-aged gentleman in a suit was walking toward us when, just as he got close to Patty, she jumped up into the air and came down in the middle of one of the puddles, splashing water all over including onto the legs of the Korean man who had just passed her by. He had a pained and exasperated look on his face as he turned his head to look back at Patty, who was now skipping merrily along oblivious to the fact that she had splattered this man's suit pants, socks, and shoes with muddy water. Tim said to me while shaking his head, "When is someone going to tell Patty she's in Korea?" "Not sure," I replied, "but seems like it would be a good idea."

About halfway through the training program, we held a talent show, or a "lack thereof" show. Most of the volunteers took part in one capacity or another. Some of the staff from Seoul also came down for the momentous occasion including Peace

Corps/Korea Director Jim Wixom. A hall next to the New Grand Hotel was rented, and beer was flowing. I even had a couple myself.

Because I was always walking around singing and I'm a fairly high tenor, a couple of the gals in our group suggested that the three of us sing "Stop! In the Name of Love" by the Supremes with me being Diana Ross and singing the lead part. So I sang the verses such as:

> Baby, baby I'm aware of where you go
> Each time you leave my door.....
> ("Stop! In the Name of Love" written by Holland-Dozier-Holland,
> performed by The Supremes)

Then my Supremes would join in for the chorus, and we of course had some choreography worked out. When we sang, "Stop" we'd hold our arms out straight with our palms facing the excited audience. Then we'd sing, "in the name of love," and we'd cross our hands over our left boobs, and so on. Back in those days without computers and Google to look up the right lyrics, I'm sure I just made up half the words, which I did most of the time anyway, but we had fun and got a rousing round of applause.

There were other singers too. Several trainees wrote a song about our training program to the tune of the old folk song "Tom Dooley."

> Landed in Korea, there was red-haired Russ
> Met us at the airport, waited by the bus.....

And so on. Some others wrote a song to the tune of "Frere Jacques" about *Chungcheongbuk-do* (North Chungcheong Province). All of the South Korean provinces with coastlines on the peninsula had a midnight to 4:00 am curfew during our Peace Corps years because of the threat of North Korean spies or military personnel landing. The only two provinces that didn't have a curfew were *Chungcheongbuk-do*, because it was landlocked, and *Cheju-do*, the southern-most island province in the East China Sea. So to the tune of "Frere Jacques" several of the trainees sang:

> Chungcheongbuk-do, Chungcheongbuk-do
> Where are you? Where are you?
> Right here in the middle, right here in the middle
> With no curfew, no curfew.

Then to the tune of "Pretty Baby" (written by Tony Jackson, as sung by Doris Day, Dean Martin, and many others) that my father always sang as:

> Every party has a pooper that's why we invited you,
> party pooper, party pooper.

Three female volunteers sang:

> If you're homely and you're lonely and nobody talks to you,
> Join the Peace Corps, join the Peace Corps.
> If you're ugly and you're fugly and nobody talks to you,
> Join the Peace Corps, join the Peace Corps.

All of these songs got rave reviews, too.

There were also a few comedians. In our TESOL classes we were learning about diphthongs and bilabial fricatives and such. One of our trainees did a whole comedy routine about these linguistic intricacies that, for some reason, we were studying. His routine was hilarious, although the only joke I remember is, "And here is a bilabial fricative." Then he pushed out his lips and forced air out between them. With his lips vibrating, he made a buzzing noise that the Brits call "giving the raspberry."

Another guy did a brilliantly funny routine in Korean using our still rather limited language knowledge. One joke was about how many restaurants and bars in Korea at this time had only one bathroom. Some of these bathrooms had a urinal against the wall and then right next to it a door to the toilet. Sometimes I would be standing and peeing in one of these unisex bathrooms when a woman would come in, stroll right behind me as if I were not there, open the stall door, walk in and close the door behind her. If I was in a bar and the woman was around my age and cute, and if I was slightly to heavily inebriated, I'd say, "*Annyeonghasaeyeo,*" the Korean equivalent of hello. She/they would always ignore me and traipse on by. The trainee's joke started with, "In America men's and women's bathrooms are separate," but said in Korean. Then the punch line was, "But, in Korea they are *ttoggataeyeo* (the same)." The fact that he said this all in Korean made us laugh, but it's probably one of those you had to have been there kind of things to fully understand how funny this was. Having a couple of beers under our belts also helped. A second joke he told is harder to explain, but has to do with a Korean greeting *Oregon maniaeyeo!* which means, "I haven't seen you in a long time." *Maniaeyeo* means many or much. So, our comedian said, "Oregon *maniaeyeo, kurochiman* (but), California *hanna pakae upsaeyeo* (only one)." Which could mean, "There are many Oregons, but only one California," although to a Korean it wouldn't mean much of anything. The last joke I remember him telling was in regards to the Korean word *insa. Insa* means a greeting. This time in English he said, "If *insa* means a greeting, then when parting, shouldn't it be an out-*sa?* He too got a huge round of applause and out-*sa* became an often-used expression among us K-23s. "I'm leaving now, so let me give you an out-*sa*—Goodbye."

Then the last act of the night was Nick Mack. Of course, he was the same Nick who had told dirty sex jokes for four hours straight on our original bus ride down from Seoul to Daegu on our first day in Korea. Naturally, he did a comedy routine for the talent show. He had gone to Columbia University, as mentioned before, and had, or so he said, done comedy at local clubs around Columbia in New York City. He began by announcing that his stage name was Uranus Farts. This got a smattering of laughs, but cracked me the heck up. Of course, all of our Korean language instructors were also in the audience, and they didn't have the foggiest idea what we were laughing about. Then Nick started into a long and drawn-out story about being in New York City and getting in trouble with the cops, and then something else happened, followed by another occurrence with more problems of this and that description or another and..... The language instructors were getting up and walking out, and even many of us trainees were getting fidgety, but Nick just kept on going. I liked Nick and his off-the-wall sense of humor. I had even stuck up for him when he called Karen an idiot for not knowing Mt. Kilimanjaro had snow on top and not eyes, but I could not follow his long convoluted story, hard as I tried. He finally finished his marathon joke, and a handful of us clapped, mostly thankful that he had stopped talking more than anything. And so ended the Peace Corps K-23 official Talent Show!

Everyone stayed and continued drinking after the entertainment. In a short while, I got bored and wandered back to the New Grand Hotel. There I ran into Nick in the hallway on the second floor where we ate our meals and had classrooms. We stood there talking for a while, and then Jim Wixom came up the stairs and into the hallway. He was obviously drunk, and he walked straight up to Nick and said, "There's not room enough in this country for the both of us. Let's go up on the roof and have it out." I thought I was in the middle of *High Noon* or a spaghetti western or something. I glanced over at Nick, and he had an incredulous look on his face but didn't move and continued leaning against the wall as he had been when Jim walked up to him. Jim had an irate look on his face, and I kept trying to think of something to say to change the subject. Of course, nothing came to mind, but I finally blurted out, "Jim, wasn't the talent show good?" He looked over at me like he was surprised I was there and began talking about the talent acts. Nick leaned over and whispered in my ear, "I'll catch you later." He walked behind me and through the door into the stairway that led upstairs. I carried on a short conversation with Jim and then suggested we return to the hall next door, which we did.

As soon as Jim and I entered the hall where the party was still going on, I wandered off and got as far from him as I could. Soon thereafter I returned to the second floor of the New Grand. There were a number of fellow trainees now in the room where we ate our meals. After our meals were done, the tables were folded up and stacked in the corner so the room could be used as a lounge. The room had a raised floor about four inches above the hall level. At each of the two doors, there was a small area where people left their shoes. The raised floor was covered by traditional shellacked, heavy paper which had a lovely mellow-yellow color. I kicked my shoes off, entered the room and sat against the wall. Someone suggested that we sing and said, "Hey Don, start singing something." So I started singing "Blackbird" by the Beatles, and everyone joined in. Then others among us started other songs, and we all threw our voices in with reckless abandon. I heard a clopping sound and looked over to see Jim Wixom walking across the floor in his clunky wing-tip dress shoes. We all gasped at this horrible example of CISness. Jim plopped down and after our initial shock wore off, someone started singing "Morning Has Broken." Again everyone joined in and we all quickly forgot about Jim Wixom's amazing lack of cultural awareness. When we finished singing Jim blurted out in his drunkenness, "What does that song mean to you?" The question was asked to no one in particular but just thrown out to the dozen or so of us trainees sitting around the edge of the room. Someone began to answer, "It's a song about how every day is a new day, a new beginning and....." Jim broke in, "That's BULLSHIT." I leaned over to whomever was next to me and said, "I'm outta here." I walked over to the door, slid my feet into my shoes, and walked off hearing Jim explaining why the song was "bullshit" and telling the trainees that they were all naïve.

I walked upstairs to our room and found Nick sitting and reading by himself.

"What was that all about in the hallway with Jim?" I asked Nick.

"I don't know," he replied. Then I told him all about Jim's clodhopper wing-tips and his "bullshit" comment.

"That guy's one loose cannon," I said.

"Yeah," replied Nick.

"Do you think he has a slight drinking problem?" I suggested.

"A distinct possibility!"

"Well, I'm exhausted. Catch you in the morning."

"Yeah, goodnight." It had been a long day, and I hit the sack thinking about Jim Wixom and thought to myself, *"Glad I don't place much importance on first impressions."* My first impression of him was favorable. He'd had many interesting and important positions in Michigan's state government, and that impressed me, but I was impressed no more.

Jim Wixom was eventually recalled. Word must have gotten back to the Peace Corps headquarters in Washington, D.C. that this guy wasn't exactly the epitome of what a Peace Corps Country Director should be. Interestingly enough, over a decade later I heard about Jim's transformation while I was the Resident Director of the Pearl S. Buck Foundation (PSBF)/Korea Branch from 1979 to 1988. PSBF was founded by Pearl S. Buck, the Nobel Prize-winning author, to help the displaced children of the world with an emphasis on the fatherless Amerasian children born throughout East and Southeast Asia in every country where American forces were or had ever been stationed since WWII, or in the case of the Philippines, since 1898. During the late 1980s, I got to know the director of Save the Children in Korea. Save the Children/Korea had replaced their American director with a Korean national in the early 1980s and ended up having problems. They hired Jack Burns, who had a Ph.D. from Harvard, to straighten things out. I was the Chairman of the Korea Association of Voluntary Agencies (KAVA) at the time and a Director of the Rotary Club of Seoul. Jack joined both of those organizations. I often sat next to him at the meetings of these groups and got to know him pretty well. At some point he mentioned that he had been the President of Cuyahoga Community College's (CCC) downtown Cleveland Campus, whose acronym should have been CCC-CC but probably wasn't. I had told him before about having been a Peace Corps volunteer in Korea, and he asked if I had known Jim Wixom. Of course, I told him I had and that Jim had been the Peace Corps Country Director when I first came to Korea in 1972. Jack informed me that Jim had been an instructor for him at the CCC downtown Cleveland Campus.

"Did he tend to drink a little too much?" I inquired.

"Oh, no," Jack said, "in fact he didn't drink at all and was a real health nut. He was out at the crack of dawn every morning and ran several miles."

"Really," I said, "Glad to hear it. He was a bit of a drinker during his Peace Corps director days." That's all I said. I could have added that I thought he had been a flaming asshole when drunk, but I saw no reason to bring up his transgressions, and I was happy to hear that he had sobered up, straightened out, and was flying right as Nat King Cole sang that one should. ("Straighten Up and Fly Right" written by Nat King Cole and Irving Mills, performed by The King Cole Trio)

Every few days during our training one of the active Peace Corps Volunteers would show up and hang out in the corridors talking with our Peace Corps trainers and with all of us trainees during our breaks and after classes. I quickly decided I didn't really like talking to some, even many, of them. They often complained about how much they disliked Korea and Koreans. According to many of them, the Koreans were dumb and lazy. Now that South Korea is one of the biggest trading nations on the planet and their international test scores in math and science are always right at the top, these remarks seem funny. I just tended to steer clear of these volunteers. If I saw an American I didn't know in the hallways of the New Grand Hotel, I'd just waltz by and ignore him or her. If I heard them being positive I might stop and listen, but at the first hint of negativity, I was out of there. So far I loved Korea, and I was sure I was going to enjoy my stay. *"To hell with them,"* I thought.

One of the things that Koreans did, which Americans would laugh about, was when they touched something hot, they would quickly grab their earlobe with their thumb and index finger. This seemed strange, but I remember Russ explaining to us that because your earlobes hang down they are cooler (Russ didn't say this, but I was thinking, *"Like your scrotum."*), and if you grab it—your earlobe, not your scrotum, although the scrotum might work too (only kidding)—with your burnt/hot thumb and index finger it helps dissipate the heat quickly and cool them off. Try it, it works.

The Koreans count money differently than we do, and again some volunteers would laugh at this too. Where we hold bills in our left hand, grab one at a time with our right hand and throw them down on a table while counting, Koreans fold the stack of bills in half around the index finger of their left hand with the ends of the bills sticking up like wings. Then pushing away against one bill at a time with their left thumb, they grab each bill one at a time with their right thumb and index finger and count as they pull this half of the bill down toward them. It is faster and easier and the bills never leave your left hand. Again, I suggest you try it.

A third thing that Koreans do that seems strange to Americans is something I learned to do later, which is using an ear spoon. East Asians use a small and short spoon, like a tiny demitasse spoon, to clean wax out of their ears. I grew up in America being told never to put anything smaller than your elbow in your ear. Of course, how anyone could ever stick their elbow in their own ear always perplexed me. On one of my trans-Pacific flights back to Korea in the early 1980s, I ended up with impacted wax in my ear and got an infection. I then had recurring ear infections for a few months. During this time, I learned about using an ear spoon. I have been using one to clean my ears once a week or so for the past thirty-some years and have never had any more ear infections or problems of any kind with my ears.

Probably the one Korean activity that got the most laughs and accusations of laziness by volunteers was the way that it took three Korean workers to operate one common-sized shovel. Upon occasion we'd notice this activity at construction sites. One man at the back guided the shovel with the handle. At the base of the handle, two ropes were tied just above the shovel part and the other two men each grabbed one of the ropes. The man guiding the shovel pushed it into the ground while the other two men in front of the shovel part, one on each side, pulled the ropes up and over to one side throwing the dirt aside. Then the next time they threw the dirt to the opposite side. Again, it looked funny at first, but good ole Russ explained that for digging a trench three Koreans working with one shovel can outdig three Americans using three shovels.

It was not new in the 1970s for Americans to think that Koreans were lazy. There are photos taken by Americans in the late 1800s showing one Korean worker guiding a shovel and two, three or even more Korean men holding onto each of the two ropes. Koreans never actually worked this way with more than three men total, but the Americans living in Korea back in the olden days must have staged these pictures in jest.

At the end of the Yi Dynasty (1392–1910), Korea's economy was stagnant, and most foreigners thought that it was because the Koreans were just plain lazy. The Yi Dynasty taxation system was to blame, though, not the Korean people. Years later, when I read Isabella L. Bird-Bishop's book *Korea and Her Neighbors*, I found that there was at least one foreigner who figured this out in the 1890s. Isabella Bird-Bishop was an intrepid British world traveler and author. For this book, she visited Korea, Japan, North China/Manchuria, and Far-East Russia and traveled to areas no Westerner, male or female, had ever traveled before. She found that the Koreans in Manchuria and in Russia, who had emigrated from Korea in the late Yi Dynasty to find more opportunity, were very energetic and hard working. Near Vladivostok the Koreans were supplying virtually all of the fresh vegetables for the city. In places where they were allowed to sell their excess crop and make money, they worked very hard. In Korea, the Yi Dynasty allowed Korean farmers to keep only enough food to feed their families for a year and took

Charlie, Lisa, and Don with matching shirts and boys' school uniform caps taken on the roof of the New Grand Hotel in Daegu.

any extra grain or produce as taxes. Consequently, Korean farmers tried to grow only enough to feed their families and no more than that.

Charlie Sarnia and I spent a lot of time together outside of class. One of the female trainees, Lisa Golly, also hung around with Charlie and me a lot. One day we were out shopping, and we all bought identical navy blue and white, wide-striped T-shirts. Then we found a shop that sold middle and high school student uniforms. Korean students all wore uniforms in middle school and high school in those days. The boys' school winter uniforms were black. They wore plain black slacks, a black Nehru collar-like jacket (which to me always looked like a Prussian military officer's jacket), and a black hat that looked like a Greek fisherman's hat. We all three bought one of these hats. Then we went back to the New Grand Hotel and changed into our new outfits. We thought we were so snazzy that we needed to have our pictures taken. We found one of our fellow trainees who had a camera (none of us had one). Then we asked him to take our picture a few times with all three of us in tennis shoes (mine were white leather Adidas), blue jeans, our new T-shirts, and our soon-to-be famous boys' school hats. I was the only one who had tucked in my T-shirt to accentuate how slim and trim I was in those days. The pictures were taken on the roof of the New Grand Hotel with the three of us together, and we then coaxed our Korean language teacher Miss Kim into putting on Lisa's hat and posing in between Charlie and me. Then we took another picture where we were doing the "hear no evil, see no evil, speak no evil" hand gestures. Lisa was hear-no, I was see-no and Charlie was speak-no. For a few days we wore those outfits around town until it got old and the hats were too hot, so we retired the winter hats and didn't wear the shirts on the same days anymore. I'm not sure that we weren't a little CIS wearing the hats around anyway, although none of our trainers or language instructors seemed to be bothered by our shenanigans at all.

One afternoon, for our TESOL session, they brought in some Korean middle school boy students. Ron Schwartz, the TESOL Advisor for the K-23 Training Program, gave a demonstration teaching lesson. All I can remember of his lesson is how he taught the students his name. He told the students, "My name is Mr. Schwartz." He then had the students repeat after him, "Mr. Schwartz." Of course, they had a hard time with the Schwartz part, though they did pretty well with "mister." So he drew a stick figure on the blackboard, and he then drew a T-shirt and instead of long pants a pair of Bermuda-length shorts on the stick figure so that it wouldn't be naked any longer. Then he pointed with his pointer at the Bermuda shorts and said, "Repeat after me, shorts." "Shorts," the students said. But Ron still wasn't pleased with their pronunciation of his family name which he was actually mispronouncing himself now. He had them over and over again repeat "shorts," and then "mister shorts." Not only did I think this was awkward and ridiculous, I felt sorry for the students. I myself was wondering, *"What the heck has this got to do with anything? Who cares if the students can or can't pronounce your name correctly? How many Mr. Schwartzes are they likely to run into in their lives anyway? They are almost certain to never meet a Mr. Shorts. I never have."* Here again is where I saw the great value in American teachers having a Korean name. Mr. Schwartz should have had a fine Korean name like Suck, No-crap, or something. There is a Korean family name So. He could have used So – So, No-shorts, maybe. (There is also a girl's given name of Sue-me, and Charlie and I used to joke that it would be a great name for a female lawyer to be named So, Sue-me, especially if she was also Jewish by chance.) At any rate, his over-emphasis on his family name turned me off, and I pretty much daydreamed the rest of his teaching exhibition, which is probably why I don't remember anything but this embarrassing family name part.

After a couple of months of training we broke up into three smaller groups and headed for other cities where we would practice our newly honed TESOL skills. I was with the group that went to Gwangju, the capital of Jeollanam-do (South Jeolla Province). Kim, Dae-Jung, who many Koreans and foreign observers felt won the 1971 presidential election against Park, Chung-hee, was from Jeollanam-do, and this province and the people in it were discriminated against by the Park, Chung-hee government. Park, Chung-hee was a general who seized power in a military coup and ruled with an iron fist from 1961 to 1979. He governed under more than one constitution in order to keep running over and over for reelection. The first constitution had a term limit for the president. Oh, hell, just scrap it and write a new one then run again, Park seemed to feel. Although he was instrumental in modernizing Korea by promoting its export-oriented growth, it was at the cost of a lack of personal freedom for his people. This was the reason we Peace Corps men had to cut our hair short before coming. In 1979, in what can only be called poetic justice, Park, Chung-hee was shot and killed at a private dinner party by the head of his own South Korean CIA.

On Sunday, we took a bus from Daegu to Gwangju, and when we got there, the ten of us trainees and a couple of the trainers, Russ and Tim, checked into a *yeogwan* (inn). Again, I ended up in a triple room, but this time it was with Charlie and Nick. Jack had been sent off with one of the other two groups. We had just gone into our rooms to drop off our bags when we heard a blood-curdling scream. It sounded like the shower scene from *Psycho,* directed by Alfred Hitchcock. We all ran out into the hall, and Patty Olivet had a look of horror on her face. "Did you see the toilet?" she cried. We hadn't, so we all went to check it out. There was the very same ceramic white, trough-like thing set into a tiled floor like the one that I had seen and stared at in a photo on the wall at the hotel in Denver during the PRIST. On the wall above this flush-style East Asian toilet was a rectangular metal contraption about two feet wide, eight inches high and six inches deep. Hanging on a chain coming out of it was a wooden pull thingie. I pulled the chain, a swoosh of water came out of a hole at one end of the ceramic trough and crashed into the other end that looked like a small band shell where there was a much bigger hole in the bottom into which the water and waste went down.

"Wow, neat," I said.

"Neat? How do you use it?" Patty still in shock replied.

"Very carefully," I said.

"Looks like we're all going to have to figure it out," Charlie said.

"True enough," I responded.

This didn't help, as Patty still looked very pained. We calmed Patty down and returned to our rooms to settle in. Shortly thereafter we all figured out that you had to pull your pants down around your ankles, squat down, hopefully without losing your balance and crashing into the walls or door, or without sitting down into the trough—especially after one had defecated into it because it was only a couple of inches deep and maybe eight inches wide.

The next day we awoke early to the typical morning din in Korea. In Daegu we were not on a large main street at the New Grand Hotel, and we had air-conditioning there. Here in Gwangju we were on a main street, and we had the windows open for the cooler night air and ventilation. At dawn the racket began: sweeping sounds, street vendors, and the ubiquitous *Saemaul Undong* (New-Village Movement) song blaring out of loud speakers. Every morning throughout every nook and cranny of Korea—except near the New Grand Hotel, it seemed—the *Saemaul Undong* song mysteriously, miraculously played to wake everyone up and urge them to clean and build up their village, town, or city. To a very peppy tune the first and fifth verses as well as the refrain translated into English are:

> Dawn bell tolls, new dawn breaks
> Let us get up you and me; building Saemaul   (New Village)
> (Refrain)   My village a good place for living,
> Let us build with our hands
> A new age unfolds; we all pooling our energies
> Let us create a new history of democracy, welfare and peace.
> (From: *Saemaul in New Age,* Republic of Korea, 1982)

Or, in Korean the first verse is:

> *Olokchongie, ulrungnea, sae achimie, palgungnee*
> *No doe na doe illona; saemaul mandulsay*

Supposedly this song was written by none other than President Park, Chung-hee. And if you believe that George Washington told his father after chopping down a cherry tree, "I cannot tell a lie," and fessed up, then I'm sure you'll believe this story, too. At any rate sleeping after sunrise was nigh onto impossible in much of Korea. The funny thing is that the name for Korea during the last dynasty, the Yi Dynasty, was Chosun/Joseon, which means Land of the Morning Calm. The Japanese also called Korea Chosun during their occupation from 1910 to 1945, and the name is still sometimes used in tourism publicity encouraging foreigners to visit the Land of the Morning Calm. After our first morning in Gwangju, Nick, Charlie and I decided that Korea should change its nickname to the Land of the Morning Racket.

The brochure that we all had received along with our invitation to become Peace Corps Volunteers (PCV) in Korea titled "Koreagraphy" had warned us about how noisy Korea was in the early morning. On the second page is a picture of a married PCV couple lying on a thin mattress looking half-asleep. The caption next to the photograph reads:

> It's hard to sleep
> 4:00 A.M. roosters
> vendors clanging brass

children screaming
scrambling rats
cacophony.

    Charlie, Nick, and I rolled over and pulled our pillows over our heads, but to no avail. We got up and started getting ready to go to a nearby college to teach. The Education Ministry had invited—or, more accurately, told—many English teachers from throughout the province to come to the college this week for conversational English practice/training/learning. The building we taught in was a very ugly, nondescript cement building. The classrooms were small, had little windows, and a wire hanging from the ceiling with a single low-watt light bulb hanging from it. Each of us taught a class of a half dozen Korean-English teachers for several hours. Their English wasn't very good, but then that is part of the reason that we were in Korea, wasn't it? This first day I learned something about my Midwestern accent that I hadn't known. While teaching I said the word "often." I never realized it previously, but I said it then and I notice now that Midwestern people often pronounce it with the "t" in often and a hard "t" at that. So I said, "I off-TIN go downtown." The Korean teachers in my class jumped all over this. One of them immediately said, "Mr. Ha, the 't' in often is silent." The others nodded in agreement. I mentioned that in the part of the U.S. that I'm from, many people off-TIN throw the "t" in for good measure. They again informed me that this was incorrect. After that, I never pronounced the "t" in often again because I knew the Koreans would call me out on it every time.

Don teaching in a classroom in Gwangju.

    On the way back to the hotel, sirens suddenly wailed. Russ and Tim had warned us that this was the monthly National Civil Defense Drill day. We had been warned that if we were out on the street we had to duck into a store or seek shelter somewhere. When the loud siren went off we hid in the closest store we could find. It was an open-to-the-street small market stall-like shop. As we stood there a South Korean Air Force jet fighter plane began sweeping low over the street we were on as if it were strafing the area with heavy machine-gun fire. We asked if this was normal, and our trainers said, "No!" In fact, in the almost fifteen years in total that I ended up living and working in Korea, I never again saw a jet fighter flying over a city during any of the monthly National Civil Defense Drills I witnessed. I think it was a warning to the people of Gwangju not to protest against President Park, Chung-hee.

Years later, in 1980, in an event called the Gwangju Uprising, students and the citizens of Gwangju rebelled against another ex-general president, President Chun, Doo-hwan, from May 18 to 27. The people took over the city and drove the police out. Then the army moved in. I was later told by U.S. Embassy personnel that President Chun had pulled a crack paratroop unit of Korean soldiers off the DMZ for this operation without informing the U.S. military and thus leaving a gap in the defenses that North Korea could have exploited had they known about it and wanted to. I was also told later by American missionaries who were working in a hospital in Gwangju in 1980 that the troops used dumdum bullets aginst their own citizens, which spread upon impact to cause maximum damage, rather than just regular bullets. There were also claims of atrocities perpetrated by the paratroopers, such as using their bayonets to cut off the breasts of female students they had captured. Government estimates that only 200 people died during the uprising seem very low compared to the stories I heard and the rumors that persisted afterwards.

On our second day of teaching in Gwangju, Tuesday, Carrie Anne Tawas hadn't felt well in the morning, and by evening she was running a high fever. Tim took her by taxi to the Gwangju Hospital, one of the hospitals where casualties of the uprising would be taken 8 years later. The next day, the remaining nine of us trainees went off to the college to teach. In the evening after dinner, a few of us went to visit Carrie Anne in her hospital room. She told us that the nurses had stuck an IV in her arm and somehow had collapsed her vein. I'm not good with medical jargon and had no idea what that meant exactly or the consequences of it, but it didn't sound good to me.

That evening Charlie, Nick, and I went to sleep, and everything seemed fine until I woke up in the middle of the night. I felt sick with an upset stomach. I wobbled and hobbled my way to the toilet as fast as I could. Just inside I puked like there was no tomorrow, and as quickly as I finished puking, hurriedly dropped my u-trou, squatted down, and even before my behind got near the porcelain trough the diarrhea started flowing as if my kiester were a fire hydrant.

I felt like the power of the brown watery stool coming out of my heinie might propel me through the roof, I was also groping with my hands for the side walls of the toilet to help keep from passing out and falling over. No sooner had my butt stopped pumping when I began upchucking again. I quickly swiveled and with my head between my knees again positioned my hands against the walls to steady myself. I felt weak as hell and finally after several minutes, I was able to clean myself up with the very rough, light-brown colored toilet paper. I stood up, pulled my underpants back up and yanked the chain to flush away the disgusting slush.

Weaving my way back to the room, I laid down and tried to sleep, but a short time later I was off to the races again. This time I was almost jogging my way back to that little room where I repeated my earlier escapade. This went on a couple more times before daybreak, except that, by the end, I was just dry-heaving as there was nothing left in my stomach or my intestines to expel.

In the morning Charlie and Nick knew just by looking at me that I wasn't feeling too well.

"What's wrong?" Charlie asked.

"I don't know. I woke up sometime in the middle of the night, ran to the bathroom, and man it was like the biggest existential dilemma of all time. I had the runs, and had to puke at the same time, and I had no idea which end to empty first. They both were screaming, 'ME FIRST!'" Nick called in Russ and Tim.

"You'd better take Don to the hospital," Russ said to Tim. All I could think of was that the nurses would put IVs in my arms, collapse all of my veins, and I'd surely perish.

"No, I'll be fine, just let me rest today. Wow, I feel a little better already." They looked at each other and agreed to let me have a day of rest. I crashed and just slept the whole day.

On Thursday I was still a little shaky, and they left me in the *yeogwan* again, but Carrie Anne got out of the hospital late in the afternoon and was feeling better. That night I went out for dinner with everyone, but ate very light and had no *kimchi* or anything the least bit spicy. We went shopping in an open market. Many people bought things, but the largest purchase anyone made was a brass gong 18" in diameter that Patty Olivet bought.

Friday I was able to teach again even though I felt very feeble. Somehow I made it through the day.

On Saturday I still felt pretty lousy when we got on the bus to take us back to Daegu. There was no Gwangju-to-Daegu expressway then as there is now, and we retraced our way back to Daegu over the same two-lane, pothole-infested roads that wound their way up and down the hills and mountains in between these two cities. I felt nauseous the whole way and sat with my head bouncing and crashing into the window over and over. I wasn't the only one traveling with a headache though. Patty had placed her brass gong wrapped in newspaper in the overhead rack where there was a place near the front of the bus right above where Brian Pewabic was sitting. Not too far outside of Gwangju the bus hit an especially deep pothole and the brass gong came tumbling down. It landed right on top Brian's head and nearly knocked him out. Brian looked almost as bad as I felt, and Patty apologized to high heaven. They say "misery loves company," but I never have liked to share my misery, and I felt bad for Brian. Several hours later we reached Daegu and the New Grand Hotel.

I spent Sunday sleeping most of the day, and then Monday morning I woke up feeling sick as a dog again. They took my temperature, and it was well over 100.

"You're going to the hospital," they said.

"Wait, which hospital?"

"The dispensary at Camp Henry, the American army base here in Daegu."

"Oh, Camp Henry, OK," I said. It turned out that the U.S. military gave medical assistance to Peace Corps when a volunteer near one of the bases was in need. This suited me just fine, as I was confident that no American military nurse would collapse any vein of mine. So I took another taxi trip to Camp Henry, this time not with Jack to buy pot at one of the nightclubs, but instead with one of the trainers. We got to the main gate of the base, got out of the regular Korean taxi, had our IDs checked, and went into the camp. Just inside we grabbed a U.S. Army-authorized taxi, and it took us to the dispensary/medical place. Inside they gave me a light green hospital gown, which I put on and climbed into a bed. A male army nurse came over and said he was going to draw blood. He wrapped the rubber cord thingie around my upper right arm, slapped my vein a couple of times, rubbed my inner arm with an alcohol swab and stuck the needle into my vein while I watched closely. Blood spat out from the hole he'd made in my arm and left a red splatter-line on his white gown from just below his neck down to his waist. I began to think that maybe I should have gone to the hospital in Gwangju when another army nurse nearby hurried over, pushed the red-striped guy aside, and said, "Give me that." He grabbed the needle and test tubes from the first guy and said to me, "Let's try that again. We'll use your left arm." He took a couple of test tubes full of blood without squirting it all over. I felt relieved, but I also wondered why they needed so much blood. It seemed like with all I'd been through I needed that blood more than they did.

They stuck me in an observation room that made me feel like a fish in a fishbowl. The room had glass from about four feet off the floor to the ceiling with no blinds or any privacy. I laid there for the rest of the week in bed. I really don't remember getting any medicine. The only thing I do remember is them giving me bottles of juice to drink and having me pee into a measuring beaker. They were monitoring how much I drank and how much came out. Once or twice a couple of our trainers and Charlie, Nick, Jack, Lisa, Carrie Anne, and others came to visit. They brought language materials for me to study, so I wouldn't fall even farther behind everyone else. I lay there thinking Peace Corps would probably ship me home because I was a sickly dude who'd never be able to teach more than a couple of days at a time without getting ill again. I had already had strep throat, and now the army doctor told me I had a case of dysentery. After having walked around with it for several days before seeing the base doctor, he said they would just let it run out its course. By the next weekend they released me. I kept singing over and over again the last couple of days I was there:

> Please release me let me go.
> For I don't love you any more.
> ("Please Release Me," written by Eddie Miller, Robert Yount
> and James Pebworth under the pen name Dub Williams,
> performed by Engelbert Humperdinck)

I especially didn't love the male nurse who splattered my precious blood all over his smock. Funny thing is once I got to my Peace Corps site, I never got sick again and never missed a day of teaching due to illness except the time I got carbon monoxide poisoning. But that story will come later.

As we started getting toward the end of our three-month training, they told us to begin thinking of where we'd like to be stationed. There were differences in dialects between provinces that we might want to consider. Or maybe we had spoken with one of the many volunteers who had stopped by and visited over the past several weeks and had heard something about one province or another that might have piqued our interest. I had no preference for one part of the country over another, other than wanting to work in a town or city on either the Sea of Japan or the Yellow Sea. I wanted to be right on the water, but I didn't care which side of the peninsula or which province I might end up in.

John Schoolcraft and Kathy Fowlerville, the very same couple Carrie Anne had tried to get as our roommates in the New Grand, asked to be placed in the same town together, and they were told that was not possible. The staff knew that they had lived together in college for a couple of years and guessed correctly that they would live together if they were stationed in the same place. Because many Koreans were very conservative when it comes to matters of a sexual nature, Peace Corps would not put them in the same town unless they were married. So Kathy and John announced that they were going to marry during our K-23 training program. They picked a date and began planning. On a Saturday toward the end of training, they had their wedding at the same hall next to the New Grand Hotel that had been used for our famous talent show. All the staff and all of us trainees were, of course, invited. The wedding went off without a hitch—or actually, with the two of them getting hitched. Afterwards at the reception in the same hall, everyone drank beer, and a good time was had by all.

There were a couple of weekends during training in which Charlie Sarnia and I took off on excursions. The first weekend trip was to a Buddhist temple near Daegu. It was probably Charlie's idea, but I too was very interested in learning more about Buddhism. I had taken a comparative religion class at Albion and studied all the major world religions, and one of my favorite books of all those that I read in college was *Siddhartha* by Hermann Hesse—"Buddha lite" as I sometimes call it. We got information about how to get to a nearby Buddhist temple from one of our language instructors who knew Daegu well. He told us that if we took one of the city buses to the end of the line toward the north, we would then be able to hike up the side of the mountain to a temple. One Saturday we followed his instructions, took the bus he suggested, and rode it to the end of the line far outside of downtown Daegu. We followed the signs with a swastika, the symbol of Buddhism, and climbed far up the mountain. (The Buddhist symbol is the mirror image of the Nazi swastika, and if it were a pinwheel, the Buddhist symbol would move in a clockwise motion. This version symbolizes Vishnu, the preserver or the protector. Hitler's swastika would move counter-clockwise if it were a pinwheel and symbolizes Kali, the goddess of destruction. I wonder if Hitler knew that when he picked this symbol.) After hiking a while, we reached the temple. We began in our very limited Korean to ask one of the monks if we could stay overnight. He asked us to wait, walked away, and brought back another monk who spoke English quite well. We repeated our request in English, and he told us this could be arranged. We told him we'd pay for our room and board, but he told us to just put a donation in the donation box in the main temple building. Just off to the side of the statue of Buddha there was a collection/donation box. He took us to our room and showed us where the outhouse was and a place with a water pump where we could wash up. He took his leave and explained that he would return later.

Charlie and I visited the main temple with the large golden statue of Buddha. We took our shoes off, went in, and walked around admiring all of the intricately painted walls and ceiling. Koreans love basic colors, especially red, yellow, dark green, and dark blue, and these colors were predominant in the patterns. Then we sat cross-legged on cushions and attempted to meditate for awhile. After some time, when my legs were beginning to fall asleep, I got up and went outside. Charlie followed shortly thereafter, and we checked out the smaller temple building dedicated to the Mountain Spirit. Almost all of the Buddhist temples in Korea had a smaller building off to the side dedicated to the Mountain Spirit, which is a vestige of the Shamanism that has existed in Korea since ancient times and which was still a part of the belief system of many Koreans. Just like Christianity picked up many aspects of pagan German and other earlier religious beliefs in the Middle East and Europe, so too Buddhism incorporated this aspect of Shamanism in Korea in order to draw the people to this new religion when Mahayana Buddhism first entered Korea from China in the fourth century CE.

We returned to our room, and dinner was brought to us by a young novice monk. It was served on a small low table, and we sat cross-legged on the floor next to it. The food was amazing. It was a typical Korean meal with an individual bowl of rice and a bowl of soup for each of us. In the middle of the table were several dishes filled with different vegetables. These center dishes are called *banchan* in Korean and usually include fish and sometimes meat, but since this was a Buddhist temple there were only vegetable choices. Many were mountain plants, and neither Charlie nor I knew what they were, but they each had different and unique flavors. We ate all the rice, every drop of the soup, and all of every vegetable center dish. This really made the New Grand Hotel food seem horrible by comparison, and we looked forward to a couple more meals on Sunday of the same or similar treats. Traditionally in Korea breakfast, lunch, and dinner were all the same: rice, soup and *banchan*. The soup might change meal to meal, and the center dishes might be different, but there were no specific ones for the time of the day one might be eating them.

After dinner the monk who spoke English well came back, and we talked with him and asked him many questions. The one question I remember asking was what he thought of Jesus' message. "Jesus outlined one path to reach the goal," he said. Though he felt the Buddha's way was better, he told us there were many roads to the same place. I found this interesting. There seemed to be more acceptance and more tolerance in Buddhism than I felt existed in Christianity or Islam. Instead of the "my way or the highway" message of many religions, I found this aspect of Buddhism to be a breath of fresh air. It has always seemed to me that any religion that teaches/preaches peace, love and tolerance is a good religion, while any one that teaches/preaches intolerance is an evil one. All religions and all cultures should be looking for and accentuating the similarities amongst all humans and not the often minor and trivial differences.

Later Charlie and I walked around on trails in the forest around the temple. We came to a cliff looking out over the basin that Daegu sits in, and we could see the lights coming on in the city off in the distance to the south as dusk set in. The young novice monk who had brought us dinner appeared next to us, and we talked to him in Korean. Charlie and I started singing a Korean pop song, and he joined in. The title in English would translate as something like "I Really Love You." In Korean we sang:

> *Saranghae tangshenul, chungmalro saranghae*
> (Love you, really love you)

Then after finishing the first verse, we moved into the very repetitious refrain:

> Yeah, yeah, yeah, yeah, yeah, yeah, yeah, yeah, yeah…..

We threw in a few extra yeahs just for good measure. The novice monk, who looked to be a teenager, sang along pretty well during the verse part, but when we broke into the complicated "Yeah" chorus part, he was so far off key that he seemed to have lost not only the key but also the lock and the door. Charlie and I looked at each other. I shrugged my shoulders, and we plowed on through with the rest of the verses and choruses. After we finished the song, the monk thanked us, bowed, and walked off back to the temple. Charlie and I cracked up laughing after the monk was out of earshot. During our training thus far we had been told over and over by our American Peace Corps trainers that all Koreans sang well because they got superior music education in school compared to that in the U.S.

"I thought all Koreans could sing well," I said.

"I guess you can throw that sweeping generalization right out the window." Charlie responded as he moved his hands as if using a broom.

"He was absolutely the worst singer I've ever heard. He couldn't carry a tune with a bushel basket," I said. And, hardy, har, har, we laughed for quite a while.

We sat and watched the sun slowly set off to our right, and as it was getting dark we found our way back to our room. After reading for a while, we both hit the hay. It seemed like a couple of minutes later when we were totally sound asleep that suddenly the loudest sound we had ever heard in our lives woke us up with a crash. I leaped from a prone position up onto my feet, and my ears were ringing—not just figuratively but quite literally ringing. The sound was coming from just outside our room. We went to the window and looked out. It was pitch black out, but a couple of feet from the side wall of our room we could make out a pavilion with a big bell hanging in it. The bell was about six feet high. We hadn't walked around the corner from our room in that direction, so we hadn't even noticed it was there. The bell was hanging from the rafters of the pavilion by two chains, and next to the bell was a large log about the width of a telephone pole and five feet long, also hanging from the rafters by chains. A monk was holding the chains just above the log, and when the bell's ringing was no longer perceptible he swung the log back a few feet and then flung it into the bell again. Bwonnnnnnnnnnng! Our eardrums just about burst, we put our fingers in our ears and moved to the far side of the room. A few more rings and then finally there was silence. The monk must have gone off to morning prayers, and we went back to sleep for a couple of more hours.

When we got up after sunrise and washed up, our breakfast was brought in. It was almost the same as the night before, and again Charlie and I ate everything but the plates. We both thought it might be worth becoming Buddhist monks just to get this wonderful food every day until we remembered the early call to prayer bell ringing and decided maybe we'd just visit once in a while. We spent most of the day taking a long hike in the forest, talking more with the monks, and meditating cross-legged in front of the Buddha statue. We also enjoyed a wonderful lunch.

Late in the afternoon we got ready to leave. We went up to the temple and put a few thousand *won* notes into the donation box in the main temple (a thousand *won* was worth a couple of dollars in those days), paid our respects to the monks who had been so kind to us, and said our goodbyes. We moseyed on down the mountain and got back on the bus that took us back to the New Grand Hotel.

Karen Gibraltar, the same Karen whom Carrie Anne hadn't wanted to room with and the same one whom Nick overdramatically chastised for thinking that Mt. Kilimanjaro had eyes instead of snow, talked Charlie and me (as well as two other trainee guys, Elton Benzonia and Bernie Riverview) into going to the small seaside town of Guryongpo and its beach near the harbor and industrial city of Pohang. We left in the morning on a Saturday and took the bus to Pohang. I sat next to Karen on the bus even though I was sure she had a crush on Charlie, although he seemed to have no cognizance of her infatuation. Karen was a couple of years older than I and already had an MA in education. I asked her questions, and she told me about her college and grad school. At one point the bus was going over a bridge across a river.

"I wonder what river that is?" I absentmindedly said.

"Oh, let's ask."

"Ask?"

"Sure!" She turned to the Korean sitting across the aisle from us and asked. "*Musin kang imnika?*"

"*Kumho-kang ieyeaow,*" (the Kumho River), the man replied.

"Kumho? Interesting, I have never heard of it," I remarked. (Strangely enough, during my Pearl S. Buck Foundation years in Korea my first wife and I lived for a while in *Kumho-dong,* the Kumho area of Seoul where she had grown up. It's also the name of a tire company.)

"How come you speak Korean so well?" I asked.

"I visited Korea after I got my BA and before starting my MA. Also I had a Korean friend in grad school, and she taught me Korean for several months before I joined the Peace Corps."

"That's great."

The five of us got out of the bus at the Pohang bus station. Karen found out which bus was headed across the small peninsula to the east of Pohang, which forms the small bay north of the city. We got tickets and boarded the bus just as it was leaving. It traveled on a two-lane dirt road like some of those between Gwangju and Daegu. When we reached Guryongpo we reconnoitered and found a *yeogwan* and got a couple of rooms. Then we went and checked out the beach. It was getting late in the evening, so we just waded in the water a little. When it was starting to get dark we headed off to find a place to eat. After dinner we went to a Korean *sul-jip* (bar, alcoholic beverage house). Karen ordered beer for us all and some snacks. She was in her element being better at the language than any of the rest of us. She loved speaking Korean and translating for us when we didn't understand or couldn't say something we wanted to say.

Sul-jips always had young ladies working in them as waitresses. The ladies came in and sat by the men (usually only men went to bars) prodding them to eat and drink more. Later in my Peace Corps town, I found out that often the men would force their drinks on the ladies and try to get them drunk, and then they'd try to take advantage of them or just feel like big shots because they could hold their liquor better. Since Karen was with our group things never got out of hand in that regard. But I was wearing a heavy cotton Sigma Nu T-shirt with the Greek letter sigma that looks like an "E" and the "N" for nu. A Korean taxi driver had turned around one day in Daegu and called me "Mr. En," so I began wearing the shirt inside out. After we'd had a few beers and were feeling fairly happy, one of the bar girls (who happened to be the cuter of the two, as luck would have it), noticed that my shirt was on inside out. She began talking quickly in Korean and started twisting the collar of the shirt to make sure it was, in fact, on wrong. Then she began pulling the shirttail out of my jeans and proceeded to pull it up over my head. As I sat there now naked from the waist up, she began fondling my pecks. Then she said something, and she, the other bar girl, and Karen began laughing.

"What did she say?" I asked Karen.

"She said your breasts are bigger than hers," Karen replied while cracking up.

"Yeah, but I bet hers are cuter," I jokingly said. After playing with my pecs a bit, she turned my T-shirt right side out and then put it back on me. We drank for another hour or so and then asked for the bill. As we were dividing it by five and putting together our payment, the cute bar girl, Miss Lee, asked through Karen if I would like to go to church with her the next morning. I agreed, and Karen said that she'd like to go too.

Sunday morning Karen and I got up to go to church. We met Miss Lee and then went into a very small Presbyterian church. I was thinking we'd sit together, but it turned out in this small town's church that women sat on one side and men on the other. In addition, there were no chairs or pews and everyone sat on the floor. So I ended up sitting alone, cross-legged, while Karen got to sit with Miss Lee. I, of course, didn't understand a word that was said, nor did I recognize any of the tunes to the hymns that were sung. It wasn't a Lutheran church, or they might have had a rousing rendition of "A Mighty Fortress Is Our God" or "Onward Christian Soldiers," but no. After the service, Karen and I said goodbye to Miss Lee and went back to our *yeogwan* to pick up Charlie, Elton, and Bernie. We then had breakfast and spent some more time on the beach before heading back to Daegu and more training.

We had one big cross-cultural trip during our training to visit Haein-sa (Haein Buddhist Temple). In Haein-sa resides the Tripitaka Koreana, the complete canon of Buddhist scriptures carved onto more than 80,000 woodblocks. Each of these blocks is about the size of a portable electronic piano keyboard. They are carved on both sides to produce over 160,000 large pages in total when printed onto paper. Each side is covered with dozens or even hundreds of Chinese characters, the written language of Korea at the time they were made. It is the oldest version of the Buddhist canon in Chinese characters in the world, and it is estimated that there are more than 52 million individual carved characters in total. All the characters are carved backwards so that when they are rolled with ink and then transferred to paper they come out the mirror image or correctly faced. These woodblocks were carved during the Koryo Dynasty, which ruled from 918 to 1392 CE. Between 1232 and 1259 the Mongols invaded Korea several times. The Korean royal family fled from their capital, which was north of today's Seoul, to Gangwha Island just off the east coast of Korea near where the Han River flows into the Yellow Sea. The Mongols were not able to dislodge the king and his family from this sanctuary. The original Tripitaka Koreana woodblocks had been destroyed by the Mongol invaders during the first invasion in 1232, and consequently Koryo's King Gojong ordered that they be reproduced. Buddhist monks cured the wood used for the woodblocks in a special process using saltwater and aging, which took several years, after which the monks carved them hoping for Buddha's assistance in driving out the Mongol forces. These woodblocks, carved from 1236 to 1251, are the very ones that are stored at Haein-sa. In 1259, even though Gangwha Island had never been captured by the Mongol intruders, the Koryo dynasty sued for peace. Their peninsular nation had been devastated by the fighting, and for the sake of their people the king accepted the Mongol peace terms. The peace terms specified that each crown prince of Koryo would be taken to Beijing as a youth to learn the Mongolian language and culture. They forced every crown prince to marry a Mongol princess, and then he was returned to Korea to rule. This went on for nearly 100 years until the Mongol Yuan Dynasty in China was overthrown. At the end of the Yi Dynasty in 1910, the court language of Korea still had vestiges of the Mongolian language picked up during the late Koryo period of intermarriage with the Mongols.

In addition to the Tripitaka Koreana, the Koryo dynasty was famous for its lovely pale green celadon pottery and for inventing the first metal moveable type used in the world in 1234 CE. This was two hundred years before Gutenberg replicated their feat and helped to bring about the Reformation and the dissemination of knowledge that led to the Enlightenment, the scientific revolution, and the modern era in Europe and the world. Koryo also gives us the English name for the country—Korea.

So our bus rolled into the mountains surrounding Haein-sa and reached the unpaved parking area. We all excitedly got out and hiked our way up to the temple. As we got close there were many stalls with Koreans selling snacks, souvenirs, and trinkets. Just in front of the temple even the monks joined into the act. They had a stall selling copies of various pages printed from the over eight-hundred-year-old woodblocks, as well as other Buddhist memorabilia.

Inside the temple compound were several buildings, two of which were long, one-story structures that housed the woodblock collection. In the walls of

One of the two buildings housing the 80,000 woodblocks comprising the Tripitaka Koreana.

the buildings were sections of wooden slats. There was no heat in these buildings, and the openings between the slats meant that the inside of these buildings was the same temperature as the outside. The slats allowed the breeze, whether with summer's humid heat or winter's freezing chill, to waft its way through. Over the past eight centuries not one of these specially treated woodblocks has cracked or warped. All 80,000 are perfectly straight and can still print every page of the Buddhist scriptures in perfectly legible Chinese characters. They can still be read (if you happen to understand the Chinese characters as used in Korea in the thirteenth century). We were given a tour of the temple by one of the monks. Our tour included the main temple building with the obligatory large golden statue of Buddha himself, the smaller temple building off to the side dedicated to the Mountain Spirit, and the two long buildings housing the Tripitaka Koreana woodblocks. We were invited to walk through and view the floor-to-ceiling rows of shelves in the front and back of these buildings with each woodblock edge individually labeled and ready for printing. After walking through the buildings the monk brought out one of the blocks and allowed us all to touch and hold it. It weighted about five pounds. Some members of our group held it while others took pictures for posterity's sake. I had no camera, so I didn't take pictures, but I think it was my roommate Jack who gave me a copy that he had taken. Of course if you visit Haein-sa today tourists can only look into the buildings through a Plexiglass partition and they are no longer able to walk through or hold any of the woodblocks in their hands.

Tripitaka Koreana woodblock.

On the bus back to Daegu, one of our fellow trainees, Nancy Juniata, who was sitting in the seat in front of me, began complaining about all the stalls selling food and souvenirs, as well as the monks selling pages from the Tripitaka Koreana and Buddhist items. She went on and on about how disgusting this crass commercialism was. I finally had enough.

"Have you ever visited a historical church in the U.S.?" I asked her.

"Why?"

"I visited St. Augustine, Florida, just before leaving for Peace Corps. The old Catholic church there built by the Spanish is tiny, and yet right next to it is a much larger building that is the gift shop run by the local Catholic church. How is that any different from these stalls and the monks making a few bucks off selling trinkets?"

"I don't know. None I guess."

"Exactly! Let them make some money to help support the temple. What's wrong with that?"

She and the others who were joining in with her condemnation didn't say more about this after my outburst. They might not have appreciated my comparison, but I didn't care. As described before, I was already sick of the negative comments of some of the active volunteers who had visited the New Grand Hotel during our training thus far, and I'd noticed some of our fellow K-23s were joining in too. Although it was always easy to complain about perceived differences, I thought it was more important to look for the underlying similarities.

I had been to St. Augustine one other time with my parents when I was fifteen years old. We began by spending a few days in the Miami area visiting my father's cousin, Jackie. Jackie's husband, Jim, was in charge of all the recreation facilities at the Fontainebleau Hotel. We stayed at this luxury hotel, the swankiest in Miami, for free thanks to Jim. Part of many movies had been filmed at the Fontainebleau over the years, and there were numerous giant posters from all of these flicks hanging on the outside wall of the hotel. Among the movies that had scenes filmed there were *A Hole in the Head,* starring Frank Sinatra; *The Bell Boy,* a Jerry Lewis comedy; and the James Bond movie, *Gold Finger.*

After a few days in the Miami area, we left and drove up to St. Augustine where my parents and I visited the same old Spanish fort and church that I was to visit again many years later just before entering Peace Corps. Even as a teenager, it seemed incongruous to me that the store was bigger than the historic church. (Talk about crass commercialism!) I did, though, buy a beautiful coffee table-type book in the store about early Catholic missions in Florida.

I have always loved books, and often my souvenirs from vacations with my parents were books and/or bookends. I still have a pair of carved onyx horse-head bookends from the Southwest and a pair of wooden acorn-shaped bookends from the Smoky Mountains. Also, I still have the book *Buffalo Bill's Life Story: An Auto-biography* signed:

> June 28th 1964
> To my good friend Don
> From Fred Garlow, grandson of "Buffalo Bill"
> In memory of your stay at Absaroka Lodge

I bought this book on our way home from California where we went to see my grandmother Emma and step-grandfather Lyman. The front cover has one damaged edge where *Pupchen* (Little Doll in German), my Aunt Ruth's dachshund who traveled with us, chewed it. (He wasn't always a little doll.) I had already bought the onyx horse-head bookends on the way out to California. Pupchen had not tried to chew on them.

Meanwhile, back in Korea, Charlie had not gotten his hair cut as short as I had mine cut before joining the Peace Corps, and after a couple of months it was starting to get scraggly and was hanging over his ears a bit. One of the trainers told him he had to get a haircut. He told me he refused. I said, "What if they send you home?" "I don't care. It's the principle of the thing," he replied. I was thinking mostly of myself because he and I were together much of the time, and I didn't want to see him shipped home. *"Who the heck else would I hang around with?"* I thought to myself. I tried to talk him into trimming his hair just until we got to our sites, but Charlie was as stubborn as hell. Luckily, the matter was dropped, and life went on.

Near the end of training each one of us went for a few days to stay with an established volunteer for what was called a "site visit." School was back in session by this time even though we were still in training. Charlie went to a town called

Yeongju in Gyeongsangbuk-do where none other than "Porto Hwanta" Tim Metamora, who nearly fell out of the cab in Daegu while hollering to a Korean lass walking by, was assigned. I went to the town of Cheonon where Byron Redford was living and teaching. When I got off the train Byron was waiting for me. He led me to his accommodation, a small room off to the side of the main house of the family he rented from. I stayed with Byron for three nights, watching him teach and taking a try at teaching some of his classes myself using all the skills we had been learning in our ESL classes. Of course, the first morning after I got there he introduced me to all of the other teachers at his school in the teachers' room, a large room with a separate desk for each teacher in it. He also introduced me to the principal of his school.

The meals that we ate at the boarding house, breakfast and dinner, were typical Korean fare with rice, soup, and center dishes of mostly vegetables and maybe a piece of mackerel. There was almost always a dish of soybeans that had been soaked in soy sauce, which turned them black. We had not had them often at the New Grand, but they were served with each meal at Byron's place, and I loved them. I ate all of them at every meal. Only problem was they gave me gas. I was farting the smelliest farts of my life all that week, and poor Byron complained to high hell, or is that heaven, about the odor. He actually quite understood about it, and I have to give him credit for that.

The first time he went out to get something and came back into the room, I paraphrased my father's "Emma Christ" joke and I said, "Lord, Byron, are you here again?" Knowing I was stealing my dad's joke, it was probably funnier to me than to him, but still he chuckled good-naturedly.

Just behind the neighbor's house and right next to Byron's room was a chicken coop. It wouldn't have been too bad, other than the smell, except that they also had a rooster. Every freaking morning at the crack of dawn the stupid, damn thing would start crowing to the new light and his heart's delight. "Morning has broken"—now I knew what that song meant. Where was Jim Wixom? I needed to let him know. There was no sleeping in late at Byron's place. He didn't seem to mind, but I did. I made a mental note to myself, *"Don't get a boarding house near a chicken coop when you get to your town."* Of course, if not roosters, it was often the *Saemaul Undong* song.

After an enjoyable couple of days of practice teaching with Byron, I headed back to Daegu. When I met Charlie we both had stories. Mine were about poor Byron having to put up with my flatulence and the crowing rooster, while Charlie told me he had found his town and school.

"What do you mean you found your school?" I inquired.

"Tim told me that the girls' middle school in Yeongju has asked for a volunteer. We walked up there, and it's perfect. It's high up the side of a hill, and the buildings and playing field are just great. That's where I want to teach." Charlie told me.

"But the Korean Education Ministry doesn't allow male Peace Corps Volunteers at girls' schools," I pointed out.

"Don't care. That's where I want to be placed."

Charlie would consider no other school than that one. The training staff tried to argue him out of this idea, but Charlie wouldn't hear of it. He dug in his heels and made it clear he'd take no other assignment.

Brian Pewabic came back with a great story from his site visit. He went with the volunteer in the town to visit the *mogyok-tang* (bath house), or for short we PCVs called it the *mog*. There were no bathtubs in any of the average houses and people went to bath houses where they could take a hot bath for a small fee. When you enter a Korean bath house, you first pay your fee and then go into the changing room where there are lockers. After placing your clothes in a locker, you lock the door, take the key, which is on a bracelet, grab a towel, and go into the bathing area. There is a large, steaming hot tub in the middle. Along the side walls there are sometimes high (stand up) shower spigots, but if not there are always low water spigots a couple of feet off the floor. You soap up and use the shower or squat down and use the low spigots, pouring water into a plastic bowl and then pour this water over you to wash away the soap suds. Only then, after thoroughly cleaning, are you ready to enter the piping hot, large tub. I could not for the first year in Korea just plop into the water, though. I would ease my way in one foot at a time, then slide my legs in up to the knees and gingerly sit down onto the higher ledge under the water with the water now just over my belly button. Then after acclimatizing myself to the intense heat, I'd ease down to the lower ledge where just my head would be above the water line. Usually, after sitting for a long, long time in the hot tub, I'd get out and sink into the always smaller cold water tub. After I sat in the cold water until I was starting to shiver, I'd head back to the hot tub and this time walk right in and sit down on the lower ledge. Ahhh!

Well, Brian had never been to a *mogyok-tang,* and he walked in with his glasses on. Of course, the minute he entered the bathing area and hit the hot, humid air, his glasses steamed up. He kept walking without being able to see where he was going and fell right into the hot tub, splashing all the Korean men both inside and outside the tub. All the Koreans gasped at this faux pas. Then the volunteer with him began laughing when Brian's head popped up out of the water unhurt but glasses askew and his face beat red from the heat and the embarrassment. Sitting around the dinner table listening to Brian recap his experience had everyone busting a gut.

By now it was getting near the end of training. We continued with Korean language classes everyday, and I still wasn't very good. I was starting to worry again that maybe they'd cut me and say, "Sorry, your language ability is subpar." In fact, even if it were putt-putt golf, I still would have been subpar.

As usual, one Saturday night, I went to bed early, and I was sound asleep when the door opened. I looked up, and Vickie Vermillac, Karen Gibraltar, and Deric Gratiot, one of the TESOL Staff, walked into the room laughing and carrying on.

"What're ya doin'?" Deric asked, obviously three sheets to the wind.

"Trying to ….." and before I could finish he grabbed the thin coverlet that was covering me and pulled it off.

"Voilá!" he exclaimed. There I was, naked, except for my yellow, thin, nylon-material, bikini briefs. I stood up and tried to get the blanket from him, but Deric hid it behind his back. Vickie and Karen were giggling and checking me out, or at least that's what I was hoping. Maybe they were giggling at the size of my????? No, I'm sure that couldn't have been it!

One day a couple of the trainers started talking to several of us trainees in the dining room, which we used as the lounge during non-meal times. The low tables used for meals were folded up and stacked in the corner when we were not eating. This left the room wide open for fun. One of the trainers said that we K-23s didn't have "group spirit."

"You have less group spirit than other groups I've helped train," he said.

"In a couple of weeks we'll be done with training, and each of us will be in a different town. What the hell good is group spirit going to do us?" I replied.

"But all the other groups had it, and group spirit is a good thing," he stated.

"Maybe so, but I for one don't need it, thanks anyway."

No real response was forthcoming after that; I think because I was right. I've never been much of a "Rah, rah!" kind of guy anyway, and one of the things I was looking forward to was being alone, getting away from everything and being on my own, immersing myself in a whole new culture and way of life with all new people. That was why I had joined the Peace Corps, not to have K-23 group spirit. *"Screw that,"* I thought.

Another afternoon in the meal room, a bunch of us were sitting around while a couple of the trainers had brought in a brand-new video tape machine. This was long before even the bazooka-sized handheld video tape recorders were invented, let alone today's cell phones. It was a very large camera with a cord attached to an even larger video recording tape deck-like machine, which was plugged into an electrical wall socket. They were testing it to see how it worked and then were going to video some of our practice teaching the next week. Nick walked in and said, "Wait a minute, tape me." The camera operator pointed the camera at Nick. Then Nick said, "Keep recording." He turned around, unbuckled his trousers, and pulled down his pants while he pointed his rather large rump still covered by his boxer shorts at the camera.

"Nick, I can't believe you just did that," I said while laughing.

"I've always wanted to do that," he said, while pulling his pants back up.

"Quite the view, I bet," I said to the camera man.

"Yes, and in high resolution."

Another day Nick walked in and I said, "Hey, it's Nick, big as life." He said, "No, bigger." And he was!

During our last week in training, we all practiced teaching in a couple of classes at a local middle school. Several of us would stand in the back and watch each other teach. Charlie and I were watching Nick when, near the end of his hour, he taught his class the words and tune to "The Bear Went Over the Mountain." When he started singing, his right hand was behind his right ear, and while singing on every downbeat he pushed his ear way down, let it back up, and then pushed it down again on the next downbeat. It just looked hilarious, and Charlie and I laughed like crazy throughout the song. We asked Nick about it later, and he didn't even seem to know he'd been doing it.

On the last day of our practice teaching, some of our group decided we should sing for the students. They suggested that since I sang all the time, I should be the song leader for the song "Do-Re-Mi" from *The Sound of Music*. Then a couple of people said, "But don't start it in too high a key." I replied, "No, get someone else. I'm not a choir director." But they insisted I do it. So the time came when all the students we had been teaching were assembled. A couple of the trainers gave short speeches, and then we trainees gathered at the front of the room. I stepped out in front of the twenty-eight other trainees in our group, and I started, "One, two, three, 'Doe a deer...'" ("Do-Re-Mi" written by Oscar Hammerstein II, composed by Richard Rodgers, performed by Julie Andrews) As soon as I started I saw a couple of dirty looks coming from some of the trainees, and as we got up near the higher notes in the song there were fewer and fewer of my fellow trainees singing along with me until I sang almost alone "That will bring us back to doe, oh, oh oh, Doe a deer..." and everyone joined back in again. Afterwards, a couple of angry trainees started hassling me about starting too high, and I said, "I told you, I'm not a choir director."

The day quickly came when our nearly three-month-long training was over and where each of us had to appear before several of the training staff members. We were first interviewed in Korean by one of the language staff with the other trainers listening and watching. I dreaded this part and spent a somewhat sleepless night worrying again that I'd be rejected as a volunteer for my lack of language skills. It turned out to be less oppressive than I had worried it would be, and I was able to muddle my way through pretty well actually. After further questions and answers in English about training and my readiness for service, I was told that I would be assigned to Mukho Middle School. Mukho Middle School was the boys' middle school in the town of Mukho on the Sea of Japan, or the East Sea as the Koreans called it, in the province of Gangwon. I was happy as all get out knowing that I would be in a seaside town on the coast. Charlie was assigned to the girls' middle school in the city of Yeongju that he had seen on his site visit and loved so much. Lisa was also to go to Yeongju, and she would teach at one of the boys' middle schools there. Bobbie Socks, Suck, I mean, Shin, No-bean was assigned to Samcheok, the town about a half hour bus ride south of Mukho. All of us of course were interested in where everyone else was going to be for the next two years, and sure enough we were spread out all over the peninsula.

Our program's first casualty came right at the end of training. "Complain all the time" Carrie Anne announced that she was not interested in continuing as a volunteer. She was the first of many in our group who did not last the two-year commitment we had all signed up for. This was accepted by Peace Corps. Anyone who for emotional, psychological, or health reasons felt they couldn't continue was sent back to the States. It was not healthy for the volunteer to stay if they were not happy, nor did it advance Peace Corps' goals to have a disgruntled volunteer serving. Unfortunately, many disgruntled volunteers didn't extricate themselves and stayed even though they disliked being in Korea. Carrie Anne decided on her own accord to leave, and I thought it was better for her, for Peace Corps, and for Korea that she did. So much for group spirit and all that!

The next day, we all headed for Seoul. Upon arrival we visited the Peace Corps office, which was in the Korea Educational Association Building on Shinmoon-ro (Newspaper Street) in the Cheong-ro-ku (Bell Street Area) of Seoul. It was very close to Gwanghwa-mun (the Gate of Transformation by Light) which is the spiritual heart of downtown Seoul and was the main gate to the most famous (or at least most popular now) of the royal palaces of the Yi dynasty. Behind it was the capitol building, which had been built by the Japanese during their occupation of Korea. Korea was a colony of Japan from 1910 to 1945. The Japanese built their capitol building inside the main royal palace to make it clear who was in charge. In addition, when seen from the air it was built in the pattern of the Chinese character for sun which is part of Japan's name. *Nippon* in Japanese, *Ilbon* in Korean, is made up of two Chinese characters which mean sun's source. The Korean government later decided to demolish the building and cart the rubble away. The demolition began on August 15, 1995, the fiftieth anniversary of South Korea's Liberation Day, with removal of the dome. It was finished a year later, returning the palace closer to its original state during the Yi dynasty (1392 to 1910).

After visiting the Peace Corps office, we wandered down the side street and headed toward Gwanghwa-mun looking for a *yeogwan* (inn) to stay in. Many of us went into the Daeji Yeogwan, which was an old-fashioned, one-story building with a tile roof surrounding a small inner courtyard. I stayed in this *yeogwan* dozens of times over my next three years of Peace Corps service.

After checking into the *yeogwan*, Charlie and I ran into Russ and a couple of others from our group. We wandered off with them to explore Seoul. It was a windy day, and Russ was walking ahead of Charlie and me while talking to the others. Russ had red hair, and he was bald on top, so he parted his hair way down by his right ear and combed it over the bald top toward his left ear. As we walked along the wind was blowing from Russ' left side toward his right. The long hair from above his right ear was streaming off to a point nearly a foot away from the right side of his head while the hair on the left side of his head was very short and his bald head in the middle was shining in the afternoon sun. I jabbed Charlie with my elbow and said, "Charlie, look at Russ, his hair looks just like Bozo the Clown's on one side." We laughed at Russ' expense as we followed behind.

I caught up with Russ and pointed at a large statue near the intersection closest to the Peace Corps office.

"Who's that?" I asked.

"What? Oh! You mean the statue?"

"Yes, who is he?"

"That's Korea's most famous military hero, Admiral Yi, Sun-sin."

"What did he do?"

"He defeated the Japanese Navy in many battles during the Hideoshi invasion in the 1590s."

I stopped for a minute and stared at this statue that dominated the street. Being a history major, I later made a point of reading up on this Korean hero. The year before the Japanese invasion of 1592, Yi, Sun-sin was given the post of

Commander of the Left Jeolla Naval District. He began preparing for the upcoming campaign and to increase the strength of the small Korean Navy, he had ships built that resembled turtles. These turtle-shaped ships were ironclad with metal spikes sticking up to discourage boarding by the enemy, and the ironcladding also insured that the ships would not be harmed by flaming arrows from opposing ships. The Japanese had what should have been an overwhelmingly superior number of ships, but in nearly two dozen battles Admiral Yi defeated the Japanese in every engagement. Like the British Admiral Nelson, Admiral Yi, in the last naval battle before Japan withdrew all its forces from Korea, was killed by an enemy bullet while standing in full view on his flagship, which was not one of the turtle-shaped ships. His forces went on to win this battle in addition to all the earlier ones. Consequently, I think it is only fitting to call Horatio Nelson "Great Britain's Admiral Yi, Sun-sin" since Admiral Yi came first.

Friday of this last week before going to our sites, Peace Corps planned a trip to Panmunjom in the DMZ (Demilitarized Zone) between North and South Korea. Charlie came up with the idea of not going to the DMZ and instead visiting Ewha University in Seoul. Ewha University was, and still is, the largest women's university in the world. It had been founded in 1886 by an American missionary. I thought Charlie's idea was brilliant and agreed immediately to join him. Bob Kern, who was the first fellow trainee I had met in San Fran, also decided to join us. So while the other twenty-six K-23s went to look at stone-faced North Korean guards across the demarcation line at Panmunjom, we got on the regular city bus to Ewha.

Ewha's campus had buildings that looked like one of America's Ivy League schools—beautiful stone structures. We wandered around the grounds and went into some of the buildings. Around noon we were hungry, and so we found the cafeteria. We walked into a large open area filled with tables around which sat dozens of lovely coeds. I praised Charlie's extremely intelligent decision to come here instead of the DMZ. I was hoping to get into a conversation with one of the young ladies and get an address to start a long-term relationship with what I was sure would be one of the most intelligent of all the young women in Korea; if not, she would never have gotten into this prestigious university. We found a table, staked out a claim to it, and then went up to the cafeteria counter to order something to eat. We all got pastry-like bread things and small bottles of milk. These milk bottles looked just like the quart size Twin Pines milk bottles that we used to get delivered to our house back in the 1950s and 1960s, which were deposited into the milk chute next to the side door of our little Allen Park bungalow. These bottles in Korea were only about half the size of the Twin Pines ones. The wide mouth openings at the top of the bottles were covered with cardboard-like disks. Bob, Charlie, and I sat down, and while they were talking I started attempting to open my milk bottle. I pushed and shoved the disk but it wouldn't move. Then I used as much pressure as my right thumb could muster as I held the bottle with my left hand. Suddenly the disk popped out and my thumb drove down into the bottle, spilling the lilly-white liquid contents all over the table and all over me. I think I also let out a loud gasp at the same time. All the cute, young coeds looked over at us and laughed. Korean women were never supposed to show their open mouths, and so they always covered their mouths with their hands when they laughed. It was always very sweet to see. But it wasn't sweet to see them all with their hands in front of their mouths while laughing at me. Charlie and Bob gave me "if looks could kill" looks. I said, "Oops!" Charlie went and found some paper towels to clean up the mess I'd made. Then they both helped clean up the table while I tried to soak up the milk that had drenched my shirt and the crotch of my pants. Oddly enough we never got the chance to speak with any of the Ewha students. News of the clumsy American guy probably traveled throughout the whole campus at the speed of light. For the rest of the day, Charlie and Bob blamed me for our lack of luck in catching the eyes of any of the pretty coeds.

On Saturday morning we K-23s met at the Peace Corps office and were told that we were to go to the old Japanese capitol building where we would have an induction ceremony with Korean officials from the Ministry of Education in attendance. We were given a copy of the Peace Corps pledge, which we would be reciting together in front of the ministry mucketymucks. I started reading it, and it sounded very much like the oath that the president takes on inauguration day. It was OK until I got to the part about defending the Constitution of the United States against all enemies domestic and foreign. I balked. "Wait a minute," I said, "this sounds like we're joining the Army and not the Peace Corps. I did not join the Peace Corps to defend the Constitution against all enemies, and we are in a foreign country so, what is this "domestic" stuff about?" Some of the others also complained, but most of our fellow trainees were fine with it. As our complaints went on for a while one member of the Peace Corps staff explained, "We can't have you making a fuss about this in front of the Korean Education Ministry people. That would not be good. How about if those of you who are bothered by this one sentence just not say it, but do recite all the other parts? OK?" It seemed ludicrous for me to be saying I would defend the Constitution against domestic enemies when I was going to be living in Mukho, Korea, for the next two years at least, but I agreed to this idea of just not saying that one sentence. Everyone else agreed also, and after some further information about how the rest of the day would go, we walked together over to the capitol.

We went into a large room and heard a speech by a Ministry of Education official welcoming us and thanking us for our impending service teaching in middle schools across the land. Jim Wixom (Mr. "What does that song mean to you?") gave a speech, and then we read our oath of office with a few of us not saying the sentence about defending the Constitution. Then we were led into another room where we met our principals and our co-teachers whom we would be working with once we got to our schools. I was introduced to the principal of Mukho Middle School, Mr. Yoo, Hyung-sul and the English teacher with him, Mr. Jong, Chul-chin. Mr. Yoo spoke in English and asked me a couple of simple questions.

"What is your hometown?"

"Detroit, Michigan."

"How many brothers and sisters do you have?"

"None, I am an only child."

"Excuse me, please," Mr. Yoo said as he walked away to talk to someone he knew. Just to make conversation, I turned to Mr. Jong, who looked to be middle-aged, and asked him a question. I enunciated very slowly and precisely.

"Mr. Jong, how many children do you have?" He replied after an inordinately long lull, "One thousand and four hundred." Obviously he must have thought I asked how many students there were at Mukho Middle School, but never one to miss an opportunity for a joke, even when I'm the only one who understands it, I added, "Wow, you have been very busy!"

"Yes, very busy," he responded.

"Oh shit," I thought. *"With his level of English this is going to be trying to say the least."* I looked around at everyone else from our group in conversation with their co-teachers and principals, and I said to myself, *"Great, I must have gotten the worst English speaker of the bunch."* Luckily Mr. Yoo returned, and his English was quite good. Soon we all left and went out to lunch together.

After lunch many of our group left to head to their sites with their principals and co-teachers. Mr. Yoo informed me that we would be staying overnight in Seoul and leaving the next morning by airplane over to the east coast.

That evening we went to the hardware-market area of Seoul where there were many small shops— and I mean many, one after another, all carrying similar things. The area we concentrated on had shops with metal pipes, fittings, and plumbing supplies. Mr. Yoo explained to me that Mr. Jong was looking for a heater to heat water for a bathtub. This seemed strange because I didn't think

Korean homes had bathtubs, but I didn't try to ask too many questions as we were walking through this amazingly crowded, busy, and loud shopping area. Mr. Jong went into shop after shop asking for a heater and being told no. Just before I passed out from exhaustion, we found a shop that had a heater. Mr. Jong and the shop owner haggled for a while over the price as I waited outside on the sidewalk just watching the din of humanity, mostly men out on a Saturday night shopping for pipes and stuff. Mr. Jong finally came out with his treasure, we took a cab back to the *yeogwan* we were sharing a room in, and he put the large heavy box in our room. Then we went out for dinner and to bed early.

CHAPTER 5

The Fall Semester of 1972: Greasy French Toast

The next morning, we got up, took a taxi out to Kimpo Airport where we K-23s had landed three months prior, and got on a small prop plane. We flew to the Bupyeong Airport. During the flight Mr. Yoo told me that I would be living in Mr. Jong's home, but that my co-teacher would be another English teacher named Mr. Jun, In-kook. He also told me to sleep in late the next morning, come to school at 9:00 am, and report to his office. In no time we reached the east coast of Korea. The Bupyeong Airport was on the beach of this small town about a fifteen-minute bus or taxi ride south of Mukho. As we flew in I thought the plane was going to set down on the sand. When we got off the plane I saw that there was a narrow tarmac strip across the sand that we had landed on. That explained why the plane didn't sink into the sand as we landed, flip over, and burst into flames, which is what I thought was going to happen. After getting our luggage, and Mr. Jong his new heater, we took a taxi to Mukho.

Mr. Jong and I got out of the taxi and walked the short distance to his house. Korean houses were usually surrounded by walls. In this case it was a six-foot-high, cinder-block wall. Often, the top of the walls had broken jagged pop bottles sticking up out of the cement to discourage thieves. Mr. Jong's wall had such a high-tech security system of broken Coke and "Podo" (grape) "Hwanta" bottles. When we got to the gate, Mr. Jong rang a buzzer. (I never got a key and always had to ring the buzzer and wait until someone came to open it during all the months I lived here.) I could hear someone walk to the gate, and I heard it unlock. As we walked into the small courtyard, his family all came out to greet me. I met his wife, Mrs. Lee, who was a very pretty woman, and their two-year-old son Chong-ho. Korean women do not change their family name when they marry, so she was Mrs. Lee. After having a child, women were thereafter known as so and so's mother. So Mrs. Lee was known in the neighborhood as Chong-ho's *eomeoni* (mother). Husbands often introduced their wives as *uri jip saram* which translates as "our house person." Both ways of referring to married women gave an indication of women's place in traditional Korean society. Next to his wife stood Mr. Jong's mother who was introduced as *halmeoni* (grandmother) and a young girl who looked to be around twelve years old named Soon-mi. I never did quite understand Soon-mi's relationship to the family, but she seemed to be the grandmother's child. I always thought that maybe she was an adopted child, but Koreans didn't often adopt children unless there was some family connection. I never asked and was never told what the girl's relationship to the grandmother was exactly, but I was told by other teachers at the school that Mr. Jong's mother had owned a bar in Mukho and was quite wealthy. The house looked brand-new, and it was large compared to virtually all the other homes in Mukho. I was shown my room, which was through the living room and at the end of a hall. It was right across from the bathroom. The bathroom had a modern Korean-style squat toilet and a small bathtub, now with the addition of the new heater just bought by Mr. Jong in Seoul. It was late afternoon, and I was left to organize my room. When dinnertime came, my food was brought to my room on a small individual table by Soon-mi. (I always ate alone while the family ate together in another room.) It was a typical Korean meal with rice, soup, and *banchan* (side dishes). The beverage was *bori-cha* (barley tea). Barley tea is a golden color. We were told during training never to drink plain water. If the water is a yellow or gold color, even if served cold, we were told we could assume that it was *bori-cha* and had been boiled and was thus safe to drink. I sat cross-legged on the floor and ate heartily off the low table. No fish head soup here.

Broken bottle security system along the top of a six foot high wall around a home (notice the fish drying on the line behind the bottles).

I went to bed and slept like a log, oak maybe. In the morning I heard everyone up early, pans banging in the kitchen and people talking. Then I heard Mr. Jong leaving, and I thought I'd better get up. After washing up in the bathroom, I came back to my room and Soon-mi brought in the low table with my breakfast on it. My breakfast was greasy—very greasy—French toast. It was pretty bad. Just like the New Grand Hotel didn't do American-style food well, this French toast was not very appetizing. Funny that I was the lone voice trying to get the K-23s to agree to asking the New Grand to serve only Korean food because I argued that's what we'd be eating three meals a day for the next two years, and here I was served French toast for breakfast. When Mrs. Lee came in to get the

Mukho Middle School and its play area as seen from a hill at the southern edge of town.

table I said in Korean, *"Chal mogusemneda."* ("I ate well.") I didn't have the heart to tell her it wasn't very good. Here she had specially made this for the American guest to please me. For months, every morning I ate greasy—very greasy—French toast. I decided to grin and bear it.

The back fence of Mukho Middle School was only a hundred yards or so from Mr. Jong's house. I walked around to the school's front gate, as there was no back entrance, and entered the schoolyard. This was the only large flat and open piece of ground in this part of town. It was a little larger than a soccer field and consisted of yellow clay-like earth packed down hard from thousands of feet trampling on it daily. As I walked in, it was deserted. I crossed over to the large two-story, cement building that was painted white, although much of the paint had worn off and cement grey showed through. I walked up the front stairs and through the main doors. There I took off my shoes and put them into one of the cubby holes along the side wall specifically built to house outdoor shoes. I slipped on a pair of plastic sandles and walked in. A young lady who worked as an assistant to the teaching staff came running up, bowed low, and motioned for me to come with her. She escorted me to the principal's office. Yoo, *Gyojang-nim* in Korean (honorable principal), greeted me as he always would every day from then on with a happy look on his face. He ordered the young lady, Choi, Yong-sook, to bring us both tea. Mr. Yoo, as I called him when it was just the two of us because we always spoke in English, had a large office with a large desk, a couch, and two large chairs in a seating arrangement around a coffee table, some cabinets with books and mementoes, a Korean flag, and a couple of other flags behind his desk with paintings and calligraphy on the walls. He invited me to sit in one of the chairs, and he sat on the sofa across from me. Two cups of tea were brought in by Miss Choi while Mr. Yoo and I conversed in English. This scene would be replayed almost every day for the next several months until Mr. Yoo, unfortunately, got transferred to another school in another town.

The first-year middle school students, along with a female teacher preparing the soil to plant flowers just outside their rickety classroom building.

After finishing our tea, Mr. Yoo said that he would give me a tour of the school. We walked down the hall into the school office, and I was introduced to the employees there. Then we walked into the teachers' office, a large room with thirty-six desks, one for each of the teachers in the school. These desks were pushed together in four groups of eight and one group of four. At the far end of the room was one larger desk, and behind it sat the Vice-Principal, Lee, Tae-hyang, who stood up and walked around his desk to greet me as Mr. Yoo introduced us. Most of the teachers were off teaching their classes, but I was introduced to a couple who happened to have their break period at this time. We continued down the hall, and Mr. Yoo pointed out the music room, science lab, and library, all of which were locked. Then we went upstairs to see the third-year students' classrooms. As we walked by each room, I noticed the excitement of the students in seeing an American in their school's hallway. At the far end of the hall we took the stairway down and went back to the main entrance where we put on our shoes. Then we walked out toward two other classroom buildings off to the side. Behind the main building Mr. Yoo showed me a small greenhouse filled with plants. We went up a stone stairway. To our right was a wooden building, which Mr. Yoo told me had been built during the Japanese occupation (before 1945). We continued walking past and around this structure. Then behind it was a little more, but not much more, substantial one-story building where the second-year students studied. We walked between these two buildings. I could see the same excitement on the faces of the first- and second-year students as we walked by. The older structure caught my attention. It was made of wooden boards. In some places there were knotholes where you could look through from the classroom to see outside or vice versa. I could see that there was absolutely no insulation. The windows, which ran the length of each classroom, had rickety, wooden frames with eight single panes of glass in each. Mr. Yoo had told me that this building housed the first-year students' classrooms, where I would be teaching.

After walking past these classroom buildings, Mr. Yoo led me over to the fenced-in volleyball court right next to the front gate of the school. As we were walking away from the volleyball court, the school bell rang. We had just started walking across the schoolyard. Hundreds of students, all dressed in their black fall uniforms—the Nehru-collared jackets that looked like Prussian military officers' coats, black pants, black Ringo-style hats (like the ones Charlie, Lisa and I had worn around Daegu), and virtually all with black tennis shoes—came running directly toward Mr. Yoo and me. It reminded me of walking in the woods near the world's biggest tire along I-94 in downriver Allen Park, Michigan, and how my friends and I would sometimes come across ant hills. These small mounds, maybe one to two feet high and three feet in diameter, were built by large black ants. Sometimes we would take a stick and dig into the ant hill. Hundreds, even thousands, of these black ants would scurry around in what seemed like a rage trying to attack whatever was destroying their nest. It seemed like hundreds of black creatures were now running down the steps from the two older lower-level class buildings of Mukho Middle School as well as coming out of the front and the two side entrances of the main two-story school building where the third-year students studied. Like giant ants in a cheap horror movie they were swarming toward us. As they got closer I thought Mr. Yoo and I would be crushed to death. I was feeling dread and alarm. Mr. Yoo reached out to me, grabbed my left hand with his right, and we walked hand in hand, which was common for Korean men to do. But the monsters kept getting closer and closer, and I felt like the oxygen was being sucked out of the playground by these hundreds of huge insects attacking us. I'm sure the terror was evident on my face. I looked over at Mr. Yoo, who was happy as a clam at high tide or low tide, whichever it is that makes clams the happiest. He had a huge smile on his face. He held my hand tighter, and we walked slowly as if we were lovers on a Sunday stroll in the park. He was just beaming with pride. He told me later that he had always wanted a Peace Corps Volunteer at his school and that my coming was a dream come true for him. I was his first Peace Corps Volunteer. It also turned out that I was the first Peace Corps Volunteer to have ever served in Mukho. For me, at this moment, it was a nightmare. All one thousand and four hundred of "busy" Mr. Jong's children (remember his answer to the question, "How many children do you have?) were swarming across the schoolyard. Just as I thought death was near, the students all seemed to stop at the same time after having encircled us. Even though it was fall, it was a warm day, and I was wearing a short-sleeved dress shirt. As Mr. Yoo and I continued walking hand in hand I could feel dozens of student hands rubbing my arms. Most Koreans do not have as much body hair as European-Americans do, and this fascinated them. Also, it was like the parting of the Red Sea—or in this case, the Black Sea with Mr. Yoo as Moses and with me as, literally, his righthand man. The students stepped out of the way to open a pathway for us to walk through. The kids were all smiling and happy and didn't look at all like the angry insects I had envisioned as they had come lemming-like toward us. They did all look alike to me though. Every student had on the same uniform and the same haircut, a buzz cut, so that with or without the hat on they still all looked alike. They all had dark, almost black eyes, small noses and black hair, what little there was of it sticking out from their almost bald noggins. (Of course, very quickly thereafter, they didn't all look alike to me.) Mr. Yoo then led me back into the main school building.

One of Don's students with an injured leg studying while his fellow classmates were taking gym class on the playground. (Notice the rustic chairs and desks.)

Once inside I met Mr. Jun, In-kook who was to be my co-teacher. He was on the tall side for a Korean—taller than I was—skinny, and rather gangly. He reminded me of a Korean Ichabod Crane from Washington Irving's story, *The Legend of Sleepy Hollow*. He was young, probably in his early twenties like me, just out of college, and not married yet, although I did meet his fiancée the following spring. This first day I just went to class with him, got introduced to his classes' students, and watched him teach.

The classrooms had fifty to sixty desks and chairs in each one. The desks and chairs looked homemade and very rustic. The chairs were probably the most uncomfortable chairs ever produced in the history of furniture-making, while each desktop was just slightly larger than a standard breadboard. At the front of each classroom was a large blackboard with a Korean flag mounted on

Front of classroom.

the wall above it. The classrooms were very Spartan. In fact, I bet Mukho Middle School's first-year classrooms would have made classical Grecian schools in Sparta look downright luxurious.

The next day (Tuesday) there was a morning meeting, as there would be most days of the school year, with all the teachers in the teachers' office. Principal Yoo came in and Vice-Principal Lee vacated his desk and sat in a chair off to the side while Mr. Yoo sat at Mr. Lee's desk to officiate the meeting. Mr. Yoo formally announced my arrival, and while he was discussing other items on the agenda, I noticed that all the students were lining up by class on the playground facing toward the front of the main building. Mr. Yoo finished his remarks, and as he exited the office the Vice Principal and all of us teachers followed him out to the schoolyard. Mr. Yoo walked up to the microphone on the raised metal platform, which sat near the front door of the main building. The teachers lined up behind the platform. Mr. Yoo made a speech to the students, telling them what a momentous occasion it was to have an American Peace Corps Volunteer teach at their school. Then he introduced me, and I went up to the mic and gave a speech in Korean. All of us trainees had worked on our speeches the last week of language classes. After a generic greeting, mine went something like this:

My American name is Don Haffner. My Korean name is
Ha, Doe-young. I am an English teacher. My hometown
is Detroit, Michigan. Detroit is famous for the five Great
Lakes and for automobiles. I am happy to meet you.

Short, but sweet! When I bowed, thunderous applause followed as if I had given a wonderfully brilliant speech.

Several years later in the late-1970s, I was back in Detroit before going to grad school for the first time. One day I was reading our local newspaper, the *Detroit Free Press,* and I noticed a short article written by Byron Redford, the same Byron Redford whom I had stayed with on my site visit to Cheonon during our K-23 training. His article was about the speech he gave when he first started at

Cheonon Middle School. He wrote about getting up to the mic and speaking slowly and succinctly, pronouncing each and every word as clearly as he could. When he finished, the students applauded wildly. Later in the semester his students told him that they had not understood a word of his speech that day, but they all agreed it was the best speech they had ever heard. I have the feeling the Mukho Middle School students probably didn't understand a word I had said either, but they appreciated my effort.

At the end of the PRIST, I had been given a "Peace Corps/Korea: Korea Middle School TESOL Program, Summer 1972" seven-page handout. TESOL was explained in the pamphlet as meaning **T**eaching **E**nglish as a **Sec**ond **L**anguage. During our training, it was also often referred to as Teaching English to Speakers of Other Languages, which makes more sense to me considering the acronym. The Volunteer Job Description started as follows:

> Volunteers in this program have been requested by the
> Ministry of Education to assist in its endeavor to
> strengthen English teaching at the middle school level.
> Most English teachers in Korean middle schools still use
> the grammar-translation method of English instruction, but
> Korean education officials and English teachers have begun
> work on developing methods that will produce students able
> to read, write, and speak English effectively. The proposed
> program will complement this Korean effort to shift the
> current English education program from grammar-translation
> to communication. Volunteers will assist in this effort by
> working with skilled Korean linguists and educators in devel-
> oping and implementing modern TESOL methods and materials,
> especially in workshop activities where English teachers
> will be re-trained.

Beginning on page five in the "Remarks: Job Related" section there are some not-so-subtle hints that things might not evolve as planned:

> ….. The volunteer must see the value of the teamwork approach
> and be willing to modify any disposition for quick or tangible
> results from his efforts, because the fruits of his labors will
> not always be immediately visible.….. He will be only one of
> thousands of teachers, and it is not likely that his efforts over

two short years will radically change a national education system or even the teaching of English at the middle school level.

To maintain intellectual and emotional stability and to be maximally effective in Korea, a volunteer must have a realistic set of expectations. Many volunteers fail in their Peace Corps/Korea service because their expectations are totally unrealistic….. Volunteers should realize that Korea is one of the most advanced developing countries in Asia and that the Asian concept of time and change is very different from that of most Americans…..

Personal appearance, conduct, and mannerisms are an important part of the professional manner in Korea, especially in rural oriented districts which tend to be conservative in most respects. *No volunteer is permitted to wear a beard or a mustache in the Korean middle schools.* (Italics added by the author.) The volunteer with a people-oriented personality is required, since he will have to work closely with less sophisticated rural people. He will also have to work sometimes with poorly motivated teachers in the middle schools…..

He should come to Korea, not for personal or selfish goals, but primarily for altruistic reasons…..

Volunteers must be sensitive enough to work successfully within a rigid culture based on a set of values very different from their own. Volunteers need not accept the traditional Confusian (sic) standards behind many Korean behavior patterns, but they must be prepared to understand their basis. A strong authoritarian government influences much of the social and economic life of the people.

All foreigners are considered outsiders in the Korean society and receive treatment that is a mixture of curiosity, hospitality, and exploitation. In certain areas of Korea, this mixture is compounded with xenophobia. Both black and white Americans are subject to some racial rejection.

There are two areas of political sensitivity in Korea. One is the constant harassment from the North and the resultant security arrangements and restrictions of freedoms in the South (for example, a 12 midnight to 4 a. m. curfew). The other is the large U.S. commitment in the country and the tensions between feelings of dependency and desire for freedom that this has developed. Open debate on issues of Communism, the Indo-China War, and unification with the North are limited, and the volunteer must stay within limits on these subjects in order to remain effective on the job.....

(signed)
Linda Ecker
Korea Desk Officer
North Africa, Near East,
Asia, and the Pacific Region

Indeed, expansive expectations were sometimes why some volunteers left before finishing their two years. Somehow some volunteers seemed to have thought that just by their presence the whole Korean educational system would miraculously change for the better. It just didn't happen that way.

As noted earlier, Carrie Anne Tawas had left either just before training finished or shortly thereafter. No surprise there with how much she'd complained about everything. I wrote to her for a while after she returned to Kentucky, but if I asked her why she left so quickly I no longer remember her answer. Before our two years were completed nearly half of the K-23s had left early. All three of the married couples left early, and yet I explicitly remember some of the trainers babbling about how usually married couples were more likely to finish their service than single volunteers. It is funny how often the trainers seemed to have been wrong. They were wrong about all Koreans being great singers. Of course, there are always exceptions to sweeping generalizations. I thought they were wrong about the K-23s needing more group spirit, and they turned out to be wrong about married couples being more likely to finish their commitment, unless the lack of group spirit among us K-23s was the reason the married couples all cut short their stay. But I doubt that.

The poorly motivated Korean teacher described in the pamphlet from PRIST certainly turned out to be true. I started out with the best of intentions as far as having an English workshop for all the English teachers in Mukho. Our principal, Mr. Yoo, invited all the English teachers from the boys' high school, the girls' combined high school and middle school, and, naturally, the English teachers from Mukho (Boys') Middle School. While Mr. Yoo and my co-teacher, Mr. Jun, attended religiously, as the weeks went by, most of the other English teachers skipped class for one reason or another more often than they came.

Another difficulty with the class was the speech habits of the third-year English teacher at our school, Mr. Lee Kwan-sup. Mr. Lee's English speaking ability was actually pretty good, and his hearing fluency was quite good. The problem was that when he had served in the Korean Army he had been a KATUSA (**Korean Augmentation To the United States Army**). KATUSAs were Korean soldiers assigned to American units. Mr. Lee had picked up all the US military slang that is used in Asia. For example, instead of "quickly" he always said "chop, chop." The first time he said this to me, "Mr. Ha, let's go chop, chop." I replied, "No, Mr. Lee, 'chop, chop' is not good English. Please say 'Let's go quickly." "Right, let's go chop, chop." He refused to drop the slang or use complete sentences much of the time. Every time he spoke in class it caused problems because much of what he said was not proper English, and he had no desire or ambition to learn the correct usage. He was a nice guy and fun to talk to one on one, but he was a real distraction in my workshop.

After a few weeks I suggested to Mr. Yoo that we end the teacher training workshop. He agreed, and I never bothered to try again. Instead I concentrated on working full time with Mr. Jun, teaching alongside him every hour that he taught, including Saturdays. I also invested a lot of energy on my five extra hours a week for the special class of the fifteen best first-year students. They never skipped. I wish I could have bottled and sold their enthusiasm and energy—I'd be rich!

It was interesting for me to note the names of the middle and high schools in Mukho. The boys' middle school's official name was "Mukho Middle School." The boys' high school's official name was "Mukho High School." The combined girls' middle and high school's official name was "Mukho *Girls'* Middle and High School." This seemed to reflect the Confucian, male chauvinist Korean culture. The schools with no gender indicated in the name were obviously schools for male students. Schools with female students had to have the gender identified in the name.

I later found out that Mukho Middle School was once the combined boys' and girls' middle and high schools. That explained why Mukho Middle School had the oldest building, the one in which I taught every day, of the three schools and why it was the closest to the center of the town.

Life quickly fell into a rhythm for me. There were eight third-year middle school classes in the school, nine second-year classes and nine first-year classes. Middle school and high school were not free and not compulsory in Korea at this time. Parents had to pay tuition, and, consequently, there were fewer classes in the third year of middle school and in high school because some parents were not able to continue to pay for their childrens' education.

Mr. Jun and I taught the first-year students. Peace Corps Volunteers who taught at the middle school level in the 1970s all taught first-year students. By the second and especially the third year, the students were preparing for the high school entrance exam, which concentrated exclusively on grammar. (So much for the pamphlet handed out at the PRIST, which stated the Koreans wanted to shift from grammar translation-centered English teaching to more emphasis on communication.) With first-year students we had the freedom to emphasize spoken English, although the students were starting from scratch since they had not studied English in primary school. In addition, there were more than fifty students in each classroom, which put a damper on each and every student getting a lot of practice speaking individually. Mr. Jun and I taught six or seven class periods a day Monday through Friday and four hours on Saturday mornings. In addition, I taught the Special Class of the brightest fifteen of the first-year students for an extra hour after school Monday through Friday, and, as mentioned, I also taught an English Teachers' Workshop once a week for the first couple of months or so. I went home every day exhausted, but in a good way, and I spent most evenings lesson planning or reading before going to bed and getting ready to head back to school the next morning.

Every day Mr. Yoo would check to see when my free hour was, as it changed day to day. I'd enter the teachers' office, and the phone would ring. Miss Choi would usually answer it, and it would be Mr. Yoo asking her to send me to his office. He and I would sit for the free hour, drinking tea and talking in English. Mr. Yoo religiously read the *Korea Herald* and the *Korea Times,* the two English language newspapers, everyday. He would ask me questions about the day's news, or in some cases he'd find a sentence that didn't sound right to him and ask my opinion. Of course, some of the writing in the paper was not grammatically correct. He would often spot these errors.

I asked him about his education. He had the equivalent of a BA in English from Yokohama University in Japan. He must have been a very good student to have been accepted as a Korean to a university in Japan. He said that when he was studying English at Yokohama University the Japanese professors told all the students to study hard, as English was needed for their empire. This was in the 1930s when Japan was at war with China, but they obviously already had their sights set on an even bigger empire, and they needed people proficient in English to help them rule it. After college he returned to Korea and began teaching English in the Chosun (Japan's name for its Korean colony) school system. By 1972 he had already been a school administrator for over a decade. I was so very lucky to have been sent to his school. I wish I could have bottled his desire to learn along with that of my Special Class students. He was better in English than all the other English teachers in Mukho, and yet he had this constant drive to learn more. Most of the other teachers had a daily drive to get out of any extra work or studying, although my co-teacher Mr. Jun's English was good, and he also strove to learn from me.

One day during lunch, shortly after I'd arrived in Mukho, one of our fellow teachers said, "Mr. Ha, you look like Gene Hackman." Many other teachers joined in, "Yes, very very similar."

"Who's Gene Hackman?" I asked.

"You know, 'Popeye' in *The French Connection.*"

Mukho harbor. (Notice the elevated train tracks just in front of the Ssangyong cement towers.)

"Oh, yes, Popeye, I remember him. That's Gene Hackman?"

"Yes, you look very much like him."

"Oh, really, yes, I guess I do look a little like him. He's very handsome, don't you think?"

"Yes, of course, very handsome," several said in unison while laughing. *The French Connection* had been a big movie in 1971 in the States, and it was big in Korea too. Throughout my Peace Corps years, many Koreans told me that I looked like Gene Hackman.

Mukho was not a beautiful town by any means. It was a port town, a harbor town. It had a small harbor, but medium-sized freighters showed up upon occasion. Mukho shipped out cement and coal, and once or twice I noticed a freighter bringing in barley. I was told it came from the States. The largest cement plant in Korea was down near Bupyeong where the airport runway on the beach was. Coal mines were scattered throughout the mountains in Gangwon Province. In the Port of Mukho area—

Rather primitive-looking entrance to a coal mine near Mukho—just behind the three minors who posed for the author.

Mukho's fishing fleet. (Notice the strings of large light bulbs on each boat.)

the only other large flat open place in town besides the school playgrounds—were four huge SSangyong (Twin Dragon) Cement Company cement silos. In addition, an elevated train track came into the port from the south, and coal trains came in. They stopped, and then the coal cars all opened up from the bottom and the soft bituminous (not hard anthracite) coal tumbled down to the ground from each car as black clouds of coal dust floated away and descended on the town. Between the coal and the cement everything was covered with a grey or black dust throughout the surrounding area.

There was also a very large fleet of fishing vessels that jumbled up at the north end of the harbor. They were an absolute mess of one boat after another jammed together facing every which way when in port. It looked like a bumper car game gone haywire. All around town were large drying racks with mackerel, squid, and huge six-foot-long octopi hanging in the sun to dry until they were like pieces of cardboard. I'm not sure what flavor was added to the fish by the cement and coal dust, but I ate fish every day for all the three years that I ended up living in Mukho and I'm still alive to tell about it, so it couldn't have been too bad. The drying fish did add an odiferousness to the whole town. Still, I loved the place.

Squid drying on racks.

Six-foot-long octopi drying on racks.

Sometimes when the squid were running—or should I say swimming—by Mukho all the fishing vessels would be out at sea not too far off shore. At night the boats had strings of large light bulbs that they turned on to attract the squid. It looked like a floating city of light off in the distance and was very beautiful and fun to watch as the boats bobbed up and down and the lights moved and seemed to twinkle.

There were no old buildings from the Yi dynasty or before in Mukho, although there was one old, small pavilion with a stone-carved stele in it commemorating some Confucian scholar. I think that the first-year middle school building in which I taught, built during the Japanese occupation, was the oldest building in town. There were also some interesting Shamanistic towers about twelve to fifteen feet high or so on the top of a hill west of town made out of small rocks that were chipped to fit together perfectly without mortar. I often hiked there and sat to contemplate my navel or eat a snack. Unfortunately, I never saw anyone who seemed to be worshipping there. The towers and the area around them were obviously well cared for, and yet I have no idea who might have been the caretaker.

After a few days, I was ahead of the game with my lesson planning, and one night I decided to explore. A couple of hours after dinner, I headed down the two-lane main street, and when I got to the only real intersection in town, I turned right. The road only went about fifty yards and then ended at one of the two movie theaters in Mukho. Behind the creatively named Mukho Theater was the Port of Mukho. At the theater I took a right turn and walked to a dead end where there were two *yeogwans*. I stopped and turned around, and a couple of young ladies walked up and said, "Hello," as each one took one of my arms. I panicked and shook my arms to get them to let go. I think I said in English, "No thanks, trying to quit," which was Jack Fisher's line (my roommate from training). I had no idea how to say, "I'm not interested in what you are selling," in Korean. So I walked fast, turned left at the movie theater, and headed back to the main street. As I walked away I could hear the young ladies laughing. I went back home quickly, lest anyone think I had been visiting prostitutes—not a reputation a Peace Corps Volunteer would want, especially not during the first month in his town.

The next day I told Mr. Yoo that I had walked downtown. He warned me to be careful and not to go downtown after dark. I didn't tell him that I had been accosted by a couple of ladies of the evening. Obviously, because Mukho was a port town with ships coming in and out often, there was a demand for prostitues. Maybe most small towns would not be able to support these women, or at least not as many, but Mukho could, and did.

A few nights later, not heeding Mr. Yoo's advice, I wandered downtown again. This time I just stayed on the main street past the intersection where I'd turned a few nights earlier, and I walked down past the port area to where the fishing boats docked and where you could walk around and watch the activity. I often visited this area during the day on the weekends. There was a two-story building with offices in it at the north end of the harbor, and a stairway led up to the roof. I loved standing on the roof and watching the fishermen working on their boats or fixing their nets. On my way back to my room this night, I saw an American-looking guy walking toward me. I greeted him, and he turned out to be another Peace Corps Volunteer. He was a K-24, a health volunteer, working in Tuberculosis (TB) control at the Mukho *Bogun-so* (health center). His name was Joe Zug. He had just finished his training and been assigned to "my" town. We talked for a few minutes, and then he told me that he had to meet the head of the *bogun-so* and a couple of the other employees for a drink. We both said, "See you again," and I went home. The next morning, I told some of the teachers who sat near me in the teachers' office that I had met another American Peace Corps Volunteer. Maybe a couple of weeks later, I was told by one of the teachers that he had heard this new volunteer had left Mukho and returned to the U.S. I never heard why he left, and I never bothered to ask either. In a way I was just as glad to have the town to myself again.

On one of the first Saturdays after arriving in Mukho, Mr. Yoo, the Principal, Mr. Lee, the Vice Principal, and a couple of the English teachers took me after classes ended to see the beach at Bupyeong. The public beach was south of the airport with the narrow tarmac landing strip on the sand. It was a lovely beach where a narrow river ran into the sea. There were several restaurants there, and we had dinner in one of them with a fine view of the East Sea (Sea of Japan).

The next weekend, on Sunday, we visited a waterfall near Bupyeong called Yongchu Waterfall. To get there we took the bus past the Ssangyong cement factory up the Mureung Valley west of the town. The cement plant itself was ugly, and they were strip-mining the mountain north of it, which was made of limestone, and this limestone was then used to produce the cement. The strip-mining made this part of the valley even uglier. Once past the factory and farther up the valley there was a small village with several restaurants and the end of the line for the bus. From there we walked up to the small Samhwa-sa (Samhwa Temple), which was a handy place to rest before the more difficult and more steeply inclined part of the trail. As we walked up between rocky cliffs on either side and followed the mountain stream, which higher up formed the waterfall, we walked through a National Guard training site. There was an obstacle course that included a thick rope across a crevice, chin-up bars, and such. On a large, bare rock face off to the southwest was a map of Korea. The map included not only the peninsula of present day North and South Korea, but it also showed a large part of Manchuria as being part of the country. Historically, this part of Manchuria had once belonged to the Korean kingdom of Goguryeo, during what is known as the Three Kingdoms period. Goguryeo was conquered and absorbed by an alliance of the Korean Silla kingdom and the Chinese Tang Dynasty. Silla got the southern part of Goguryeo, and China took all of its Manchurian possessions and the northern part of today's North Korea. That was in the seventh century CE. Korea has not controlled any part of Manchuria since then, although there is one province in Manchuria today in which Korean is the official language because many Koreans settled up there during the late Yi Dynasty in the nineteenth century. As we walked by this map I wondered if the South Koreans really thought that someday they might get this land back from China. I certainly doubt it, but stranger things have happened—look at Israel.

Continuing our journey, the path got narrower and steeper as we progressed. About a half hour after resting at the temple, we reached the first of two consecutive waterfalls. At the bottom of this first one a small pool had been carved into the rock by the falling water. We walked past the pool and then up a very steep trail that led to a very narrow path around a rock face. The path was only about eighteen inches wide, and everyone had to nearly make love to the rock face, hugging it for several steps in order to get past. After that erotic excitement, though, we were greeted by an even larger waterfall and a much larger and very deep mountain pool. The water from this large pool then ran out between two boulders and cascaded down the lower falls and into the lower and smaller pool. By the upper falls we

Yongchu Waterfall—starting at the far left in the front row Mr. Jong, Chul-chin, Principal Mr. Yoo, Vice Principal Mr. Lee's son, and Vice Principal Mr. Lee. Don is kneeling, and three other teachers are shown.

broke out our *kimpop* (literally seaweed rice or, in Japanese, sushi) for lunch. We spent a wonderful afternoon looking at the lovely scenery and listening to the rhythm of the falling water. Many photos were taken by the teachers, and they later gave me copies. I was to return to visit this valley and the two waterfalls many times. On my very last visit there in the spring of 1975 a young lady fell into the water, and I jumped in and saved her from an awful fate, but more on that later.

As noted earlier, the students quickly stopped looking alike. They each looked different from one another. Many students reminded me of friends and relatives. They also had very individual personalities, which I got to know over the course of the school year. I couldn't help thinking that the uniforms allowed them in some ways to be more individual than American students who didn't wear uniforms. Not able to express their personalities and preferences in their clothes, they were freer to express them in other ways.

Especially the first few weeks, I did not leave Mukho to visit any other volunteer. I wanted to acclimatize myself to these new surroundings. As mentioned, I worked five and a half days a week just as the other teachers at Mukho Middle School did. Some Peace Corps Volunteers told their school that we only had five days a week of schooling in the U.S. and insisted that they had to have Saturdays off. These were the volunteers who every weekend took off to another town where there was another PCV or more than one. Many of them would congregate and commiserate about how much they didn't like Korea or complain about their school or their co-teacher. Oh, the self-pity!

On Saturday afternoons and most Sundays, if I had no other plans, I would just take off hiking in any direction except east since the East Sea (Sea of Japan) prohibited it. There were a couple of valleys heading west that I'd follow for miles. Often, instead of hiking on the pathways through the valleys, I'd head up to the crest of the hills and low mountains that surrounded Mukho on three sides. All the hills and mountains around Mukho were virtually treeless. There were some small, three-foot-tall pine trees here and there, but as I walked in any direction from hilltop to hilltop I could "see for miles and miles and miles and miles and miles, oh, yea." ("I Can See for Miles" written by Pete Townshend, performed by The Who)

Other days and weekends I'd follow the railroad tracks south with great views of the shoreline, rocks, and lovely small beaches. I couldn't walk the railroad tracks to the north, as they quickly entered a tunnel through the large hill that went right to the sea at the north end of town. The road heading north through town also stopped at Mukho's ice plant, and this is where the hill fell precipitously into the sea. But if I walked to the only real intersection in town, the one where I had turned right and ran into the nice ladies described earlier, and instead turned left I could head out of town. The road went off in a northwesterly direction past the girls' middle and high schools, through a pass between the two large hills that hemmed the town in on the north, and then curved back toward the east to a lovely beach called Mangsang. I'd usually have the beach to myself. In those days Koreans only went to the beach from June 15 to August 15. That was the summer beach season.

Just off the beach, there was a small military base with caves carved into a hill. The Korean soldiers there would often wave, and sometimes I would go up to the front gate and talk with them. They were obviously bored and happy to have someone new to talk to. On other trips I noticed the soldiers having war games where they'd attack up the hill with rifles in their hands. I'd stay a safe distance away and watch for a while. The beach stretched for almost a mile, and once past the army base I would walk in the sand and surf to my heart's content. After several trips this long way around the large hill, I took a chance and walked through the neighborhood of small houses built willy-nilly to about half way up this rather steep hill. I walked up the zigzagging pathways between the homes always trying to head higher, and eventually I found a way through the maze and up onto the treeless area past all the dwellings. At the very top of the hill there was the foundation of a small building. I climbed down into it and stood there for a while thinking this must have been a military observation post at one time. Then I hiked over to the Mangsang side and down to the beach this new way.

Almost wherever I went, young preschool aged kids would point and yell, "Hello!" Or they'd yell, *Miguk* (America) or *Miguk saram* (American). All western foreigners, black or white, were considered to be Americans by most Koreans. With 30,000 GIs and the vast majority of other western visitors being Americans, it was an obvious assumption to make. Sometimes, when the little kids followed me, always at a safe distance, I'd turn around and say in Korean, "Not American—German." They'd look a little puzzled, but then just start yelling, "*Miguk!*" some more. There was an urban legend-like story that the use of the term "gook" as a derogatory name for Asians by American soldiers came from the Korean War when kids yelled what sounded like "ME GOOK" and the US GIs said, "OK, you're a gook."

Another similar language-based story is about Pork Chop Hill where the famous Korean War battle, which was later made into a movie, took place. In Korean the word *bokjop-haeyo* means complicated or confused. During the heat of the battle, so the story goes, the KATUSAs (Korean Augmentation To the United States Army) were running around saying "*bokjop-haeyo*," and the Americans thought they were saying the place was "Pork Chop Hill." Another version of the story is that the hill looked like a pork chop from the air. Take your pick. Either way, the constant yelling of the children got old very fast. Some days it was worse than others, but it never went away completely. During my three years of living in Mukho, there were times when, if I could have gotten away with it, I would have wrung the necks of a few of those noisy brats. Of course, that would have been CIS (CULTURALLY INSENSITIVE)—after all, killing children *is* frowned upon in all cultures. So even though the thought often crossed my mind, I never acted out on this urge.

I also had trouble with Mr. Jong's son, Chong-ho. The kid didn't like me for some reason. Often, his mother would be holding him in her arms, and when I walked by the little bugger would give me a dirty look. One Saturday afternoon I left my room door open while I was sitting on the floor reading a book. Chong-ho walked up to my doorway and looked in at me. It was still warm, and he was walking around with only a T-shirt on and no pants as Korean kids often did in those days. I started to get up from the floor when he began pissing into my room. "You little shit," I said in English. I grabbed him from behind and walked him a couple of steps down the hall while he just continued taking a leek. After putting him down, I went back into my room and closed the door. I grabbed a towel, soaked up the pee in my room and opened the door a crack to see if the little pisser was gone. He was. I went across the hall and washed out the towel and then carefully headed back into my room, walking around the wet areas in the hall. I have no idea where Chong-ho's mother had been during this little adventure, but she must have noticed the yellow puddle still left outside my room because later, when I left the house, it had been cleaned up. After that incident, I never left my room door open, and I kept an eye out for Chong-ho.

One Sunday a few weeks after arriving in Mukho, Mr. Jong asked if I'd like to take a bath in the small bathtub in the house. I said, "Yes, that would be good." It would be nice not to have to head downtown to one of the three *mogyok-tangs* (bath houses). So Mr. Jong started up the heater that he had bought in Seoul. I had not seen him use it before and had the feeling as the American guest they wanted me to be the first to have the pleasure. The kerosene heater was outside the house. There was a small door in the outside wall of the house which was opened to allow this heater to throw a flame at a metal plate attached to the outside of the bathtub. Mr. Jong had filled the bathtub with cold water, the only kind that came out of the tap, and got this heater, flame-thrower-like thing going. It sounded exactly like the kerosene generators used by some Americans when the power goes out. Mr. Jong told me the water would be hot shortly. I continued lesson planning, and time seemed to stand still. Over an hour went by, and Mr. Jong finally told me the water was hot. I got my towel, soap, and a change of u-trou and went in for a nice hot soaking—except when I got in the water it was only tepid. *"Oh, my God, after more than an hour of the flame thrower going like gangbusters all we got was lukewarm water? You've got to be kidding me,"* I said to myself.

I wanted to get back out of the tub and leave, but after an hour's worth of kerosene having been used up, I didn't want to seem ungrateful. So I sat in this very unsatisfying small tub for as long as I could stand it. I sang through in my head several songs to mark out the time as I always do when walking alone or doing any activities that don't require concentration. After a few songs I dried off, put my clothes back on, thanked Mr. Jong, and returned to my room. Luckily, he never asked me if I wanted to bathe at home again. I never saw him use the heater again for himself or the rest of the family either, so I assume he realized it had been a failure. I returned to using the *mogyok-tangs.*

Another daily activity was writing letters. I wrote to my parents, other relatives, and to numerous high school and college friends back home. (My parents, aunts, and uncles often commented throughout their lives that I always remembered to send them birthday wishes even during all the years I spent in Korea.) Several days a week during my second free period after regular classes ended and before my special class started, I'd walk down to the post office. (After the regular classes ended the students had a home room class where, among other things, they'd sweep the floor, clean the windows, and perform other janitorial services. The schools had no janitors; the students did all the cleaning.) At the post office I'd mail letters and buy aerograms. Aerograms were like origami. They were light blue, very thin sheets of paper that, when folded up and sealed, became an instant pre-stamped air mail envelope. You wrote directly on the portion that ended up inside after folding. Sometimes, when I wanted to write longer letters, I would write on notebook paper and put the pages in a regular envelope. Then I'd need to buy actual stamps. In addition, I was writing to Charlie and some of the other volunteers. Walking down to the post office was always pleasant. It was only a ten-minute walk or so, as

Mukho was a very small place. There was very little land to house the 50,000 people who supposedly lived there. The houses were mostly small and overly crowded together even by Korean standards of the time. Mukho residents told me that because there were over 50,000 people in the town that it should be Mukho City, but for some reason the change had not yet been made. It was still officially called a town. Walking from the school down to the main street and to the post office, I was never bothered by little urchins as I was in many other parts of town. There were never groups of preschool aged kids on the main street, thankfully. So I'd leisurely stroll past the small shops along my route. There was very little traffic, and many people walked in the middle of the road. They'd get out of the way for the occasional bus, taxi, or truck that would lumber by.

Every day I looked forward to the mail delivery at school. I'd often get a letter from the States or from Charlie or one of the other K-23s with whom I corresponded. One day I got a letter from Sam Okemos at Albion. My senior year there were two freshman guys named Sam on my corridor, Sam Okemos and Sam Boisblanc. I got along really well with both of them and enjoyed their company. Often, in the afternoons, we'd get talking about one thing or another and have discussions that sometimes lasted hours. The longest discussion I remember was about an article that appeared in the *Wall Street Journal* about the death of Lake Erie. Lake Erie was horribly polluted at the time; the river in Cleveland had so much trash in it that it twice caught on fire, and the city of Cleveland itself was called the "mistake on the lake." One Friday afternoon one of the guys on the corridor brought in a *Wall Street Journal* article that suggested a series of locks be put in south of Detroit on the Detroit River, a new canal be made around Niagara Falls, and Lake Erie be dropped to the same level as Lake Ontario. Doing so would flush out the lake and turn it into a river. The two Sams were both in the room, as well as three or four other guys from our corridor, and we began to argue for or against this plan. I took the devil's advocate position and said, "I agree the lake is dead, so get rid of it." Most of the guys were against the idea. The article mentioned on the positive side that both Canada and the U.S. would increase in size and gain a lot of additional farmland. Of course, one has to wonder if it wouldn't have been horribly polluted farmland, but the article didn't mention that. A canal could be dug and locks put in up to Cleveland from the new Erie River so that Cleveland could still be a port, and in the biggest flight of fancy, a geodesic dome would be placed over what had been Niagara Falls. It would now be dry, and it would be turned into the world's largest hanging gardens. Babylon, eat your heart out! Today, seeing what has happened with the vanishing Aral Sea and Lake Chad, I'm just as glad the U.S. and Canada didn't decide on this radical quick fix. Lake Erie is not as polluted as it was back then. It has been cleaned up nicely, although it does have algae blooms upon occasion. Cleveland has had a rebirth, and its river has been cleaned up as well. No more fire on the water. In his letter Sam told me about how he and the other Sam were both living in the Deta Tau Delta fraternity house and enjoying their sophomore year thus far.

Sam Okemos was one of many Albion friends I kept in contact with by mail during my Peace Corps years. In many of the early letters to friends and family I talked of the town, the mountains, how much I enjoyed teaching in general, and the special class with the best fifteen students where I could really work on their speaking skills. Also, I wrote about the upcoming American election, how I hoped McGovern would win, and how the war in Vietnam troubled me. When my absentee election ballot came, I held it up and announced to all the teachers that I was voting for McGovern and pushed the tab out next to his name. I'm not sure what they thought about the U.S. election, as I never talked politics with them— especially not Korean politics. Korea was under martial law at the time. But I just couldn't resist letting them know I didn't support "Tricky" Dick Nixon.

Another Albion friend I wrote home to was Fred Barbeau. Fred was in my graduation class and had also been an RA in Suzy Hall during our senior year. He kindly kept all the letters I had written to him and later returned them to me. In one of these letters, I wrote about how my appearance had changed due to Koreans not liking hippies:

> I too look a little different than when I last saw you. My hair
> is shorter, no longer over my ears, for Peace Corps won't let you
> become a volunteer here in Korea with long hair. Also, my
> mustache went at the same time as my hair. The more my
> hairs (sic) this way the more I want it long. I wish it would
> grow long overnight and say to the Koreans that I am still
> me. They think anyone with long hair is a hippie and they
> don't like hippies to say the least. (2 Nov 1972)

Because I had not cut my hair since the day before leaving for San Fran to meet the other K-23s, it was getting longer by this point, though, and I pushed it behind my ears for the time being.

To keep up with the news, I had a subscription to the English language newspaper, the *Korea Herald,* and read it every day. Of course, that was the source for many of the daily discussions with our principal Mr. Yoo. I also had a subscription to *Newsweek's* Asian edition, and for part of the time I was in Korea we received free of charge the *New York Times Week in Review*. Any news that wasn't in those periodicals, I wouldn't hear about. There were no more discussions about *Wall Street Journal* articles in Mukho.

One weekend, after having been on the east coast for a couple of months, Bob Saks invited me down to Samcheok to visit. It was a half-hour bus ride south along the coast. We were on a cement road for the first fifteen minutes of the trip. The Ssangyong Cement Company had paved the road from its cement plant near Bupyeong to the harbor in Mukho so that its trucks would have an easy drive. After that it was a dirt road the rest of the way south, but the view of the shoreline was beautiful in many places. Samcheok was similar in size to Mukho, but its population was a little smaller than Mukho's. Also, there was a river running through it, and it was flatter being situated in a valley. Samcheok was semi-famous because of something that happened there during the Korean War. General MacArthur sent the *USS Missouri* to bomb Samcheok on September 15, 1950. This was a diversionary tactic while the Incheon Landing was taking place on the other side of the peninsula. The *USS Missouri* was the Navy's most famous ship because it had been the site in Tokyo Bay of the surrender of the Empire of Japan at the end of World War II. The North Koreans, it was felt, would not think any major battle would take place without this famous battleship being a part of it. The landing at Incheon did catch the North off guard, so this diversion seemed to have done the trick.

Bob met me when I got off the bus, and we went to visit where he lived. He was in a lovely *hanok* (traditional Korean-style) house. He rented a room in the house, as I did, but I liked his house a lot more because it was old and looked like a home from the Yi dynasty (1392–1910 CE). After seeing his accommodations, we walked around the town. Samcheok actually had an old Yi dynasty open pavilion on a rock at the shore that had been used by Confucian scholars for poetry writing contests. This pavilion was very impressive compared to Mukho's near total lack of ancient structures. After wandering around town, the only thing left to do was to visit a tearoom and have a cup of tea or coffee. Tearooms were as ubiquitous as Starbucks coffee shops are in the U.S. today. Virtually every corner had one, and Koreans almost always met their friends in one whenever they went out. Although they were called tearooms and did serve tea, most everyone drank coffee there. It wasn't freshly ground, exotic coffee mind you; it was instant Maxwell House. So, I had a cup of tea, as I didn't drink coffee yet, and Bob had a coffee. It was always about half of a cup of whatever you ordered. The drink wasn't really that important. The tearoom was an institution—a place to meet friends and converse. That was its importance. People would sometimes sit and talk for hours. After we sat and talked for a while in the tearoom comparing our schools and our co-teachers, Bob and I went out to dinner and then went back to his room and talked some more. Before it got too late Bob walked me back to the bus station, and I boarded the last Mukho-bound bus before curfew and went back home.

A couple of days later, while talking about the day's *Korea Herald* articles, Mr. Yoo told me that I was invited to help chaperone the third-year students on their class trip to Sorak Mountain and Soraksan National Park, the most famous of South Korea's national parks. It was a couple of hours by train and bus north of Mukho and not too far from the DMZ. In fact, the whole park is north of the thirty-eighth parallel, which was the dividing line between North and South Korea after World War II and until the Korean War started. Due to the vagaries of war and the fact that the DMZ now lies on the truce line where the fighting ended in 1953, on the east side of the peninsula the DMZ is north of the thirty-eighth parallel, and in the far west it is slightly south of it.

Mr. Yoo, eight other teachers, and I escorted the four hundred or so third-year boys on this trip. We took the train up to Kangnung City, which was a one-hour train ride north of Mukho. We got on buses in Kangnung and went to the home of Yi, Yul-gok on the outskirts of the city. Yi, Yul-gok (1536–1584) was a famous Confucian scholar born in this house near Kangnung. Among other things, he wrote a lot about Korean national security and warned of the threat from Japan. He suggested that Korea build up its military, but no one listened to him. Shortly after his death, Japan invaded Korea in what is called the Imjin War in the 1590s. (This is the same war in which Admiral Yi, Sun-sin defeated the Japanese Navy in battle after battle.) Unfortunately, Yi, Yul-gok's warnings had not been heeded, and the Korean peninsula was devastated by this invasion because the Koreans had lost battle after battle on land. Consequently, he is considered a national hero. His home was surrounded by a residential area at this time. The buses were parked alongside the road, and we walked through narrow passages between the walls surrounding these homes until we reached Yi, Yul-gok's home. It was a wonderful *hanok* house with a wall around it and an inner courtyard. Once inside the home, after taking off our shoes, we saw interesting exhibits—although it would have been nice if there had been English translations of the descriptions for the objects from his life. Included in the exhibit were also several paintings and calligraphy works done by his mother, Shin, Sa-im-dang, who was famous in her own right for her art as well as for having given birth to this great Confucian scholar. Her paintings of flowers and insects were very life-like and reminded me of some of the works of Germany's most famous artist, Albrecht Durer.

Years later I returned to revisit Yi, Yul-gok's home. The neighborhood around it had been removed. There was a large parking area, a new stone wall built around the complex, and there were English translations for all the exhibits' descriptions.

After leaving this historic home we went by bus to a lovely beach area just north of Kangnung called Gyeongpo Provincial Park. We stopped for only a few minutes on this trip with the students, but I later went there many times during my Peace Corps years.

Next we visited Naksan-sa (Naksan Buddhist Temple) near Sorak National Park. Naksan-sa is right on the coast, and the main temple building is perched on a rock outcropping. Part of the building is hanging over the sea, and through a hole in the floor you can watch the waves crashing upon the rocks below. It is a lovely sight. While the students were still wandering around, Mr. Yoo and I were standing and talking on the path a few yards from the main temple when an elderly Korean man walked up to us. He bowed low in front of me, and I bowed too. Then he began talking in what I could tell was in the highest level of Korean, even though I couldn't understand what he was saying. When he finished he bowed low again. I bowed along with him, and he walked away. I asked Mr. Yoo if he could translate what had been said. Mr. Yoo told me that the man was thanking me for the United States' efforts in fighting to save Korea from the Communists. I was the first American he had ever seen, and he wanted to thank me personally for America's help. I was flabbergasted. His obvious deep sincerity and his heartfelt gratitude profoundly touched me.

Don and Principal Yoo standing in front of Naksan Buddhist Temple.

We again boarded the buses and headed up to Sorak National Park. There we unloaded and went to the *yeogwans* where we all stayed. Mr. Yoo, the eight other teachers, and I all stayed in one large room; each of us had a traditional *yo, ibul,* and *begae* (quilted mattress, coverlet, and beanbag-like pillow). I remember Mr. Yoo remarking the next day about how I was sleeping on my stomach in the morning, and he found this interesting. We made sure all the kids were up, went for breakfast, and then began hiking. We hiked alongside a mountain stream, often on very precarious narrow paths, and over a rope suspension bridge with wooden slats across the bottom. We ended at a beautiful waterfall. The next day we repeated the whole drill except we hiked in another valley and visited Shinhung-sa (Shinhung Buddhist Temple), which is inside the park. The following day we retraced our route by bus and train back to Mukho. It was a wonderful trip and a great introduction to Sorak National Park where I would return many times during my Peace Corps years.

Don in his Sigma Nu jacket, Principal Yoo seated in front with his hat in his hands, and and seven of the other teachers in front of a suspension bridge in Sorak National Park.

After the class trip, one morning I noticed Miss Choi, Yong-sook, the teachers' office assistant, was using a silk screen-like contraption that looked straight out of a medieval workshop. Like all the students' chairs and desks, this machine (if you could call it that) looked hand-made. The top, which was a wooden frame covered with silk, lifted up, and Miss Choi would put a piece of cheap, beige-brown colored paper, which often had small holes here and there in it, onto the bottom part of the device. Then closing the top, she would put a piece of wax paper over the silk. Using a stylus, the teachers had scratched the wax away to write their tests. Finally, after closing the top and putting the wax paper engraved with the test on top of the silk screen, she would cruise a heavy roller over a large ink pad and then pressing down heavily run it across the wax paper page. The ink would leak through all the scratched letters and print onto the toilet paper-like, cheap beige paper resulting in an almost readable copy of the test. This would be repeated hundreds of times for each page of each test for all of each teacher's classes. By the time she finished, Miss Choi's right arm looked like Popeye's while her left arm had nearly atrophied away.

Every few weeks Mr. Jong would grab me, and we'd go out drinking, sometimes the two of us, but more often with other teachers. Although it broke up the monotony of my day-to-day and week-to-week existence, I also dreaded going most of the time. Korean men (traditionally only men went out drinking) turned social drinking into a competition. Everyone tried to get everyone else more drunk than they. There were fun drinking customs to follow and games that were played, but some parts of it got old quickly. The basic drinking customs were interesting though. You never pour your own drink. When I finished a shot glass, metal cup, or beer glass depending on whether we were drinking *soju*, a clear liquor that I always described as tasting like lighter fluid, *makgeolli*, a rice wine that looked like skim milk and had very little taste, or *maekju* (beer), either OB (Oriental Brewery) or Crown, I would always quickly pass the drinking vessel to another drinker at our table. (Usually, in Mukho the teachers didn't drink beer because it was more expensive than the other two alcoholic beverages.) Then I would fill the shot glass or cup as the other person held it in his hand. When pouring you always hold your left hand under your right forearm. This was polite and supposedly comes from the fact that Korean men and women wore puffy-sleeved garments traditionally, and the left hand would be holding up the material so it wouldn't get into any of the food on the table. There was always food on the table because you never drank without some *anju* (snack) of some kind. *Anju* could be simple like some peanuts or some elaborate fish dish.

A fun thing to say after giving your glass to another person at the table who had not finished his first glass was, "*Angyeong issayyeo*," which means, "You have spectacles." The two shot glasses looked like the two lenses of eye glasses when sitting together. It implied that the person with the *angyeong* should quickly drink up one of their glasses. Glasses, though not spectacles, were always being exchanged around the room, and I'd always try to give everyone at the table my glass at least once before the end of the drinking. Of course, everyone else was trying to give the others their glasses and trying to get others drunk before them. So if one member of the party was known as being a weak drinker, they'd barrage him with glasses early. Luckily, I could hold my own, so they didn't pick on me. Also, I always cheated. I would put an ashtray under the table in front of me. We were at low tables always sitting cross-legged on the floor. I would hold my glass in my lap, surreptitiously pour it out into the ashtray, put it up to my mouth and pretend to gulp it down and then pass it to someone else. If there was a potted plant in the room I would strategically sit next to it and, while pretending my back hurt and I was rubbing it, pour my drink into the potted plant. Lucky I didn't kill the poor plants! Of course, as the evening wore on, everyone would lift their glass as it was being filled, thus pushing up against the spout of the bottle or metal pot to try to make sure their glass wasn't filled all the way.

Another part of the game was giving drinks to the bar girls. There were always bar girls. Giving the glass to a bar girl and forcing her to drink it would empty the bottle faster and mean that one might hold out longer before getting shit-faced drunk. Sometimes the girls would become so drunk they'd start crying. I always thought this was cruel. Often the men in the group would grouse and puff out their chests like they were great he-men having gotten the poor young lady drunk. Mostly I just found it all rather sad.

There was often flirting going on and lewd comments being made. Barroom girls were notorious for earning extra money by sleeping with guests. Of course, tearoom girls were notorious for delivering tea to men in offices, *yeogwans*, or wherever and turning tricks for cash. There were often articles in the *Korea Herald* about lewd barber shops too. Barber shops usually had young women who did the shaving. For some reason the police would raid barber shops every once in a while, and there would be coverage in the paper about how lewd services were being performed in these barber shops. I have no idea if this was true about barber shops. I only went into a barber shop once during my Peace Corps days, and my visit there will be covered later. But I often heard all the male teachers raving about how wonderful the treatment was in barber shops. (Maybe they were talking about the lewd services, now that I think about it.)

An ever-present aspect of going drinking was singing. Usually someone would suggest one of the group members sing a song. This person would sing and then suggest someone else to be next. Almost always the singer who couldn't carry a tune in a basket, like that young monk at the Buddhist temple near Daegu, would sing "Ave Maria" and miss most of the high notes. Most Koreans loved "Ave Maria," and everyone applauded wildly because, by then, everyone was drunk and didn't seem to notice how off-key and off-note the singer had been. Usually we'd go around the table until everyone had sung at least once. I always had to sing twice. They'd want a song in English. A couple of songs that were always big hits were "Proud Mary" or "Ob La Di, Ob La Da." I'd sing one or the other of them, and then they'd want me to sing a song in Korean. I'd always sing *"Newtki Junae,"* (Before It's Too Late) as sung by the famous female singer Kim, Chu-ja. I had bought a cassette of one of her albums and memorized this song after a couple of weeks of playing it over and over. Recently I read that this song was intended to be an anti-Vietnam War song about a Korean woman whose boyfriend was among the South Korean Marines sent to fight in the jungles of South Vietnam.

I never did use the lyrics of the many songs that I had written down the last couple of days before leaving Detroit. I had written down lyrics to my favorite songs by the Association, Donovan, the Beatles and others, but they were all songs that were not known by the Koreans. "Proud Mary" and "ObLa Di, Ob La Da" had both been big hits in South Korea, so I just sang them over and over again.

There were always jokes flying around during these drinking bouts. One of my favorite jokes was often used and yet drew laughs every time. The restrooms, whether modern ceramic indoor squat toilets or outhouses, often had W. C. on the door. W. C. is short for "water closet," which is the British common term for toilet. Almost every time we went drinking someone getting up to go hit the head, as they say in the Navy, would announce, "I am going to Washington College." Another later would say, "I am going to Winston Churchill." Each time laughter would then permeate the room.

One of the funniest jokes I ever heard while out drinking with Koreans was told a couple of years after my Peace Corps service while I was teaching in the evening for the adult education program at the Hankuk University of Foreign Studies in Seoul. My students took me out for drinks at the end of our six-month-long semester. As we were each taking turns singing, Mr. Lee, Myung-bok, who had just finished his song, called on another of the adult students to sing. The man he called on worked for the company that made Kotex feminine hygiene products in Korea. Mr. Lee said in English, "Next I will call on Mr. Kotex to sing a song." Everyone laughed heartily, but then Mr. Kotex replied, "No, I am not Mr. Kotex, I am Mr. New Freedom," which was the name of Kotex's latest product. What had been a chorus of snickers, turned into an actual roar of thunderous laughter. When it finally quieted down a bit, Mr. New Freedom sang the John Denver song "Country Roads." He sang very well indeed.

Back in Mukho one night Mr. Jong suggested we go drinking, and we picked up the gym teacher, Mr. Choi, Gil-rang. I didn't care for Mr. Choi much, but I didn't say anything. So we drank at a *sul-jip* (bar), and then Mr. Choi suggested instead of going to a second place, which was a common occurrence, we should go to his house. (Often we'd leave one place, and at first I'd think we were done, and then we'd walk into a second place or even a third after that.) So this night we headed to Mr. Choi's house. He was gruff and mean to his wife, ordering her around. "Bring *soju*," then a minute later "bring *anju* (snacks)" and when she quickly brought these items in he'd complain that it wasn't fast enough or the *anju* wasn't good enough. I was very uncomfortable with his demeanor. Then he brought in his son, a boy of maybe four. He ordered him around as if the poor child were a soldier. He stood the boy on the table and ordered him to salute and sing. The young boy looked frightened. Mr. Choi, obviously very drunk, ordered his son to sing one song after another. In between he urged Mr. Jong and me to drink up. It seemed like we were there an eternity, but we finally left. I started watching Mr. Choi more at school. Many times I noticed he looked drunk in the afternoon. Even though he was new at Mukho Middle School that semester, and usually teachers spent a few years at each school, after winter break he was gone. Our principal, Mr. Yoo, had pulled some strings or called in a favor and got him transferred away. I, for one, was relieved.

In Mukho, saluting was something all the male students did when they passed a teacher even in town and after school hours. They also had to say while saluting, *bangong* (anti-communism). When I passed by students they'd stop, stand at attention, salute, and say *bangong*. Sometimes they'd then say in English, "Good morning, sir." I'd smile and say "Good morning!" back and always loved it when they did so. I was told that a few years before I got to Mukho, North Korean commandos had landed nearby and murdered a family before being surrounded and killed by South Korean soldiers. Possibly this is why all the students saluted and said *bangong* in Mukho. In other parts of Korea, I was told by other volunteers, the students didn't do this.

I loved my life and teaching, and in a letter to Fred Barbeau, I wrote:

> It's beautiful here and my life here, for me, is beautiful. I
> love teaching. It's not work, for I enjoy it too much to
> be work. I hope the rest of my life I can find something
> or things to do that make me as happy as being here does.
> Today as I was leaving school many students were playing
> soccer. As I walked alone by them several of them turned
> and said, "Good bye, Sir!" Those three words make my
> whole self almost unconscious, and I feel happier than if
> someone told me I had won the Irish Sweepstakes. It
> makes me feel like I'm the richest person in the world –
> Good bye, Sir! The kids are beautiful simply beautiful.
> When I enter the room there (sic) faces light up like a
> Christmas tree and they say, "Good morning, Sir" makes
> me feel drunk and I forget everything for an hour. The
> world could crumble around me, and I wouldn't even know
> it.

I don't think really it's so important if the kids are learning more with me here, but the fact that I am here is the important thing. The fact that I'm living here for two years, trying to learn the language, eating the food, teaching the classes all these things together are the important things. To show them Americans are people not just soldiers, to show them Americans want to learn from them as well as teach to them, to show them Americans admire there (sic) customs, land, people, etc. This is why I'm here I think. (21 Nov 72)

The students were amazing in their zeal to learn. Even though there were fifty to sixty kids in each classroom at any given time, you could hear a pin drop. Never did we have any disciplinary problems in the classes I taught. It was a joy to be in the classroom.

I take that back. There was one time when the students got rowdy. It was the first time I was teaching a dialogue. I wrote some key words for the dialogue on the blackboard with underlines for the words that I didn't spell out. There were two speakers whom I labeled A and B. Part A started, "What time is it? Part B answered, "I don't know," and so on. So I modeled the dialogue. I stood on one side and said, "What time is it?" Then I moved to the other side and said "I don't know." While I said "I don't know," I shrugged my shoulders and held up the palms of my hands in what I assumed was a universal gesture. I then explained that I would be Part A, and all of the students would in unison be Part B. I said, "What time is it?" The fifty-some students in the class all said together "I don't know," while all shrugging their shoulders, holding up the palms of their hands in exaggerated motions, and all bursting out in uproarious laughter. Turns out shrugging one's shoulders to imply not knowing something is *not* a universal gesture. They thought it was absolutely hilarious. It took several minutes to get them quieted down. When Mr. Jun, In-kook and I taught the same lesson to other classes throughout the rest of the day I held my arms at my side and forced myself not to shrug as I said, "I don't know," with my body frozen. It's hard as hell not to shrug when saying "I don't know," but I forced myself. Of course, I was robbing the other classes of the mirth the first class had enjoyed, but it had taken a long time to get them to stop laughing.

During the evenings after I had finished lesson planning and on weekends when not hiking or if the weather was bad, I also read books. The Peace Corps office had a library, and we could borrow as many books as we wanted. I took a dozen or so before heading for Mukho. During the first four months up until

Christmas some of the books I read were *The Journey to the East*, by Hermann Hesse; *Death in Venice*, by Thomas Mann; *Snow Country*, by Yasunari Kawabata; *The Moon is Down*, by John Steinbeck; *The Catcher in the Rye*, by J. D. Salinger; *Women in Love*, by D. H. Lawrence; and *Wuthering Heights*, by Emily Bronte. I had it in my mind that I would read every classic novel in English and American literature while I had this opportunity as well as some German and Japanese fiction.

Peace Corps turned me into an avid reader. I had read some rather difficult history books while in high school, such as *The Rise and Fall of the Third Reich*, but I took a whole summer to read that, and I never read anything extra during the school year. But I have always loved books even though I wasn't always reading them. Also, as described earlier, my mementos from vacations were often books and/or bookends. My most cherished books came from my Great Aunt Lena. Lena was my Grandfather Otto Haffner's older sister. When I was thirteen years old, Aunt Lena, who was a widow by then, decided to move to Florida. My father and I visited her home in Detroit while she was having an estate sale. I spotted a white Bavarian china polar bear.

"Aunt Lena, I want to buy this polar bear," I said.

"You like this bear?"

"Yes, it's very beautiful."

"Here, you take it, it's yours."

"Oh, thank you, Aunt Lena." Then I looked and saw a bookshelf next to the fireplace with wonderfully gorgeous old books. The polar bear had had a price tag on it, but these books didn't.

"Aunt Lena, what about these books?"

"Oh, no one wants them."

"May I take them?"

"Sure, I was going to throw them out with the trash." *"Oh, my God!"* I said to myself. Even at such a young age, this seemed like sacrilege to me.

"Can we take them, Dad?" I asked my father.

"Well, as many as we can fit in the car." He had already loaded a beautiful antique chair, which I still possess, and some other things that Aunt Lena had wanted my parents to have. There was very little room left, but I was able to fit in five sets of books, twenty-one precious volumes in all, into my dad's car along with the cherished white Bavarian china polar bear. These treasured books have a place of honor at eye level on our living room bookshelves today. The polar bear is in our china cabinet. Some of the covers of the books are a little worn, but that just adds to their intrinsic value for me.

The first set that caught my eye the day we visited Great Aunt Lena's home was the five-volume set of James Fenimore Cooper's *Leatherstocking Tales*. With caramel-colored backs/spines, these beautifully bound books have light green and teal marbling on the covers, the top edge, fore edge, and bottom edge, as well as fancy floral patterned paper on the free endpapers front and back. On the title page of each volume is the title, subtitle, and for four of the five, a quote:

THE PIONEERS; OR, THE SOURCES OF THE SUSQUEHANNA.
A DESCRIPTIVE TALE.

Extremes of habits, manners, time and space,
Brought close together, here stood face to face,
And gave at once a contrast to the view,
That other lands and ages never knew.

Paulding

THE LAST OF THE MOHICANS A NARRATIVE OF 1757.
(NO QUOTE)

THE PRAIRIE. A TALE.

Mark his condition, and th' event; then tell me,
If this might be a brother. – Tempest.

THE PATHFINDER; OR, THE INLAND SEA.

Here the heart
May give a useful lesson to the head,
And Learning wiser grow without his books.

Cowper.

THE DEERSLAYER OR, THE FIRST WAR-PATH

What terrors round him wait?
Amazement in his van, with Flight combined,
And Sorrow's faded form, and Solitude behind.

Each title and quote is then followed with:

"BY J. FENIMORE COOPER, NEW YORK: NEW YORK PUBLISHING COMPANY, 26 CITY HALL PLACE. 1895." "A TALE."

The largest of the books are the two volumes in the set entitled *The Portrait Gallery of Eminent Men and Women*. Each of the two books is three inches wide, eleven inches tall, and nine inches deep. Both have a dark brown, leather-bound cover which is a half inch thick. They are massive. These two volumes have lovely marbling on the free endpapers front and back and lithograph copies of paintings of each of the eminent people presented in each volume. On the first of two title pages is an engraving of a pretty young lady sitting on a settee wearing a head-band, a Grecian-like dress, and sandals while holding a tablet and a pen in her hands. Above her in very fancy Gothic font it says "Portrait Gallery of Eminent Men and Women" while below her in equally impressive lettering "with Biographies by E. A. Duyckinck." On the second title page, in standard font is repeated, "PORTRAIT GALLERY OF EMINENT MEN AND WOMEN OF EUROPE AND AMERICA EMBRACING HISTORY, STATESMANSHIP, NAVAL AND MILITARY LIFE, PHILOSOPHY, THE DRAMA, SCIENCE, LITERATURE AND ART. WITH BIOGRAPHIES BY EVERT A. DUYCKINCK, author of "Portrait Gallery of Eminent Americans," "Cyclopedia of American Literature," "History of the War for the Union," etc., etc. *ILLUSTRATED WITH HIGHLY FINISHED ENGRAVINGS* FROM ORIGINAL PORTRAITS BY THE MOST CELEBRATED ARTISTS. In Two Volumes. NEW YORK: JOHNSON, WILSON AND COMPANY, 27 BEEKMAN STREET. 1873." Unfortunately, James Fenimore Cooper did not make Duyckinck's cut and is not included in either of the volumes.

Two of the sets have six volumes in each. One is *A Popular History of France*. The spines are in a burgundy color with gold lettering and gold filigree-like patterns on them. All six volumes of this set have beautiful marbling on the covers, endpapers, as well as on the top, fore and bottom edges. The title page reads, "A POPULAR HISTORY OF FRANCE, FROM THE EARLIEST TIMES. BY M. GUIZOT, AUTHOR OF 'THE HISTORY OF CIVILIZATION IN EUROPE,' ETC. ETC. WITH 300 ILLUSTRATIONS BY A. DE NEUVILLE. TRANSLATED BY ROBERT BLACK, M.A., TRANSLATOR OF 'LEOPOLD I., KING OF THE BELGIANS,' ETC. ETC. BOSTON: DANA ESTES AND CHARLES E. LAURIAT, 301 WASHINGTON STREET. 1869." Being part French on my mother's side makes these books seem even more valuable and important to me.

The second set of six volumes is *Globe Encyclopaedia of Universal Information*. Each volume is almost as big as *The Portrait Gallery of Eminent Men and Women* except that they are only two inches wide instead of three. The brown leather bindings are very similar to *The Portrait Gallery*'s binding. All six volumes have matching marbling on the endpapers as well as on the top, fore, and bottom edges. The title page reads:

THE GLOBE ENCYCLOPAEDIA OF UNIVERSAL INFORMATION. EDITED BY JOHN M. ROSS, LL.D. FORMERLY ASSISTANT EDITOR OF "CHAMBERS ENCYCLOPAEDIA." VOLUME (I THROUGH VI) BOSTON: ESTES & LAURIAT, 301 WASHINGTON STREET. 1876. This is the same publisher as for Guizot's history of France set.

The last cherished set is two volumes entitled *The War Between the States*. The spines are in a caramel-colored material similar to the *Leatherstocking Tales*. The front and back covers have burgundy and red marbling as do the front and back endpapers. The top, fore, and bottom edges have a lighter colored marbling of pink and green. The title pages in this set read: "A CONSTITUTIONAL VIEW OF THE LATE WAR BETWEEN THE STATES; ITS CAUSES, CHARACTER, CONDUCT, AND RESULTS. PRESENTED IN A SERIES OF COLLOQUIES AT LIBERTY HALL. BY ALEXANDER H. STEPHENS. 'Times change and men often change with them, but principles never!' IN TWO VOLUMES. VOL. I (or II) NATIONAL PUBLISHING COMPANY, PHILADELPHIA, PA.; CINCINNATI, OHIO; ATLANTA, GA ZEIGLER, McCURDY & CO., CHICAGO, ILL.; ST. LOUIS, MO." There are numerous wonderful lithograph engravings in this set, too. The above quote after the author's name interests me, as I can't help thinking that one side's principles are the other side's blasphemy. We can guess where Mr. Stephens' bias lay.

Every three months during our Peace Corps years, we had to get more inoculations. On July 15, 1972, Dr. C. J. Coe, the Peace Corps doctor, came to the New Grand Hotel, and we got another cholera shot as well as typhoid, Japanese B encephalitis, and gamma globulin (an antibody). Every time after getting the gamma globulin shot, which we received in one of our butt cheeks, we ran up and down stairs to try to get the stuff to move around our bodies. If you didn't, your upper thigh would tighten up in a couple of hours, and you'd limp around the rest of the day. Then at the end of training in September we received tetanus-diphtheria and a rabies shot. Come December it was time to get more shots, and we were told to travel to Seoul one Sunday. Bob Saks and I took the train up to the city of Kangnung and then took a bus to the Kangnung airport. Kangnung's airport was bigger than the one at Bupyeong. It wasn't on the beach, and it had a normal runway. When Bob and I got to the terminal we met Vickie and Jim Middlebelt, who lived in Kangnung and were almost finished with their two years of service. We also found out that the flight was delayed by a couple of hours. After a few minutes a green military truck pulled up, and a couple of American GIs jumped out and met some young Korean women who were in the terminal. The soldiers saw us and came over to talk with us. They were part of a small U.S. base next to the airport where they manned a radar station. They invited us to visit their base, and seeing that we had a couple of hours to kill we jumped in the truck with them and five minutes later entered the base. It looked a little like something out of M*A*S*H except there were only a handful of guys at this facility. We went into the snack bar with the two guys and the gals they brought. Once inside, we had beers and talked with several of the soldiers there, who were obviously lonely and thoroughly enjoyed having some new people to talk to. An hour or so later one of the GIs drove us back to the terminal. A couple of months later Bob and I heard that this base had been turned over to Korean forces, so we never got a chance to visit those guys again.

I knew the base looked like M*A*S*H because I had seen the movie M*A*S*H while in college. Later, after Peace Corps, I enjoyed the TV series too. But in the winter of 1972 I noticed the Quonset huts on this base, and it did remind me of the movie set of M*A*S*H. Four years after finishing Peace Corps and just after finishing the course work for my master's degree in International Administration from the School for International Training in Brattleboro, Vermont, I was hired by the Pearl S. Buck Foundation (PSBF) as Resident Director of their Korea Branch where I worked for ten years. In December of 1979, there was a M*A*S*H episode called "Yessir, That's Our Baby" which featured a storyline about a baby abandoned by her Korean mother at the 4077th MASH unit with a note saying the father was an American GI. The doctors Hawkeye, B.J., and Winchester try to help this baby but are met by indifference from Korean bureaucrats, the Red Cross, and the American military. They find that this poor baby is totally abandoned by both sides of her heritage. In the end, at the military chaplain's suggestion, they leave the child at a monastery. At the end of this episode the Pearl S. Buck Foundation is credited with being the source of information about Amerasian children. In fact, Pearl S. Buck is credited with coming up with the term Amerasian, which I feel is much better than the term "mixed-race" that some people use. After all, there is only one "race" on this planet—the "human race."

Fast-forward several years and after the last special hour-long episode of M*A*S*H aired in 1983, Alan Alda, the star of M*A*S*H, and his wife, photographer Arlene Alda, published a book of photographs, notes, and commentary titled *The Last Days of MASH*. On the inside front cover it states: "The authors' royalties from the sale of this book are being donated to the Pearl S. Buck Foundation for the benefit of Amerasian children." Pearl S. Buck, the Pulitzer- and

Nobel Prize-winning author, started the Welcome House adoption agency in 1949 to help place fatherless Amerasian children into American homes. By 1964 she saw that in Japan and Korea, as well as in the other Asian nations with an American military presence, many of these children were still being born, and in many cases were raised by their mothers and/or other family members. She realized that these Amerasians needed assistance in their country of birth. So she established the foundation that bears her name to help these innocent children to get an education and become productive citizens in their home lands.

After having been driven back to Kangnung's airport by the GIs at the M*A*S*H-like U.S. Army radar station, the Middlebelts, Bob, and I flew to Seoul. On Monday, we got the following shots at the Peace Corps Office from Dr. C. J. Coe: another cholera shot, gamma globulin, polio-sabin, rabies, and a TB test. We all did more hiking up and down the stairs, this time in the Korea Educational Association Building where the Peace Corps Office was located. Monday afternoon we flew back to Kangnung in the same type of small prop plane that I had first flown in with Mr. Yoo and Mr. Jong in September and that had, just the day before, taken us to Seoul. Jokingly we East Coasters (east coast of Korea) always said that we might not quite be "jetsetters," but we were "prop setters." Bob and I bid farewell to Jim and Vickie, as they were leaving Peace Corps at the end of the semester and we'd probably not see them again.

CHAPTER 6

First Winter Break '72–'73: The Runs Again

I t was nearly time for winter break. Korea has weather very similar to that of my native Michigan. Because Mukho was on the coast, its weather was a little milder than up in the mountains, and it didn't get very much snow, but the temperature was similar to Detroit's during all four seasons. Up in the mountains, and especially in North Korea, it was like the Upper Peninsula of Michigan in the winter with lots of snow and much colder. Because the schools had no central heat—and, in fact, the classrooms in most of the country had no heat at all—the winter vacation lasted from before Christmas until the end of January.

Charlie and I had been writing back and forth, and he was bent out of shape about the third-year English teacher at his school, Mr. Kim, Yong-sam, with whom he was in some kind of power struggle. He alluded to the trouble, but he said it was far too complicated to explain by letter and he'd tell me during winter break. I planned to head down to Yeongju when the break started and then after hanging out there a few days, both of us would head up to Seoul to chill out for awhile. I hopped on the train in Mukho. This mostly single line of track started in Kangnung, passed through Mukho, and then went all the way to Seoul. Although Seoul, as the crow flies, is due west of Mukho, the train continues due south when it leaves Mukho. This is because the highest mountains in South Korea run along the coast through Gangwon Province and down into Kyongsangbuk-do (North Kyongsang Province), which is the province Charlie and Lisa's town of Yeongju is in. After Bupyeong, on the coast, the tracks headed into the mountains and straight south for a couple of hours before heading in a southwesterly direction till they reached Yeongju. This was about a five-hour train ride from Mukho. The engine then decoupled, and another engine went up another track at the station and coupled to what had been the last car and headed out in the opposite direction. It would then turn northwest for four more hours until it reached Seoul.

Charlie met me at the station when I got to Yeongju, and we started walking toward his rented room. I asked about Mr. Kim, but again he said it was too long a story to tell while walking. He'd tell me when we were sitting down. We walked through the downtown area and then up a hill into a residential area to the house where Charlie lived. He lived in an older house, surrounded by a wall as usual, with a small inner courtyard of pressed-down, yellow clay-like earth. The house was on the right as you walked in, and the wooden outhouse was in the far left corner. Charlie's room had its own separate door, which opened onto a narrow, three-foot-wide wooden veranda. We sat on the veranda, took off our shoes, and went in. His room was smaller than mine and just barely had enough room on the floor for our two *yos* (mattresses), which would be rolled out when we were ready to sleep. Charlie suggested we go back to town and hit a tearoom, which we did. Finally, after sitting down and ordering coffee for Charlie and tea for me, Charlie began to tell me the saga of his and Mr. Kim's struggle. It went on and on and didn't seem all that serious to me, but was obviously important to him. When he finished, I suggested that maybe things would work out over time. (They did. Later Charlie and Mr. Kim became good friends.) We'd both had enough talking by then. We each grabbed a magazine or book and started reading, as was our habit, which continued for the next two and a half years (Charlie and I both extended for a third year of volunteering). I always carried a small nylon bag, about the size of a laptop computer, which I had bought at the Kolon Store in Seoul. I'd always have the latest *Newsweek* magazine, for which I had a subscription, and/or *The New York Times Week in Review*, which we PCVs got free during at least one of the years of our volunteering; a book; my English-Korean/Korean-English dictionary; a notebook; a pen; and a pencil in my bag.

I pulled out the November 27, 1972, *Newsweek*. I had not finished it yet and began reading the business section.

"No shit!" I blurted out.

"What?" Charlie looked up with a quizzical look and asked.

"My father was right."

"Right about what?"

"Right about my college sweetheart's father."

"How so?"

"My dad said he'd be the next president of Sears, Roebuck & Company, and so he is. He's the new president of Sears."

"You're kidding! And that's in *Newsweek*?"

"Yeah, right here. 'The board chose A. Dean Swift, vice president for the thirteen state Southern territory. Metcalf said the board wanted a president with field experience.'"

"Wow, guess you blew that one."

"Big time."

I told Charlie the story of how Sara and I had dated our whole sophomore year. How I'd given her a fraternity lavaliere (a necklace with a pendant of the

Greek letters Sigma and Nu), which meant we were going steady, and then my fraternity pin, which implied being pre-engaged. Then I told him how after that wonderful year she had dumped me.

While we were dating my father had told me that he knew a top exec at Sears who said that Mr. Swift was sure to be the next president of Sears. At the time I thought, *"Yeah, big deal. Who cares?"* But now I kind of cared a little. What if we were still together? What if we were now engaged? What if????? No, I'd still be here, and even more importantly, I'd still rather be here. I'd still be happiest living here with very few material possessions, very little money, and teaching in a Korean middle school. Although I was happy for Sara, her father, and their family, it really did not matter to me. I picked my path, and I'd follow it to the end. No amount of money, fame, or glory of any kind could sway me.

When we got back to Charlie's house, the woman of the house met us. Charlie introduced me, and she said, "So, you went to Rose Tea Room." She always knew where we went because someone she knew would see us and report to her before we got back. Even though Yeongju was bigger than Mukho and was a city, we couldn't go anywhere without being noticed.

That evening we met Lisa Golly for dinner. She invited us the following evening to visit her room. She was going to have a Christmas party for the boys in her special class and wanted us to attend. The next night about a dozen or so first-year middle school boys, Lisa, Charlie, and I ate snacks, drank Cokes and sang Christmas carols. When we got to "Deck the Halls" and started singing, I began loudly, and my voice carries well anyway, singing "Deck the Halls with Lisa Golly," over and over. The boys all loved this and quickly joined right in with me. Lisa was a little ticked off about this, but we all had a lovely evening.

The next day, Charlie and I ran into Tim Metamora of "porto hwanta" fame. Tim taught at another boys' middle school in Yeongju, not the one in which Lisa Golly taught. He invited us to a tearoom. There he regaled us with a story of how he was having wild sex with one of the female teachers at his school. He roomed in a large two-story home that rented out several rooms to people. Tim was on the second floor, and so was this fellow teacher, a Miss Cho. At night he climbed out of his window, walked around on a narrow ledge to the other side of the house and into Miss Cho's room through her window. Later, he'd climb back out her window and return to his room. He thought this was hilarious. After a while, we switched to other topics, and we finally left with Charlie and I saying goodbye to Tim. Charlie and I both thought his actions were very regrettable. If it was found out at the school that this was going on, Miss Cho's reputation would be ruined and maybe even her career. If worst came to worst, Tim could just pack up and leave Peace Corps, and he was near the end of his second year as a volunteer anyway. I was reminded of Tim ridiculously hanging halfway out of the taxi in Daegu during training and whistling and yelling at a pretty girl.

Walking back toward Charlie's place we ran into two of his students from his special class. Charlie introduced me to Miss Chae, Sun-hui and Miss Ko, Myung-shim. They were both cute girls, and their English was very good for only having just finished the first semester of English as a subject. We invited them to a *ppang-jip* (bakery). The *ppang-jips* sold donut-like items that were not too bad. The cakes in Korean bakeries looked great, but the frosting always tasted like lard to me. We steered clear of them. But we ordered Korean donuts and glasses of milk for each of us and talked to these students for a while.

Charlie and I headed to a *takgu-jang* (ping-pong parlor) to play some ping-pong. In Mukho I often went to one or another of the *takgu-jangs* around town. Growing up we had a ping-pong table in our basement, and my father and I often played. Being the amazing athlete that my father was, for years he always won. Sometimes he even played me left-handed, and he'd still win. That always riled me, and I still remember the night when I was fifteen years old or so when I first beat my father. Oh, the joy! After that we were pretty evenly matched, and we'd split wins and losses most evenings. We played ping-pong holding the paddle the way people hold tennis rackets and not the way most professionals and all the Koreans did, which was holding the handle between your thumb and index finger with the paddle pointing down. Whenever I played with Koreans, my playing style would initially confuse them, and usually I'd win the first two or three games until they figured me out, and then they'd destroy me. So Charlie and I walked in and started playing, and we noticed that several of the Korean young men were watching us—normally only men were in *takgu-jangs*.

We also noticed that there was in this ping-pong parlor the weirdest heating contraption we'd ever seen in Korea. It was a bizarrely shaped metal heater with a big funnel sticking out of the top. At one point there was a loud blast, and Charlie and I nearly jumped under the table. Then the *takgu-jang* owner walked over, shook the contraption, opened a large wooden box near the wall, scooped up sawdust, and poured it into the big funnel. Instead of the usual kerosene heater, this was a sawdust heater. Not only was this the first time we had ever seen such a monstrosity, we never saw one like it anywhere else during our three years of Peace Corps service. It must have been homemade.

As we finished our match and I had defeated Charlie this time, one of the young men watching us asked if he could play me. Charlie said, "Hey, have at it." So we began a match, and as we warmed up a bit everyone else in the ping-pong parlor stopped playing and came over to watch. Koreans play ping-pong standing quite far back from the table. They hit the ball as hard as they can and always aim for the opposite far left side of the table, which puts the ball on the opponent's right side. That player then aims it right back to his far left, which is his opponent's right side. I hit the ball back hard one time and soft the next, sometimes with English (spin) on it and often straight across to my opponent's left side, and I was driving my opponent nuts. The more frustrated he got the more mistakes he made. I won easily. The next game he started to do better, but I still won. Then I stretched and said to Charlie, "I'm getting tired. How about you? Shall we quit?" Charlie replied, "Sure, let's go." I could tell my opponent was chomping at the bit to play some more, but I said in Korean, "Sorry, we have to get going." I bowed and thanked him for playing with me. He was almost shaking because he wanted to play another match with me so badly, but Charlie and I went and paid for our time and left. After we got outside we both burst out laughing because we knew if I had played him once more he probably would have annihilated me.

After spending Christmas Day in Yeongju reading and relaxing, we decided to visit Gyeongju, the ancient capital of the Silla Kingdom (57 BCE–935 CE). During the days when the Romans had their empire in the Mediterranean world, Korea was in its Three Kingdoms Period. The three Korean kingdoms were Silla, Baekje, and the largest of them all, comprising today's North Korea and a large part of Manchuria, was Goguryeo, the same kingdom whose borders were shown as part of Korea on the rock face near the Yongchu Falls near Bupyeong. For part of the time, there was a smaller fourth area, a confederation known as Gaya, which was located between Silla and Baekje in the south central part of today's South Korea. (Korea's most well-known traditional musical instrument is known as the *gayageum*, as it was developed in the Gaya region.) Gaya was overrun by Silla in the sixth century CE. In the mid-seventh century CE, Silla also overran Baekje. Goguryeo, which had repelled several invasions by the Sui and Tang dynasties of China, fell by 676 CE in a war fought by Goguryeo on two fronts in a coordinated attack by Tang China from the north and Silla from the south. Silla ended up controlling about two-thirds of today's Korea with the Chinese Tang controlling the upper one-third of the peninsula and all of Goguryeo's Manchurian possessions. Korea became a vassal state to China and remained so until 1895. But Silla had succeeded in uniting Korea for the first time, and it remained one united country until 1945.

Silla's capital, Gyeongju, then became the capital of the unified country in 676 CE. It was purportedly a large city with a population of nearly a million. Modern Gyeongju is a city of maybe a quarter of a million people and is known as the "museum without walls."

One of the first things we noticed when we arrived in Gyeongju was a series of large pimple-shaped hills on the edge of town. There were more than a dozen of them on the southeast side of town, one after another, and some with the bases overlapping. Off to the west in the distance across the Hyeongsan River that runs by Gyeongju were a few more. We found a *yeogwan* to stay in and then explored. Heading toward the large hills we realized that they were not natural formations, but instead man-made. They were large burial mounds for the Silla dynasty kings and queens. Burials are still done with burial mounds, but today's are small (four to five feet high) while some of these mounds in Gyeongju were as high as a four-story building. When we got near them we were walking through a neighborhood, zigzagging our way around the walled-off houses and slowly getting nearer to the burial mounds. Some of the houses were even built partway up the sides of some of the mounds. (If you visit now, there is a large stone wall around Tumuli Park where these houses were when Charlie and I first visited.)

After visiting the mounds, we walked around town and passed by the Cheomseongdae Observatory, the oldest astronomical observatory standing in East Asia. From there we walked up to a plateau-like area into the Panwol Fortress site with a stone ice house built into the side of the plateau area. Ice would be hauled there in the winter from the river and put into this cave-like ice house, and then it would stay frozen and last most, if not all, of the summer for royal use.

Then the next couple of days, we took buses to see the other ancient sites. One bus ride took us to a small park with the famous Poseokjeong (Pavilion of Stone Abalone) with an abalone-shaped stone water course. This was a party place for the king and other elites of Silla society. It is a small stream course with a stone bottom and edges only about six inches wide. Wine cups would be put into the slowly moving water to deliver drinks to the partygoers sitting along the edge of the water's course. It sat in a grove of pine trees outside the city, although this area was once inside a palace grounds. (There is a replica of this carved granite water feature in the inner courtyard of the U.S. Ambassador's residence in Seoul.)

Another site a short bus ride from town was Bunhwang-sa (Famous Emperor Temple). Built in 634 CE out of stone, it now has three stories where originally it had at least seven and possibly nine. It is unusual because Koreans rarely made temples out of stone, preferring wood. A sign there said that the Mongols, during their thirteenth century invasion of Korea, knocked down the top stories. (It was during this invasion that the Tripitaka Koreana woodblocks were carved.) This large stone pagoda-like temple was my favorite point of interest in Gyeongju.

Two other temples that were farther away from downtown are the two most famous in the Gyeongju area. The largest temple is Bulguk-sa (Buddhist Nation Temple) southeast of the city. There are several large temple buildings made of wood and all in typical Korean style. The wooden parts are all painted with multicolored, mostly prime colors in geometric patterns and with roofs made of earthenware tiles. All of these buildings have been rebuilt after being destroyed during one or another of the several invasions of Korea by the Mongols, the Japanese, and the Manchus since its unification under Silla in the seventh century CE. My favorite parts of Bulguk-sa were the stone entrance steps, bridges, and the foundation walls, which are made of granite blocks pieced together without the use of mortar. They are all original. Also at the top of the steps and inside the temple compound are two famous stone pagodas, Seokka-tap and Dabo-tap, each with its own unique style.

The last temple that we took an early morning bus ride to see was Sokkuram (Stone Cave Hermitage) Grotto. Sokkuram is a man-made cave with a large and beautifully carved stone seated Buddha inside. Often during the year on clear days when the sun rises off the East Sea (the grotto is facing east) the rays of the rising sun hit the Buddha's face and illuminate it. Charlie and I dutifully got up before sunrise and took a bus to near the grotto. Then we climbed the rest of the way and waited in anticipation. Sadly, it was a cloudy day, and there was no illumination or mystical conversion on our part akin to Paul's conversion on the way to Damascus. In our Peace Corps days, though, we could enter the grotto and get a 360-degree look at the statue of Buddha and closely examine the precise carving. A few years later a Plexiglas wall was erected at the opening, and tourists can no longer enter for a closer view.

Our last stop was the Gyeongju Branch of the National Museum of Korea filled with objects found in the archaeological excavations in the area. The most famous relics are the beautiful gold crowns, belts, and earrings that were buried with the royals. The most extravagent crown is made of construction paper-thin gold sheets cut into three tree-like shapes that are about 18 inches high and which protrude from a golden hatband. It also has antler-like extensions on each side. Dangling from the trees and antlers are glass and jade beads and very small gold circles all hanging by thin braided gold threads. There are also pendants hanging down like dreadlocks from each side of the headband. Inside of this crown a laced golden skull cap was worn. These crowns look very fragile. Some scholars believe they were not worn, but only used for burials. If they were worn it would obviously only have been for very special occasions. Crowns of the other Korean kingdoms were also similar, and so were crowns used by some of the Asian steppeland peoples. This is interesting in that the Korean language is a Ural-Altaic language related to the Turkic and Mongolian languages.

After three or four days in Gyeongju, we returned to Yeongju for a couple of days, and then we took the train into Seoul. Trains from the west came into Seoul at the Cheongnyangni Station on the western edge of the city. From there we had to catch a bus and take the hour or so slow ride to the Peace Corps Office. The Republic of Korea was building its first subway line, which would stretch from Cheongnyangni to Gwangwha-mun and beyond during this period of our service, and we looked forward to the time when that would be finished. Pyongyang, the capital of North Korea, already had a subway line, and the South Koreans, not wanting to be outdone by their Communist rivals, were playing catch up. They would not only catch up but very shortly thereafter fly by the stagnating regime in the north. Upon arrival at Gwangwha-mun, we got rooms at the Daeji Yeogwan as usual.

Seoul was the big city of ten million people. The streets in downtown Seoul were wide—really wide. Some of them were eight lanes across and filled with taxis and buses by the thousands. Later in the 1980s, when I worked for the Pearl S. Buck Foundation (PSBF) and was a member of the Seoul Rotary Club, I got to know the man who was the first mayor of Seoul after the Korean War. Unfortunately, I don't remember his name, but he was a Senior Active member of the club (Senior Active members were the elderly retired members). The former mayor told us one day about how after the war, with the city totally destroyed, they decided that someday Seoul would be a city on wheels. His administration widened all the downtown streets even though there were virtually no vehicles, except a few army jeeps in the beginning, using these wide avenues. He was in his nineties when I knew him and was the oldest member of the club. His favorite joke was to call to other Senior Active members who were only in their seventies or eighties and say, "Young man! How are you today?" That always got a big laugh from all the other members.

In 1972, there were virtually no private cars, and those few we'd see were always black, the only car color used by the politicians and rich Koreans. Most of the cars on the streets were made by Hyundai, Kia, and Shinjin. Shinjin meant "new beginning," but I always thought it meant "new engine" which would have been a funnier name. In 1972 Shinjin became a joint venture with General Motors, and the name was changed to GM Korea. The taxi cabs were mostly made by Hyundai and were small and brightly colored, but virtually all the private cars were larger than the taxi cabs and black. This started to change during the 1980s. Again, through the Seoul Rotary Club, I got to know the man who began to change this infatuation with black cars among the wealthy and influential people in Seoul. In 1982 the U.S. Congress passed the Amerasian Immigration Law that allowed some Korean Amerasians to immigrate to the United States provided that they had an American to sponsor them. It took a full year for the Immigration and Naturalization Service to establish the procedures and create the necessary forms to use. But then from 1983 to 1988, when I stopped working for the Pearl S. Buck Foundation (PSBF) and left Korea for the second time in my life, PSBF (with the assistance of many other nonprofit agencies) helped more than 500 Amerasians immigrate to the States. So beginning in late 1983, I began going to the American Embassy at least a couple of afternoons a week to work on immigration matters. Every Wednesday after the Rotary Club lunch at the Silla Hotel on Nam-san (South Mountain), I would proceed to the U.S. Embassy near Gwanghwa-mun. Most Wednesdays our PSBF driver would drive me in our Kia Bongo van, and he would wait in the parking lot until I finished. But one Wednesday every other month our van was used to take our driver, the bookkeeper, a counselor, and Mr. Ryu, Je-il, our director for the Republic of Korea's (ROK) Amerasian support program, on a four-day swing through the southern provinces of Korea to present the Amerasians with their PSBF stipend and the ROK support funds. On these Wednesdays, I went to the Rotary Club meetings by taxi instead of being driven by the PSBF van. The first time this happened after I had started to do immigration work, I asked the Rotary Club's secretary if he knew which members might work near the U.S. Embassy, as I was hoping for a lift in that direction. He suggested that I should talk to Rotarian Heiki. (In the Seoul Rotary Club, everyone had a Rotary name, and most people used their first name. For example, I was Rotarian Don.) Heiki Latvanen was the Finnish chargé d'affaires at Finland's Consulate in Seoul. It turned out that the Finnish Consulate was very close to the U.S. Embassy, and when I asked him he said he'd be happy to give me a ride.

After lunch we went out to his car with Finland's flag flying from the front bumper, and I was surprised to see that it was a white, not black, Mercedes Benz. After we both got into the backseat, where one sits when one has a chauffeur, I asked him about his vehicle's color. Heiki was quite proud to tell me that he had been the first diplomat in Korea to have a car that wasn't black. He told me that since he'd broken the "color barrier" a few other ambassadors had also begun using non-black vehicles.

It was always fun to ride with Heiki in the official Finnish Consulate vehicle on those Wednesday afternoons every other month. When his car pulled up to the U.S. Embassy the Korean staff who worked at the main door would come running out and open my door for me. They'd always quickly get a look on their face that seemed to say, "Oh, it's just you." I'd laugh and say, "Good afternoon!" They'd greet me, but their extreme attentiveness would cease as soon as they realized it wasn't Heiki getting out.

In 1972 the streets were filled, as mentioned, with taxis, buses, and black private cars. The "Heiki Revolution" had not yet taken place. After having checked into the Daeji Yeogwan, Charlie and I went up to the Peace Corps office. I usually walked around the Peace Corps area, which occupied two floors in the Korea Educational Association Building, singing and greeting everyone. I was soon known by all the Korean staff, if not by name at least as the "singing volunteer."

On the sixth floor of the Korea Educational Association Building was the Peace Corps library and volunteers' lounge. The seventh floor had the reception desk, offices of the director, the doctor's office, the business office, etc. We ran into "Uranus Farts" Nick in the lounge. He had also just rolled into town. We invited him to crash with us, and the three of us hung out for a few days together. A lot of PCVs camped out in the Peace Corps Office while in Seoul, often complaining about how much they disliked Korea, their school, their co-teacher, the other teachers at their school, their principal, or just life in Korea in general. As mentioned before, one thing volunteers often complained about was how lazy the Koreans were. This is really funny because by the 1980s, when I was back in Seoul working for PSBF, one common joke was that the Koreans were the only people in the world who made the Japanese look lazy because of the break-neck speed with which South Korea was developing. Charlie, Nick, and I would buzz in, return the books we'd read, borrow some more, and buzz back out.

Charlie and I, having already visited Ewha Women's University when most of the K-23s went to Panmunjom, suggested visiting Yonsei University, the largest and most prestigious private university in Korea. When we walked through the main gate and onto the campus, we saw Severance Hospital off to our right. Yonsei University was formally established in 1957 with the union of Yonhi College and Severance Union Medical School. The hospital is the oldest part dating back to 1885, only three years after the treaty between the United States and the Kingdom of Korea, which opened up what had been known as the "Hermit Kingdom" for the first time. An American Presbyterian missionary by the name of Horace Allen opened the hospital, which later took the name of Severance. We walked farther in and came upon some buildings that looked like they would fit in on Harvard's, Princeton's, or Albion's campus. The front one was Underwood Hall, and there was a statue of the founder of the original college, Horace Grant Underwood, in front of this building. He founded Chosun Christian College here in 1915, which later changed its name to Yonhi. When Yonhi and Severance merged, they took the first Chinese character from Yonhi, Yon, and the first Chinese character from Sei-bu-ran-suh (four Chinese characters that approximate the

English word severance), Sei, and got the name Yonsei. They then used the first letter of the two syllable clusters that form the sounds Yon and Sei in *Hangeul* (Korea's phonetic alphabet) to form the school's coat of arms-like symbol.

The Underwood family is very famous in Korea. Five generations now have lived, worked and many were born in the country. I got to know two of Horace Grant Underwood's grandsons, Horace and Dick, who were both Rotarians, during my Pearl Buck years. While their grandfather was the famous missionary who came to Korea, their great uncle, their grandfather's brother, was the founder of the Underwood Typewriter Company, who went into business to make money while Horace Grant Underwood was into saving souls.

In the mid-1980s, the President of Albion College, Dr. Melvin Vulgamore, and his wife visited Korea. They contacted me before coming, and I invited Dr. Vulgamore to come to our Rotary Club's Wednesday luncheon meeting. I introduced Dr. Vulgamore as a visiting Rotarian from Albion, Michigan's Rotary Club and the president of Albion College. After the meeting, Horace and Dick came over to talk and told Dr. Vulgamore and me that their mother was a graduate of Albion College. She married Horace and Dick's father after graduating, and the two of them then moved to Korea and spent most of their lives here as missionaries. They had lived on the Yonsei campus, back behind these beautiful stone buildings that Charlie, Nick, and I were admiring, where there was faculty housing. In 1949, their mother was having tea with several Korean ladies at her home on the campus when Communist Koreans entered the home and murdered her in front of her guests. It seems the Commies thought that this would gain them support from the South Korean general population, but of course it had the opposite effect and helped to turn the South Korean people even more staunchly against this horrible and brutal ideology originally from the Soviet Union and China.

Horace and Dick had many interesting stories. One they told was about their school days in Korea. During the 1930s every school, because Korea was a Japanese colony, had a shrine on the grounds to Emperor Hirohito. Dick and Horace said they would sometimes leave one shoe untied and then when in front of the shrine, but not too close mind you, they would bend over. While pointing their rear ends toward the Emperor and laughing to themselves because they were in essence mooning the dude, they would retie the shoe.

During the Korean War, Horace and Dick were both in the U.S. Army and served as translators. Dick told me once that early on they were getting many prisoners who were Chinese and spoke no Korean. He obviously reported this to his commanding officer. Dick is sure that a few weeks later when MacArthur went to Hawaii and told President Truman there was no way that China would send troops into Korea that Mac had to have known the Chinese already had entered the war. General MacArthur had lied to the president on purpose.

Horace once talked about the difficulties of translating when he was at Pan-munjom near the end of the Korean War. One example he gave was when the American general he was translating for said to the North Korean general: "Your words change directions like a weather vane." Horace had to think quickly as there are no weather vanes in Korea and hence no word for them. He said something like, "Your words change directions like rice stalks being blown this way and that by the wind." It got the point across. Depending on how the previous day's fighting had gone, the North Koreans would change their demands.

Whenever in Seoul, all of us Peace Corps Volunteers would walk all over downtown. From the Peace Corps office in the Gwangwha-mun area we would walk to Myeong-dong (Bright District), the main shopping area of Seoul. Seoul was divided into nine *gus,* and each *gu* into numerous smaller divisions called *dongs.* Myung-dong was about a mile from the Peace Corps office. On the corner of the main entrance to Myung-dong from the west side was the Cosmos *Baegh-wajeom* (department store). *Baeg* means one hundred, and so a department store was called a place with one hundred shops or departments. Cosmos was a less expensive department store that had different areas rented by independent people or families to sell goods. At the back, southern end of Myeong-dong was Shin-segae Department Store, which was a higher-end store. West of Shinsegae was the Namdae-mun Shijang (South Gate Market), which was similar to the hardware area I had visited with Mr. Yoo and Mr. Jung the day I first met them. Except at the Namdae-mun Shijang shop after shop sold clothing; in another area, material for Korean traditional outfits, *Hanbok;* and even more areas specialized in other goods, but not hardware.

We often visited Myeong-dong for people-watching. Usually there were no cars in Myeong-dong, just thousands of people cramming the streets everywhere. Lots of young and lovely Korean ladies shopped here. Besides many stores, there were restaurants, coffee shops, night clubs, and street vendors selling items off of carts. These carts were technically illegal, but usually the police looked the other way. Every once in a while there would be a crackdown, though. We'd be wandering through the street when all the vendors suddenly seemed to grab their carts and shove them away, disappearing up side streets, and it would be as if there had never been even one vendor around. A group of policemen would walk through with determined looks on their faces. Then a few minutes later all the vendors would return, and it was business as usual. Myeong-dong always warranted a few visits during each of our trips to Seoul.

Shopping in bookstores was another popular activity. Just across from the Peace Corps office was one bookstore that had a small selection of books in English. Then there was another larger bookstore up toward the east on Chong-ro (Bell Street). Chong-ro literally had a large bell in a pavilion, similar to the one that woke Charlie and me up at the Buddhist temple near Daegu, only bigger. Until the Japanese annexation of Korea in 1910, Seoul had been a walled city with large gates in several places. Most of the wall has been torn down except on Nam-san (South Mountain) and Bukhan-san (North Han Mountain). One of the gates, Namdae-mun (South Great Gate), stands in the middle of a busy intersection and is Korea's number one national treasure. During the Yi dynasty, this bell on Chong-ro was rung at dawn and dusk to order the opening for the morning and closing at night of all the city's gates. Just past the bell pavilion was the larger bookstore that occupied several floors. Also, just off of Chong-ro and a little past the large bookstore was the Royal Asiatic Society's office and bookshop. They published many books in English about Korea, such as Bishop Richard Rutt's books *Korean Works and Days* and *A Biography of James Scarth Gale and a New Edition of His History of the Korean People.* We'd often browse there too.

Under many of the main intersections in Seoul were underpasses. Pedestrians were fair game, and taxi drivers gave no quarter, so streets had subterranean walkways at the big intersections and stairway overpasses at other places along the streets. In the underpasses were more shops. In one of them there was a used bookstore where I found and bought a book in English, *The Great Khan* (a biography of Genghis Khan), by Dong Sung Kim, published by The Korea Information Service, Inc. There is a picture in the front of Mr. Kim with British and American journalists at a garden party during the Washington Disarmament Conference in 1921. It says he represented the *Dong-A Ilbo* (Dong-A Newspaper) and that he was the first Korean correspondent to attend an international conference. One of the people in the picture with him was H. G. Wells, who represented Great Britain. (Mr. Kim graduated from Ohio State University in 1912, but I don't hold that unfortunate error in judgment against him any more than I did against my K-23 roommate, Jack.) Mr. Kim claims, in the Foreword that, "this turns out to be the first English work on the Khan done by an oriental." My favorite paragraph from the book is on page 14:

> After the Yuan Dynasty was well established, Kublai
> sent his daughter to be the queen of Korea. Since then
> for generations until the downfall of both the Yuan
> Dynasty and Korea (Koryo Dynasty), the Mongol

Princesses of Blood became the Korean Queens.
Naturally the Court Language was the mixture of the
Mongolian and Korean, even during the succeeding Lee
(sic, Yi) Dynasty, the Court Language was still a mixture.
A Mongol queen of Korea was of political convenience
and necessary. *The Mongols in Peking (Beijing) preferred
to marry Korean girls who were then as now the most
beautiful women in all of Asia.* The last emperor of the
Yuan Dynasty was a son of a Korean beauty. He was
driven back to the Gobi Desert to become king of the
Mongols.....
(Italics added by the author of this book.)

Mr. Kim may be a little biased on the beauty of Korean women part. I agree personally, but then my first wife, Mi-yun (from the Chinese characters for beautiful and soft), was a Korean beauty.

Mi-yun's family name was also Kim. There are only about 40 family names in Korea, which are used by all seventy-five million Koreans in North and South Korea. Kim, Lee, and Park are the three most common. So when two Kims meet, to find out if they are distantly related or not, they ask about each other's hometown. Mi-yun was a Kangnung (the city just north of Mukho) Kim. Supposedly, a couple of the Koryo queens, I assume before the Mongol invasion, were Kangnung Kims. My son is proud of this bit of family lore, and back in his school days he would tell his classmates about his royal connection.

Between Gwangwha-mun and Myeong-dong was the Chosun Hotel, the most upscale hotel in Korea at the time. In the garden behind it sat the Temple of Heaven, a beautiful building from the Yi Dynasty that could be seen from the fancy restaurant off the lobby. We'd always walk through the lobby of the Chosun Hotel and then check out the shops in the basement. One shop sold Irish-style wool sweaters made by Korean women on Cheju Island under the direction of Irish Catholic nuns. They raised sheep on the island and knitted these heavy and beautifully made sweaters with Irish patterns. I bought a burgundy crew-neck one this first winter in Korea and often wore it when teaching on cold winter days, as the classrooms were nearly the same temperature as outdoors.

After a day of running around Seoul and dinner one night, Charlie, Nick, and I were sitting in our room at the Daeji Yeogwan. All three of us were reading with our door open when a young American popped his head in and started talking. His name was Tom Munising. He and a girlfriend, another American, were exchange students studying at Wasada University in Tokyo, Japan. They had come across for their winter break on the ferry from Shimonoseki on the main island of Honshu, Japan, to Busan, Korea, and then had hitchhiked up to Seoul on the expressway. A truck driver had given them a ride all the way. Tom was a bubbly, talkative, hyperactive kid who quickly got on our nerves. I remember that I was reading Aleksandr Solzhenitsyn's book *Cancer Ward* when he waltzed in, while Charlie and Nick were reading equally intellectual fare. Tom was impressed by what we were reading and started asking us questions about these books, about Peace Corps, where we had gone to college, and our majors while also telling us all about himself. When he found out that Nick had been a literature major at Columbia, he asked, "Can you explain William Blake's cosmology?" Nick replied, "I could, but I'm not going to." Tom didn't take the hint and kept badgering Nick, almost begging him to answer his question. I stood up and went to the out-house-like latrine—the W. C. "I am going to Winston Churchill," I said. On the way back, I noticed an open door and a young American gal sitting in the room reading a book. Tom hadn't told us what his traveling partner's name was, but I poked my head in and said, "Hi, you must be traveling with Tom." I was thinking maybe I'd plop down and talk to her, but her reply was very cold and stand-offish. I thought the better of it and sat out on the stoop on the edge of the small inner courtyard for some fresh air and so as not to hear Tom's annoying prattle.

After he left, I returned to our room. "So, what did Tom Tokyo have to say while I was gone?" "Nothing worth repeating," Charlie said. We all returned to our books. Years later, when I watched the movie *Volunteers*, John Candy's character, Tom Tuttle from Tacoma, reminded me of Tom (Munising) from Tokyo. Whenever we mentioned Tom Munising from then on we always called him Tom Tokyo.

Charlie wanted to get back to Yeongju and do some lesson planning and prep for his classes, and Nick also took off, but I decided to stay a couple of more days at least in Seoul. When I visited the Peace Corps office, Miss Jang, Yong-sook, one of the secretaries, asked if I'd like to accompany her to Chuncheon. Chuncheon is east of Seoul and the capital of my province, Gangwon. Not only did I claim Mukho as mine, I claimed the whole darn province, or at least the majority of it that was under South Korean control. Chuncheon was the site of the K-25 middle school TESOL Training Program (the K-24s were a Health Group that had trained during the summer of 1972, one of whom had briefly been in Mukho). Miss Jang needed to deliver some papers. We'd then spend the night there (although not together, of course) and return the next day.

So we got to Chuncheon in the late afternoon. I hung out and talked to the

K-25s, but I obviously didn't complain about Korea as so many had during my training program. Instead I told them how much I enjoyed teaching and being a PCV. After classes ended, Miss Jang, along with Ryan Grayling, who had also worked as a PCV Assistant Trainer on our K-23 training, a couple of the K-25s, and I went off to dinner. The famous Chuncheon specialty is *dakgalbi* (marinated chicken roasted on a charcoal grill), which we had for dinner, and then went out to a *sul-jip* (bar) to drink. We sang, and Ryan, who had an amazing voice, sang "Danny Boy" because that was another song the Koreans really loved. Ryan did it justice and then some. In fact, Koreans were often called the Irish of the Orient. I always thought it was because their relationship with Japan is so similar to the Irish relationship with England. Also, both nationalities like their booze and like to sing. I stayed with Ryan in his room while Miss Jang stayed with a couple of the female Korean language instructors.

The next afternoon, Miss Jang and I returned by bus to Seoul. Ryan had left on an earlier bus, but we had made a plan to meet him at the *bulgogi-siktang* (marinated beef roasted on a charcoal grill restaurant) across from the Peace Corps office in Seoul for dinner. Pretty much the minute the bus pulled out of the bus station in Chuncheon and for the three-hour bus trip back to Seoul, my stomach was churning. I knew I had the beginnings of diarrhea, the likes of which I hadn't had since the dysentery during training. I clinched the sphincter muscle in my butt shut and pretended nothing was wrong. Miss Jang started talking about romantic love and some book she had read about a knight in shining armor, or the Korean equivalent thereof. She spoke about her desire for that to happen to her and how she hoped someday she would meet the perfect mate, and I…was in agony. My eyes were floating in blocked-up shit; I think it made my blue eyes brown. (Richard Leigh and Crystal Gayle got it backwards.) I just wanted to jump up to beg the driver to stop (there were no bathrooms on buses in Korea in those days) and let me run out behind a rock and just let it rip, but I couldn't. When we got to Seoul, we then took a taxi from the bus station to the Peace Corps Office. I told Miss Jang I'd be right back as she went into the restaurant and that I would get my room at the Daeji Yeogwan, drop off my bag, and return. I got to the Daeji, ran to the latrine, and opened up the floodgates of my arse, as they pronounce it in England. I nearly passed out from exhaustion and pain, but I waited until I thought the contents of my intestines and stomach were completely ejected and went back to the restaurant. When I got there, Ryan said, "What took so long?" "Oh, I got into a conversation with the owner of the Daeji Yeogwan. He was real talkative today, and I couldn't get away." I ate sparingly, no kimchee or anything spicy, and I'm sure I deserve an Academy Award for my acting performance through all the pain and suffering.

How the bowel movements were going was a common topic of discussion among PCVs. The spicy food the Koreans ate often caused gastric anomalies. This day's case was the worst, other than my dysentery episode during training. I never again had it as bad, but then the timing was what made it so troublesome on this day. Had it hit an hour earlier, and had I been able to get most of it out before boarding the bus, things would have gone much more smoothly and less explosively. As it was, I spent most of the next day gingerly resting and hardly eating anything.

CHAPTER 7

Spring Semester 1973:
Don't Americans Look Good with Mustaches?

Don with medium-length hair and his mustache.

It was time to return to Mukho. Not only was my hair covering half of my ears, but I had also let my mustache grow during winter break, and it was fully grown out by this time. The first morning of classes, I walked into the teachers' office. Mr. Lee, Tae-hyang, the vice principal, called me over and invited me to sit in the chair next to his desk. He began talking quietly and very seriously, telling me that having a mustache was not acceptable. I was thinking that I would go home and shave it during my break hour if it was going to be a problem when our principal, Mr. Yoo (Yoo *Gyojang-nim,* "Honorable Pricipal"), walked into the room. He got about halfway to the vice principal's desk when he stopped and said in a loud voice for all the teachers to hear, "Don't Americans look good with mustaches?" No one said a word. I excused myself and returned to my desk, the vice principal moved to the chair I had been sitting in, and Mr. Yoo took his place at the vice principal's desk to welcome everyone back from the winter break and to conduct the morning meeting. No one in the school or in the town of Mukho ever said another word about my hair or my mustache. During the rest of my Peace Corps days there were times when my hair was parted in the middle and it hung down nearly to my shoulders. Part of the time, I also grew a full, somewhat bushy beard to go along with my "stache,'" and still no one ever commented about my appearance in Mukho. I'm sure that Mr. Yoo was responsible for the acceptance of my hippy-like hair, mustache, and beard.

It was still cold and often below freezing when the semester began. None of the classrooms were heated. The only three rooms that had any heat were the principal's

The old, wooden slat, Japanese-era building with the metal drum outside where students burned any scrap paper between classes for warmth.

office, the school office, and the teachers' office. They had kerosene heaters in these rooms. When the bell rang for class to begin the teachers would hang by the stove for seconds and even minutes before tearing themselves away. At the end of class all of us teachers would make a beeline back to our office. Every teacher huddled around the stoves and got as close as he or she could. The poor students froze their butts off. There was an old oil barrel that had been cut in half and had thin metal legs, which sat just outside our old, wooden slat, Japanese-era building. Sometimes the students would take all their scrap paper and throw it into this metal drum and light it all on fire, holding their hands over the flames.

Some of them, but not all, had gloves. They had to take the gloves off when they needed to write, and many of them would bend over and put their gloves on over their stocking feet. Only a few of the students could actually afford indoor shoes. But it was cute as hell to look down under the rickety, roughhewn desks and see these gloved feet waving at me while I taught.

I got a letter from Peace Corps asking if I'd be host to one of the winter K-25 trainees from Chuncheon for his site visit before completing his training. I replied that I would be happy to do so. A letter came with the dates for the visit, which train he'd be coming on, and his name—Bill Comb. I met him at the train station.

Some of the fish drying around Mukho.

"Oh my God! How can you stand the smell?" was the first thing he said.

"What smell?" I asked.

"What smell? That rotten fish smell."

"Oh! That. It's like perfume to me. You'll get used to it." The fish smell from the drying racks was always the first thing Americans noticed when they visited.

He had arrived after school was finished for the day. We went out for dinner and talked for a while. The next morning, I took him to the school with me and introduced him to all the teachers in the teachers' office. They all laughed when I told them his name. One teacher said in English, "Ah, Mr. Comb. Like comb your hair?" He was making a combing motion with his right hand while asking the question. "Yes," I said, "exactly like that." Bill took it very well and laughed right along with all the teachers. The first day Bill watched me teach my classes. Then on the second day I asked if he'd like to teach, and he said yes. He did very well and worked well with my co-teacher, Mr. Jun, In-kook. Then that evening after dinner, he began blurting out his story of how the training staff wanted to terminate him and send him back to the States. "Why?" I asked. He didn't know, but he said they told him his attitude was bad. "I don't get it," I said. "Your attitude seems fine." Through tears he again said they wanted to send him home. He asked if I would write a letter he could take back to Chuncheon. I agreed and wrote what was the truth—he had done very well here in Mukho. He had interacted with the students and teachers admirably. His attitude had been great. He had done an excellent job teaching and worked well with my co-teacher. I put the letter into an envelope, sealed it, and gave it to him to take back and give to the training staff. I later heard that he had been allowed to stay. I was glad to hear it and to have been of assistance.

A month after getting back to Mukho, Bob Saks in Samcheok wanted to meet. Again, I took the bus down to his town on Saturday after school. We went to a tearoom and talked. He was very upset because of the corporal punishment in the Korean school system. I had seen some in Mukho Middle School too, but I just ignored it. Sometimes the teachers would have the kids pull up their pant legs above their knees, and they'd use a switch to whip the heck out of the boys' calves. I told Bob that I too had been paddled in junior high school and high school. Some of our teachers had wooden paddles made by the shop teachers with many holes drilled in them so there would be less drag and more oomph to each swat. I told Bob about my teacher in seventh grade. His name was Rocky Donahue, and he had been a New York Giants football player before he came to Dasher Junior High School in Melvindale, Michigan. I was an angel in his class, but sometimes female teachers would bring a problem child, always a guy, down to his classroom and say, "Mr. Donahue, this young man has been a bad boy." "Bend over, son," he'd say and then wind up and paddle the young man's tuckus. The boys always looked rather contrite afterwards.

Before gym class one day, I walked into the gymnasium at Dasher Junior High School. There was no one around, and a rope was hanging from the rafters down to the floor. I ran out across the beautiful wooden floor with my street shoes on and jumped onto the rope, swinging like Tarzan. In my exuberance, I probably did the Tarzan yell too. As luck would have it, that's when the gym teacher walked in. He ordered me off, told me to wait, came back with his paddle, told me to bend over and touch my toes, then proceeded to give me one hearty swat. While changing in the locker room I checked my buns, and there was a four-inch-wide red stripe across them both – talk about cheek to cheek. In high school once, I had finished my work early in history class. History had always been my best subject, and I would finish all assignments and tests before everyone else. I began blabbing away to the gal sitting next to me about a movie I had seen over the previous weekend.

"Don, that's one," our history teacher, Mr. Kaltsas, said to me.

"For what?" I blurted out.

"That's two."

"Yes, sir," I said. (One of the few times in my life that I've ever said, "Sir.") After class, he swatted me twice, and since it was my last class of the day, I ran out of the school to get on my bus to head home. I didn't sit down though. Instead I stood the whole way home. My rear end hurt far too much to sit.

So I told Bob these stories and advised him to just walk out of the room when the children were being swatted. He told me that he had complained to his principal and that the atmosphere now was very tense at his school. I told him that it probably wasn't a good idea to complain. "Maybe it will blow over and things will be OK," I suggested. "I sure hope so," Bob said.

A couple of weeks later Bob came up to Mukho and told me he was leaving the Peace Corps. One teacher who especially loved to punish the kids who caused any problems in class would bring them into the teachers' office and hit them with the switch right in front of Bob's desk. He did it on purpose in front of Bob just to torment him. Bob said, "Mr. Pak hits the students harder and longer than he used to, just to antagonize me. I can't stand it, and I don't think he'll stop. The principal obviously doesn't care." I told Bob how sorry I was and that I'd miss him, but I understood his feelings. He left a few days later.

There was, though, a new volunteer up in Kangnung. One of the K-25s, Glenn Vriesland, was teaching at Kyongpo Middle School. I visited him on a Saturday afternoon, and we went to his school. This school was much more impressive than Mukho Middle School, bigger with much newer and more substantial buildings. Of course, Kangnung was a city and had a larger population. Mukho

**Glenn's principal in his office
at Kyongpo Middle School.**

was just a town. The principal was still in his office and invited us in for tea or coffee. His office had better trappings, and the furniture was much more expensive looking than in my principal's office. The walls were paneled with beautiful built-in cabinets. Behind the chair that Glenn's principal sat in was a huge stuffed hawk, a couple of lovely bonsai trees, a large strangely shaped rock in a carved wooden stand, and other accoutrements that looked like they were from one of the royal palaces in Seoul. That night Glenn and I got very drunk at a *sul-jip* (bar) and spent most of Sunday hung over. Late that afternoon I returned to Mukho.

While buying some cookies at a small *gage* (convenience store) one Friday evening, a Korean guy, Mr. Pak, Chi-jin, who was around my age began talking to me in English. He was home for a break from college and asked if I'd like to visit a *dabang* (coffee house or tea-room) with him. So we went to the nearest tearoom and sat and talked for quite a while. His English was better than that of most of the English teachers in town, and I enjoyed talking with him. He told me that the first time he had ever seen an American with blue eyes like mine he had thought that the person was blind. Light-colored eyes are common with blind people, he explained. I laughed along with him and thought this was strange. But that same story was told to me over and over again throughout my years in the country by several different Koreans. As we were leaving the *dabang,* he suggested that we visit Mureung Valley and Yongchu Waterfall on Sunday, and I agreed.

That Sunday we met, took the bus past the Ssangyong cement plant, hiked past the map of Korea painted on the rockface near the National Guard training area, and reached the upper waterfall. Mr. Pak had a knapsack with a camp burner, a pot, a couple of bowls, chopsticks, and some food to cook. First, we boiled rice. Then he had carrots, potatoes, onions and a package of curry powder.

He also pulled out a cutting board and knife. We sat there slicing up the vegetables while water heated up in the pot. We threw the vegetables and curry powder in, and we ended up with a great lunch. Then he mentioned that his father was the principal of the Mukho Girls' Middle and High School near the pass toward Mangsang Beach. His father was wondering if I might be willing to teach a couple of days a week at the girls' middle school. I told Mr. Pak that I'd think about it, but I would also like to visit and take a tour of the school. We planned this out, and I met Mr. Pak the next Saturday after I had finished teaching. We walked together up to the girls' school and met his father.

The Monday after that, I asked Mr. Yoo during my free hour in his office if I could teach a couple of days a week at the girls' middle school. Without hesitation he told me that would be no problem. I had assumed he would hesitate, but he didn't. He said he knew the girls' school principal well, thought this would be a good opportunity for me, and told me that he would discuss this with Principal Pak. I thanked Mr. Yoo. From then on I taught three and a half days a week at the boys' middle school and two days, Tuesdays and Thursdays, at the girls' middle school. Mrs. Hwang, Soon-hui was my co-teacher at the girls' middle school, and I had a special class of the fifteen best students from the first-year class just as I did at the boys' middle school. I don't know of any other PCV who had such a setup. Usually, the principals of the schools were very possessive of their American English teachers, although sometimes, like the principal of Bob Saks' school, they were at the same time not supportive. Again, having Mr. Yoo as my principal was the greatest stroke of luck I could imagine.

The special class students at the girls' middle school were as sweet as could be. They were so much more fun to teach than the boys because their enthusiasm was even more amazing. Also, they sometimes came as a group to visit me, and I taught them to play American card games.

As mentioned before, the students no longer all looked alike to me. Each, of course, was different from the others, and each had his or her peculiar personality and idiosyncrasies just as American students do. One of my special class students at the girls' middle school reminded me of Linda Ecorse, who lived across the street from our house in Allen Park where I grew up. I got to know many of the students as individuals during the course of each school year and grew to cherish their differences.

On my way to the post office one afternoon, I saw three guys walking toward me who looked to be Americans. When they got close I said, "Hi! How are you?" One of them answered with a Spanish accent, "Good, how are you?" We stopped and talked for a few minutes, and I invited them to a *dabang* (tearoom). It turned out they were Chilean, and their ship was picking up cement and was heading for Taiwan the next day. Only one of them spoke English, and he wasn't fluent, so after finishing our tea and coffee, I told them I had to get back to teach.

The next Saturday in the early afternoon I was sitting at my desk in the teachers' office eating one of the muffin-like things that I ate for lunch every day at the school, and I heard a crack. I felt the upper molar second from the back on the left side with my tongue. This tooth had had a root canal job done on it during my junior year in college. About a quarter of the tooth on the outside had broken off at the gum line. It was hanging on by a thread and was flapping back and forth as I pushed it against my cheek with my tongue. I knew this was not good, and I immediately went to the principal's office and told Mr. Yoo what had happened. Not knowing any dentist in Mukho (and I would not have trusted a local dentist with something this complicated anyway), I told Mr. Yoo I would need to fly to Seoul and see the Peace Corps-approved dentist on Monday. He had a secretary check the flights out of Bupyeong Airport (if you could call it that—maybe Bupyeong Tarmac would be more accurate). There was a flight leaving later in the afternoon, and she made a reservation for me.

After quickly packing a few things, I got on the next bus headed down to Bupyeong and got to the airport with a few minutes to spare. After purchasing my ticket, I got into line for boarding. While in line I was telling the guy behind me about my tooth breaking and how I was heading to Seoul to see a dentist when the jackass Korean airport security guard began asking me a lot of questions. After several questions about why was I on the east coast to start with and then why was I flying back to Seoul, I finally got pissed and opened my mouth as wide as I could with my left index finger. Then I pushed the broken off part of my tooth that was barely attached to my gum line back and forth with my right index finger. I had already told him that I had broken my tooth and needed to see a dentist in Seoul. I guess my demonstrative performance convinced him that I was not a Russian spy or whatever the hell he thought I was, and he let me board the plane. It never ceases to amaze me how the wearing of uniforms by petty people goes right to their heads, and they think they can lord it over everyone else.

There was nothing exciting going on in Seoul over the weekend and no one around, but on Monday I went right into the Peace Corps office early and saw Dr. Coe, Chae-jun, the Peace Corps physician. He sent me right off to the dentist they used in Seoul. I needed a crown. After dislodging the quarter of the tooth that had broken off, the dentist ground down what was left of this tooth to a stump and he said he'd have a crown made. When I returned to have the new crown permanently put on, he told me he was installing a gold crown, even though Peace Corps had told him to use a cheaper kind, because he felt gold was best.

This crown lasted for about fourteen years. Around 1986, I went with one of the Pearl S. Buck counselors to do a site visit in order to talk with the grandmother of one of the Amerasian boys we were helping. He was an eight-year-old Amerasian named Kim, Young-min. Young-min's father was a white American. His mother had recently married a black American soldier and gone to the U.S. with him. She left Young-min behind because her black American husband told her he could not handle the shame of raising a white Amerasian child. Young-min was being raised by his maternal grandmother. Our caseworker, Mrs. Paik, Mi-young, told me that he was having emotional problems and had begun wetting his bed at night. Consequently, I accompanied Mrs. Paik to get a better idea about what was going on. After meeting the grandmother, I suggested that we get some professional counseling for Young-min. Before heading back to the Pearl S. Buck Foundation's office in Seoul, we stopped to have lunch. I ordered *kalbitang* (beef rib stew) and when I chomped down on some beef I hit a bone with my gold crown. Again, I heard a cracking sound, and something heavy landed on my tongue. It was my gold tooth, which had completely broken off right at the gum line.

When we got back to the PSBF office, I had Mrs. Paik call Yonsei University's Severance Hospital Dental Department to make an appointment for me. She told me I had an appointment for the next morning at 10:00 am. At 10:00 a.m. sharp, I walked into the dental area at Severance Hospital, and the receptionist asked me to follow her. We walked out into a hallway, up a flight of stairs, and into a large office. The office had one wall lined with bookshelves and a huge desk at the far end of the room. Near the door was a seating area, which had a large sofa, coffee table, and two large upholstered chairs with an end table between them. The receptionist motioned for me to sit and politely told me to wait. I sat in one of the chairs and looked around wondering if Mrs. Paik had told them that I was here for a dental problem. An older Korean man in a suit walked in and introduced himself as Han, Jin-ho, Dean of the School of Dentistry at Yonsei University and Severance Hospital. He sat down. Tea was brought in by the receptionist, and Dr. Han asked me questions about my work at the Pearl S. Buck Foundation. Just as I was about to interrupt him and mention that I actually had a tooth problem, he suggested we head back downstairs to where the dental chairs were.

I guess it was because Mrs. Paik had told the receptionist that I was the *Chibu-jang* (Korea Branch Resident Director) of the Pearl S. Buck Foundation that I got the red carpet treatment. Dr. Han had me sit in a chair, took a quick look, and called over his gum specialist, Dr. Wrigley (just kidding, his name was actually Dr. Lee). They decided that I needed to have gum surgery. They would trim some of my gum off around what little part of the stump of the original tooth was left and that would give them enough of a base to put another crown on. I came back a couple of days later and started that process.

Later, back in the States in the 1990s, I had further gum surgery when one of the roots got infected on that very same tooth, and the infected root was extracted, leaving me with three out of four roots to hold the tooth in and the crown on. Another few years later, the Yonsei/Severance crown crashed, and I now have a bridge over where the second molar from the back on the upper left side used to be. It finally had to be completely pulled out. That one tooth sure caused a lot of problems over the years. But, "C'est la vie," as my French-Canadian ancestors on my mother's side used to say.

All of us K-23s received a letter from the Peace Corps office inviting us to an end-of-our-first-year conference in March at Songnisan National Park on the border between Chungcheongbuk-do (North Chungcheon Province) and Chungcheongnam-do (South Chungcheong Province). We were told to arrive on a Thursday night, and we would stay until Sunday at the Songnisan Tourist Hotel. It sounded like fun to me, but Charlie wrote and told me that he wouldn't be going. I traveled alone since there was no other K-23 on the east coast now that Bob had left. By the time I got there it was late afternoon. I checked in and hung out with everyone. We had dinner and drank in the bar together until someone suggested we walk in the dark up to Popchu-sa, the Buddhist temple inside the park, which was not too long a walk from the hotel. A little tipsy, several of us walked into the temple compound "by the light of the silvery moon." ("By the Light of the Silv-ry Moon" words by Edward Madden, music by Gus Edwards, as sung by Doris Day among others.) There was a huge Buddha that looked like it was chiseled from stone. We stood staring at this statue of Buddha and waxing poetic about how ancient it must be. The next day when we returned in daylight, we discovered that it had been built in the 1960s and was made of cement. So much for ancient! The temple itself was originally built in 653, but the main buildings were destroyed by the Japanese during the Imjin Invasion (1592–1598) and rebuilt after that.

On Friday we held discussions about teaching, cross-cultural issues, food, and other topics. Dr. Coe, Chae-jun, the Peace Corps physician, spoke about the Korean diet and how healthy it was. One thing I remember him telling everyone was that we should all be eating *myulchi* (anchovy). *Myulchi*(s), small minnow-sized anchovies, were fried up whole, head and all, in soy sauce. Many volunteers refused to eat them—that fish head thing again—whereas I always ate and enjoyed them. Dr. Coe told us they were a good source of calcium because we were eating all the bones as well as the flesh.

In the afternoon the discussion turned to women having a much more difficult time working in Korea than the men did. Women were usually not invited out drinking, but the male volunteers were often invited out by their fellow male teachers. Nice women didn't frequent *sul-jip*(s). Also, women did not have doors opened for them, men didn't get up on buses to offer them a seat, nor did men offer to let women enter the buses ahead of them. In fact, the city bus stops were like roller derby rinks. We always said that those with the sharpest elbows got on first. Buses would often hardly stop but rather just glide through the stops. At each stop there would often be numerous buses, all with different route numbers, all cruising by the same pick-up area. Some drivers would cut in where there was a gap, and if you didn't run your ass off and get there fast they'd pull away and leave. They were evidently paid by how many times they completed their route each shift, and they were always in a hurry. The female volunteers went on and on about this and about the fact that most Peace Corps men hung around with Korean girlfriends and/or bar girls, tearoom girls, lewd barbershop girls, or prostitutes and didn't spend any time with Peace Corps women.

Even though I agreed with what the ladies were saying and I had a lot of empathy for their situation, it seemed like we were talking about this topic forever. I began running through songs in my head, which is my usual way of tuning out. Suddenly, Steve Moross, the married volunteer in our group who had been in charge of herding us through Tokyo's airport, said, "Maybe this is all a self-fulfilling prophecy." If looks could kill! Every female volunteer in our group just stared at Steve. I whispered to whomever was sitting next to me, "I don't think Steve will be getting any tonight." He nodded in agreement. Several gals verbally jumped all over Steve at the same time. A cacophony of deafening screeching sounds filled our ears for quite awhile; Steve had truly hit a raw nerve with his comment, and I personally didn't agree with him either. Eventually this topic wound down, and we proceeded onto something else.

Late in the afternoon, I noticed the Peace Corps Director Jim ("That's bullshit!") Wixom, passing a note that went around the table to one of the Korean Peace Corps employees. A few minutes later the Korean employee passed a note in my direction, and it went around the table until it got to me. I glanced at it, and it had my name on it. Inside it read, "Mr. Haffner, I am Mr. Song, Jun-ki, the Supervisor for Gyeonggi and Gangwon provinces. After the meeting can we talk?" I looked up, and Mr. Song was looking at me. I nodded. I had not known he was my supervisor because he had never visited Mukho before, and if I had met him at the end of training, I had forgotten.

After all the discussions ended, I walked over to Mr. Song and introduced myself. He apologized for not having made it to Mukho yet. I told him that was no problem. I understood that Mukho was a long way from anywhere. It was also not a big tourist attraction or easy to get to or anything. By this time, we were the only ones left in the room, and he got very serious.

"Tomorrow officials from the Ministry of Education will be coming to our morning meeting. Mr. Wixom would like you to cut your hair short and shave before tomorrow," Mr. Song informed me.

"You know, Peace Corps is a two-way street. We are here to show Koreans what America and Americans are like. In America, we can have long hair and mustaches," I replied.

"Yes, but we want to make a good impression on the ministry officials."

"And I think it would be good for them to see what freedom is all about."

"Please, consider trimming your hair and shaving your mustache."

"I will think about it, but I don't think I can do that. I will see you at dinner," I said, just to end the awkward conversation. Then I bowed slightly and walked away.

I walked back to my room filled with trepidation. I asked myself many questions. *"Should I or shouldn't I shave and cut my hair short? What if they threaten to send me home? But how could they after all the money they've spent training me? Besides I'm a good volunteer, aren't I?"* I went down to dinner, and we drank some more, but my stomach was tied in knots. I hardly slept due to all the tossing and turning because of my worrying. By morning I thought, *"Screw it, I'm showing up as I am. If they threaten to send me home, then I'll trim and shave."*

No one said another word about my hair or mustache. We all met the Ministry of Education muckety-muck officials, and I didn't notice them giving me the evil eye or even a second glance for that matter. Sunday I traveled the several hours by bus and train to get back to Mukho for Monday's classes.

After this weekend, in a letter home to Fred I wrote:

> About my hair it was the point of contention at the meeting
> that we had last month as I was told by a PC staff member
> to cut my hair and shave by the next morning. I explained
> to him how I felt, my reasons for looking the way I do and
> apologized for causing problems cuz I wish to cause
> nobody any problems and then said I was sorry but I could

not cut my hair and shave. One staff member said they
would send me home. I doubt it and I would not be the
only one. Also if it came to that I would shave and get
a haircut & grow it long again. Sort of a non-violent protest.
I'm not so convicted (sic) to my hair I could give up this
beautiful life for a little protein. (April 28, 1973)

Mr. Yoo got notice by telephone a week later that Mr. Song from the Peace Corps office in Seoul would be paying an official visit to our town on Wednesday. It was funny how I had not seen him even once in the previous eight months or so, and now, all of a sudden, he was about to show up. On Wednesday he arrived in the morning. He asked if he could observe one of my classes while I taught, and naturally I agreed. He also asked if we could have a private conversation during my afternoon free hour. Again, I agreed. When my free hour came around he asked if there was some place where we could be alone. I got the key to the music room, which was not being used that hour, and we went there.

"Do you have anything you'd like me to talk to the principal about?" Mr. Song began.

"No, everything's fine," I said.

"Do you want me to speak with your co-teacher?"

"No, everything's fine."

He continued asking if I'd like him to talk with any of the other teachers, did I have any problems with my housing that he might help with, or anything else. Each time I replied, "No, everything's fine." He asked me so many times I was getting real sick and tired of having to answer over and over again, "No, everything's fine." Finally, he stopped asking questions.

"I have never been to a school before where the school had nothing they wanted me to talk to the volunteer about and where the volunteer had nothing to complain about," he said with a puzzled look on his face.

"I'm happy. I teach just like all the other teachers. I ask for no special favors, except for my mustache and hair. Otherwise, I am just one of the staff, exactly like every other teacher. I try my best, and I love teaching."

"Good. I'm surprised, but that's good," he replied.

But he was still scratching his head in disbelief as we left the room. We went back to the principal's office to visit with Mr. Yoo. Mr. Song, I found out later, had had private meetings with the principal, the vice-principal, my co-teacher, and had talked with several of the other teachers. Not one of them had any complaint whatsoever about me, and I, in turn, had no complaints either.

That night Mr. Song invited Principal Yoo, Vice-Principal Lee, and all of us English teachers out to dinner at a very nice restaurant that I had never been to before. We had some fancy food, the likes of which I had not eaten before either. I started hoping Mr. Song might visit often to wine and dine us all, but alas he never visited Mukho again while I was there.

As the weather warmed, the students switched from their winter uniforms to the summer ones. The boys now wore light blue pants, light blue short-sleeved shirts with two breast pockets that had buttoned flaps, and matching baseball caps. The girls switched from black slacks with black jackets to black skirts with white blouses.

Boys' summer uniforms.

Also in the late spring came the boys' middle school annual All Sports Day. Each class had teams or individuals in several different sports that competed against each other to see which class—first-year, second-year, or third-year—had the best athletes and could win the All Sports Award. Among the sports were volleyball, track and field events, wrestling, and the "pull-down-the-large-log" event.

Starting position in Korean-style wrestling.

The wrestling matches were Korean-style wrestling. A long piece of material was tied around each competitor's waist and then around his right upper thigh. The material was twisted so that it was the thickness of a rope. The two boys in competition bent at the waist, wrapped their right hands inside the material on the opponent's left waist, and

"Pull-down-the-log" game at students' All Sports Day.

their left hands under the material on the right thigh of their opponent. Then they would make a fist around the material in those two places. The starter blew a whistle, and the boys stood up still holding the material in each hand. They tried to push or pull their opponent down. Whoever landed on the top when they fell won the match.

The "pull-down-the-large-log" game was also very unique. A log about twelve feet high and about six inches in diameter was wrapped with rope from bottom to top. There were about twelve students on each squad, and one team's responsibility was to keep the pole standing upright for as long as possible while the other team's members tried to pull it to the ground.

These events went on all day long, and the students who were not participating cheered on their class's athletes. One class had all of their cheerleaders wear hats that looked like dunce hats. Others had headbands on. One of my favorite students had on a women's *hanbok* and led the cheers of the freshman class. The third-year students won as usual, but everyone had a great time.

Students cheering their team – notice the student dressed in a woman's *hanbok* (traditional dress).

In a letter I wrote to Fred, I told him that April 28, 1973, had been the day of the annual spring school picnic. We hiked that day with all 1,400 boys up into the mountains. I sat with Mr. Yoo and the teachers for lunch and "had a groovy time," I wrote. I caught a toad in a rice paddy and turned it over to

Mr. Yoo and I sitting at the boys' school picnic.

find that the Korean toads had a bright red-orange stomach. In the letter I also talked about how beautiful spring was. On the hike, I noticed tobacco growing, as well as barley and rice seed beds. The farmers were busy diverting water into the paddy fields and plowing. And I mentioned how I would often play soccer after school on the playground with the boys.

Another story I wrote about was at the beginning of the letter:

> Using the freaky purple ink one of my students gave me.
> Teachers here receive all kinds of little things like ink, food,
> cigarettes and it goes further than that. One day quite a
> while back now about 10 at night I went with another
> English teacher—a Korean—to a wine shop. It turns out
> the woman who runs the place has a boy in my class. So I
> met her boy (sic) drank beer and as almost all wine shops have
> girls to keep you happy enjoyed the little ladies (sic) company.
> Well the woman wouldn't let me pay for the beer & I spent
> the night with the little lady who works for her while the
> other Eng. Teacher also spent the night with one of the other
> little ladies. (April 28, 1973)

So much for not messing around in your own town, except she was a bar girl, so that was OK. And my student's mother encouraged it, even insisted. Who was I to argue with her?

There was this strange dichotomy in Korea between the prurient and the puritanical. Woman faced the puritanical side of the coin. From the beginning of the Yi Dynasty (1392–1910), Confucianism was established as the state ideology. Women lost many rights that they had held in the previous Koryo Kingdom when Buddhism was dominant. Women had to conform to Neo-Confucian ideals of purity, obedience, and chastity. Especially *Yangban* (upper-class) women were completely segregated from the rest of society. They were kept in female-only sections of the houses. On the rare occasions that *Yangban* women were allowed to leave their homes, they wore clothing that covered them from head to toe, including veils that completely hid their faces, and they were carried in palanquins (sedan chairs) that were completely enclosed. Even as late of the 1970s there were still vestiges of these paternalistic Neo-Confucian ideals for women.

Yangban men in the Yi Dynasty, on the other hand, could have concubines. They were also free to visit wine houses and at official functions were entertained by *gisaeng* (geisha), female entertainers' adept at singing, dancing, and playing instruments, as well as reciting poetry. There were still vestiges of this prurient freedom for men alive in the 1970s, too.

What I didn't tell Fred was that the English teacher with me was Mr. Jong, Chul-chin. When I got home early the next morning, I was suffering from a bad hangover. I pulled out my *yo, ebul, and begae* (mattress, coverlet, and pillow) and tried to get some extra sleep, but Chong-ho's mother, Mr. Jong's lovely wife, came in demanding to know where Mr. Jong was. I told her I didn't know, and I honestly didn't as he'd left while I'd stayed in a room at the *sul-jip*. It was then that I decided I really needed to move. I was sick and tired of the greasy French toast that I had never gotten the nerve to comment about, and I wanted to get away from Mr. Jong because he was obviously a bad influence on me. Also, I didn't really want to go to any more alcoholic beverage houses, especially not with him.

A couple of weeks later I broached the subject with Mr. Jong. He agreed to help me find a place. We went downtown together, and he headed right up the alley near the Mukho movie theater where I had been accosted by ladies of the evening my first night out alone. We walked into the Changshin Yeogwan, which was the last building on the right next to the wall surrounding Mukho Harbor. Mr. Jong worked out a good deal for me to rent a room there. A couple of days later I bid farewell to *halmeoni* (grandmother), Mr. Jong, Chong-ho's mother, and the kids. I carried all my possessions in a couple of duffel bags downtown to my new digs.

Shortly after I moved into the *yeogwan*, around 10:30 pm, just as I was getting ready to go to sleep, there was a knock on my door. A Korean in a suit walked in, flashed an ID, and explained that he was a policeman and needed to interview me. He began asking many questions.

"What do you do on the weekends?"

"Hike in the mountains and read books."

"What cities in Korea have you visited?"

"Seoul, Daegu, Gwangju, Yeongju, Kangnung, and a few others."

He continued for quite a while. I was cranky and tired. After a couple of questions I started getting more and more pissed off. I finally told him that I had to teach in the morning and needed my rest, and I shooed him out the door.

The next morning in the teachers' office I began telling the teachers around my desk about this policeman and how rude he had been. As I was telling the story more and more of the teachers began gathering around, and I raised my voice higher and higher to make sure they all heard. I ended with, "I am going to complain to the Peace Corps Director about this harassment. The U.S. Embassy has already been informed that some Peace Corps Volunteers have had similar problems, and I'm going to make sure it is known that I have been mistreated here in Mukho." Part of that I just made up on the spot, but I had heard that a couple of PCVs had had similar experiences. Word must have gotten back to the police in Mukho about this because I was never bothered again.

In early May, on a Friday, I went with Mr. Yoo to Wonju, the second-largest city in Gangwon Province, and we took the five-hour train ride from Mukho to a Peace Corps/Provincial Board of Education meeting there. Glenn from Kangnung and his principal were also there, as well as all the other volunteers in the province. After the meetings on Friday afternoon and Saturday morning, Glenn and I decided to head into Seoul to party, and we planned to get a Korean Air Lines prop plane back to the east coast on Sunday. The weather was so bad Sunday that the planes didn't fly. On Monday morning we had one of the Peace Corps secretaries call our schools. All the flights were cancelled on Monday also. It wasn't until Tuesday that we got a flight out and "prop-setted" it back to the east coast.

On May 29, 1973, I wrote to Fred again, after which I didn't hear from him or write to him until October 1974:

> Received bad news this week – my principle (sic) at the boy's (sic) school is being transferred to a different school. He has become almost like a father to me and is the most beautiful person I have met in Korea. I will miss him immensely. He is 56 years old yet he would often come to my classes and repeat along with the students. He has told me many times that he is also my student but I have learned much from him. I hope I am like him when I'm his age that would be truly beautiful. (May 29, 1973)

I was in Mr. Yoo's office having tea when the call came. I had never seen or heard him angry before, but he raised his voice and argued that he did not want to go to another school. In frustration, he finally agreed that he would go if he absolutely had to. I couldn't help feeling that one of the biggest reasons he didn't want to go was that he wanted to continue to spend more time with me and learn more English. After he hung up the phone he explained that they wanted him to go to Sokcho High School, the boys' high school. Sokcho is the city north of Sorak National Park and near the DMZ. He told me that being the principal of a boys' high school meant many more disciplinary problems and that at his age he didn't want to have to deal with them, but he had no choice; the provincial Board of Education had ordered him to go.

The next morning, Mr. Yoo announced to all the teachers at the morning meeting that he would be leaving. His last Saturday at Mukho Middle School, there was a morning assembly with all 1,400 students standing at attention on the playground, and Yoo *Gyojang-nim* (Yoo, Hyung-sul) made his farewell speech to the entire student body as tears rolled down my cheeks.

The next Monday our new principal, Chai *Gyojang-nim* (Chai, Young-sun) conducted his first morning meeting. Our relationship was very businesslike. There were no more visits to the principal's office every day for a cup of tea and conversation. Otherwise, there were no changes for me; I still taught the same classes at Mukho Middle School and continued to teach on Tuesdays and Thursdays at Mukho Girls' Middle School.

Don with his Aleksandr Solzhenitsyn look-alike hair and beard style, along with his first co-teacher, Mr. Jun, In-kook.

By the end of the semester my hair had gotten pretty long, I had let my beard grow out, and I looked pretty handsome. Mr. Jun, In-kook and I took a hike up Mureung Valley with his fiancée, and she took a picture of the two of us. I've always said that this was my Aleksandr Solzhenitsyn look-alike hair and beard style.

One of the many books that I read during the spring semester (besides finishing *Cancer Ward* that I was reading when we met Tom Tokyo and *The Great Khan* that I bought in an underpass shop near Gwanghwa-mun) was *The Hound of the Baskervilles,* by Sir Arthur Conan Doyle. I started reading *The Hound of the Baskervilles* one rainy spring evening. As I got deeper into the book the rain picked up with thunder and lightning crashing and brightening the night sky. When I got to the scary parts in the book with the scenes on the foggy moor, the noise and flashing outside got louder and more frequent, right on cue, as if someone was turning off and on the lights and beating on loud cymbals. I read the book cover to cover in the midst of this storm. It seemed as if I was in a theater with great staging in my imagination and the all-too-real lightning and thunder stage effects. I was a bit groggy while teaching the next day, but what fun it had been.

CHAPTER 8

Bike biking in Japan: Ohio, no, Michigan

In our letters back and forth, Charlie wrote about wanting to go to Japan during our summer vacation and biking around Kyushu, the southernmost of the four big islands in the Japanese archipelago. I wrote back that I was game. We discussed how it was odd that none of the senior volunteers we knew had ever mentioned anyone doing this before. We both thought it was a brilliant idea.

We had asked Peace Corps for permission to travel to Japan, and Charlie and I separately went into Seoul to get our passports and money for our trip. All the PCVs' passports were held at the Peace Corps office in Seoul ostensibly so that PCVs wouldn't lose them, or even more likely have them stolen. We also got a special summer vacation check in dollars. I cashed this check at a bank in Seoul, exchanging it for Japanese yen. When I went up to the Peace Corps office and went to the seventh floor to get my check for summer expenses, I saw my supervisor Mr. Song, Jun-ki from across the large room where the secretaries and bookkeepers had their desks. Mr. Song was coming out of his office. When he saw me he waved and in a loud voice called out, "Mr. Ha, the best volunteer in Gangwon-do." I laughed and waved back. For the next two and a half years, every time I saw him he called me the best volunteer in Gangwon Province.

Walking into the Peace Corps lounge that afternoon, I ran into John Sturgeon who had married Kathy Fowlerville during training.

"John, where's Kathy?"

"She left Korea, and now they're kicking me out."

"Why?"

"Peace Corps policy – if one spouse leaves, the other is sent home too."

"You're kidding. I thought we had freedom as Americans."

"Yeah, not if you're a Peace Corps volunteer."

"Can't you fight it?"

"I'm trying, but it doesn't look good. Seems they used to allow one spouse to leave and the other to stay. Then one couple got divorced and blamed Peace Corps for the divorse, so then Peace Corps changed its policy."

"Seems a bit of an overreaction, doesn't it?"

"Yeah, it does. I have to run. I'm going upstairs to meet with Jim Wixom to argue my case."

"Good luck."

But luck wasn't with him. We heard later that he was forced to leave.

I took the train and met Charlie in Yeongju, and of course, the first thing we talked of was the news about Kathy and John. The next day, Friday, we headed down to Busan. We bought our tickets for that evening's ferry to Shimonoseki, Japan. The ferries left in the early evening and sailed to Shimonoseki at the bottom of Honshu, Japan's biggest island. They arrived around midnight and anchored in the harbor with everyone sleeping on the ship. The next morning it then pulled up to the dock, and everyone disembarked.

About an hour before we were to board the ship, Charlie announced that he needed to find a bank to exchange some Korean currency into Japanese yen. I knew this would be a problem. We went into the closest bank to the ferry dock, and the teller informed us that it was impossible to exchange Korean currency (Won) into a foreign currency unless Charlie could show a voucher proving that he had exchanged a foreign currency to get the Korean Won in the first place. We flashed our Peace Corps IDs. He and I both argued that because we were American Peace Corps Volunteers, this money obviously originated with U.S. dollars. It came to Korea and was exchanged for Korean Won, and then paid to us as our salary, but because the exchanging was done by the Peace Corps' Korea Office in Seoul we had no such voucher. "Sorry! No vouchie, no cashie," was basically the response we encountered. We asked to see the manager. He told us the same thing. Of course, we knew there were strict currency controls in Korea, that the Korean Won was not an international currency, and that it certainly was not exchangeable in Japan. We begged, we pleaded, and we explained again that we were American Peace Corps Volunteers. We were here in Korea teaching English to help Korea's development. This money had come to Korea from the U.S. government to pay for our salary and so had been exchanged from a foreign currency (the American dollar), and we just now wanted to exchange a small percentage of it back again. Finally, the nice bank manager agreed and exchanged Charlie's pile of Won notes. We ran from the bank, Charlie with his new yen hoard, and got to the ferry just before they yanked up the gangplank. Whew!

As we made our way onto the ship, I began singing and paraphrasing, to the tune of Rod Stewart's song, "Every Picture Tells a Story":

> On the Shimonoseki ferry, we was feeling merry,
> Sailing on our way to Japan.
> ("Every Picture Tells a Story" written by Rod Stewart and Ronnie Wood,
> performed by Rod Stewart)

We found the closed-in deck area where we poor folk slept on a wide-open carpeted floor. There were also cabins, which were, of course, more expensive. We both grabbed the thin pads, light blankets, and pillows that were supplied by the ferry company and located an area to lay them out and stake our claim for sleeping space. In walked a white guy with long hair hanging down below his shoulders, a scruffy beard, and mustache. He saw Charlie and me, grabbed his bedding, and headed our way. We exchanged pleasantries. His name was Fred Interlochen. He was an American living and working— sort of underground— in Japan. The reason he had come to Busan was to renew his tourist visa for Japan. He was a real hippie in looks as well as deeds. He told us that he drove around Japan on a motorcycle. He made and sold silver and abalone shell jewelry on street corners. The abalone shells came from California, and he'd head home once in a while to get a fresh supply. He used silver wire to fashion jewelry from pieces cut from the shells and would sit on the corners in one city after another making jewelry while showing a small table full of finished earrings and pendants for sale. He was, he told us, married to a Japanese bar girl who lived in Tokyo, and whenever he got the equivalent of a few hundred bucks' worth of yen, he'd send a money order to his wife and/or return to Tokyo and spend a couple of days with his woman. He did not have a license to sell his jewelry, but as long as he didn't look like he was making a lot of money, the Japanese police let it slide, he told us. Consequently, he never wanted to have too much cash because if the police realized he was making a killing they'd force him to have the appropriate legal licensure. I couldn't help wondering, *Were Japanese bar girls like Korean ones? Did they too sometimes spend the night with their customers?* Fred seemed to anticipate my thoughts. "Japanese bar girls aren't like the ones in Korea," he told us, "They only serve drinks." I wasn't sure if he was also trying to reassure himself while assuring us, but that was his problem—or not. *Was Fred really married? Why would he need to keep renewing his tourist visa, if he was legally married to a Japanese woman?* I pondered these questions, but Charlie and I were more interested in grilling him on the practical matters of traveling in Japan as inexpensively as possible.

Fred told us that he usually camped out at Shinto shrines. No one minded, and it was one of the few places around where there would be flat land that wasn't used for buildings or growing crops. He would just pitch his tent and crash each evening. This was good advice, we later discovered. We asked about buying used bicycles, and he assured us there were used bikes for sale in shops around any city, and certainly in Shimonoseki we would find some. Another helpful hint was to make sure to get mosquito coils, as the pests were ubiquitous and voracious bloodsucking monsters. Otherwise, he assured us, it would be no problem to bike all over and that the Japanese people would be very kind.

The ship was pulling into Shimonoseki harbor after midnight when we finally exhausted our questions for good ol' Fred. We also had told him a little about our Peace Corps experiences. Most of the people around us were sleeping already, so we hit the hay (or rather padded mats)—Charlie and I with great expectations for our bike-hike vacation.

The next morning, Saturday, we went through customs and immigration and disembarked from the ferry. A wave of fear came over me as I realized we were in a foreign country where neither Charlie nor I had any knowledge of the language. Korea had been the first non-English speaking place I had ever been to, and there were Peace Corps Trainers there to greet us. Here, Charlie and I were on our own; we had to use our wits. We bid farewell to Fred Interlochen, put our bags in lockers at the ferry terminal, and wandered off. Shimonoseki is the southernmost city on the largest and main Japanese island of Honshu. We would need to get our bikes and camping equipment. After that we planned to head south, either across the bridge or through the tunnel under the Shimonoseki Straights and over or under to Kyushu, the southernmost of the four large islands in the Japanese archipelago. We reconnoitered the town, found a small park with public restrooms, and located a nearby Shinto Shrine where we could try crashing this first night in Japan. In a shop near the shrine, I bought a long-sleeved denim shirt in case of cool evenings. I think I bought it mostly because I needed a Japanese size XL, while in the U.S. I was a medium. It made me feel downright Herculean.

Item number one on our list of items we needed to purchase for our biking/camping expedition was sleeping bags. After a lunch of noodles—always cheap, good, and filling—we found a department store. We checked out their sleeping bags, which seemed to be selling for a reasonable price, and purchased one each as well as mosquito coils and some matches with which to light them. After putting our purchases into the lockers at the ferry terminal, we then began searching for bike shops. We found one store with a reasonably priced used bike, but we needed two bikes. We explained as best we could that we needed another similarly priced bike and that we'd probably be back.

By evening we still hadn't found a second bike, and we sat in the park reading until it got so dark we couldn't read anymore. So we got our sleeping bags and duffel bags out of the lockers, washed up in the park's washroom, and entered the Shinto shrine. Problem! All the flat area around this Shinto shrine was paved with stone. It would not have been comfortable for sleeping, so we climbed a wooden staircase alongside the shrine leading to an elevated wooden walkway that went around the whole building and was about four feet wide. There we laid out our sleeping bags, rolled up some clothes to make pillows, and quickly fell into a sound sleep.

Sunday we were up at the crack of dawn and out before anyone might decide to walk around the walkway we had slept on. We went over to the park restrooms for morning face washing and tooth brushing, and then we were ready for another day.

We tried to do some shopping, but we found a lot of the small shops were closed. Looking at a map, we noticed a beach off to the north of town and decided we'd try to make our way there. After lunch, we somehow managed to get on the right bus and made it to the beach. We sat out in the sun and then under a tree for a while reading. After dinner, we were again sitting on the beach when five or six Japanese high school-aged students came up and began talking to us in English. From the beginning, the conversation went something like this:

"Where are you from?" one of the students asked.

"Well, we're Americans, but we live in Korea."

"What do you do there?"

"We're teachers."

"You look too young to be teachers." We heard this often in Japan. Evidently, it took longer in Japan to get teaching certification than it does in the U.S., and Japanese teachers are in their late twenties or even early thirties when they start teaching.

Their English was quite good, but Charlie got tired of them and said he'd walk back down the beach toward the entrance where the bus had let us off. I enjoyed the conversation, though, and stayed to continue talking to the students.

"Well maybe so, but I am a teacher in Korea."

"What do you teach?"

"I teach English in a Korean middle school."

"How did you come to Japan?"

"We came by boat." They looked puzzled, and one began making motions with his arms as if he were rowing a boat.

"By boat?" he asked.

"Well, you know, a big boat."

"Ah, you mean a ship."

"Yes, a ship," I said while laughing.

"How do you like Japan?"

"Oh, very much, I like your mountains."

"No," one of them said, "these are hills. In America you have mountains, the Rocky Mountains, but these are hills."

"Yes, OK, I like your hills. My hometown is Detroit. It is very flat there, so these look like mountains to me." I pointed at their "hills."

"No, these are hills," one of them further reminded me.

The conversation dragged, and I finally said, "What does your pin mean?" And I pointed to a pin on his collar.

"Ah, this is not a pin, it is a badge."

"Yes, indeed, what does your badge mean?"

"It is our school badge."

"Oh, very nice."

We talked for a while longer, and they continued to correct my errors. By this point in time I was imagining that these Japanese students were probably thinking, how the hell is this guy an English teacher when he makes so many vocabulary mistakes? So I took my leave and went off looking for Charlie. Quite a bit of time had gone by, and when I got to the parking lot, dusk was approaching. I walked around and couldn't find Charlie anywhere. I finally thought that maybe he had returned to downtown Shimonoseki. Panicking, I held out my thumb to a passing car, and they stopped and picked me up. Back in town, I went to the park, but Charlie was nowhere to be found. Consequently, I returned to the Shinto shrine and slept there again. I slept so soundly that when I woke up it was already bright daylight, and I could hear someone sweeping the paved stone area below me. Quietly, I turned and could see a monk in his light gray baggy slacks and jacket mindfully sweeping the already clean and tidy area. I was sure this was a morning ritual, and the last thing I wanted to do was disrupt it by suddenly making noise or otherwise drawing attention to myself. I wondered if he didn't already know that I was there. I stayed there as still as I could until he worked his way around the corner and out of view. I then quietly wrapped up my sleeping bag, picked it and my duffel bag up, climbed down the steps, and left the compound.

On my way to the restroom at the park, guess who I saw walking toward me? Emperor Hirohito? No. None other than Charlie! With a mixture of profound relief and displeasure, I walked quickly toward him as he was walking quickly toward me.

"What the hell happened to you last night?" I blurted out.

"What happened to you?" he replied.

"Oh, good! Very Socratic," I thought.

"Where were you? I looked all over around the parking area at the beach."

"Didn't you see the pavilion? I was sitting in there," Charlie responded.

"No, missed that. Where'd you sleep?"

"In the pavilion. What happened to you?"

I explained how I hitchhiked back and slept at the Shinto shrine again. We both, I'm sure, had puzzled looks on our faces as we both processed this information.

But it was Monday, and we had shopping to do. We began our search again, and finally in the afternoon we found another bike shop with one good and cheap used bike. I bought it, and then we went back to the first shop and Charlie bought the other. We also bought some bungee cord-like rope to tie down our sleeping bags and duffel bags to the racks on the back of each bike.

By now it was late afternoon, too late to start heading across the straits, and so we rode our bikes back to the beach. We watched the sun set and then went to the pavilion where Charlie had waited for me the night before. There were piles of tatami mats about three feet by six feet and a couple of inches thick in the pavilion. We decided to make a tent-like structure out of our bikes and these mats on the beach. We parked our bikes in the sand and draped mats over and around the bikes with a small opening to get in and out. With our sleeping bags rolled out inside we were all set for a good night's sleep. Things were great until I heard Charlie screaming. I jumped up, knocking over our bicycles and the mats covering them. Charlie had woken up by this juncture and looking about at the devastation asked, "What happened?" Standing in the middle of the fallen bikes and mats, I responded, "You screamed, and it startled me." (I probably dreamt it.) We decided we were too tired to try to reconstruct our edifice and just plopped back on top of our sleeping bags. Mosquito city! There were dozens of them buzzing around our heads. We lit a mosquito coil, but they ignored it. Finally, even though it meant sweating the rest of the night, we each crawled into our sleeping bags, zipped them up and buried our heads inside, out of harm's way. From then on it was an uncomfortable, mostly sleepless night.

Up again at the crack of dawn, if not before, we packed up and headed back to Shimonoseki and the park with the restroom to wash up, shave, and brush our teeth. We obviously needed a tent, so we went back to the department store again and bought a two-person pup tent.

Back to the park one last time, and we changed our clothes. I put on a T-shirt and a pair of Albion soccer practice shorts, sweat socks, and my Adidas athletic shoes. I was ready for serious action, and Charlie was similarly attired. As we started riding toward the entrance to the tunnel, which we had decided to use rather than the bridge, Charlie announced that he needed to cash his Peace Corps summer pay/vacation check.

"You're kidding, right?" I asked.

"No," was all he said.

"You've got to be kidding? Why didn't you cash it in Seoul when you picked it up like I did?" I questioned him in exasperation.

"Why? It shouldn't be a problem."

I had the sneaking suspicion it would be, but we rode along until we spotted the Chinese characters for bank on a sign (Chinese characters are used extensively in Japan). We parked our bikes by the bank's main door and walked in. Many of the doors in Japan were like magic, and this one at the bank was that way. They opened by themselves whenever you got near them. We had never seen this in the U.S. or in Korea, and we were amazed by this ultra-modern technology. But we didn't have time to admire the door because we wanted to get Charlie's money and get on the road headed south.

Again, as in Busan, we walked up to the teller and Charlie explained slowly, in English of course, that he wanted to cash this U.S. government, U.S. dollar check and exchange it for yen. The sweet young Japanese lady looked at it with jaundiced eyes and said, "Excuse me, please wait," while bowing ever so politely. She went into the manager's office behind a floor to ceiling glass partition. We watched as they discussed the matter. She came out and said, "Please, follow me," and she led us into the manager's office. He approached us in his dark suit, white shirt, and tie, and I felt just slightly under-dressed in my short shorts and already sweaty T-shirt. We formally shook hands and bowed. Then he invited us to sit down on the lovely upholstered sofa and chairs around a coffee table. We hesitated, not wanting to get the beautiful fabric dirty or damp, but he motioned again for us to sit and so we did. He asked Charlie why he had a U.S. government check. Charlie showed the manager his Peace Corps ID, and we explained about the Peace Corps being a government program and how we were English teachers in Korean middle schools.

"Ah, I see," he replied. "But, why issued at Manila, Philippines?"

"Manila, Philippines?" Charlie and I both quizzically said.

"Yes, see! Manila, Philippines."

"Ah!" we both said together. Charlie then suggested, "The U.S. government must issue checks there for East Asia."

The bank manager didn't look convinced, and we really didn't have the foggiest idea why it said Manila, Philippines, on a U.S. government check. After a couple of minutes in thought, the manager suggested that he would have someone call the nearest U.S. consulate in Fukuoka on Kyushu and inquire about this. We both heaved a sigh of relief. He left with the check.

"If I can't cash this check I will only have enough money for a few days," Charlie said.

"Great. Why didn't you cash it in Seoul when you were there?"

"I didn't think it would be a problem," Charlie repeated. I just shook my head in disbelief. The manager returned and asked if we would like a cup of tea or coffee. I asked for tea. Charlie ordered coffee, and the manager relayed our order to one of the lovely female employees. She brought in the beverages as we sat having a nice conversation with our new banking friend, telling him about our planned bicycle trip around Kyushu. A few minutes later, one of the female employees came in with the equivalent in yen of the dollar amount on the check neatly piled on a cute little money tray. Charlie stood up. The young lady ever so formally presented the tray to Charlie, bowing while holding it with both hands. Charlie bowed back and received it equally formally with two hands. "Please count," the bank manager advised. But Charlie said, "Oh, that's OK." We thanked this kind gentleman ever so profusely and also bowed our way out of the bank, thanking all of the employees, who had so graciously assisted us two sweaty, but jauntily dressed, young Americans.

Now that Charlie had his money, we both wanted to make one more stop before heading across the straits—a camera shop. We'd had both spent a year in Korea without a camera and obviously without taking any pictures. (All the photographs in the book so far were either taken by others or by me after the summer of 1973, but of the same people, places, or things mentioned.) Just up the street we saw a small shop with hundreds of cameras, and in we went. They had Nikon, Canon, and Minolta cameras. As each brand had many models, it took a while to figure out what we wanted. We both ended up buying Canon FTBs with black bodies instead of the usual stainless steel color because black is ever so much more stylish. We also bought cases to put them in. Mine was an attractive burnt orange colored case. Now we were ready to cross the straits to Kyushu. Near the bridge we found an elevator that took us down into the tunnel. There was a sidewalk along the edge of the road where we could ride our bikes, as there were no other people walking or biking at the time. We went up another elevator on the other side and emerged in the city of Kitakyushu. Now we began seriously bike riding in a southwesterly direction toward Fukuoka, where the U.S. consulate that the nice bank manager had called was located. After a couple of hours or so of riding, we found a nice park along the beach with restaurants, outdoor showers, and restrooms. We set up our tent there for the night.

Up early the next morning, we ate rice and vegetables for breakfast and hit the road again. Around noon we found a small restaurant and stopped for lunch.

The best part of restaurants in Japan was that virtually all of them had a glass case with plastic imitations of the meals on plates so we could just bring the waitresses to the case and point at what we wanted, since our Japanese never got past knowing how to say a few simple things. We had figured out that *"Ikura desuka?"* meant "How much is it?" But when the people answered we couldn't follow even though we learned a few of the lower numbers. So we'd say, *"Ikura desuka?"* and then hold out a note pad and pen for them to write down the amount. As we were sitting in a small restaurant, one customer ordered coffee. The man behind the counter hand ground some beans and put them in a small filter. Then he poured steaming hot water through the grounds. We watched as the brown liquid slowly dripped into the cup below it, and the smell of coffee wafted by us. Charlie started raving about the smell, and he ordered a cup. In Korea, as mentioned before, it was all instant Maxwell House coffee at all the tearooms, and I had heard the coffee didn't taste all that great. I didn't know personally as I always drank tea. This Japanese coffee did smell good, but having never had a cup of coffee in my life, I just watched and listened to Charlie as he waxed poetic about how good this coffee tasted. At the next similar restaurant, I too ordered a cup and have been a heavy coffee drinker ever since. It's all Charlie's fault.

We continued for two or three more days riding hard all day and camping on the beach each night. Surprisingly, we started seeing Americans going by in trucks and jeeps as we were riding along, most of them in sailor suits. Then we saw two American guys in civilian clothes standing on a corner, and we were able to stop and talk to them. They told us that the Sasebo American Naval Base was not too far away.

After a couple of more days, we pulled into the city of Nagasaki. Our first stop there was at the Nagasaki Peace Park. This park is at ground zero where the second atomic bomb was dropped on Japan near the end of World War II. Code named "Fat Man," this bomb was dropped by the U.S. on August 9, 1945, just three days after the first one, "Little Boy," had been dropped on Hiroshima in an effort to force Japan into surrendering more quickly. There is an imposing statue, the Peace Statue, of a muscular, almost naked man sitting with material wrapped around his waist and loins. Some of the material is draped over his left upper arm, which he is holding out straight, parallel to the ground. This symbolizes tranquility. His right arm is pointing straight up with his index finger pointing toward the sky, and this symbolizes the threat of the bomb. He is sitting on a boulder with his right leg folded up under his left thigh in a semi-Buddha-like pose. His left leg is bent at the knee, and his left foot is resting on the ground in front of the boulder, which symbolizes moving to help. Oddly, his facial features didn't look

The Nagasaki Peace Statue.

very Japanese or Asian to me but more like a Norse god, maybe Thor or Odin. He was very burly looking with shoulder-length hair; a large, strong nose; and almost Germanic facial features—needless to say, he looked a lot like me.

We entered the Nagasaki Atomic Bomb Museum nearby. As we walked around the exhibits and saw the devastation and the degree of suffering caused by this one bomb, I wished I'd had a Canadian flag on my shirt so I could have pretended not to be an American. This is the only time in my life that I really felt ashamed of my country. I'm a historian, and I can intellectualize the reasoning for these two bombs being dropped. But when I saw the exhibits depicting the suffering of innocent civilians, including, of course, women and children, I questioned the humanity of it. I walked around with tears streaming down my cheeks. I also knew that dropping these two bombs on Hiroshima and Nagasaki has given the Japanese an excuse to not truly and fully address the horrible things that they did during the war. Instead they fixate on being the only country to have ever had atomic bombs dropped on it. Some Japanese suggest that they were the victims in the war rather than addressing the fact that they started the damn thing, and they in fact were the victimizers.

It is interesting to note that the Japanese started and fought three wars since America's Commodore Matthew C. Perry USN got them to open up to the United States and the rest of the world in 1854: the Sino-Japanese War (1894–1895), the Russo-Japanese War (1904–1905) and World War II. In all three of those wars the Japanese started them by attacking the opponents' navy in surprise attacks. Japan needs to come to terms with its own history. In addition, all the nations in the modern world must find a way to guarantee that Nagasaki is the last city to ever suffer an atomic or hydrogen nuclear blast. Unfortunately, civilization seems to be but a thin veneer over our animal nature. The *Los Angeles Times* is famous for the saying: "The superman has created the airplane and the radio, the ape-man has got hold of them." I remember reading somewhere that a more succinct version of this was expressed by a British author when he saw bombers flying overhead in World War II: "Man invented the airplane and then the ape got hold of it." Either way, I couldn't agree more, although this may be unfair to the apes. Apes, after all, don't fight wars the way we do, except in movies with Charlton Heston in them.

As we drove away from the museum we noticed a Catholic church and stopped there. This church had been completely destroyed by the A-bomb and was rebuilt. I took a picture of Charlie taking a picture of a stutue of Mother Mary.

While pedaling out of Nagasaki, we passed by a junkyard and stopped there to rest a while. I struck the pose of the Nagasaki Peace Statue and had Charlie click a photograph of me using my camera. Possibly a little CIS, but I just had this urge to duplicate the statue's pose here where no one would see me except, of course, Charlie.

Charlie Sarnia taking a picture of Mother Mary at a Catholic church in Nagasaki.

Don striking the Peace Statue pose.

We headed south out of Nagasaki down the narrow Nagasaki Peninsula to a lovely beach resort area and pitched our tent on the south end of the beach. The beach had some restaurants, and in one of the restaurants there was a computer game—the first computer game either of us had ever seen—called

Pong. It had one vertical line down the center of the screen that represented the net and then two short lines on either side of the screen that we could move up and down with controllers. A ball bounced back and forth, and if you were able to hit it with the line representing a paddle you volleyed the ball back to the other side. If you missed, then you lost a point to your opponent. It was pretty primitive by today's standards, but we played this newfangled game over and over all evening the first night we were there.

The next morning, we hung out on the beach and jumped back and forth in and out of the water. At one point, we were playing catch with a Frisbee when I noticed a gorgeous young Japanese gal in a bikini sitting on a rock near the shore. I also noticed that she was watching us play catch. Upon noticing her interest, I threw the Frisbee to Charlie and while stretching and yawning said, "I'm getting tired, let's quit." Charlie agreed, and I headed toward said rock. When I got close to the rock, the young lady spoke to me in English.

"Excuse me, are you an American?"

"Why, yes. Yes, I am an American."

"Do you live in Japan?"

"No, I am visiting."

"Where are you from?"

"Well, my hometown is Detroit. Do you know Detroit?"

"Yes, the Motor City."

"Exactly, but I live and work in Korea. What is your name?" I asked.

She obviously wanted to practice her English, and she spoke very well. She told me her name was Misako Yamato, and I told her my name.

"Would you like to see our tent? 'Come and I'll show you my etchings,'" I suggested.

Misako at the beach near Nagasaki.

"Please, say again," she responded.

"Only joking, please, come and meet my friend."

We walked to shore, and I introduced her to Charlie, who was sitting near our tent.

Then I asked if she would mind my taking some pictures of

her. She didn't, and after taking a few photos, I realized I was famished. I suggested the three of us go to a restaurant for lunch. Charlie said he wasn't hungry, so Misako and I went off together. After lunch we walked across a narrow channel to a small island, and I followed behind Misako as we walked up the steep incline to a small shrine at the top. I nearly fell several times because instead of watching where I was going, I was staring at Misako's cute rear end. We talked for a couple of hours or more while sitting at the top of the island. Finally, Misako told me she needed to leave.

"Where are you going?" I asked.

"I have to go back home," she said.

"Oh, where do you live?"

"I live in Kurume."

"Did you come here this morning from Kurume?"

"Yes."

"How far away from here is it?"

"It takes about two and a half hours. I must take a bus to Nagasaki and then by train to Kurume."

I had absolutely no idea exactly where Kurume was, but I asked her if I could get her address and write to her. She eagerly agreed. We walked back down the steep hill and then into the narrow channel of water separating this tiny island from the peninsula. The tide was moving in by this time. The water was up to our chests, and the current was very strong. I held Misako's hand very tightly as I led the way gingerly one step at a time because of the rocky bottom. Misako went into a changing room to put on her clothes, and I waited until she came out. She had a notebook and wrote down her address for me. I wrote mine down for her and we both promised to write to each other. I returned to the far southern end of the beach walking on air with thoughts of a letter writing campaign leading to romance.

Charlie and I stayed a couple of more days on this beach and then headed back up the peninsula past Nagasaki to where we turned in a southeasterly direction and along the shore of another larger peninsula, the Minamishimabara Peninsula. (Too bad the Japanese language doesn't like to use a lot of syllables; it would be more fun if they did.) We ate an early supper this day and decided to keep on riding. Then it started raining and raining and raining. We finally stopped by an open field that was mostly mud. We had no idea how far we were from the nearest town. We also didn't know how close or far we were from the shoreline and a sandy beach. In the rain we got out the tent and put it up, securing the tent stakes as well as we could. It was nearly dark by the time we got into the tent and rolled out our sleeping bags. We were both soaking wet and changed into dry clothes and tried to get to sleep. The wind started howling and the rain was coming down in buckets. Suddenly the tent stakes pulled up on one side and the tent folded down on top of us. We unzipped the tent and went out in the pouring rain and wind and pulled the tent back up. We again set the stakes into the wet soil and pushed them down as far as we could get them in the hope that this time they would hold against the typhoon-like winds. I imagined this was what it was like for the Mongol fleets that twice tried to invade Japan during the thirteenth century only to be largely destroyed by typhoons that the thankful Japanese called *kamikaze* (divine winds). The Mongols failed both times, but Charlie and I succeeded our second time and the stakes held.

We got up the next morning and rode down the peninsula to the bottom. Then we headed north along the shore of a body of water known as the Anake Sea. At the north end of this sea we turned again in a southeasterly direction heading toward the city of Kumamoto.

At one point we were again off the coast and came to a fork in the road. Charlie and I both stopped our bikes in a parking lot in front of a fairly large, modern three-story rectangular building. We pulled out our map and were both looking at the Chinese characters on the street sign above us and trying to find the same characters on the map to try to figure out which way we should go. About thirty yards away, the front door of the building opened, and a policeman in uniform walked out carrying a metal tray with two glasses of ice water on it. We both watched incredulously as the policeman walked toward us. "Where do you think he's going with that tray?" I asked Charlie. "I don't know, but he's heading our way," Charlie responded with the obvious. He walked up to us, bowed, and offered us each a glass. We bowed and accepted this wonderful bounty. We explained as best we could that we wanted to head toward Kumamoto, and he pointed off to the right, which is what we had thought anyway. After gulping down the water we thanked him profusely saying, *"Arigato gozaimasu"* (thank you). Then we watched as he carried his tray back into the building, which we cleverly now assumed was most likely a police station.

"Can you imagine an American cop coming out and offering a couple of young sweaty foreign guys two glasses of ice water?" Charlie said.

"No, not really," I said. "In fact, I can't believe it just happened here."

"Amazing, isn't it?"

"Sure is, I'm flabbergasted!" I exclaimed.

Before reaching Kumamoto we again pitched our tent on the beach. We ate dinner at a small restaurant and then headed up the road toward what looked like a school. As usual I broke out into song and ran through a couple of Crosby, Stills & Nash songs, Neil Young's "Don't Let It Bring You Down," a Beatles tune or two, and then I sang the Dylan song that contains my all-time favorite Bob Dylan line:

> Genghis Khan and his brother Don
> Couldn't keep on keepin on."
> ("You Ain't Goin' Nowhere" by Nobel Prize Laureate Bob Dylan)

"As the Japanese say, 'No man is an island, but I can sing archipelago,'" I said.

"Not if you're Easter Island," Charlie retorted.

"Good point," I added.

By this time, we were nearly up to the school. I then ended my mini-concert with "The End" from Abbey Road. After I finished singing it, I contemplated the words of the song.

"You know; I don't agree with that. It's a bankrupt philosophy. If, when you die, the love you take and the love you make are equal, then you might as well not have lived."

"Yeah, it means your life changed nothing," Charlie said.

"Exactly, it should go," I started singing and I sang the last line my way, "the love you make should be greater than the love you take."

"That is better," Charlie said.

"If you create more love than you take, then your life has meaning. You've changed the world for the better, even if just a little bit. I think I'd better write Paul and tell him."

"Right, set him straight," Charlie said.

My version totally sums up my philosophy of life. Luther stated that it is faith alone that saves us, but I disagree. If faith alone saves us, then if Hitler, Pol Pot, Stalin, Mao, or insert your favorite murderous megalomaniac dictator's name here, on his death bed sincerely had faith then, according to my understanding of Luther, he'd be welcomed into heaven. Yet all the millions of people throughout history and even today who die without ever knowing of Christ or his message couldn't possibly have faith, and so they, I assume, are condemned to hell. Does this make any sense? The French theologian, John Calvin, on the other hand, expounded the doctrine of predestination, which again leaves me scratching my head. If we are predestined by God to do what we do, then how could God punish any of us after death? We just did what he predestined us to do. If there is any life after death, then I believe only by giving more love and kindness than we take in life can we possibly be invited to heaven, nirvana, Valhalla, or any other after-life. That, to me, is the only system that seems worthy of God. We won't get to heaven through faith alone, or by predestination, but only by doing good works. And, in addition, "You'll never get to heaven if you break my heart," I guarantee you that. ("You'll Never Get to Heaven" composed by Burt Bacharach, lyrics by Hal David, performed by Dionne Warwick)

Charlie and I walked up to the school and wandered into the gym where there were high school-aged young men doing Kendo. Kendo is a martial art where the opponents whack each other with wooden sword-like weapons. They wear helmets and padding for protection. They face off like fencers, and then all of a sudden one or the other of the pair would explode and lunge, often smacking the other person on the head with the stick. It seemed like they'd both end up with headaches, but it was fascinating to watch. Charlie and I stayed for an hour or so taking it all in. Then we hiked back to our tent, read for a while, and then crashed for the night.

The next morning, as we walked past the restaurant where we'd had dinner the night before, the elderly lady who had waited on us and who probably owned the place was out front sweeping the sidewalk. After we had just passed her she looked up and saw us. *"Ohio,"* she called out. I turned and said, "Michigan," while Charlie blurted out, "Texas," and we both laughed at our amusing jokes. *Ohio* must mean good morning we figured, although the higher form would be *Ohio gozaimasu!* Because she was elderly, it was perfectly acceptable for her to just say *Ohio* to us. Of course, she probably thought that Michigan and Texas meant good morning in English, thanks to us. This incident did teach us another Japanese word, adding to our ever-enlarging vocabulary of maybe a dozen words by this point.

As we neared Kumamoto, we saw off in the distance a hilltop stone-walled fortress with beautiful wooden buildings above the fortifications. This, we learned as we drove up to it, was Kumamoto Castle. I couldn't help thinking of a line from my college fraternity, Sigma Nu's, opening ceremony for its meetings, "The sentinels are vigilant, and the castle is secure." It's strange that I'd remember this having never been a "rah-rah!" fraternity kind of guy. Back in college I went on spring break to Fort Lauderdale for four years in a row. Walking around I'd often have a Sigma Nu shirt on, and we'd run into Sigma Nu frat brothers from other universities. Sometimes they'd give me the secret handshake, and I'd stare at my right hand as if to say, "What the hell?" The gung-ho frat guys would usually say, "Don't you know the secret handshake?" "Oh! No, I learned it and forgot it," I'd respond. Then, after a couple of minutes of conversation, I'd say, "Nice talkin' with ya," and get away. I was not interested at all in talking to some frat guys—gorgeous ladies, yes, frat guys, no thanks. Yet, oddly enough, the old castle line from the Monday night frat meetings came to mind, probably because I always thought it was a funny line.

When we reached the castle, we parked our bikes. Leaving everything except our new cameras on the back racks of the bikes and the bikes unlocked, we went in to sightsee. We never even bothered to buy locks for the bikes or our stuff because we had been told by many experienced travelers that stealing was unheard of in Japan. For whatever reason, this was the opposite of Korea, where stealing was rampant. No one ever dared leave anything unbolted, or it would go missing. Houses were never left unmanned (or unwomanned) in Korea. Someone always had to be at home in every house; if not, a thief would break in and steal the place blind. Apartments in large complexes were different—they were left unattended—but not individual houses. So being in Japan and not having to worry about theft was a real treat for us. One urban myth-type story about Japan is that an American once had something stolen. He began badmouthing the Japanese saying, "Right, who says the Japanese never steal anything?" Later, the Japanese police caught the offender, and it was another foreigner. *"Ah, sou desuka?"* (Is that so?)

Kumamoto Castle was originally built in the 1400s and is considered one of the three premier castles in Japan. The stone walls around the fortress were fascinating in that they curved up from the ground. It almost looked like you could run halfway up before it got too steep, and then you'd fall flat on your face and slide back down. I could see the cast of Monty Python doing just that in a movie. It wasn't until near the top that the walls became vertical. Inside the fortress there were numerous buildings, some with Samurai armor exhibits and all with beautiful silk-screens with nature scenes on them. We toured the castle buildings for a couple of hours and then returned to our unmolested bikes.

South of Kumamoto we came to a small town and decided to stay there for the night. On the edge of town was a small Shinto shrine where we placed our tent, sleeping bags, and duffel bags inside a pavilion. Rather than put up our tent, we decided to go into town for dinner first, and then we'd set up our camping site later. We rode our bikes to a restaurant and leisurely ordered and ate our dinners. Suddenly, it began pouring rain with thunder and lightning. We sat hoping it would let up, but even after we had finished our meal and waited for another hour it continued to come down intensely. We finally asked if there was a *ryokan* (inn) nearby. One patron spoke some English and suggested we follow his car, and he would lead us to the nearest one. He jumped in his car. We rode along behind him on our bikes, and by the time we got to the inn, we were dripping wet. After creating a good-sized lake under us in front of the check-in desk, we were taken to a room. We took off our shoes and entered. After more than two weeks of camping out, what a treat this was! There were cozy navy blue and white patterned cotton robes, which we got into immediately after getting out of our wet clothes. Then we flipped a coin. Charlie won and got to shower first. In our room were the cutest legless chairs. I sat down in one with my legs crossed under me, turned on the TV, and watched a Japanese soap opera about pre-industrial Japan. I couldn't understand a word of what was going on, but it was fun to watch the action and see the costumes. After I showered, we discussed whether to keep heading south, circumnavigating the whole island, or heading inland and up toward Mt. Aso, Japan's largest active volcano in Aso Kuju National Park. We decided to head inland. Shortly after deciding, we quickly both hit the hay and slept like babies without colic.

We paid our bill the next morning and headed back to the Shinto shrine to retrieve our stuff. After strapping down our bags and tent onto our bikes we headed a little north and then turned onto a two-lane road heading east and inland toward Mt. Aso. At first, the incline wasn't too bad as we headed east and into the interior of the island.

The farther we got from the shore, the more sparsely settled it became. After a while there were areas of grassland with herds of cattle grazing, and it seemed like we were in the western U.S. We half expected to see cowboys riding the range. The road kept heading upward though. At one point, a couple of Japanese guys on bikes passed us by. This was fine with me, but it got Charlie's goat, and he started riding faster to catch them. I tried for a while to keep up and then said to hell with it. Charlie was trucking on ahead, and I fell back. I lost sight of him around the next crurve in hot pursuit of the Japanese guys. I moseyed on along taking it easy and eventually ran into Charlie waiting alongside the road. I don't think I bothered asking what happened to the Japanese bikers. I really didn't care.

As we got closer and closer to Mt. Aso and higher and higher above sea level, we sometimes had to get off our bikes when the incline got too steep and walk them up the steepest places. At those times we mispronounced Mt. Aso, dropping the "o," adding another "s," then an "h" and three other letters. "Ah, honorable Mt. Asshole," we'd say and then laugh our rear ends off, which made it harder to ride our bikes, of course. Then we'd double down, keep pumping those pedals, and head ever higher. As we got closer, off in the distance we could see smoke rising from the cauldron. "Double, double toil and trouble; Fire burn and cauldron bubble," as ol' William Shakespeare said oh, so well in Macbeth.

The third afternoon after leaving the coast, we rode past a huge hotel and resort complex. Charlie and I both looked with longing eyes at this Shangri-La and both blurted out at the same time, "Why don't we stay here tonight?" Good idea, that, and we drove up to the entrance, parked our bikes, and walked inside. It was a bit pricey, but we booked a room. Exhausted and soaking wet with sweat, we again took turns showering. Then we turned on the TV, and there was an American special on with Sammy Davis, Jr. and many famous jazz musicians and singers. The most amazing part of the show was when a jazz drummer played what seemed to be several improvised drum solos, and then Sammy Davis, Jr. would replicate the exact same sound with his tap dancing. American music and entertainment is second to none, we both agreed. Later in the afternoon, we both napped for an hour and then we decided to try the bath house attached to the hotel. It was huge and looked great—all hot and steamy—until we walked in and the sulphur smell nearly bowled us over. Deciding we would not be able to take the odor, we backed out and went off to dinner instead.

At the crack of dawn, we were up and chomping at the bit to get on the road again. As we were strapping our stuff onto the back racks on our bikes we noticed a big tour bus with its door opened. We looked in, and there was a television sitting on the dashboard. We watched as the driver got in and started up the engine. When he put the bus into reverse the television came on showing what was behind the bus. There was a TV camera in the back of the bus giving the driver a view of everything that was behind him. What a brilliant idea! It was two decades or more before I noticed any American bus with a similar setup. It was like we had entered a science fiction movie here in Japan. There were so many technologies we had never seen before, from self-opening doors to computer games to buses with rearview cameras and television screens.

We climbed aboard our bicycles, and up, up we pedaled for hours. Then finally the road started heading downward. We hung on for dear life and held our brakes tight the whole way for kilometer after kilometer of windy, hairpin turns and steep, downward slopes. After a couple of hours or more of coasting and constantly clutching our brakes, we arrived in the eastern coastal city of Beppu. The whole city is powered by thermal energy. There are pipes sticking out of the ground all over the city with steam pouring out of them. It didn't seem to smell like sulfur, but the whole town was covered in misty clouds from all these pipes bringing up the steam from deep within the bowels of the earth. We rode through Beppu heading in a northerly direction as dusk was descending on the town.

The town seemed to go on and on along the coast, and we needed to find a place to pitch our tent. Off to our left we saw a building that looked like it might be a Buddhist temple. We decided to ride up the side street and check it out. As we drove through the large wooden main gate into the temple complex, we saw a young Japanese boy standing on the wooden porch of a building next to the main temple. As we made what we thought must be the universal gesture for sleep (holding the palms together and putting the hands next to the head while tilting the head sideways) we said in English, "Can we sleep here in our tent?" The boy, sounding like any American kid, said with no accent whatsoever, "Wait for a minute and let me ask my father." Charlie and I looked at each other dumbfounded. His father came out along with the boy we had just spoken to and two other children. We explained to the father, a Buddhist monk (there are some sects of Buddhism in which monks can marry), that we were caught late here in Beppu and wondered if we could pitch our tent in the grassy area next to the temple and sleep here. He told us that would be OK as long as we were packed and gone before 8:00 a.m. because there was an event happening the next morning. We assured him that we'd be up and out at dawn.

Naturally, we asked how it was that he spoke English so well and how his son spoke without any accent at all. It turned out he had been in charge of a Buddhist temple in California for many years, and his children had all been born in the States. They had just a few months earlier returned to Beppu and this temple. We sat for a while talking with his kids and enjoying their fluency. We had not met anyone else fluent in English on the whole trip except, of course, for the American sailors we had run into near the Sasebo Naval Base.

At dawn, we were up and out before we saw or heard any activity in the monk's household. We left a thank-you note and took off heading north. It was only a couple of days of easy riding before we reached Kitakyushu, the northern-most city on the island. We took the tunnel again back to Shimonoseki and rode our bikes to the same two shops where we had bought them. We asked if the owners wanted to buy their bikes back, and they did. They made offers that seemed very reasonable to us, especially seeing that we had put a lot of wear and tear on the bikes; the tires were well worn and the brakes pretty much shot after our long descent from Mt. Aso (Asshole). There were tickets available for that evening's ferry back to Busan, and we bade our fare-thee-wells to Japan.

We had enjoyed Japan immensely. Some of the differences between Korea and Japan were startling. It was not only the technological differences noted earlier, which even made the U.S. seem backward by comparison, but also the personality differences between the two. Japan was a developed, modern, industrialized country. Korea, although it had already come a long way by 1973, was still developing and still throwing off some of the old feudal mannerisms. In

Japan we were never followed by youngsters yelling "Hello!" at the top of their lungs. We did once hear some school kids call us *gaijin* (foreigners), but that only happened once and they weren't yelling it, just pointing out the obvious. The lack of petty thievery was nice, as was the lack of bargaining all the time as the Koreans loved to do. Another difference was that the Japanese controlled their emotions much more than the Koreans did. The Koreans wear their emotions often on their sleeves. You know when a Korean is mad. With the Japanese, you're not sure. Sometimes, the Japanese would bow and smile when we had the sneaking suspicion they were really angry and gritting their teeth. After nearly a month in Japan, both Charlie and I were happy and anxious to get back to Korea and the Korean people we loved. The Koreans just seemed more honest, more down to earth, and less tightly wound than the Japanese. We missed that. Some of these differences may be due to the contrasts between an island people and a continental people. In Japan there is nowhere to run, nowhere to hide. Koreans could and sometimes did take off to Manchuria or the Russian maritime coastal area. That's why one of the provinces in China along the border with North Korea is a semi-autonomous Korean-speaking province today and why there was a Russian gymnast named Nellie Kim who won several gold medals at the 1976 and 1980 Olympic Games. (She was of Korean ancestry.)

Another thing that bothered me about Japan was the food portion sizes. They seemed tiny to me. I often left the table still hungry. In Korea we always got a big bowl of rice; in Japan it was half the size. I always easily ate all the rice in the Korean rice bowl. In addition, Korean restaurants would always give you more kimchee and other side dishes if you asked for them. I'd often eat every scrap of food on the table in Korea and ask for more. In Japan I'd often leave the table with a half-empty stomach. While Koreans were happy when you heartily ate and obviously liked their food, the Japanese didn't seem to care about that. The Japanese seemed more interested in the visual presentation of the food. They wanted it to look nice. Again, the Koreans seemed more down to earth and cared more about the quantity than about how attractively arranged it was. I was always popular with Koreans because I ate like a horse, and this made them glad that I appreciated their culinary efforts.

It wasn't just the quantity that I missed, though. It was also the flavors. Japanese food just seemed bland to me compared to the heavy use of hot peppers and garlic in Korean food. I needed quantity and flavor—some would say pungency. Supposedly, the Japanese used to call the Koreans "garlic eaters" as a derogatory term. I was happy and downright proud to be a "garlic eater," thank you very much.

After returning to Busan on the ferry, Charlie headed back to Yeongju, and I went up to Seoul on my own. Walking around in the Peace Corps office singing (as per my usual), I ran into Miss Lee, Soo-yun, one of the secretaries. We started talking, and she asked if I would like to accompany her and the Peace Corps driver to take some papers down to the new summer training site located in Cheongju, the capital of Chungcheongbuk-do (North Chungcheong Province)—the province "with no curfew." Always anxious for a new experience, I agreed to go with her. So in the Peace Corps vehicle with the Peace Corps driver at the wheel, we headed down to Cheongju. When we got to the training site Miss Lee told me she needed an hour or so, and then we would be returning to Seoul. I wandered into the trainee's lounge and during their break talked with some of them about how much I loved both teaching and Korea. Having drunk too much coffee, which, thanks to Charlie, I was now addicted to, I walked into the men's bathroom. While standing at the urinal, emptying my dragon (as we PCV men sometimes said), I was singing:

> Lies, lies, you're breakin' my heart.
> ("Lies" written by Beau Charles and Buddy Randell, performed by
> The Knickerbockers)

A guy walked in, sauntered up to the urinal next to me, and said, "The Knickerbockers, 1965."

"Yeah, I think that's right."

"I know it's right," he cockily responded. The voice sounded familiar. I looked over to my left and, lo and behold, it was Tom Tokyo.

"Wait, your name's Tom, isn't it?"

"Yes, hey, I remember you. I met you in Seoul last winter. How's Nick?"

"Nick's fine as far as I know," I said, already getting tired of conversing with Mr. Smarty Pants, but I asked, "What are you doing here?"

"Oh, after talking with you guys last winter, I applied to the Peace Corps. I got accepted, and here I am."

"No kidding?" I added for emphasis.

I walked out of the bathroom, and Miss Lee was looking for me. It was time for us to get going back to Seoul. I waved back to Tom, who was just coming out of the john too and said, "See you around." Oddly enough, though, I never did see him again, so I have to imagine that he crashed and burned like so many other overly energetic and often overly idealistic PCV trainees.

Back in Seoul, walking near the Kolon building on my way to Myeong-dong, I ran into Alan Custer. Alan had been in the same group as Glenn up the coast from me in Kangnung. On a couple of occasions when in Seoul, Charlie and I had hung out with Alan and his friend Larry Lathrup. I was surprised to see Alan as I'd heard that he'd left Korea early.

"What are you doing back in Korea?" I asked.

"I'm teaching in Japan, and we had a couple days off, so I came for a visit."

"You're kidding. Where in Japan are you teaching?"

"In Kobe at the YMCA there."

"Really!" I said.

You'd think I would have broken into the song: "YMCA, why don't we stay at the YMCA, A!" ("Y.M.C.A." written by Jacques Morali and Victor Willis, performed by the Village People) But unfortunately, in 1973 it hadn't come out yet. It came out in 1978.

"Yes, I got back to the States and found out about this teaching opportunity in Japan, so I jumped right on it. Unlike Peace Corps, they pay really well."

"Neat. You remember Charlie Sarnia, don't you?"

"Sure, I remember Charlie."

"Well, he and I just spent the summer bike hiking around Kyushu and had a blast. I met a cute Japanese gal on the beach near Nagasaki, and I hope to return to Japan sometime soon to see her again."

"Hey, if you do, stop in the Kobe YMCA and look me up. You can crash at my place."

"Sounds good, you may see me before you know it." We parted, and I planned to take him up on his offer sometime.

It was now the end of my first summer vacation in Korea. Charlie and I had had a blast bike hiking around Kyushu, but it was now time to get back to Mukho and my beloved teaching.

Fall Semester 1973: Dog Pancake

Don and Mr. Hyun in front of the largest of the Shamanistic towers.

Quickly back in the groove in the fall, I was teaching the same schedule as the previous spring with Mondays, Wednesdays, Fridays, and half the day on Saturdays at Mukho (Boys') Middle School and Tuesdays and Thursdays at Mukho Girls' Middle School, but the students were all new, as this was the beginning of a new school year. I again had a special class at each school with the fifteen best new first-year students. My co-teacher stayed the same at the girls' middle school, but I had a new co-teacher at the boys' middle school. Mr. Jun, In-kook was transferred away, and my new co-teacher was Mr. Hyun, Jong-jin. He had just graduated from college and was also as yet unmarried. His English was very good. We quickly fell into a routine and taught together well.

Mr. Hyun and I sometimes would hike together on the weekends. The first time we did so, I took him up to the Shamanistic towers not far outside of town. We were standing there talking when I noticed a man, who looked to be a farmer, walking up from the west side of the large hill that these towers stood on top of. Every few minutes I looked down and saw him getting closer and closer. When he reached the top, he walked right up to me, bowed, and began talking in very honorific Korean. I bowed back. After he finished speaking, I asked Mr. Hyun what he had said. The gist of his story was that many years ago an American had sent him a Bible just after the Korean War—probably through some nonprofit organization. I was the first American he had ever seen, and he just wanted to thank me for the kindness some American had shown him. Again, as with the man who thanked me at Naksan Buddhist Temple for the United States of America having expelled the North Koreans, I was deeply moved by this farmer's gratitude. After Mr. Hyun finished translating, I said in Korean something like, "Don't mention it." The farmer then turned around and walked back down the hill and headed back to work in his field.

One of the first days back at the girls' middle school I was up on the roof of the building during a break. The stairways at both ends of the middle school building went up to the roof, and students and teachers could go up there to a deck-like area and get some fresh air. Since the school was right near the crest of the pass that led between the small mountain (or large hill) to the east that fell into the East Sea (Sea of Japan) and the one to the west that rolled on into larger and larger mountains, there was an excellent view of much of Mukho from up here. As I was gazing off into the distance, one of my new first-year middle school students began talking with me. She saw a taxi going by on the road and asked in Korean, "How do you say taxi in English?" There was no word for taxi in Korean, so they used the English word and pronounced it "tak-she." I laughed and explained in Korean that "tak-she" is an English word, and we say "taxi" in English. "No," she informed me, "that's the Korean word. What is the English word for tak-she?" I gave up and said, "Cab." "Oh," she said and happily wandered away.

Mr. Jong, Chul-chin, the English teacher whose home I had lived in during my first several months in Mukho, was transferred from the boys' middle school to the girls' this fall of 1973. I had to think that Mr. Jong's mother must have bribed someone to get this special treatment. All of the other teachers I had known so far who were transferred were sent to a different town or city. Not once before or after did I see another teacher transferred to a school in the same town. Also, all of the teachers I knew whose spouses were also teachers were assigned to different places than their spouses. Some of them were in sites that were hours apart by train or bus, and they only saw each other on holidays. There was no effort by the provincial education ministry to place married teachers together, and yet here Mr. Jong got to transfer across town to a school that was still only a twenty-minute walk from his home instead of his two-minute walk to the boys' school.

I'd often run into Mr. Jong on my way up the hill from downtown going toward the girls' middle school on Tuesdays and Thursdays, and we'd walk together on our way to work. Then one day he shot by on a motorcycle. He saw me and stopped and said in Korean, "Mr. Ha, please get on." So I did, and he often gave me a ride up the hill after that. The next Saturday after class he saw me and invited me to ride with him south to Bupyeong. I jumped on, and when we were about halfway to Bupyeong he pulled over and said, "Here, you drive." So I jumped on the front, and I drove off with him on the back through Bupyeong and part of the way down to Samcheok, where Bob Saks had been assigned until he left early. Then we switched, and Mr. Jong drove back. In the middle of Bupyeong we saw an army truck coming from the opposite direction. Because the streets were very narrow, we got as far over to the right side as we could. A dog was startled by the truck noise, ran into the front tire of the motorcycle, and fell under the tire of the large truck. Its head was sticking out toward us, and Mr. Jong and I watched as it writhed in agony while the truck made a pancake out of its body. I was sickened and nearly upchucked my lunch. Mr. Jong began laughing this high-pitched grotesque laughter that was just eerie. His laughter made the horror of the event even worse. The truck driver stopped with the dog trapped under the tire. One of the soldiers in the back bed of the truck looked down saw the dog and motioned for the driver to continue on. Thankfully, Mr. Jong hit the throttle, and we also left the scene.

Several months earlier, while I was living at Mr. Jong's house, I was on the cement slab porch in front of the house when their small dog began yelping and running around in circles like a headless Banshee hen. Then it fell over dead with foam coming out of its mouth. Again, I was horrified, especially because Mr. Jong had laughed the same high-pitched squealing way he did this day in Bupyeong. In both cases, I came to the conclusion that it was a nervous reaction and decided that he should not be reported for animal cruelty. I had the feeling their dog must have eaten rat poison, but I never asked him what had happened.

One Tuesday a couple of weeks later, I came out of the side street that went back to Mukho Theater and my *yeogwan* and onto the main street that led up to the girls' school when I saw Mr. Jong walking towards me.

"Mr. Jong, where's your motorcycle?" I asked in Korean.

"My mother made me sell it."

"Oh, sorry to hear that," I replied. We walked along for quite a while in silence. I didn't want to ask him for any more details, and he obviously didn't want to give any. But, as I had been told by some of the teachers at the boys' middle school, his mother controlled the purse strings in the family, and she owned the home in which they all lived. If she decided he shouldn't have a motorcycle, then that was that.

One morning, while sitting in the teachers' office at the boys' middle school, one of the Korean language teachers walked up to me in the teachers' office.

"Mr. Ha, there's an American Peace Corps Volunteer at the *bogunso* (health center)."

"Really? Do you know his name?" I asked.

"No, but he just arrived a few days ago."

"Have you seen him around town?"

"No, just heard he had begun working last Monday."

"Thanks, I will have to try to find him."

So, there was another PCV in "my" town. I was kind of hoping he'd go away like the previous one had the fall before, but I soon ran into him on the street downtown. His name was John Hudson, and he was living in the home of the *bogun-so* director—his boss. A few days later, I ran into him again, and he asked if I would like to study taekwondo with him. The *bogun-so* director had introduced him to a semi-retired taekwondo instructor who had a local *dojang* (gym). Charlie and I had always joked that taekwondo was where you kicked someone in the crotch and then ran away. Then we'd both crack up. But it sounded like a good way to get into better shape, so I told John I'd be interested. "Meet me tonight at the Rose of Sharon Tearoom at 6:30 pm," he suggested. "Then we'll go over and meet Mr. Chae, Myung-ho, the taekwondo instructor." "OK," I said, "sounds good."

John and I drank a cup of coffee together at the tearoom. Then we went over to a tailoring shop that Mr. Chae's wife owned. After we'd talked a while with Mr. Chae, he suggested we have class five nights a week from 7:00 to 8:00 pm Monday through Friday. We'd be his only students during that time period, so it was essentially private instruction. He did teach a youth class, but it was earlier. He named a fee, which seemed very reasonable, and we both agreed. "Come with me," he said. We followed him to his *dojang* up the hill behind his wife's shop. It was an old wooden slat building not unlike the school building I taught in at the boys' school and also with no heat. He unlocked a combination padlock on the door, turned on the lights, and we looked around. There was a small area behind a wall to the left to change in and hooks to hang our clothes on. Also, near the door was a large punching/kicking bag filled with sand. The rest of the room was open with a wooden floor and some benches on the sides. On the far wall there hung a large Korean flag and Mr. Chae's sixth-degree Black Belt certificate. He asked for some money to purchase our *dobok* (taekwondo clothing), which we gave him, and we agreed to return the next night. From that point on every night Monday through Friday, John and I got taekwondo lessons from Mr. Chae. After a few weeks, I asked for the padlock combination, and I went every morning around 6:15 a.m. and worked out by myself for a half hour or so, mostly kicking and punching the living shit out of that very heavy, solid punching bag. Quickly we learned the different stances, as well as hand and foot techniques. Once proficient in these, we also began learning the set patterns in order to earn the different color belts and move up in rank.

John was from New York and was very clean cut; he kept his hair short the whole time he was in Mukho and never grew any facial hair. But he did have an earring, which for men was quite unusual even in the States in the mid-1970s. I can't remember which ear he had the earring in, nor can I remember which side meant what. Many said an earring in one side meant that you were gay and in the other straight or some such nonsense. I really couldn't have cared less, except that one evening after taekwondo we stopped for a coffee at a tearoom, and we ran into a couple of my fellow teachers. After we'd been talking a bit, one of them asked John why he had an earring, and he replied, *"Miguk gwanseub,"* (American custom). Under my breath, I said in English, "Don't tell them it's a damn American custom, cuz then they'll wonder why I don't have one." Then he turned and explained that it was really a state of New York custom. "That's better," I told him.

Down in Samcheok, where Bob (Suck, No Bean) had been a volunteer until he left early, there was another PCV also from John's training group at the Samcheok *bogun-so*. His name was Chris Sombra, and every once in awhile John and I would head down to Samcheok to see him, or he'd swing up to Mukho. Most weekends, though, John would go his way, and I'd go mine. Usually I still walked for hours every Saturday after classes ended and on Sundays too. On days of inclement weather, I'd read and lesson plan.

I got a note from Glenn up in Kangnung saying that Bill Comb was going to visit him because Bill's school was doing testing and he was skipping out. I always stayed when our students did their testing, but evidently Bill didn't think it important for him to be there. On Saturday, Glenn said they'd come down for a visit. Of course, I met them at the train station. Upon getting off the train Bill again said, "How do you stand the smell?" "You'll get used to it just like you did the last time," I responded. We wandered around town for a while and then hit a tearoom. We all ordered coffee, and the tearoom lady brought us three half-filled cups of coffee as per the usual. Bill yelled at the young tearoom hostess in Korean, "I want a full cup of coffee." She looked scared. This was obviously CIS (Culturally InSensitive) and just outrageous behavior. The Korean male patrons in the place were staring. I looked at Bill and said under my breath, but I'm sure still rather loudly in English, "If you want a damn full cup of coffee, order two and pour them together. You know perfectly well every tearoom always serves half a cup. Don't act like an idiot and yell like that in my town. I have to live here, and

I don't want them to think Americans are all jackasses. If you want to act like one, then get out of my town." Bill looked kind of sheepish and apologized to me. I turned to the tearoom gal, who still looked frightened, and apologized in Korean to her. The conversation dragged, and I sat thinking I should not have written the letter on his behalf last spring when he visited. Maybe the training staff was right, and they should have sent him home. I had heard from others that he was a problem, and though he'd only been in Mukho for a couple of hours, I already wanted him gone. We ate dinner at a restaurant and then had a couple of beers. When Bill went to the bathroom, Glenn apologized for Bill's behavior, and when he returned to our table Glenn suggested that they catch the late train back to Kangnung, which they did. *Good riddance!* I said to myself.

During a long holiday weekend in the fall, I took the train down to Yeongju to see Charlie. Rhonda Romulus, a fellow K-23 trainee and good friend of Lisa's, was visiting Lisa Golly the same weekend. When I got off the train Charlie told me we were going to have dinner with them. They came up to Charlie's place.

"I'm still mad at you," Lisa said right away.

"Why?" I asked innocently.

"Some of my special class students from last year are still singing, 'Deck the halls with Lisa Golly,' whenever they see me."

"My, they have long memories, don't they?"

"So do I, and you better be careful."

"I will, cuz I don't like it when you're mad at me." We both laughed. The conversation wandered to other topics, and we talked until after dark. Then we decided to head downtown for dinner. As we were getting our shoes on outside of Charlie's room, I said, "Hang on a minute. I have to hit the outhouse first." Off I went into the dark far corner of the open space where the wooden outhouse sat. I opened the door and went in, aiming the stream as best as I could in the dark. Then, as I stepped out, I began singing "Monster Mash" and dancing like the Frankenstein monster:

> As my monster from the table began to rise
> He did the mash, he did the Monster Mash.
> (Written by Bobby Pickett and Lenny Capizzi, as performed by Bobby
> "Boris" Pickett and the Crypt Kickers.)

Charlie, Rhonda, and Lisa joined in. All four of us were singing and dancing in the dark while laughing uproariously. After several encores, we ran out of energy and headed off for dinner.

Back in Mukho a few weeks later, I walked into the post office one after-noon to buy several aerograms and some stamps. I walked up to the counter and noticed there was a new young lady working there. She was very lovely with long, thick, beautiful jet black hair. I began babbling as per my usual, mentioning the good weather, sunshine, and whatever else came to mind. Then she asked if I lived in the Changshin Yeogwan. I was taken aback, but I quickly gained my composure and told her that she was correct. Of course, being the only American living downtown, everyone probably knew where I lived.

The next Sunday I was reading *Buddhism: Its Essence and Development,* by Edward Conze, after having taken a long walk when a knock came at my door. I opened it to find the post office gal standing there with a pair of ice skates over her shoulder. I was surprised but invited her in.

"Hi, what's your name?"

"Cho, Myung-hui."

"Miss Cho, I'm Ha, Doe-young."

"I know," she said.

"What are the skates for?" I asked.

"I told my parents I was going ice skating," she replied.

"Oh! Do you live in Mukho?"

"No, in Bupyeong."

"Is that so?" I responded and thought to myself, *"That's good!"* It wouldn't be kosher for a Mukho gal to be visiting my room unaccompanied. She told me that she had graduated from high school a couple of years earlier and had been working off and on at different places. Her father was a doctor in Bupyeong. Through connec-tions he had gotten her the job at the post office, but she didn't like it. We talked a while, and then she announced that she had to go back home. I walked her out to the main entrance of the *yeogwan* and thanked her for visiting.

The next week when I went to the post office Miss Cho was nowhere to be seen. *"Guess she 'really' disliked her job,"* I thought. Then the next Saturday night, a knock came at the door of my room. When I opened it the lady who ran the place told me I had a phone call. This was a first. I had never gotten a phone call at the *yeogwan* before. When I picked up the phone it was Miss Cho. She was drunk. She was at another place with her friend, Miss Shin, Kyung-ok, and two Korean soldiers. She told me that she didn't want to stay with them. She wanted me to come and get her. She was at a place called Daehung Hasuk on the corner, where the theater was, only about fifty yards away from the Changshin Yeogwan where I stayed. (*Hasuk* technically means boarding house, but in this case most of the rooms were rented out nightly like a *yeogwan*.) I told her I'd be right over and

Cho, Myung-hui at Kyungpodae.

nearly ran down the alley. There she was standing in front of the place. As I got near her, I could see a Korean soldier in uniform just inside the doorway of the Daehung Hasuk glaring at me. I glared back and escorted Miss Cho back to my place.

After that night, every few weeks she'd call or stop by my room and tell me to get on the Saturday 1:15 p.m. train going north to Kangnung. She'd get on it in Bupyeong, and then I'd get on in Mukho. I'd look for her, and then we'd sit together for the hour-long train ride to Kangnung. Once there we'd either hang out on the beach of Kyungpodae or in downtown Kangnung somewhere. I had no way to contact her, and sometimes weeks would go by before she'd contact me again.

The fall semester was drawing to a close. Meanwhile, on the culinary front, new and better cookies suddenly appeared in all the small *gages* (stores) across South Korea. The British company McVities entered the Korean marketplace. The McVities Digestives were my favorite. They were such a huge improvement over the previously available Korean brands. Of course, over time the Korean brands also improved in order to compete, and all was well in our little world.

Korean *gages* were almost always run by women. If the husband was around he'd be sitting like a bump on a log while the wife did all the stock work, the selling, and usually the cashiering. The women seemed to have also done all the selecting of merchandise and the bookkeeping too. Charlie and I always joked that without the women, who seemed to run all the small stores and many small businesses, the whole country would collapse. The women all seemed to have an intelligent gleam in their eyes; many men, in the countryside at least, not so much.

One of the first things I had done after returning to Mukho at the end of summer vacation was to write to Misako in Japan. She wrote right back, and we began a voluminous correspondence. I told her that I wanted to see her again and that I would visit her during our winter break around Christmas. She invited me to come, and she told me that I could stay at her brother and sister-in-law's house, as they would be away over the holidays. Oh, there were amorous thoughts a-running through my head. The semester came to a close before Christmas 1973, and I again went to Seoul to get my passport.

CHAPTER 10

Winter Break '73–'74: Better late than never, but better never late!

I still have the official Peace Corps "Leave Request" form that I filled out for this winter vacation trip to Japan. The "Period of Leave" was from December 20, 1973, to January 5, 1974, and under "Itinerary, Place" I wrote Kurume, Japan—Misako's hometown. This form was signed by my Regional Representative, Song, Jun-ki, and the Director PC/Korea, Jon Kalkaska. Jon was the new director and had taken Jim Wixom's place. So five days before Christmas Day, I headed from Seoul down to Busan and got on the ferry—alone this time. But now I had no worries, as I was an experienced Japan traveler by this point. I knew a few phrases in Japanese and had the lay of the land figured out. As soon as I got off the ferry the next morning, I headed to the Shimonoseki Train Station and bought a ticket to Kurume. Misako met me at the station and announced that she had a bad cold. Her parents had told her not to leave the house, but thankfully she told them that she must do so; otherwise, I would have been a lonely *gaijin* (foreigner) stranded in a nondescript Japanese town.

But there was further bad news. Her brother and sister-in-law had not left town, so I couldn't stay at their house. Misako instead showed me to a *ryokan* (inn). The *ryokan* was a lovely traditional Japanese-style building. It was late in the afternoon by then. She was feeling very ill and, apologizing profusely, told me she would see me the next morning after resting. So much for the enchanted evening I had been looking forward to. I wandered out, had dinner, and bought a can of beer out of one of the vending machines out on the sidewalk that you would see all over Japan. Anyone could walk up and use them, but evidently this didn't cause the problems that such a system in the U.S. would obviously cause. I went back to the *ryokan*, took a bath, and watched Japanese television while drinking the beer. The movie I watched was interesting. It had something to do with a whorehouse. Suddenly, a fire broke out and topless ladies of the evening started running out of their rooms and out onto the street followed by a lot of semi-clothed, rather heavyset, older men. That was fun—the topless women part, not the semi-clothed older men—but I had no idea what the plot was supposed to be. After a while I shut off the TV and read *Gullible's Travels, Etc.* by Ring Lardner, for an hour or two. At some point I looked at the back of the door and saw the nightly rate for the room. *"Holy shit!"* I thought. At that price I'd be out of money really quickly. I decided to ask Misako to take me to a less expensive place the next day. She obviously didn't understand that as a Peace Corps Volunteer I was not making much money. She must have figured that because Japanese teachers made a good salary then I must be making a boatload (or is it a shipload?) of money too.

Next morning, I explained my predicament. She understood, and we went down to check out. This took some time, as she had to explain why I was leaving early when she had already told them I'd stay for a couple of nights. It involved a lot of talking and apologizing and bowing back and forth by all three of us.

Misako took me to a much more affordable nondescript, western-style, motel-like place. Then we were off to visit her home, so I could meet her parents and have lunch there. I presented them with a large box of Korean Ginseng Tea, which is purported to be the best in the world. They seemed pleased, but then Japanese always do, don't they? Anyway, we had a lovely lunch, and I explained to them with Misako translating about how I had volunteered to teach English in Korea to help Korea develop and to increase cross-cultural understanding between Koreans and Americans. Misako's father told me about his taxi company. He had evidently done very well because they had—for Japan— quite a large house. It did not seem like the usual "rabbit hutch-sized" dwellings that most Japanese lived in. Even in the early 1970s, and even though Japan was much wealthier than Korea at the time, most Koreans had larger homes and apartments than most Japanese. Fascinating, isn't it? Again, maybe it was a matter of continental people (even if they lived on a small peninsula) versus island people.

Misako and Don in the lobby of the motel.

Following lunch Misako and I did some shopping and sightseeing. We made a visit to the local Shinto shrine. Misako explained to me that you had to wash your hands before presenting yourself before the shrine. "Cleanliness is next to godliness, after all," I said. She looked at me quizzically. Anyway, we washed our hands at a well and then approached the shrine. There Misako clapped, explaining that this was to awaken the god or gods to our presence. I'm thinking, *"If they are gods, shouldn't they know we came?"* but this time, I didn't say anything. There also was a tree with papers folded and tied to the branches, which were people's supplications. I could think of no entreaty that was an appropriate prayer to hang on the tree, so I didn't do that. After dinner and a couple of drinks, Misako again dropped me off at the motel.

On my third day in Japan (Monday, December 23, 1974), Misako and I got on the train heading north. I bought a ticket to Osaka, and then I planned to head over to Kobe where I hoped to find the YMCA and crash with Alan Custer for a few days to save having to pay for lodging. Misako was heading up to see her grandmother in a small town just south of Kitakyushu. As we sat together Misako gave me several little presents: a little ceramic frog, a 1964 100 yen Olympic commemorative coin, a little notebook, and a couple of other little things. (The Japanese love little things so much.) I was especially interested in the coin, being a longtime numismatist and all, while the other things were just tchotchkes to me. But I made a point of making a big deal over each one and thanking her profusely, especially since I had no gift for her. When we got to the town her grandmother lived in, we stood up, I thanked her, and we bowed to each other. I was disappointed that we never got past a formal friendship, but we did stay in touch with each other by mail for another year or so. By then, though, she had gotten engaged, and our correspondence ceased.

I got off the train in Osaka. Osaka is a huge city, and I walked through an underground shopping area that seemed to go on endlessly. After having a meal, I bought a ticket for the short commuter train ride to Kobe, which is very close to Osaka.

Once in Kobe, I found that the YMCA was a short walk from the train station, and I strolled on over. In the lobby, I inquired about the English Language program and asked if Mr. Alan Custer was teaching today. He was, and I was told where to find him. Walking toward his classroom, I ran into him in the hall.

"Alan, I'm taking you up on your offer!" I yelled over the noise of all the Japanese students talking in the hallway.

"Good timing and bad timing on your part," he said.

"How so?"

"The good part is that today is our last day of classes, and you can attend the staff year-end party this evening."

"Great, what's the bad part?"

"The bad part is that I'm headed to Korea tomorrow with my roommate, Sonny, and another American teacher, Cher."

"You're kidding," I exclaimed.

"No, Sonny and Cher want to see Korea, and I told them I'd be their tour guide, but you can crash at my apartment as long as you'd like while we're gone."

"Thanks, I may hang out a few days and then head down to Kyoto before my money gets close to running out. A few days here will let me extend my stay. Otherwise, I'd be heading back pretty quickly."

"Sounds good. I've got one more class, so let me show you where the staff lounge is and you can hang out there." Alan took me to the lounge where I met Sonny Sylvan and Cher Alma. They all three went back to teach their last classes for the afternoon, which were also the last classes for the semester.

At the party, Alan tried to talk me into taking part in a skit that they had planned.

"Here, take this football." He handed me a small, about eight-inch long, brown American football.

"Why?"

"Put it under your shirt, and when we give you a sign you pretend to take a dump and let it fall out of your shirt and bounce on the floor."

"You've got to be kidding!"

"No, the Japanese love scatological humor. You'll be the hit of the show."

"That's all right. I'd rather be the wallflower of the party. I'll hide over there while you guys do your little shit, I mean skit, thing."

"OK, but you're missing your chance for stardom."

"I'd rather stick with anonymity. But thanks anyway."

When they did their skit, I slid to the back of the crowd of Japanese YMCA employees who enthusiastically watched the American language teachers. They spoke in Japanese, so I didn't follow what they said, but at one point Alan squatted down and pretended to poop out the turd-shaped football. As it bounced on the floor, the roar of acclamation was deafening. Alan was right; the Japanese really loved scatological humor. Still, I was just as happy to not be a part of what seemed so childish to me. Maybe if I was still in kindergarten—but then again, maybe not even then.

During my travels in Japan, besides the Ring Lardner book, I was also reading a humorous book by a British author who wrote about what he saw as funny aspects of the Japanese culture, such as their great love for scatological humor. I finished it while in Kobe and left it there for Sonny and Alan to read. Unfortunately, I forgot to write down the title and author as I virtually always have done for every book I've read since joining the Peace Corps. Consequently, I can't remember the author's name or the title of the book, but it was funny. In one part he wrote about how using Chinese characters (as the Japanese, Chinese, and South Koreans do) was like trying to run a modern society using caveman drawings. In another chapter he went on and on about bathroom habits. The one I remember is that in Japanese bathrooms there is always a pair of easy-to-slip-on plastic sandals/slippers by the door. When you leave the bathroom you must always back out and leave the sandals facing inward so that the next visitor can easily slide his or her feet into them, even though, as he stated, the next visitor might well be you again.

At the end of the evening, Sonny, Cher, Alan, and I got on the commuter train out to where their apartments were on the outskirts of town. All the way on the train Sonny went on and on about how much he hated Japan, and he sounded to me like some of the worst Peace Corps Volunteers. He was from Hawaii and mentioned that he had once been a Catholic brother. One of his biggest complaints was about the weather in Japan—not because he had been a Catholic brother but because he came from Hawaii. "It's not like Hawaii's," he'd say. *"Duh,"* I thought. His next biggest complaint was about Japanese men in general, especially about how office workers got drunk every night and would ride home on the train thoroughly sloshed.

"At almost every stop when the door opened, one or more of the totally intoxicated men lean out and puke on the tracks," Sonny said.

"Sounds lovely," I said.

"It's disgusting; I wish I had never left Hawaii."

"Why did you?"

"I thought it would be different and exotic here. But it's just horrible."

"Why don't you go back then?" I suggested, just as I always suggested to Peace Corps Volunteers who spoke this way about Korea.

"Because I told everyone I'd be gone for at least a year, and I don't want to go back and look like a failure."

"Who cares? If you dislike it so much, leave."

"No, I'll stick it out, but I'll never come back again once I leave next summer."

"Good idea," I said with a sarcastic smile on my face while nodding my head up and down.

The next morning Sonny and Alan got up very early to catch their flight to Kimpo from the Osaka Airport. I heard Sonny in the bathroom while he was washing up. "I can't believe you left beautiful Hawaii. Why did you ever leave

Homeless man in Kobe, Japan.

Part of misspelled Happy New Year sign.

Hawaii?" He said this to himself out loud. This self-flagellation went on for about five minutes. I got up and wished them a safe and enjoyable flight and visit to Korea, and then I went back to sleep.

Once up and about, I had something for breakfast, read for a couple of hours, and then decided to take off for downtown Kobe. Backtracking the route from the previous evening, I got on the commuter train and took it downtown. I wandered around taking pictures. After awhile, I saw a homeless man sleeping on the ground in front of a low stone wall with his winter jacket on, all bundled up and his head resting on a bag that probably held all his worldly possessions. He was the only homeless person I had seen in Japan in my two visits so far. Behind him a shop window said "Happy New Yaer (sic)." I thought I shouldn't take his picture. I felt like I was imposing, maybe being CIS, but it was such a great shot. So from across the street I put the 200mm telephoto lens on my Canon FTB camera. With a quick click, I took the shot and nonchalantly walked away as if I had never taken his picture at all. I also took a shot of the "New Yaer" sign and later juxtaposed the two together.

"What to do now?" I wondered. I noticed a theater showing a double feature of two Beatles movies, both of which I had not seen before: *Let It Be* and *Yellow Submarine.* The Beatles' first two movies, *A Hard Day's Night* and *Help* I had duly

seen when they first came out, but by the time of these later two, I was busy with college. So I bought a ticket and went in. There I spent the afternoon. Both of these movies were in English with Japanese subtitles. *Let It Be* was interesting. You could feel the tension between the four lads from Liverpool as they recorded in this big, sterile warehouse-like studio. Then the grand finale of the movie, when the Beatles played all of the songs on the *Let It Be* album up on the roof of the four-story Apple headquarters in London, was amazing. The traffic stopped in front of the Apple building, and people got out of their cars to listen. In addition, people were hanging out of windows in all the surrounding buildings. Some policemen went into the front door and went up onto the roof as if they were going to shut it down, saw it was the Beatles, and then wandered back out. Fun! Then I watched *Yellow Submarine,* a psychedelic cartoon movie with Beatles songs and, of course, the song "Yellow Submarine" as the central theme. At the end the real Beatles came on and told us to watch out for the "Blue Meanies," the antagonists in the cartoon movie. Truer words were never spoken. Leaving the theater, I had the feeling that indeed there are "Blue Meanies" out there trying to stop the music. Maybe I had a premonition of Al-Qaeda, the Taliban, and ISIS emerging. "Watch out!"

The second time I saw *Yellow Submarine* was in 1979 while in grad school. I was attending the School for International Training in Brattleboro, Vermont, and working on my Masters in International Administration degree. I was the Head Resident at one of their dorms for one semester. One of the duties of the Head Resident was to show the Thursday night movie on campus. As luck would have it the first time it was my turn to show a movie the feature being shown was *Yellow Submarine,* so I got to watch it again. In those days a feature-length movie took two reels, so after putting on the first reel and starting the movie, about fifty minutes later that reel would run out, and the projectionist (me) had to take off the used-up reel and then put on and start reel number two. Even though I had seen it before, I enjoyed this clever cartoon movie again.

Back in Kobe after supper (where, as usual, I had the waitress follow me to the plastic imitation plates of food in the display case and pointed out my choice for the evening), it was starting to get dark, and I wandered into a small tavern. Sauntering up to the bar I sat on a stool and ordered a beer from the slightly heavyset bar girl. It was a slow evening, and she sat next to me and started a conversation even though her English was minimal. After I mentioned that I lived in Korea, she told me that she was Korean. *"Geuleom, hankukmal halsuisseyo?"* (Well then, can you speak Korean?) I asked. *"Jogeum,"* (a little) she replied. She was right. There are many ethnic Koreans still living in Japan whose families first came to Japan during the colonial period from 1910 to 1945, and she was one of them. Other than a few words she didn't know much and couldn't carry on a conversation in Korean any more than she could in English. She did know *Hangeul* (the Korean phonetic alphabet), and she wrote the few words she knew on a napkin, and I wrote a few things for her to try to read. She pointed at me and in English she said, "Pretty boy." I laughed, pointed back, and said, "Pretty girl." We went back and forth with this several times. She would wait on any new customers that came in and then come back again and say, "Pretty boy." I'd reply again, "Pretty girl," and we'd laugh until she thankfully finally tired of this game.

After another beer or two, I was feeling pretty darn good. She pointed at my watch and motioned that she wanted to switch with hers. My watch was an old, banged up, cheap stainless steel men's watch that I had dug out of a drawer filled with old watches that my Uncle Bob had at his cleverly named shop, Haffner Jewelry, a few days before I left to fly to San Fran. Sometimes people would trade in their old watch at Haffner's, and my Uncle Bob would give them a few bucks off whatever they were purchasing from him. He just threw these old watches in a drawer he had for that purpose behind his jewelry cases. I didn't want to take a good watch to Korea, so I had asked him if I could pick out a cheap old one, and he told me to take whatever I wanted. Her watch looked like a men's watch in shape, but was clear plastic, and you could see all the gears moving inside. It had a plain black, plastic band. I agreed to swap, and when I left I wore hers out thinking I'd switch back some other night. I got back to the apartment with no trouble and didn't see any Japanese men puking out the open door of the train at the stops anywhere before I got off. I think Sonny may have been exaggerating a tad. We hadn't seen any the first night when he was telling me his stories either.

The next morning, Christmas 1973, I got up and headed toward a bathhouse that I'd noticed the day before near the apartment building. I walked in, and there was a tall counter, about four feet high, with a man sitting behind it taking the money. To my right it was wide open to the men's side. I could see naked guys going in and out of the tub area from the men's locker area. To my left was the women's side with several naked and semi-naked women in their locker area getting ready to go into their bath area or who'd finished bathing and were getting dressed to leave. I gave the man a 10,000 yen note worth about $50.00 at the time and waited for him to give me change back while watching the women. It was interesting how open the Japanese were to nudity compared to Koreans who were very prudish. Oddly, though, the Japanese did not allow the showing of women's pubic hair in their girlie magazines. I checked. Yet, as described earlier, I had seen topless women on Japanese television shows, and now I found this interesting bathhouse setup. (In those days there was no nudity at all on TV in Korea or the U.S.) I'd heard that in the countryside in Japan there were actual coed bath houses. Good idea! I've always said that in the United States we need more nudity and less violence portrayed in our television, movies, and society in general. Maybe we'd have fewer murders and certainly more fun if we had more nudity and coed bathhouses. But no, we have goofy things like John Ashcroft in 2002 ordering that material be draped over a barebreasted statue at the Justice Department because he and/or American society is so prudish. Give me a break. I like the Japanese attitude better. After receiving my change, I went into the men's side where you could no longer see over into the women's area, took my bath, and left. I thought about going back again every day with 10,000 yen notes, but then I thought I'd better not or the guy taking the money might think I was a pervert. Besides I only had a couple of 10,000 yen notes left anyway.

Feeling squeaky clean, I returned to downtown Kobe and stopped at a McDonald's for lunch. I was sitting there reading a book while eating, as I hate to eat alone and just stare off into the distance. Then I heard from behind me, "Pretty boy." Sure enough, it was the Korean-Japanese bar girl from the night before. I pointed at her.

"Pretty girl," I said, and we laughed.

"What are you doing?" I asked. It went over her head.

"You eat?" she questioned.

"Yes," I answered. She was with a girlfriend, who looked at me quizzically.

"Bye," she said.

"*Hummm?*" I thought as I watched her walk away still wearing my watch.

After lunch I found a different theater with a different double feature: *Sunflowers* with Sophia Loren and a French film that I had read somewhere, probably in *Newsweek*, was a soft-core porn film called *Emmanuelle*. The Sophia Loren film came on first, and I was glad because I figured it would be in English seeing that Sophia Loren was in it and it was called *Sunflowers*. *Emmanuelle* would probably be in French. When *Sunflowers* came on, though, it was in Italian. "*Oh, right she's Italian, you dummy,*" I thought to myself, but still the title was in English unless the Italian word for sunflower is, well, sunflower, and I doubt it. "*Oh well, what else did I have to do to entertain myself?*" I thought. I could kind of follow the story, so it wasn't too bad. Sophia Loren was married to an Italian man just before World War II. When the war started he got drafted, and he ended up on the Soviet front in the winter where he was wounded and, while retreating, passed out and fell facedown in the snow. Then a Russian woman found him, dragged him home, and nursed him back to health. After the war, they lived together and had children while Sophia back in Italy waited, still hoping for his return. Years later, not believing he'd died in combat and hearing rumors that he was alive in Russia, she travels to the Soviet Union and finds him. I can't remember the ending. Did he stay in the Soviet Union or return with Sophia to Italy? I know what I would have done; Sophia was gorgeous. But at least I figured out and still remember much of the plot even though it was all in Italian with Japanese subtitles. Then *Emmanuelle* came on, and it was in French with Japanese subtitles. It started with a couple of skinny, rather flat-chested French gals lying topless on chaise longues talking to each other. I had no idea what they were saying, and they seemed to talk without moving off their butts for an eternity. After ten or fifteen minutes, I could stand the boredom no longer and left.

It was dinnertime, but I didn't feel like staying downtown any longer, so I took the train back to the apartment. As I unlocked the door I heard music playing, and as I went in, there was Sonny Sylvan sitting on the sofa.

"What are you doing back already?"

"Oh, I caught a cold on the plane and decided I'd better come back before I gave it to Cher and Alan." He did sound quite raspy.

"You do sound bad," I said.

"Yeah, but it feels better just to be back here."

"I'm hungry. Do you want to go to a restaurant, or are you too sick?"

"No, I'm hungry too. Let's go."

We headed out to a neighborhood restaurant. Sonny told me his life story, and I told him mine. After dinner we returned to the apartment. I told him that I'd seen all the double-feature movies Kobe had to offer in the past couple of days, had had a bath at the local bathhouse, had taken lots of pictures, and was thinking of leaving the next day. Then he could have the place to himself and recuperate.

After listening to Sonny's soliloquy the next morning as he stood alone talking to himself in the bathroom about why he should never have left Hawaii, I packed up and left the apartment. Still wearing the "pretty girl's" plastic watch, I headed northeast from Kobe for the short trip to Kyoto, the ancient capital of Japan. It's a fair-sized, bustling city, but filled with many beautiful Buddhist temples, Zen gardens, a royal palace, and Shinto shrines. I found the youth hostel, got a bunk in a room with several other young tourists, and discussed with a couple of them the order of interest of all the cultural assets in the city and surrounding area. I spent the afternoon exploring the area around the youth hostel.

The next day I visited the famous Golden Temple and the garden surrounding it and walked around the royal palace. After two more days of sightseeing, my funds were running low, and I decided to head back to Shimonoseki. I got on the train heading southwest and planned to get on that evening's ferry back to Korea.

It was Monday afternoon December 30, 1974, when I returned to Shimonoseki. I walked from the train station right to the ferry terminal. There I received bad news; the ferry shut down for several days from Christmas Eve until the Friday after New Year's. Why hadn't I known this? There must have been signs at the terminals and/or on the ferry itself when I came over, and yet, if there were, I certainly hadn't seen them. I started to panic, as I didn't have enough money to last that many days with the prices in Japan, especially if I had to stay in a hotel. I did have some reserve Korean currency, but it wasn't convertible to Japanese yen. *"OK, calm down,"* I told myself. I began looking around at the signs on the bulletin board at the ferry terminal, and there was an advertisement for a youth hostel. Whew! If I stayed there I would be all right—as long as I ate ramen for breakfast, lunch, and dinner every day. The hostel was a long way from the terminal, but I'd just have to hoof it. I started the long march up the street in the hostel's direction.

After a couple of hundred yards a Nissan Fairlady Z sports car pulled over, and a Japanese guy called out through the open passenger-side window in English, "Hey, do you need a ride?"

"Yes, thank you," I replied and got into the passenger side of the car.

"Where are you going?" he asked.

"Up to the youth hostel," I said. "How come you speak English so well?"

"Oh, I just graduated from UCLA last spring." What are the odds? I couldn't believe it. So we started talking about UCLA, his major, and so on. I told him that I had wanted to return to Korea today and didn't realize that the ferry shut down over the holidays. Before we reached the youth hostel he asked if I would like to stay with him at his apartment for free instead of in the hostel. Of course, I agreed. He turned around and drove to his apartment just past the ferry terminal and up the road a piece. I recognized the corner. Charlie and I had walked this area looking for used bikes during the summer. In fact, I had taken a picture that past summer of the old V-shaped building on the corner of the main street only about fifty yards from his place.

We entered a door and walked up a stairway to his small second-floor apartment. The stairs were creaky. They creaked loud enough to alarm a parrot in the downstairs apartment. It cried out *"Konichiwa!"* It was weird to hear a parrot saying hello in Japanese; I just assumed that parrots only said, "Polly want a cracker," and only in English.

My lifesaver's name was Muneaki Kihara. He worked for his parents' business, which supplied the main ingredient for miso soup to local restaurants in the area. I threw down my bag, and Muneaki suggested we go up the street to his parents' business and home.

"Don't tell my parents that I picked you up," he said.

"OK, what should I tell them?"

"Tell them that you also went to UCLA and that we've known each other for a couple of years," he suggested.

"Good, that's what I'll say," I replied.

We walked another hundred yards or so up the side street, and I knew when we were getting close because I could smell the odor of the miso wafting out of his parents' business. We walked through a small warehouse-like area and then into their home. Muneaki introduced his parents to me, and we all bowed. It turned out that they didn't speak a word of English, so I wondered why he bothered to tell me to say that I was a fellow UCLA grad since he had to translate our entire conversation anyway. If I said, "I'm a Martian," he could have translated it to, "He's a friend from UCLA." His mother invited us to stay for dinner, and we had a wonderful feast as if she had known I would be coming.

Tomb of the Japanese Unknown Soldier from the Sino-Japanese War in Shimonoseki.

The next couple of days we did a little sightseeing even though Shimonoseki is not the tourist capital of Japan by any means. Having told him that I was a history major, one of the places he took me was to the grave of the Unknown Soldier from the Sino-Japanese War. The treaty between China and Japan had been signed in Shimonoseki in 1895. The grave mound looked very much like the burial mounds in Gyeongju from the Silla Dynasty except it was smaller, and instead of being just a plain grass-covered hill, there was a six-foot-high stone pagoda-like structure on top of the mound. Besides a little sightseeing, we hung out with his brother and friends. I watched them as they played mahjong, but I never did figure out the rules.

On New Year's Day we visited a Shinto Shrine. Muneaki told me he had always wanted to visit Korea, and for the past couple of days I had been egging him on about going back with me for a trip. He finally agreed and asked permission from his parents to take some days off work. They agreed. Because the ferry still wasn't running yet, I got a refund on my return ticket, and the next day we flew from Fukuoka to Busan—a puddle jump if there ever was one.

On the way over he suggested that I tell the Koreans that he was an American because he was aware that Koreans disliked the Japanese due to the harsh treatment the Koreans had endured during the colonial period. Of course, I agreed. From the first time we entered a shop or restaurant, and every time thereafter, the Koreans assumed he was a Korean. They'd look at him and ask him a question, and I'd answer. Then they'd look back at him, thinking we were playing a game. I'd explain that we were both Americans, but that I was a Peace Corps Volunteer and taught English here in Korea while my friend, though he looked Korean, was in fact an American, spoke no Korean, and was visiting on vacation. Muneaki kept asking in English, "What are you talking about?" and I would explain that they thought he was Korean and believed he was faking that he didn't speak the language. We'd laugh, and the shop employees and waitresses would finally stop addressing Muneaki and begin talking directly to me. This happened everywhere we went for the two days and three nights we were touring together.

I suggested that we head up to Gyeongju and visit the museum and historic structures there. So we caught a bus and headed north. We spent a couple of nights in Gyeongju, packing in as much sightseeing as we could and with me serving as Muneaki's tour guide extraordinaire. We exchanged addresses before parting and kept in touch for a couple of years or so by mail. I got him on a bus back to Busan, and then I headed up to Seoul.

I had signed up for the Peace Corps-sponsored Korean language instruction at the Myongdo Language Institute in Seoul near Gwanghwa-mun and the Peace Corps office. The classes were to start the following Monday. Charlie and I had decided during the previous winter vacation not to bother with studying Korean, but I had not gotten much better in language in a year and a half now and decided a little formal studying might just help. I'm a little slow, but eventually I catch on.

On Monday morning I walked into the Myongdo Institute, and there was Nick Mack, my former roommate from our K-23 training.

"About time you decided to join the language training," Nick said.

"Better late than never," I retorted.

"Yes, but better never late," he re-retorted back at me.

I had no smart-ass answer to that one and decided to just agree. "True enough," I replied and added "Better late than never, but better never late!" as one of my favorite lines, which I still often use. I was quickly placed into the remedial language group, and even there I was surely the worst one out of the half dozen in the class. Nick was in the super-accelerated, high achiever, brilliant student class. I did often hang with him during the breaks and after class, though.

Larry Lathrup was also at Myongdo and in the high-level class with Nick Mack. Charlie and I had first gotten to know Larry during a long weekend the previous spring when we were in Seoul. He and Alan Custer (in whose apartment I had just stayed while in Kobe) were good buddies as earlier noted. Larry was fun to talk to. He would tell a story or give his philosophical interpretation of some occurrence, and then when he finished he'd say in a slow, methodical style, emphasizing every syllable, "What I'm tryin' to say, man, is.....," and then he'd tell the same story all over again but in a different way. He was a trip to listen to because he sounded like he was in fact tripping. His Korean was better than Charlie's and mine even though we had been "in country," as we PCV's liked to say, longer than he had been. One day the previous spring, too lazy to walk to Myeongdong, we'd gotten into a taxi (Charlie, Alan, Larry, and me) at the end of a street. This street came to a dead end right at the main intersection near Gwanghwa-mun where Chong-ro crossed Sejong-ro and near the huge Statue of Admiral Yi, Sun-sin. A customer got out of the cab, and we ran and jumped in. Evidently, the driver didn't know the area well, and where the street ended he went up the curb onto the sidewalk and then noticed that there were pylons at the far edge of the sidewalk blocking him from going back down the curb on the other side and entering the main street. Larry said, "*Ajosshi, kil-ro kapshida,*" which translates to something like "Sir, or middle aged gentleman, let's go by way of a road." We all cracked up, and even the driver got a kick out of Larry's comment. Laughing, he put the taxi in reverse and went back onto the dead-end street where he did a U-turn and headed back the way he had come in.

On the way to Myeongdong, Larry began telling us that his two new favorite words in Korean were "*ashidashipi*" and "*poshidashipi*." *Ashidashipi* means, "as you know," while *poshidashipi* means, "as you can see." "You can add one or the other to almost any sentence, and you automatically sound more erudite," Larry told us. I sat there and repeated *ashidashipi* and *poshidashipi* over and over a few times in my head. When I returned to Mukho I started throwing them into my conversations in Korean. They were fun words, and I was glad Larry had pointed them out to us.

On Wednesday at the Myongdo Institute, I noticed Larry's absence. "Where's Larry?" I asked Paul Missaukee and Art Nepessing, a couple of other guys fom Larry's training group. They told me that Larry was living for the week with a prostitute in Itaewon, the bar and shopping area near *Mi-pal-gun*

(American Eighth Army) Headquarters. He was so worried she might have a tryst during the day while he was studying that he decided to not come to class.

"You're kidding? What's he gonna do—stay in Itaewon 24/7?" I asked.

"Guess so, he's gone off the deep end."

"Do you know where he's staying?"

"Yeah, he took us there over the weekend before classes started."

"Why don't we go see him this evening and try to talk some sense into him?" I suggested.

They agreed, and though I had not visited Itaewon in the year and a half I'd been in Korea (because I wanted to avoid the artificial world around U.S. military bases and instead immerse myself in Korean culture) altruistically I decided to help Larry and go there this one time. It was worth the sacrifice. As mentioned before, I had visited around Camp Henry in Daegu with Jack Fisher during our training and had found the atmosphere strange. The Koreans around the bases were rather surly. They didn't seem to like the U.S. soldiers, and I couldn't blame them, though they obviously liked their money. The Korean shopkeepers would speak to the soldiers in low-form Korean, suitable for talking to children or animals, and then the soldiers would pick up some of this and speak it back to the Koreans, further souring the relationship. After my Peace Corps service, I taught at U.S. military bases for two years. When the Koreans around the bases spoke in low-form Korean to me and I answered in higher-form Korean, they would immediately switch up and change their mood. But as Elton John once said so well, "It's a sad, sad situation, and it's getting more and more absurd." ("Sorry Seems to be the Hardest Word," music by Elton John, lyrics by Bernie Taupin.)

After class we went to Itaewon and found Larry moping around with his sweetheart.

"Larry, you need to attend class, man," we said.

"Yeah, but I don't want to leave Miss Kim alone all day," he replied.

"She'll be fine," I countered.

"She might be too fine," Larry retorted. This went on for a while, and then we decided to order in Chinese food. A little while later the delivery boy brought the food in the neat big metal box with a handle on the top that all Chinese restaurants used for deliveries. I had ordered my favorite sea creature stew with fish, tentacles, shelled animals, and other weird things sticking out of the noodles.

After more urging, we talked Larry into coming back to class. He did, though he still skipped out early a couple of times to check up on his woman. This all seemed like much more trouble than it was worth to me, but obviously Larry didn't adhere to my way of thinking.

A couple of years later when I first started dating Mi-yun, my first wife, she told me that she had a friend who married a Peace Corps Volunteer. I asked his name, and she said, "Narry." Hummm! I was thinking family name and didn't know any volunteer named Narry, so I said, "Don't know him," and forgot about it. Months later she mentioned again that her friend had married a PCV and started describing him.

"He had long, blond, wavy hair and wore a waist-length, tan, fringed jacket."

"Was the jacket really dirty?" I asked.

"Yes."

"Oh, you've got to be kidding—that's Larry Lathrup."

"Yes, that's what I've been saying for months, Narry," Mi-yun said.

Larry, Rarry, Narry—they're all pretty similar, right?

The week of language training ended with me not feeling any smarter. In fact, I felt dumber because now I realized how poor my Korean was compared to most of my fellow volunteers. Nick was staying on for a few more days in Seoul, and Charlie was heading up to hang in the capital, so Nick and I got a room together. Charlie arrived later and he, Nick, and I went out to dinner and our usual visit to the classical music listening room. Nick had a bad cold and was coughing up a storm. He was drinking opium-infused cough syrup from a local pharmacy as if it were water. The drugstores in Korea sold all kinds of drugs over the counter that you needed a prescription for in the States. That's why they were off-limits to American GIs—and the first place many of the GIs headed the minute they got off base. Later in the evening after listening to a little Mozart, Brahms, Beethoven, and Bach, we headed back to the Daeji Yeogwan.

"Wait, I need some *soju*," (the alcoholic stuff that tasted like lighter fluid to me) said Nick, and he started heading into a small *gage* (shop).

"Nick, do you really think you should be drinking *soju* on top of all that cough syrup you've been inhaling?" I said.

"Oh, it's OK," he said, "I do it all the time."

"It still doesn't seem good to mix drugs with alcohol," Charlie said.

"Hasn't bothered me so far." So he bought a bottle of *soju,* and we headed back. When we got to the room, I couldn't stand to watch Nick drinking alone, so I grabbed a glass and said, "Hit me!" Charlie refused to join in, so Nick and I drank the whole bottle before finally hitting the *yos, ibols,* and *begaes* (quilted mattresses, coverlets and pillows). *Soju* still tasted like lighter fluid to me, but after a few shots I didn't care so much.

Nick left Seoul, but Charlie and I stayed for a few more days. At the bookstore I was looking at the music section and found a songbook of recent hit songs. On one page was John Denver's "Take Me Home, Country Roads," except country was spelled "counter." I showed Charlie, and from then on we always sang:

Take me home counter roads....
(Written by Bill Danoff, Taffy Nivert, and John Denver)

You could hear "Take Me Home, Country Roads" in Korea, but not John Denver's "Rocky Mountain High." It was banned, evidently because President Park, Chung-hui's administration decided it was a drug song. In Korea, even getting high on nature was forbidden.

I had read about Tongnip-mun (Independence Gate) and wanted to see it, so we figured out which bus would take us there. It is just west of Gwanghwa-mun through the Sajic tunnel. As we came out of the tunnel we could see it ahead of us. We got off the bus at a stop nearby so that we could see it up close and personal. This gate, which looks like the Arc de Triomphe in Paris, was built near a much smaller Korean-style gate where the Koreans would wait to meet Chinese emissaries. These emissaries were sent by the Chinese emperor every other year to renew the Korean Kingdom's vassal state relationship to the Chinese Empire. (On the opposite years Korean emissaries were sent to Beijing.) Basically, China controlled Korea's foreign relations. After having been defeated by the Japanese in the Sino-Japanese War of 1895, the Chinese were forced by Japan to give up their suzerainty over Korea. King Kojong then declared himself to be an emperor. That meant that Korea was an empire and made it equal to China. To emphasize this point, King Kojong had this Independence Gate/Arch built. He also changed the name of the country from Chosun (Land of the Morning Calm) to Taehan (Great Han). Today South Korea's official name is Tae Han Min Kuk (Great Han People Country). There are two carved Korean *Taekukgi* (Korean flags) on the gate, one on either side above the arch. During the Japanese occupation from 1910 to 1945, the only place in Korea where the Korean flag could be seen was in these carvings on Tongnip-mun. I thought about Korea's sad history of the late nineteenth century and first half of the twentieth century as the traffic of Seoul roared around us.

From Tongnip-mun we took a bus to Seoul Station, a large brick structure built by the Japanese in the Meiji restoration style. The juxtaposition of the Independence Gate and the Japanese train station built during Korea's subjugation was not lost on us.

Interestingly, as we were riding on the bus between the two structures there was a huge sign on a large warehouse-like building off to the right. The sign said in Korean writing (*Hangeul*): *"san, san, san, namu, namu, namu"* (mountain, mountain, mountain, tree, tree, tree). It's fascinating how mountain is two syllables in English but only one in Korean, while tree is two in Korean yet only one in English. Anyway, this was the most recent environmental campaign slogan in Korea. After the Korean War, many Koreans cut down trees to burn the wood to cook with and/or to heat their homes. This led to many hills and mountains in Korea being denuded. The government was encouraging reforestation with this rather simplistic slogan, but it got the point across. There were always campaigns going on like "Don't spit on the sidewalk." So I wrote a ditty to the tune of Petula Clark's hit song "Don't Sleep in the Subway:"

> Don't spit on the sidewalk people,
> Don't pee on the building sides,
> Don't elbow your way on the bus,
> Forget your foolish pride, stand in line,
> You'll get to ride soon enough.
> ("Don't Sleep in the Subway" written by Tony Hatch and Jackie Trent, recorded by Petula Clark. My apologies to all of them.)

Back at the Peace Corps office later that day, we were standing with a crowd in the lobby of the Korea Education Association Building waiting for the elevator to come back down. At the very front by the doors were two female PCVs, and behind them were some Korean men with Charlie and me at the very back. When the doors opened the Korean men elbowed and shoved their way in front of the female PCVs, filled the elevator, and the doors closed in behind them. One of the gals started crying. After a long day of fighting the crowds of Seoul where those with the sharpest elbows were always the ones to get on the buses first, it was the last straw for her. We commiserated with the gals and then ran interference for them when the elevator again came down by holding off the riotous hoards of Korean men behind us so that the ladies could safely get in.

There was a new "hamburger place" in Myeongdong that we had eaten at a couple of times before, and we headed there for dinner. It didn't really serve beef patties. They were more like some kind of veggie and/or tofu burger, but they were the closest thing to hamburgers available outside of the tourist hotels, which we couldn't afford. So we went there and had a burger. There was a young Korean girl, who was probably homeless and who always came in and asked if we wanted our shoes shined. She was a sweet girl about twelve years old. We let her take our leather hiking boots. She gave us plastic slippers to wear in the meantime. The first time we had let her take them she didn't come back for a while, and we'd started to worry that maybe she had stolen them, but then she came back smiling with the beautifully polished shoes in her hands. Since that first time, we always waited for her and gave her our shoes. There were often homeless children living in the viaducts underneath the elevated highway above Cheonggye-cheon Street. (*Cheon* means stream, and this street once was a stream. The stream was covered and paved over. In 1968 an elevated expressway was constructed above the street. Between 2003 and 2005 the expressway and street were torn up, and the stream was restored.) Sometimes the homeless children who slept in these viaducts would follow behind us and beg for money. We'd tell them not to bother us and walk faster, feeling that if we gave them money we'd just encourage them to bother all Americans even more. But this little girl was cute, and she wasn't begging, so we were happy to help.

Even though we couldn't really afford a meal at any tourist hotel, we had gotten into the habit of going to the coffee shop in the Chosun Hotel, which was situated between Myeong-dong and Gwanghwa-mun. It was the oldest and swankiest tourist hotel in Seoul. In Korean *dabangs* (coffee shops), as brought up before, the coffee was watered down Maxwell House instant coffee, and they always gave patrons only half a cup. But at the Chosun Hotel the coffee was a wonderful dark roast, and it was a bottomless cup—American-style. In addition, they had the best Black Forest chocolate cake; it tasted as if it were from a fine German bakery. Their cakes were very different from those in the Korean bakeries where the cakes looked great but the frosting tasted terrible. So, we'd order a coffee and piece of cake each and then camp out. Charlie and I would talk and talk and wave to the waitress for refill after refill of coffee. Although it was listed on the menu as a bottomless cup, after a while—a long while—the maitre d' would begin hovering near us and start giving us a menacing evil eye. Then we knew it was time to call it a night, pay our bill, and retire to the Daeji Yeogwan.

Before we knew it, the long winter break was ending. It was time to head back to Yeongju for Charlie and to Mukho for me.

CHAPTER 11

Spring Semester 1974: Soccer Star

Meanwhile, back in Mukho, it was my second spring semester. John Hudson and I returned to our taekwondo evening routine. I also continued getting up early in the morning and heading up to the gym by myself for an extra workout every day.

Both Charlie and I had become interested in a teaching method called the "Silent Way." We also heard about a book by the man who espoused this method, Dr. Caleb Gattegno, called *Teaching Foreign Languages in Schools the Silent Way.* In this method the teacher only said each new word once, and then after that only the students said it. The teacher was mostly silent. Too often, I felt, only the teacher talked in class and then the students could only understand this one person's speaking style. Gattegno's method had the students talking to each other exclusively. The method emphasized talking about colored rods. By concentrating on grammar and pronunciation, the students carried on advanced conversations about different colored short rods. So instead of memorizing lists of words but not knowing how to make a sentence with them, the "Silent Way" used only a handful of words.

To begin with, Dr. Gattegno taught the word "rod" and then the primary colors. Soon one student was telling another who had several different colored rods in front of him: "Take a green rod. Put it on the desk." Then a little later, "Take a blue rod, a green rod, and a red rod. Put them on the desk." With a few words, long sentences could be formed. The students would be speaking very fluently instead of struggling to figure out the meaning of the words. Then reading was taught with these few words printed on a poster. The instructor would pick a particular student and, using a pointer, tap out a sentence: "Take, a, blue, rod, and, put, it, on, the, desk." Then the instructor would encourage the student to say the sentence. Ooh la la! Reading accomplished! The teacher could hand the pointer to a student. Then after having said a sentence, the student would tap out the word order on the poster. Or the teacher could have a student say a sentence while another student then tapped it out or "verse visa." Listening and reading skills were both built up this way. The book suggested that students became very fluent in their use of sentence building, listening skills, and pronunciation because they focused on these skills instead of trying to memorize hundreds of words that they could not string together into any meaningful utterance. I wanted to try this in a Korean classroom. I discussed it with the principal at the boys' middle school. I had the desire to extend my Peace Corps volunteering by another year, and I wanted to use Gattegno's method starting on day one of the next new school year. I would still teach two days a week at the girls' middle school, so the class could be taught in the traditional manner on those two days by my Korean co-teacher. On the other three and a half days, I wanted free rein to use "The Silent Way" in one of the nine first-year classes at the boys' school. I would follow the textbook as much as possible but build all the sentence structure encountered in the book around talking about colored pencils. I decided pencils would make more sense than rods, and pencil is a more useful word to know anyway. The principal agreed, and I wrote up a proposal and sent it to the Peace Corps office. It was accepted, and I was now going to extend for a third year.

Chris Sombra invited John and me down to Samcheok to visit. He had met the Irish Catholic nuns in town who ran a health clinic right next to the Catholic Church. They had invited the three of us for dinner, as Chris had told them John and I were both working close by in Mukho. There were nine Irish nuns who ran this health clinic. A couple of them cooked all their meals. They even made home-made bread. We were served a wonderful Irish-style dinner with (go figure) pota-toes too. Potatoes were grown in Gangwon-do, so the nuns felt right at home. In fact, the commonly heard nickname for Gangwon province was "*kamja - pawi*" (potato - rock) because they grew lots of potatoes and the soil was very rocky. After dinner a couple of the nuns stayed with us and wanted to play cards while the others excused themselves. So we spent the evening playing Hearts with them. As it was late by the time we finished, they invited us to stay in rooms down in the lower level that they had for overnight patients. Evidently, they rarely had any patients stay over the weekend. Sunday morning we had breakfast with them and then left. We were to get invited back every few weeks for the remainder of our time on the east coast. They seemed to thoroughly enjoy having some different people in to converse with in English and to play cards with.

Suddenly, soon after our visit with the nuns, every little *gage* in South Korea got a small freezer as if someone waved a magic wand and it just happened. There must have been a big warehouse somewhere bigger than the Pentagon filled with all these freezers and thousands of trucks at the ready in an equally large parking lot. On F-Day (Freezer Day) they were distributed throughout the country. I saw the freezer in my favorite *gage* near the Mukho Theater one afternoon when I was buying my evening's supply of McVities Digestives. Then I noticed them in other stores as I walked around town after taekwondo practice. The next day every freezer in the nation was filled with American-style Foremost brand ice cream, which went by the Korean name of *Bingalae* (smile). Before this the only quasi-ice cream available, outside of the tourist hotels, was a soft serve kind of stuff often sold near bus stations that we called "cancer cones." Who the hell knew what the stuff was made of? This Bingalae ice cream was great. Another small step for mankind, but a giant leap for Korea!

The teachers at the boys' middle school challenged the teachers at the boys' high school to a friendly soccer match on a Saturday afternoon on our field. I wore my Yonsei University shirt and showed up ready to play. We exchanged greetings, and even though I had played fullback in college, "Chop-Chop" Mr. Lee, Kwan-sup, the third-year English teacher, who was the acting manager, put me in as right forward. With all the taekwondo I was practicing, I was in the best shape of my life, even better than at the end of soccer season each year in college. Not only that, but I was also the youngest person on the field. Mr. Ko, Joo-hyung, the science teacher, playing the center midfielder position, told me that when he got the ball he would kick it far in front of me toward the right side of the goal and that I should take off as soon as he kicked it but to make sure I wasn't offsides.

The match began, and the play moved up and down the field until Mr. Ko got the ball near midfield. The minute his foot made contact with the ball, I took off and ran past the high school teacher defender like he was standing still. When I reached the ball, the goalie tried to come out and cut off my angle, but I booted it into the far corner of the goal. Goal in! A few minutes later, Mr. Ko got the ball again, booted it as far as he could towards the goal on the right side, and I scored again. It was at this time that the high school team placed a formal complaint arguing that, as a foreigner, I shouldn't be allowed to play. Of course, my team-mates argued that I was a teacher at their school and had every right in the world to be on the field. I just stood there listening and laughing inside. I'm sure when they first started playing the high school teachers assumed that I wouldn't know how to play because Koreans knew that in America soccer was not only an unpop-ular sport but also still virtually unknown there in 1974. Now they wanted me off the pitch. After a while the high school teachers gave up their arguing, and I con-tinued playing, but they double-teamed me to try to snuff my stuff with one of their defensemen always hanging way back on my side. That opened up our left forward, and we started feeding him the ball, and he scored a couple of goals. Later Mr. Ko again kicked the ball ahead on my side, I dribbled around the last defenseman and scored a third goal—hat trick city! This was my first and only hat trick ever. We ended up winning by several goals, and my teammates took me out for drinks afterward to celebrate. I never felt so appreciated in any sporting event I had ever participated in before in my life—even more so than our final APAC (Allen Park Athletic Club) baseball game in which I got the only hit by our team. Of course, we had lost that game. On this day, though, in Mukho, I left it all out there on the soccer pitch, and I had a euphoric feeling as we all drank the night away.

The boys' school principal, Mr. Chae, Yong-son called the teachers' room one afternoon and asked Miss Choi, Yong-sook, the teachers' office assistant to send me into his office. Visiting the principal's office was a rare occurrence for me since Mr. Yoo, Hyung-sul was replaced. As I walked in, I was wondering what he might want to talk to me about. He had me sit down and had Miss Choi bring us coffee. While sipping our hot beverages, Principal Choi asked me if I would translate a former student's transcripts into English, and he handed me the papers. I noticed right away that this was for a female student, and it was a high school transcript. When I asked about this, Principal Choi informed me that Mukho Middle School at one time had been Mukho's only school, and it had been the middle and high school for both boys and girls. All these former records were still in Mukho Middle School's files. I had not known this before. The young lady in question was applying to be a nurse in Germany and needed her high school transcripts translated to send along with her college transcripts and other documents. Knowing that there were not a lot of German speakers in Korea, the hospital had informed her that an English translation would suffice. Of course, I agreed to take on the challenge, and with the help of my co-teacher, Mr. Hyun, Jong-jin, we were able to accomplish this task in a couple of days.

One day I got a letter from Glenn Vriesland, in which he told me that he was engaged and living with his fiancée, Miss Lee, Yong-hui. He had been dating Miss Lee for a few months. She was a lovely young lady who taught nursing at the Kangnung Technical School of Nursing. Once people were engaged in Korea, it was considered all right to live together, even with Korea's very conservative attitude towards sex. Glenn invited me up to visit, so one Saturday afternoon I took the train up and met Glenn at the station in Kangnung. We went right to his place of cohabitation with Miss Lee. I had met her before, but this was the first time I'd seen her since their official engagement. Glenn told me he was going to get married in the summer and leave Peace Corps early to return with Miss Lee to the States and start their married life together. I congratulated them, wished them well, and stayed overnight at their place.

They had a great rickety old outhouse that I was afraid would collapse on me or out from under me every time I went in, even more rickety than Charlie's was. There were many outhouse stories in the Peace Corps/Korea world. My favorite was the one about an outhouse on the side of a low hill. Below it was a pig sty, and the excrement supposedly fell into the sty and was eaten by the pigs. One weekend when a Peace Corps gal from another town was visiting, she went in and squatted in the outhouse. One of the pigs stuck its head up from below and licked her heinie. It naturally scared the heck out of her. She screamed and jumped out through the door with her slacks and underpants around her ankles, trying to run and, of course, falling headfirst into the ubiquitous yellow clay to the amusement of all the other volunteers there that day. There were, of course, other stories of the floorboards giving way and volunteers falling into the filth and so on..... Most or all of them were probably urban, suburban, or more likely rural myths.

When normal outhouses (not ones on hillsides with pigs below) filled up, they had to be emptied. South Korea is the size of the lower peninsula of Michigan. Besides being small it was also mountainous and had a population of nearly 40 million people. Michigan's total population, in both lower and upper peninsulas, was less than nine million in the 1970s. The Republic of Korea was then and still is today one of the most densely populated countries in the world. When an outhouse hole fills up, there is no room to dig another hole and move the outhouse. Consequently, men came and emptied the contents by hand or, more correctly, by bucket. We called them "honey pot men" because they smelled so "sweet." They would put a rather thick wooden rod across their shoulders with a large bucket full of human excrement hanging by ropes on each end of the rod and walk through the neighborhood down to a small tanker truck into which they would then empty the contents. These guys, as you might imagine, probably didn't love their work and were rather surly. They didn't much care if the contents of the buckets splashed out onto your pant legs or shoes and socks. No, they didn't really care! Luckily, you could always smell them coming and duck up a side alley to stay clear of them while they passed by.

In late April it was time for me to get more shots. Chris and John were on a different shot schedule than I was, so early on Thursday morning I took the train up to Kangnung and went out to the airport to rejoin the "prop set" and fly to Kimpo Airport in Seoul. I had no luck this time. The weather was bad, and my flight was cancelled. I needed to get to Seoul for the shots, so I headed to the bus station and bought a ticket for Seoul. The bus took seven hours, so it was faster than the train, which from Kangnung took ten hours. Also, buses ran more often than trains, and I was able to hop right on the next bus instead of having to wait several hours for the next train. The bus left, and it quickly ran out of paved road.

Most of the seven-hour ride was on a dirt road, and all of us passengers bounced along the whole way. In addition, the bus twice got stuck in the mud. Both times the bus driver ordered everyone off the bus. We all jumped off into the muck and rain, and then we all gingerly stepped through ruts and puddles till we reached the shoulder. The bus driver rocked the bus forward and backward until he dislodged the large vehicle and drove ahead thirty to forty yards or so until he got to terra firma. Then all of us passengers, nearly soaking wet by now, ran forward through the mud and crud till we reached the door and climbed in. Just as we were all settled and feeling snug in our seats, we got stuck again and repeated the whole operation. Six hours or so into the trip, the bus finally found paved road, and we coasted into Seoul. When I got off, I swore I'd never take the bus again, and I never did until years later after my Peace Corps experience when an expressway from Seoul all the way to Mukho had been finished.

When I got to Gwanghwa-mun it was already getting dark. As always I made my way to the Daeji Yeogwan. I was so exhausted I ran out, grabbed a quick dinner, and then went right to sleep.

The next day I went into the Peace Corps office and got my shots. As per the usual, after the gamma globulin inoculation, I ran up and down the stairs of the Korea Education Association Building from the seventh floor Peace Corps office down to ground level and back up just to make sure that my ass and thigh muscles didn't tighten the hell up. After running back up, I ran into Rhonda Romulus who lived in Chuncheon, the capital of Gangwon-do, and who had also just gotten her shots. We hung out at the Peace Corps lounge and ran into Joe Toledo, who taught in Chuncheon too. He invited us to go to Itaewon to have dinner and then drink beer at the nightclubs there that catered to the soldiers. I figured after more than a year and a half in country without having gone to the clubs near *Mi-pal-gun* (U.S. Eighth Army Headquarters), what the heck? I'd give it a whirl. After dinner the three of us grabbed a table at one of the bars and started drinking. Over at another table, we noticed another guy who we knew was also a PCV, though we didn't know his name. He was carrying on an animated conversation with a cute Korean gal who was in all likelihood a prostitute. Many soldiers and their ladies of the evening were dancing on the dance floor. Joe turned and asked Rhonda if she would like to dance. They went off, and I was sitting alone when I looked over and noticed the cute gal who had been talking to the other PCV guy was sitting alone. Our eyes met, and she came over and asked me to dance. I followed her out onto the dance floor. When the song ended, she went back and sat with the other PCV guy, who must have gone to the bathroom and had returned. After another song Rhonda and Joe came back and sat down.

"Did you miss us?" Rhonda said.

"He didn't miss us. He was out dancing too," Joe replied before I could answer.

"Who were you dancing with?" Rhonda obviously had not noticed me out on the dance floor. Hard to believe as I could really cut a rug, or so I thought. I pointed over toward the table where the Peace Corps guy and the cute Korean gal were sitting.

"I was dancing with the gal over there talking with that other Peace Corps guy."

"Oh, really?" she said as she looked over their way.

"Yeah." We all laughed, and then two seconds later the Peace Corps guy knocked my shoulder with his fist and said, "Why are you laughing at me?"

"I'm not laughing at you, man," I said while holding my hands up.

"Yes, you are. You pointed at me, and then you all laughed."

"Calm down, buddy. Rhonda here just asked me who I was dancing with, and I said with the gal who is sitting with you. No one's laughing at you, dude." He looked kind of goofy as hell and said, "Oh!" and walked back to his table.

"That guy's messed up," Joe said.

"Yeah, let's just ignore him and not look his way, OK?" I suggested.

"Good idea," Rhonda and Joe both said.

I then asked Rhonda to dance, thinking that would get us farther away from the nutcase guy. After a few dances we returned to the table, and Joe was hot and heavy in conversation with a local lass. By now it was nearly 11:30 p.m. and getting near the midnight curfew time. Joe exited with his honey, and Rhonda and I attempted to grab a taxi back to Gwanghwa-mun. As it got near midnight in all the parts of Korea with the curfew, there was always a mad rush of mostly men trying to get taxis to take them back home. It was always fun this late at night because often taxis would stop, and the driver would ask, "Where are you going?" After you told them they'd often say, "No way," and take off because their home was in a different direction. They were trying to get one last fare for the evening, but it had to be toward the direction of their home. After a few tries, we finally got a driver who was heading our way.

Back in Mukho, I was invited by Mr. Ihm, Yong-tae, a Korean language teacher, who was also the Boy Scout troop leader, to accompany Mukho Middle 0School's troop on a camping trip in late April. I was told they would have enough camping and sleeping gear to accommodate me, and I jumped at the chance to spend a Saturday night in tents with about a dozen students and a couple of other teachers.

Boy Scout camping trip.

After classes on Saturday, we met at the schoolyard, carted all the equipment with us to the bus station, and headed toward Bupyeong and the beautiful part of Mureung Valley past the Ssangyong Cement plant. Disembarking from the bus, we hiked up along the stream to an area where there was enough flat land to pitch our tents. The students, of course, did all the work while I wandered around and watched. Once the camp was set up, the students began preparing dinner. They cooked up rice and stew, and we all ate to our hearts' content. After the scouts did the cleanup, they built a campfire, and we all sat around singing songs till quite late. By then it was pretty chilly up in the mountains. I had on a sweatshirt and my fleece-lined nylon Sigma Nu jacket that I wore all winter, and I was still cold. When it was time to sleep, and after all the students had climbed into their tents, we teachers got into ours. I couldn't believe the sleeping gear. I had a thin mattress and a blanket that was about as thick as cheap toilet paper. When I held it up I could almost see through it. It was cold up in "them thar mountains" in late April, and even with all my clothes on, my teeth were chattering as I tried to sleep. In addition, the boys were talking late into the evening in hushed voices, and then every once in awhile squeals would ring out as one of the kids said or did something that cracked up the others in their tent.

The next morning, I was a basket case, but while the gung ho students made breakfast and cleaned up, I stripped down to my Mark Spitz-like Speedo bathing suit with the American flag motif and jumped into the stream running by our campground. That woke me up, as the water was, I bet, exactly 32.1 degrees Fahrenheit or even .001 degrees Celsius. There were places where the stream formed fairly deep pools as it meandered through the many boulders in the valley. In one of these pools I dove in and swam the six to eight feet to the bottom. There I noticed many beer and soju bottles, which had obviously been flung in by inebriated men on weekend excursions. I began plucking these bottles off the bottom, surfacing, and piling them on the shoreline of the stream. After a few minutes some of the scouts came over and asked what I was doing. I explained that I was going to clean up this area of the stream and take all the bottles to the nearest trash can. They pretty much decided then and there to make helping me in this endeavor their scout troop project, or at least their good deed for the day. The other teachers heard what was going on, and they also joined in. So for the rest of the morning we cleared all of the discarded glass bottles we could find in this part of the stream and carried them down to the nearest trash receptacle. I felt pretty good about bringing some environmental awareness to the Mukho Middle School's Boy Scout troop through my example.

At the girls' school picnic—Don with one of the high school students.

Each spring I got to attend the boys' middle school and the girls' middle and high school annual spring picnics. At the girls' picnic each year, I spent most of the time after eating lunch standing for pictures with seemingly every single student. This went on for hours. There are hundreds of pictures just like the one above.

The next Sunday, May 4, 1974, my co-teacher, Mr. Hyun, Jong-jin and I hiked over the large hill/small mountain north of town and then down to Mangsang Beach. It was a beautiful, warm spring day, and the beach was empty. In those days' beach season in Korea was from June 15 to August 15. Early May was far too early for anyone to be on the sand. We walked along the deserted beach, and I began to get hotter and hotter.

"I'm going swimming," I told Mr. Hyun.

"No, it's too early," Mr. Hyun said.

"The date doesn't matter, I'm hot." I stripped down to my underpants (they might have even been my famous yellow nylon ones), and I ran into the cold water. Mr. Hyun followed suit, and we both swam around until our teeth started chattering because even in the summer the East Sea never warmed up all that much, but it was fun. We ran back on shore and put our clothes back on, hiked some more along the shoreline, and then headed back to Mukho.

The next morning when I entered the teachers' office, Mr. Hyun was holding court and telling all the teachers how we swam in the East Sea even though it was only early May and far from the June 15 "Korean Beach Season" starting date. All the teachers were ooh-ing and ah-ing at our exploit.

Among the books I read during the spring semester of 1974, in addition to Dr. Gattegno's *Teaching Foreign Languages in Schools the Silent Way*, were several books about Korea: *The Dutch Come to Korea*, by Gari Ledyard; *Korean Patterns*, by Paul S. Crane; *North Korea Today*, edited by Robert A. Scalapino; *Under the Snow the Bamboo Shines*, by Ruth G. Stewart; *Traditional Korea, a Cultural History*, by W.D. Reeve; *Korea Under Colonial Rule*, by Andrew Nahm; and *The United States in the Korean War*, by Don Lawson.

The rest of the semester flew by, and before I knew it I was heading to Seoul to fill out some paperwork for my extension of one more year and to fly home for "home leave." I ran into my other roommate from our K-23 training program, Jack Fisher, and we roomed together at the Daeji Yeogwan as he was filling out his "end of service papers" and getting ready to travel across Southeast Asia and to Europe before returning home and starting grad school. I was jealous in a way because I had no idea what I wanted to do with the rest of my life, and I still didn't think I was smart enough to actually go to grad school, but I knew he was.

The first Saturday back in Seoul was Glenn Vriesland and Lee, Yong-hui's wedding. I ran into a couple of Peace Corps gals from his group, Agnetha Haggerty and Anni Paquette, who were also going to attend the wedding. They told me that Yong-hui's family was quite prominent. The wedding ceremony was to be at a government guesthouse on Namsan (South Mountain), near where the K-23s had stopped the first afternoon after we had landed in Seoul and where "no-bra" Patty Olivet had bounced along and fallen into the sewer gutter. Jack didn't know Glenn and wasn't going, so I hitched a taxi ride with Agnetha and Anni. The guesthouse was actually several buildings, all built in traditional Korean architectural style. The main building in front looked like an ancient Buddhist temple or a palace building. I picked up a brochure in English, and it listed the prominent diplomats as well as a couple of American presidents who had stayed here when they visited Seoul. The inside of the building looked like the Yi Dynasty kings' audience hall. We went in and took our seats as the ceremony was about to begin. This was a civil ceremony, and Agnetha and Anni told me that the man who married them was the equivalent of the Korean Speaker of the House. Always being very articulate, I think I said, "Wow!" In Korea there were many wedding halls where couples who were not Christian would have their ceremonies. This was certainly a big step up from the Las Vegas-style wedding halls.

It was a beautiful ceremony, and we all wished Glenn and Yong-hui the best of luck in the future. They left Korea shortly after their wedding, six months short of Glenn's finishing his two years of Peace Corps service. He was leaving early, but I was happy to be staying longer.

The main holdup for my departing for home leave was that I needed to give three stool samples before Peace Corps would give me my passport and let me get on a plane bound for Detroit—something about parasites. (Or was it parakeets? I forget, as it has been so long.) The first two dumps were produced fairly quickly, but then, as luck would have it, I got constipated. One of the running PC jokes was about a guy who was ready to take off for home leave but couldn't squeeze out the last stool sample. Instead he took his sample cup with him outside the Korea Education Association Building and up an alley where he found a pile of dog poop and scraped some of that into the cup. Peace Corps then let him leave, but when he returned a month and a half later, Dr. Chu, Un-bong, the new Peace Corps doctor, saw him and excitedly said, "You must come directly to my office; you have problems." It turns out the dog had some serious ailments, and Dr. Chu was about to administer many remedies until the PCV finally fessed up to his scam.

While waiting to get all three of my stool cultures deposited, I hung out a lot with Jack. We'd talk and/or read all morning and sometimes part of the afternoon. In the evening we'd wander off for dinner and hit a bar or two. We were sitting around one morning when three or four other volunteers wandered into our room. One of the gals by the name of Martha Vernor began talking about some volunteer who was very hoity-toity. He had bragged about how his senior year in college he was listed in that year's edition of *Who's Who Among Students in American Universities and Colleges*.

"That's no big deal. I'm in the 1971–1972 edition," I said.

"Oh! Excuse me, another Mister Big Shot," Martha responded.

"No, Don's not like that at all. I've known him for two years, and we were even roommates in training together, and I've never heard him mention this before," Jack said.

"It's no big deal, and I've never mentioned it because it never came up in any conversation until today," I said.

I don't think I had told anyone in Korea about being in the 1971–1972 *Who's Who Among Students in American Universities and Colleges.* Why bother? The minute I graduated from college it already seemed like ancient history to me. Before Martha brought it up I didn't think anyone would care anyway, but seeing that she mentioned it I told the story of how I happened to be in this "hoity-toity" (as she saw it) book. The first semester of my senior year I walked into the Kresge Gym at Albion College to register for classes. As I was walking in, I saw a student sitting behind a table with a sign that read, "Who's Who Among Students in American Universities and Colleges."

"Don, aren't you a senior this year?" she asked.

"Yes, I am," I answered.

"Then you get to vote for our Who's Who representatives."

"Where's my name?" I jokingly said as she handed me a voting form. She didn't answer, but I glanced at the form, and in fact there was my name big as life. I walked up into the bleachers and filled in my ballot. I think out of twenty-some names we could vote for a dozen. I thought to heck with everyone else, and I voted for myself only. I hoped that might give me a slight edge, though I didn't think I'd get enough votes anyway. As I handed in the form, I asked who picked the candidates. The student told me that the previous spring semester a group of students, faculty, and staff came up with this list. As luck would have it, a few weeks later I was told I was among the chosen few. Story of my life! (I wish, but not really; I don't think I'd been elected to anything since grade school when I was picked to receive the new 50-star U.S. flag for our classroom back in 1960. I still have the 48-star flag that once hung in that classroom.) I was told that during halftime of the homecoming football game we would be called out onto the field for a short ceremony and would be presented with our certificates. I had an away soccer game the day of homecoming. (It shows you how far down the pecking order the sport of soccer was at the time. They didn't even bother to schedule soccer for a home game on homecoming day.) I missed the excitement, but I did go over on the following Monday to the admin building and to get my certificate. Thanksgiving holiday weekend I took it home. My father took me right over to the drugstore to get a frame to put it in and, of course, took it to Thanksgiving dinner to show all the family. Later I got a letter from the publisher asking if I wanted to buy the book. Hell, no! I threw the form away. Of course they're not dumb; they also sent one to my parents, who unbeknownst to me purchased the book. Seeing that my parents bought it anyway I now have it placed on the bookshelves in our living room with other reference books, not far from the cherished books I was given by my Great-Aunt Lena.

I was actually very anti-hoity-toity back in college. My write-up in *Who's Who* is about the shortest one in all 1,082 pages. They asked me to write down all the clubs, honors, sports, organizations, etc. I belonged to. I sent in the following:

Haffner, Donald Richard
(Albion Coll.) 4156 Nickolas, Sterling Heights, Mich.
B. Jan. 24, 1951. B.A., History; 1972. Varsity soccer;
Sigma Nu; Choir; Resident Asst.; Empl. Mens Wear
Store; Food Service.

Short and sweet. Others put all kinds of stuff: Head of Porta Potty Brigade for special events on campus; member STP, Do Rae Me, and Wow Wow We; Chairperson of Organization for Fair Treatment of Mice and Other Rodents; "and so on and so on and scooby dooby dooby do." ("Everyday People," songwriter Sylvester Stewart, as sung by Sly and the Family Stone)

I could have added many more things to my listing, but again I just thought, *"Why bother? Who cares?"* I could have mentioned that I was not just an employee but that I actually "managed" menswear stores. I could have BS'ed and said I was the Chief Bottle Washer for the Albion Food Service. I could have mentioned that I was a charter member of the Albion College Zero Population Growth chapter. A couple of fellow soccer players and I had taken part in a program called REACH, where we went to an elementary school on the other side of Albion from the college one afternoon each week and did after-school programs for the students whose parents worked. Those two soccer players and I also coached a fifth grade basketball team in the Saturday league at the same school. I was involved in the ecology and recycling program in Albion. I would go afternoons after classes, put on safety goggles, and break up glass bottles into shards with a lead pipe in big oil drums so that much more glass would fit in them and they could then be hauled away to be recycled. (This was a good way to work out any frustrations too.) I was also a BMOC (Big Man On Campus) known far and wide, or at least as far and wide as one can be known on a small campus with around 1,500 students. But I didn't bother to write any of this down in my *Who's Who* write-up.

In addition, I was chosen again by some committee, unknown to me, to be a member of Omicron Delta Kappa (ODK): The National Leadership Honor Society. There was a luncheon for us chosen few, which I went to, and someone from the organization told us about ODK and what a great honor it was to be a member. A week or two later an envelope arrived from their national headquarters with a request for dues, as I remember, but maybe it was just asking for a donation. Either way, I threw the envelope in the trash. By this time, I had absolutely no money left in my bank account. For spending money, I was relying exclusively on my meager pay check from the Albion Food Service from my dishwashing job. I didn't care if they kicked me out or not, I could not afford to mail them a check of any amount. Decades later I received a letter from Omicron Delta Kappa saying they wanted to correspond with all past members and blah, blah, blah. I laughed because for all those years since college I had no idea if I was actually a member or not. In fact, I had forgotten all about the organization and even the name. I guess I'm a humble member. I hadn't mentioned this honorary society to *Who's Who* either!

Back at the Daeji Yeogwan, the conversation drifted away from the pompous-assed PCV who was in some edition or another of *Who's Who Among Students in Universities and Colleges* to the topic of the Korean government forcing farmers to knock down their old thatched roof houses and build more modern tile roof homes. In August of 1971, the North and South Korean Red Cross chapters began having talks. Whenever the North Korean delegation visited, the South Korean government would fix up everything within eyesight of the routes that the North Korean delegation would travel, sort of like Potemkin's villages. For example, roads would be paved as far as the eye could see off of any major thoroughfare the North Korean delegates would be driving down. On one of the visits, the delegation traveled on the expressway south from Seoul to Suwon. Before the visit, the South Korean government forced every farmer whose thatched roof house was in sight of the proposed route to Suwon to borrow money from the government and build a new tile roofed house with very beautiful red, blue, or green tiles. The South Koreans wanted North Korea to see that South Korea was no longer a developing country and make them think the Republic of Korea was now a wealthy, modern place. Of course, the South Korean economy was booming by this time. Even during our K-23 training there was talk of Peace Corps closing up shop in South Korea because the country was becoming too wealthy to justify having this American volunteer program. (Peace Corps finally did leave South Korea in 1981. North Korea, of course, never had any Peace Corps Volunteers.)

"Koreans should not improve their homes because the thatched roof houses are so quaint and cute. Foreign tourists want to see these thatched roof houses. It's stupid to build modern houses," Martha complained.

"Maybe so, but us foreigners telling Koreans they should all live in thatch roofed houses is like if British tourists came to the United States in the mid-1800s and told Americans they shouldn't improve their one-room, drafty, dark, dirt-floored, log cabins because the more modern Brits thought the log cabins were so quaint and cute," I said.

"Well maybe, but they are traditional and more interesting to look at," Martha said.

Thatched roof house near Mukho.

"Yes, and that's why we in the U.S.A. have places like Greenfield Village in Michigan, the Shelburne Museum in Vermont, Plimoth Plantation in Massachusetts, and Colonial Williamsburg in Virginia. I'm sure the Koreans will one day also have nice outdoor museums where tourists will be able to see how they lived in the good ol' days," I responded.

Of course, I later learned that a lot of farmers didn't want to give up their thatched roof cottages, not for nostalgia's sake, but rather because the huge loans they were forced to take out from the government to knock down their homes and build modern ones would take another generation to pay off. The farmers did not want to leave their children with this albatross hanging around their necks.

While we were finishing up the conversation on the positive and negative aspects of thatched roofs, Jack was fiddling with his wire-rimmed spectacles. His eyesight was pretty bad, and he couldn't see much without them. As he bent them to adjust the fit, they snapped in two. There he sat with one lens and arm in one hand and the other half of his glasses in his other hand. "Jack, what happened?" I asked. "Just lucky, I guess," was the response that he gave with the saddest look on his face that I'd ever seen. I tried my best not to laugh at his comment, but I thought that was one of the funniest lines I'd ever heard. "Just lucky, I guess," immediately became another one of my favorite lines to use just like Jack's other line, "No thanks, I'm trying to quit." Jack had used this line during our visit to Camp Henry in Daegu. As we were leaving with "the stuff," as Cheech and Chong used to call marijuana, a prostitute came up to Jack and was starting to proposition him when he replied, "No thanks, I'm trying to quit." Now I added "Just lucky, I guess," to my repertoire, and whenever something not too good happens and someone asks me about it, I reply with Jack's line, "Just lucky, I guess." Jack had some errands to run this day and took off for the afternoon. We agreed to meet later for our usual dinner and some beers. When he returned in the late afternoon his glasses were back in one piece.

"How'd you get them fixed?" I asked.

"As luck would have it, I saw a guy on a side street welding small pieces of metal together. I asked him if he could fix my glasses, and he did. Look at his work—amazing."

"That is amazing, and how auspicious that you would happen to run into him."

Jack handed me his glasses so I could admire the quality of the tiny weld that held his spectacles together. He gave the guy the equivalent of a few bucks, and his glasses were good as new or maybe even better.

Jack finished his pooping and paperwork to leave Peace Corps service before I got my pooping done, and he got his readjustment allowance and the equivalent of the return airfare so he could travel through Southeast Asia and then on to Europe before heading back to the States. Martha Vernor, a couple of other volunteers and I escorted him to Kimpo Airport. We all got there early, and Jack suggested that we head out to a grassy knoll outside the terminal. When we got there, Jack pulled out and lit up a joint. *"Oh, no, here we go again,"* I thought. I also began singing, "Pass the pipe around, and talk of poems and prayers and promises….." ("Poems Prayers and Promises" written and sung by John Denver) While singing, I was watching for the airport security and thinking I might get kicked out of Korea, not be able to extend for a third year, and never get to try the Silent Way in my class at Mukho Middle School. Thankfully, we didn't get caught. We walked with Jack back into the terminal. Each of us gave him a big hug, wished him well and watched him as he headed toward the big jet airplane that would take him off to his future and the rest of his life.

CHAPTER 12

Not a Bore! The Summer of '74

Finally, I got all my crap—I mean stool—samples in to Dr. Chu. On July 18, 1974, I too got on a big jet airplane like Jack, but I headed back to Detroit, and my summer vacation in America after two years of Peace Corps service in the Republic of Korea. I flew Northwest Orient, the American carrier, because the employees were not on strike as they had been in the summer of '72. This time we flew straight to the U.S. with a stop in Anchorage for refueling. Shortly after taking off out of Anchorage, the pilot announced that we were near the city of Juneau, Alaska. Since takeoff, I had been talking to the lady next to me who was married to an American soldier stationed in Korea.

"Did you know the Beatles wrote a song about Juneau?" I asked her.

"Really?"

"Yes." Then I started singing "Juneau, if you break my heart, I'll go," to the tune of the Beatles song "I'll Be Back." (Apologies to John Lennon and Paul McCartney) She groaned, and we resumed our conversation about her returning home because her mother was ill.

Some eighteen to twenty hours after leaving Kimpo Airport in Seoul and a transfer in Chicago, I landed at Metropolitan Airport in Romulus, Michigan. The police did not arrest me upon landing because of the aforementioned illegal pool party. Of course, they were still looking for Tony Dequindre, not Don Haffner, Peace Corps Volunteer extraordinaire. As I walked off the plane and into the terminal I saw my parents there waiting. I kissed my mother and hugged my father. It was an emotional greeting and wonderful to see them after two years.

It was late in the afternoon by the time we got back to my parents' home in Sterling Heights, Michigan. On the garage door was a huge banner that read, "WELCOME HOME DON!" I'm not sure who made the sign, but it sure gave me a warm, cuddly feeling inside. My parents announced that we'd have a quick, easy dinner because lots of relatives were coming over to welcome me back. I was running on adrenaline, so I was fine with that. I rarely sleep on airplanes. On the flight from Seoul to Chicago, I had eaten four meals, had a snack or two, and watched all four movies that they showed in between the meals and snacks. (In those days, you didn't have an individual screen on the seat in front of you; everyone had to watch the same movie on large screens at the front of each section of the plane. There was always a long line for the bathrooms right after each movie ended.) The short hop from Chicago to Detroit was nothing, but I had been up for more than a couple of days straight by this time.

Many of my aunts, uncles, and cousins came over after dinner, and we talked late into the night. My father loved to drink Manhattans in those days, and I joined in and had a couple myself. After everyone had left around midnight, my dad flipped on the lone outdoor light in the corner of the wooden deck he had built when they first moved into this home in 1971. "Come on, let me show you what we've planted in the backyard." I followed him out the sliding glass door and onto the deck. If you looked at my parents' house from above, it was an inverted L shape. The short part of the L was formed by their family room which stuck out the back towards the south with the sliding glass door on the west side of this room. The deck made the house into a rectangle as it stretched west to the far end of the back of the house. My father and mother had picked out and planted trees and shrubs all around their small backyard in every place that you could possibly plant something. Pointing at a shrub-like tree next to the stairs going down into the backyard, my dad said, "Thish ish a dwarf shpruce." My father had had at least one too many Manhattans by this point, and he was slurring his "s" sounds. I could see the dwarf spruce a little, as the light in the corner of the deck was close enough.

"Over here to the right ish a fitsher juniper." This pfitzer juniper bush was on the right side of the stairs. "Now here next to it ish a barberry bush and off the corner of the deck ish a locust tree." This far from the corner porch light all I could see was the outline of something tree shaped.

"Here at the far end of the deck ish a lilac bush," my father informed me while pointing into the darkness.

"Oh, 'When Lilacs Last in the Dooryard Bloom'd,'" I intoned with a mock New England accent. I don't think that my dad recognized this line. It's the title and first line of the poem written by Walt Whitman in homage to President Lincoln after Abe had been assassinated. I've always loved that poem and think of it whenever I see lilacs.

"Follow me," my father said, and he walked down the stairs and off to the right— west. "Now we planted another fitsher here and in the corner of the yard ish a yew."

"Oh, better a you than a me," I joked.

"Right," my dad replied, "and here next to it ish a shilver Rushian olive tree."

"Oh, are you going to press any Russian olive oil?"

"No, there are no olivesh, but ash you can see, it'sh a beautiful tree with narrow shilver leavesh." I couldn't see much of anything except again the outline of a tree, and I couldn't help being reminded of one of Larry Lathrup's and also one of my favorite Korean words, "*ahshedashipie,*" which means "as you can see," which I couldn't at this point in time. Next to the silver Russian olive heading east my father pointed out two pussy willows with a forsythia bush in between them.

"Pushy willowsh are good in schwampy placesh, and the back of the yard ish alwaysh wet," my father explained.

In the southeast corner of my parents' backyard was a storm drain. The backyards of about six houses west of the drain and six more east of it, half on Nickolas (my parents' street) and half on Cavant (the street behind them) tapered down to this low point at the corner of their yard. Consequently, at the back fence my father had left a three-foot wide swath of ground with pebbles to help rainwater drain away. Inside of that area is where the built-up beds with the trees and bushes were planted. In front of where the drain was in the raised bed on the east side of the yard was another pfitzer juniper and closer to the corner a crabapple tree. "Thish crabapple hash beautiful flowersh in the shpring," my father added. Heading toward the house was another yew, then a gate leading into the neighbors' yard with a patio stone path connecting the neighbors' deck and my parents' deck. My parents had become best friends with their neighbors on this side, Tom and Connie Hancock, and they visited back and forth so often that they put this gate in for easier access. Along the back of my parents' family room was an arbor vitae bush, then right behind the chimney, a variegated silverberry and next to it was the dwarf spruce by the stairs that my father had pointed out when we began our tour. By this time, I had been awake for more than two and a half days straight without one wink of sleep, and it was all I could do to keep my eyes open. I had patiently listened as my father told all his stories about the different shrubs and trees and how he and my mother had decided on each and where to plant them. It seemed hilariously funny to me that we were out in the dark looking at plantings that could hardly be seen. My dad didn't seem to think there was anything strange about it, though, and as he hadn't seen me in two years, I kind of felt that I owed him this attention. Finally, we went into the house, where my mother was cleaning up. I bade them good night, dropped into the bed in my old bedroom, and immediately fell asleep.

The next day I began planning out my vacation. There were numerous high school and college friends I wanted to catch up with. Most of them I had been writing to over the past two years from Korea. So they all knew I was just going to be around for only a couple of months and then return to the Land of the Morning Calm. Over the next few days I called my high school buddies, Joe Kercheval, Steve Sibley, and Tony Algonac. I invited them and their wives to a cookout at my parents' house near the end of July. My parents had suggested this, and I had thought it was a great idea.

Then I called Matt Engadine, my sophomore year roommate at the Sigma Nu house, and Billy Calumet, who was my fellow soccer teammate from the 1969 championship team and my "fraternity son," to set up a visit to see them and their wives. Matt was living with his wife Pat in Grand Rapids, Michigan, while Billy and his wife Diane were living in Niles due south of Grand Rapids and near the Indiana border. I set up to see them in early August.

I also called Kathy Pinckney, a friend since our freahman year in college. During our sophomore year when I dated Sara Swift, whose father was a VP of Sears Roebuck and Company at the time, Kathy was dating John Sebewaing, a fellow Sigma Nu. We double-dated a lot, and Kathy often said that I was her second favorite man in the world. (I'm not sure if I came in just after her father or just after John, but either way it was pretty good.) While Kathy was still going steady with John, she went to Europe on vacation during the summer between our sophomore and junior years, and she brought back for me a Donovan double album because she knew I loved Donovan. This album of lovely children's songs called *HMS Donovan* was never released in the U.S.

During my senior year of college, I hardly dated anyone. In fact, I went out of my way not to have a steady girlfriend. I knew that I was going to enter the Peace Corps after college if I had the opportunity, and I didn't want any entangling alliance with a woman to get in the way of my leaving. But when I heard that Donovan would be playing at Eastern (EMU), I invited Kathy to go with me to thank her for the wonderful gift. We remained good friends and had been pen pals for the past couple of years.

Kathy was living with her parents in the town of Mason a little more than halfway to Lansing from Sterling Heights. I borrowed my mother's car and drove over to visit her late Friday afternoon. Her father was already home from work when I got there, and I met him, Kathy's mother, and her also very attractive younger sister. Over dinner we all talked. Her father owned a tool and die shop that made special blades used to cut leather or fabric for car upholstery. These blades he sold to one of the Big Three automobile companies. He swore that his facility made the best blades in the business for this application and that no one made them that lasted as long as his did. He also told me that there was another tool and die shop just up the street from his place. This shop was owned by a

Korean-American named Mr. Moon. Kathy's parents were both quite liberal, and Mr. Pinckney told me that once when he was talking about politics with Mr. Moon, the Korean-American got so mad that he said, "You are un-Amelican." We laughed at that, but it didn't surprise me because most South Koreans were quite conservative.

Kathy and I went out after dinner to a bar for a beer or two. When we returned Kathy's sister was out, and her parents were asleep. We sat on the floor in their family room and reminisced about our college days.

The next morning Kathy took me for a walk around the property. They had a swimming pool off to the side of the house, and she told me about how she and her sister sometimes swam topless.

"Once," she said, "we looked across the street and the guy who lives in the house across the way had his binoculars out and was checking out the view."

"Why don't we get your sister and all three of us swim topless this morning?" I suggested.

"Right, I don't think so," Kathy replied.

"Why not? It'd be fun," I suggested.

"Yeah, fun for you, but that's not going to happen."

"I'm downhearted," I said.

"Too bad," she replied while laughing.

Her parents had a lot of property behind the house, and there was a stream that they had dammed up to form a small pond with a little rowboat on it. I had always dreamed of living out in the country, and this home seemed heavenly to me. But after lunch I thanked Kathy and her parents and headed back to Sterling Heights. I told Kathy that I hoped to see her again before leaving to go back to Korea, and she agreed that would be nice.

My cousin, Cherie, happened to be getting married in the summer of 1974, and of course I was invited. My mother suggested that I might want to ask Linda Boyne to accompany me. Linda had started working at my parents' gift and jewelry store, Bedon's, when she was still in high school. Her aunt had worked for my parents first, and when they needed an extra part-timer she suggested her niece. I had worked at Bedon's with Linda during the Christmas vacation of my senior year in college. At that time, Linda was a senior in high school. She was vivacious and absolutely gorgeous. I was smitten the moment I saw her, but I thought she was too young and didn't want to be accused of robbing the cradle, so I admired her from afar.

She didn't like to wrap gifts and gift wrapping was offered as a customer service by my parents' store. Whenever she sold something and the customer wanted the item gift wrapped, she'd look at me with those lovely dark eyes and say, "Don, would you wrap this, please?" She had me eating out of her hands. I would have done anything she asked me to do. "Sure, let me do it for you," I'd reply and deftly wrap the box, as I had learned the fine art of gift wrapping years before. My father was the head of display at United Shirt Distributors, and my parents had long had gift stores—the first one in Allen Park and now this one in St. Clair Shores.

I had already thought of trying to call Linda Boyne since coming back home. She was in college now, and our age difference no longer seemed as important, but I hadn't broached the idea to my parents yet. When my mother made this suggestion, it was all that I could do to not scream for joy. But I was cool and said, "Sure, Mom, I could give Linda a call. That's a good idea because she knows Cherie as well as Uncle Bob and Aunt Ruby already." That night I called, and she agreed to go to Cherie's wedding with me. I also invited her to come to the cook-out for my high school friends, but she refused and/or gave an excuse suggesting that she didn't know any of them and that maybe it was better for her not to attend that party.

I also called Barry Wyandotte, my older Allen Park High School friend from our United Shirt days and one of the co-conspirators in our airport hotel swimming pool caper. He had graduated from Central Michigan University while I was still in college, and by the summer of '72 he had already been teaching high school-level biology for several years in one of the school systems in the Downriver Detroit area. He invited me to come visit his house, and then we'd go out to lunch together. When I got there he gave me a quick tour starting with the garage, which was almost as big as the house. He was into old cars and repairing them, and he had plenty of room here to do his tinkering. We wandered back into the house. He spent much less time describing the inside of his house than he had the garage.

Then as we started to head out for lunch, his fiancée came in. When I had called him on the phone, he'd told me that he was engaged to a gal who was several years younger than he was. His fiancée had been one of his students and had just graduated from high school the year before. She walked in screaming bloody murder and calling him many names that can't be repeated in polite company or even on the pages of this book. After her initial rant, he introduced her to me. Her name was Misty Zilwaukee. Realizing my presence after having been formally introduced didn't seem to have any effect on her temperament or obnoxious behavior. Her father owned a car wash, and there was some problem with a key for the business that Barry was supposed to have left somewhere but he had brought home instead. Barry apologized and finally got her to settle down a bit. Misty ran into the bedroom, found the key, and stormed out.

"Sorry, she's a little high strung."

"Yes, so I see."

"Between the classes she's taking at Henry Ford Community College and helping her father with his business while he's ill, she's under a lot of pressure."

"What happened to her father?"

"Heart attack, but he should be OK."

"That's good to hear." But I was thinking that no matter how much pressure she was under, she had no right to behave the way she did. She seemed like a spoiled brat rich kid to me—a very attractive one, mind you, but still bratty.

After a nice lunch and a long conversation with Barry, I drove home. While driving back to Sterling Heights, his fiancée's pretty face contorted in anger, the horrible things she said to Barry and the names she called him replayed in my mind over and over. I just couldn't see this relationship lasting long. I have never seen Barry again, but I heard from another United Shirt friend, Dennis Hisperia, who graduated from Allen Park High with Barry and who just happened to marry my cousin's wife's best friend, that this marriage with Misty did not last very long.

My Melvindale High School friends came the last Sunday in July for a cookout on my parents' deck. It was great to see them all: Joe Kercheval, Steve Sibley, and Tony Algonac. They were all married, and two of them had married their high school sweethearts. Both Steve's and Joe's wives graduated the year after Joe and I had graduated from Melvindale High School. I had stood up in Steve and Martha's wedding my senior year in college. Joe and Judy had married while I was in Korea. Joe sent photos of the wedding and their honeymoon in Acapulco, Mexico. He sent a set of small photos that used to come as a bonus if you developed your film at Hite. I treasured them when Joe sent them to me and treasure them still. Lastly, Tony married Bobbi whom he had been dating while in college at Eastern Michigan University (EMU). On this summer Sunday we had a wonderful afternoon and evening together drinking beer and eating hamburgers. Also, I showed them all of my photographs from Korea; many of which are reproduced in this book. The pictures were black and white, not color, and all just loose in a big pile. Each couple looked at them one at a time and then passed them on to the next couple. I gave a running narrative as they were being passed along, often having to repeat or point out which pictures went with which story I'd already told. I didn't get my Peace Corps pictures into a photo album until more than twenty years after completing my three years of Peace Corps service. Sometimes I'm a little slow, and also I was a little too busy living each stage of my life with little regard for nostalgia until much more recently.

I thought Joe and Steve were lucky, and I envied them for having met someone in high school and falling in love. Often (without pronouncing the 't') I wish that had happened to me. There is so much commonality in marrying someone from your high school with the same background and memories. Unfortunately, I had not really dated anyone in high school; I just never met anyone I liked all that much. Obviously, my relationship with Sara in college hadn't worked out either, and after that I became very gun shy. Later I did about the exact opposite of marrying someone with a lot of similarities and instead married a Korean. I sometimes think it's too bad I hadn't met someone special with a comparable background from high school like Joe and Steve did, or at least in college as Tony did. I did do that to a great extent the second time around. Carol and I were both born in Detroit, grew up in small story-and-a-half bungalow homes in the suburbs of Detroit, and both have Canadian ancestors on our mothers' sides of our families.

The next Saturday, August 3, 1974, was Cherie's wedding at Bethel Lutheran Church in St. Clair Shores, Michigan. Linda Boyne lived nearby the church, and I picked her up on the way. We met my parents at Bethel and sat next to them up front close to the altar. This seemed strange, as my parents and I always sat in the last pew at Christ Lutheran Church in Warren where my parents attended, but then we were close relatives of the bride. At one point during the ceremony a poem by Elizabeth Barrett Browning was read. I later learned it was my Aunt Ruby's (Cherie's mother) favorite poem. The pastor intoned, "How do I love thee? Let me count the ways." ("How Do I Love Thee? Sonnet 43," by Elizabeth Barrett Browning) As he continued I held out my index finger and said, "One," then I put up my index and second fingers and said, "one and a half, maybe two, but that's it." Linda started laughing out loud, poked me in the ribs with her elbow, and I smiled and held my index finger up to my lips and she laughed some more. I knew then I was even more enchanted with this gorgeous gal who appreciated my goofy sense of humor.

I'm not sure why, but the reception was at a Polish Club. (Our family's hometown is near Danzig, which is now Gdansk, Poland. Maybe that's why it was there.) Linda and I danced the night away until we were worn out. I said, "It's warm in here; let's go out to the vestibule." We walked out there where the air-conditioning wasn't mitigated by so many people dancing and heating up the environment. Looking out the front doors, I suggested we take a walk. We walked up and down the neighborhood streets talking and holding hands the whole time. By the time I took her home I was infatuated.

My parents had heard about the Agawa Canyon train tour on the Algoma Central Railway from Sault Ste. Marie, Ontario. The week after Cherie's wedding they suggested that we three head up there in the middle of the week for a couple of days. I had always loved and still do love the northern part of Michigan, so I was more than happy to drive up through the Lower Peninsula, across the Upper Peninsula, and into Canada over the International Bridge from Sault Ste. Marie, Michigan, to Sault Ste. Marie, Ontario. The Algoma Central train heads north from Sault Ste. Marie, Ontario, through beautiful forests and canyons up to a small valley area with some waterfalls. You get off the train for an hour or so and then re-board and head back to town. It's a nice day trip, and we enjoyed it.

Thursday, August 8, 1974, on the way back to Detroit we visited Mackinac Island. Mackinac Island is how I envision heaven. It is a very historic place where the British built a fort, the American Fur Company once had its trading post, and it is where Dr. William Beaumont did his famous gastric experiments. To make it even better there are no cars allowed on the island, only bicycles and horse drawn carriages. While my parents and I were walking through the amazing Grand Hotel, which opened in 1887, and has the longest wooden porch in the world, we saw a poster that said there would be a TV placed in the ball room that evening so the guests could watch a special speech to be given by President Richard Nixon. We took the ferry back to the Lower Peninsula and stayed at a motel in Mackinaw City that evening. After dinner we watched the speech in our motel room there and heard Richard Nixon announce his resignation. I and my mother were happy, but my father, who always voted Republican, seemed less so.

The next week I had set up to visit my two college friends and fraternity brothers Matt Engadine and Billy Calumet over in the western part of the state. So I drove across to Grand Rapids on a Wednesday. Matt was working. I parked and went up to his place of work, a furniture company with offices in a downtown building. It was almost lunchtime, and Matt led me into his office where we talked for a while. Then he suggested we go out to lunch with several of his coworkers. We went to a Mexican restaurant after Matt introduced me to his fellow employees. There he suggested I might want to order my lunch mild, as their food was very hot. I assured him that the Koreans ate hot food all the time and that I was very used to hot peppers. After lunch Matt had to return to work, and I wandered around the shops in downtown Grand Rapids and checked out the library.

When Matt's workday was ended I met him again, and he suggested we go out to dinner at a restaurant. Pat, his lovely wife, had to work late, and Matt didn't feel like cooking. First, we stopped at a Meijer's Thrifty Acres store. This was a superstore with a large supermarket as well as a department store-like area all in one huge space. As we walked in, I felt overwhelmed and nauseous. The store went on forever. I had never seen such a large store before, and it was such a culture shock in reverse. Now I was used to Korea and its little *gages*. This place nearly made me faint. I was shocked at the gross amount of stuff all in one place. I let Matt go on and get what he needed, and I stayed by the doors. Thankfully, he came back quickly before I puked up lunch. Then we went to a very swanky restaurant and I remember thinking, *"Oh God, I can't afford this place."* Matt must have read my mind because as we sat down he said right away, "Dinner's on me." I, of course, protested, but not too vigorously, and Matt insisted. So we had a lovely meal with cocktails before and an after-dinner drink with dessert. I was thinking this was awfully extravagant.

After dinner Matt wanted to stop at a menswear store. This too looked like an upscale place. Matt had a shirt in mind and was looking through their shirt department while I saw a sale table and was checking it out. There was a pair of khaki-colored slacks with wide bell-bottoms that happened to be my size.

"Hey Matt, I'm going to try these on," I yelled over.

"Sure, go ahead, I'm still shopping," he replied.

"OK, great!" I tried the slacks on and they were kind of hiphugging, snug in the thighs, and then, being bell-bottoms, very wide at the ankles. In the mirror I could see that my ass looked fantastic in these tight-fitting slacks. They were expensive for me, even though they were on sale, but I really liked them. Matt came over with two shirts he had picked out.

"Yeah, those look great, you ought to get them."

"You know, I think I will," I agreed.

"Meet you at the cash register."

"Sure, I'll be out in a second." I changed back into my blue jeans and walked with Matt up to the register. He laid his shirts down on the counter and the saleslady said, "Will this be all?" Matt said, "No," grabbed the khakis out of my hand and said, "Add these, too!" This time I really did try to seriously talk him out of buying these slacks for me, and I tried to grab them back off the counter. Matt, bigger and stronger than I, stood his ground. "No, Don, I insist. You're a Peace Corps Volunteer, and this is my gift for you." I was speechless as well as much moved and very grateful. For several years after this, every time I wore these pants I thought of Matt, our year together as roommates at the Sigma Nu house at Albion College, the several weekends I had visited him up at MSU during our junior and senior years after he had transferred there, as well as this wonderful visit with him and Pat in Grand Rapids in the summer of 1974. But I was also worried. I had no idea how much money Matt and Pat made, but this seemed like a huge expenditure for one day between lunch, dinner and the shopping. I had the sneaking suspicion that this was normal behavior for Matt, and I was concerned for his finances and his marriage, and yet I had only been with him for a few hours so far. My father used to say about some of his friends that they had "champagne taste on a beer budget," or was that, "champagne taste on a wine budget?" Either way, I wondered if this were not the case with Matt.

After shopping, we went to Matt's apartment. It was an apartment in a huge, old colonial-style mansion that had been cut up into several rental units. All up and down the street were big old houses in colonial, Tudor, Cape Cod, and other old styles except for the home directly across the street from his place. That house across the street was a very modern looking, long ranch-style house with very straight lines, and I noticed it had oversized copper rain gutters and downspouts.

"Wow, that house is interesting, but very different from all the other houses," I commented. Matt explained that it was a Frank Lloyd Wright-designed house, built by a Jewish man named Meyer in 1908.

"He was ostracized by the whole town of Grand Rapids when he had this built," Matt said.

"You're kidding?"

"No, Grand Rapids was and still is a conservative place. That house was called a monstrosity, and the Grand Rapidians hated it."

"I think they were nuts. It sure looks great to me."

We went into Matt's place, and Pat had just gotten home too. I had met Pat when they were dating at MSU, but like most of my high school friends they were married while I was in Korea. (I saved a fortune, not having to buy wedding gifts, for all my friends who got married while I was away.) We sat talking about Frank Lloyd Wright, Pat's job, Matt's job, Korea, and being a Peace Corps Volunteer. I showed my pile of black and white pictures. Then we reminisced about our college days while downing a couple of bottles of wine.

Thursday Matt took a day off work and showed me the sights around Grand Rapids, none of which I remember much anymore. I stayed again Thursday night. This time we stayed in and had pizza. Friday I got up with them. As they went off to work I gave them my fond farewells, said, "auf wiedersehen" (good-bye) and headed south toward Niles where Billy Calumet and Diane Calumet née Kitchener lived. Billy and Diane had both been a year behind me in college. Billy was my fraternity son, and we had both played on Albion's soccer team together for two years before he and Diane both transferred to Michigan

State University, just as Matt Engadine had done the year before them.

Niles sits near the Michigan border with Indiana. Billy worked for a local Niles company, and Diane worked in South Bend, Indiana, where Notre Dame University is located. I got to Billy's company and met him, as I had done with Matt in Grand Rapids, before he'd finished his workday. I wandered around till Bill finished work. Then Bill and I went to his house where Diane was already home. She looked as beautiful as ever. Both Matt and Bill still looked like all-American heartthrobs with chiseled faces and short, sandy blond-colored hair. Together, Bill and Diane looked like the perfect couple. I was in awe of their beauty and handsomeness compared to my scruffy, bearded, not very good look-ing-ness. It was a pleasure to be with them, as it had been to be with Matt and Pat who were equally as attractive as Bill and Diane.

Saturday they suggested we head over to their favorite beach on Lake Michigan. As we were driving near their apartment and toward the highway, we passed a huge house.

"Holy cow, is that a house or a country club?" I inquired.

"Oh, that's the Eauclaire house. He's the owner and editor of the local newspaper among other things," Billy said.

"Wait, do they have a daughter named Sheena, who goes to EMU?"

"Yes, they do. Do you know her?" Diane asked.

"Yes, I know Sheena, she's a cute gal. I once spent a night playing cards with her until dawn." Then I told them the long story of the night of Steve and Martha's wedding, which I had stood up in. I left their reception around midnight after calling Tony Algonac, drove to Eastern in my mother's car, and met up with Tony and Bobbi. Then Bobbi called Sheena, who was pledged to Bobbi's sorority, and invited her over to play cards with us. After playing all through the night, we then went to early mass at the local Catholic church together.

By the time I finished the story we were almost to the beach. After spending much of the day at the beach and eating a picnic lunch that Diane had prepared, we began packing up the car. Next to Billy's car was a convertible with the top down. Music was playing, and it sounded like chanting, but this was long before some monks in Spain had a hit album of Gregorian chants that climbed up the American charts. I had not heard chanting like this before. It was beautiful. A middle-aged man with a goatee and mustache and his exotic-looking wife were loading their stuff into this convertible.

"That is such lovely music. What is it?" I asked.

"You don't look like you vould like sis music! You look like a shwinger!" the man said with a heavy European accent.

"Well maybe I look like a swinger, but I do like this music. I sang in my college's choir, and we did a lot of classical and religious music." I must have convinced him because he showed me the cover for the cassette tape and explained that it was Gregorian chanting.

Sunday I bid farewell to Billy and Diane and headed back to Detroit. I had by now met many of my old friends I wanted to touch base with while home, but there were still a few others I wanted to see. One was Linda Ecorse, my neighbor from my years growing up on Keppen Avenue in Allen Park. When I got home from the western part of Michigan, I called her and made a date to meet the following Friday night. I also called Linda Boyne and then Tony Algonac. I had mentioned to Tony during the party at my parents' house that I was dating a gorgeous gal who hadn't been able to come to the cookout. Tony suggested that we double-date sometime before the end of summer. Linda Boyne was free the next Saturday night, and so were Tony and Bobbi. So I had my next weekend planned. I also got in touch with Otto Peach, who had been a good friend during my senior year at Albion when he was a freshman and we both lived in the Suzy dormitory. He decided to drive up to Detroit from his home in Ohio a week from the following Saturday. The summer was flying by so quickly, but it sure was wonderful to see all my old friends.

I also got together one evening with Joe Kercheval and Steve Sibley and Steve's younger brother, Mickie, who was on home leave from the Air Force. We went out to a strip club somewhere downriver and sat watching the topless gals while talking about old times. Steve talked about how we used to be playing baseball down at the park on Arno Street when I was fifteen, he was seventeen, and Joe was sixteen, and I'd announce that I had to go home and get ready for work. I worked before any of my buddies did even though I was younger. I was able to begin working at fifteen because my father was an executive at United Shirt Distributors. There was a special work permit available in those days for fifteen-year-olds if they were working for or with their fathers. Joe and Steve both laughed about how working was far from their minds at that time, and here I was the youngest among the three of us already working.

Another college buddy I looked up was Sam Okemos. He and Sam Boisblanc were two of the guys with whom I often spent afternoons discussing different topics like draining Lake Erie. Besides the fact that he had lived on my corridor during his freshman, my senior year, we had both played on Albion's soccer team together. Consequently, we had also kept in touch by mail over these first two years of my Peace Corps service. He was off on Wednesday and I suggested we catch a Bruce Lee movie in downtown Detroit at the Adams Theater, one of the old and once opulent movie theaters on Grand Circus Park. The ornate interior was a little shell-shocked and tattered, but you could perceive how beautiful it once was. We went into the john to take a leak, but neither of us wanted to touch anything in there as the coat of grit and grime and who knows what else covering every inch of the walls, floor, and even the ceiling grossed us out. The Adams Theater was showing *The Big Boss* with the great ice factory fight scene at the end, which I hadn't seen yet and neither had Sam. In Mukho I had already seen "Enter the Dragon," Bruce Lee's big Hollywood movie, as well as a couple of his other earlier films. After the movie we went back to the northern suburbs and grabbed dinner out there.

Friday night I headed back downriver to Allen Park and drove to Linda Ecorse's house, which was across the street and one house over from the house I had grown up in. Linda was like the sister I never had. We had never dated, but were always good buddies. Throughout middle school and high school many summer evenings we'd sit together on her porch or my porch and talk late into the night. We graduated together in 1968 from Melvindale High School. Her older sister, Leslie, had graduated a couple of years earlier. The first time I ever kissed a girl was when Linda, Leslie, my Dasher Junior High School friend John Ludington, and I played spin the bottle in Linda and Leslie's basement. Leslie spun first, and the bottle stopped in front of me. She was three years older than I and a more mature high school student compared to us other three junior high students. I must have looked like a deer caught in the headlights because Leslie suggested we go behind the door into the other part of the basement to kiss. We went behind the door, and I looked at Leslie and she looked back at me.

"Well, what are you waiting for?"

"You spun the bottle, so you have to kiss me."

"No, you're the guy, so you must kiss me."

Linda and John heard this and started snickering, which made me even more embarrassed than I had been anyway. Leslie leaned in and kissed me, saving me from any further shame. Then we walked out, and I spun. It landed on Linda, and this time I leaned over and kissed her quickly. Then we went on, and after a couple more go rounds I was completely accustomed to this lip-locking stuff. (No tongue yet, though.)

As I pulled up the drive of Linda's house, Matt Munising was out on his porch next door to Linda's house. The Munisings, Matt and Carol, had five children: Mary, Tom, Pattie, Bobbie, and Anne. Mary was a year ahead of Linda and me in school. Mary, Linda, and I often hung around together during the summers after dinner, although Mary was always called in around 10:00 p.m. by her parents, while Linda and I were allowed to stay outside as long as we wanted. My nextdoor neighbors, the Houghtons, told me later that they used to argue about which one I'd end up marrying. Mr. Houghton thought Mary, while Mrs. Houghton was sure it would be Linda. Of course, they both turned out to have been wrong and off by a whole continent.

Tom, the second oldest of the Munising children, was a year younger than I, and we often played baseball together down at the park with mutual friends. Even more often Tom, my father, and I would play a game that we kids invented called curb-ball. We played right in front of our houses. In curb-ball the batter (or rather thrower) would throw a rubber ball against the curb. If it flew more than halfway across the street and wasn't caught, it was a hit—halfway across the street was a single, three-quarters across a double, onto the grass on the other side of the street a triple, and onto the sidewalk or farther a home run. Any ball caught was an out, and three throws without getting at least halfway across the street on the fly in bounds meant a strike-out. Many nights after dinner in the summer we'd take turns playing this game for hours.

This evening in the summer of '74, I started talking to Matt, and then Carol came out on the porch to greet me. None of their kids was home. Linda had heard me drive up, so she also came out to see me and greet me. Matt invited us both in to see his woodworking. After retiring he had gotten into making bird houses and wooden plaques with sayings on them and other small items made of wood. He was quite talented, and I was impressed by the quality of his work and the obvious pride he took in it.

We went into Linda's house and sat and talked with her parents, Max and Arlene, for a while. Linda had suggested that we grab dinner out and then go see a double feature that was playing at a movie theater in Dearborn. (Double features always remind me of Kobe, Japan.) The two movies were *Blazing Saddles* and *Lady Sings the Blues.* Linda had raved about *Blazing Saddles,* especially the scene where the cowboys were sitting around a campfire, eating beans, and then farting. *Blazing Sad*dles was shown first, and I thought it was a little moronic, especially the scene where the cowboys were all sitting around a campfire, eating beans, and farting. Linda laughed at this part and slapped my knee. "Isn't that hilarious?" she asked. "Right, hilarious," I answered, but I was thinking it seemed just sort of silly to me. After it finished there was a short intermission, then *Lady Sings the Blues* started. I enjoyed this movie more, and I thought Diana Ross did a good job of acting although I guess it really wasn't much of a stretch for her to play the part of the famous singer, Billie Holiday. But anyway I liked this movie much more than *Blazing Saddles,* and I really wanted to see the whole thing, but I almost didn't make it through to the end because I couldn't sit still.

I was in the best shape of my life by this point after a year of twice-daily taekwondo workouts. All summer long I continued working out most days while in America. I'd go out into my parents' backyard and kick and punch at the bushes, the very same ones that my dad had described in such detail the first evening out in the pitch-black night. I'd also sit on the deck and do yoga-like stretches and poses. There was a young boy around five years old living in the house behind my parents, and sometimes I'd hear him yell to his mother, "Mom, that guy's kicking again." She'd yell back, "That's OK. He's just exercising." I had to stretch and exercise every day, or I'd go crazy and my muscles would begin to tighten up and I'd start feeling anxious. Sitting still in a chair for more than one movie got to be nearly too much to bear. I started squirming in the seat. First I'd stretch one leg, then the other, then stretch one arm, and then the other. I'd then interlace my fingers and extend my arms out straight, then point one arm down across the opposite knee and grab that shoulder with my other hand, pulling my upper arm and popping the shoulder joint.

"Are you OK? Do you want to leave?" Linda asked several times.

"No, I really want to see this movie, but my muscles are all tensing up from sitting still so long."

"Are you sure? We can leave, if you want."

"No, I'd like to see the end of the movie. Wait, I'll be right back." I ran up into the lobby and squatted down, swayed back and forth, stood up straight and bent over, touching my toes over and over. My favorite stretch was to straighten one leg out to the side and then bend the other leg squatting down with my butt touching the bent leg's ankle and then switching to the opposite side. The theater staff stared at me like I was weirder than hell, but I just had to stretch. After limbering up, I returned to my seat and managed to make it through till the end of the show.

By this time, I had probably driven Linda nuts. But in all honesty she had also driven me nuts by this point, too. She had picked up an affectation that, by the end of the evening, had me grating my teeth every couple of minutes. I'm not sure where she got this annoying habit of hers; she was working in a downtown Detroit office and probably picked it up there. It was aggravating as hell. She would end nearly every sentence with "OK?" But it was not just a quick OK; she would drag out the kaaaaay part and make every sentence seem like a question by her inflection at the end of the "kay!" Her comments would go something like this:

I was walking down the street, okaaaay? Then I looked in the
store window and there was the most beautiful pair of shoes
there, okaaaay? I knew I had to buy them. So I went in and tried
them on, okaaaay?

By about this point in time I was ready to scream, "No, it's not OK!" I felt like
that egghead-shaped guy in the famous Edvard Munch painting, "The Scream."
"Stop saying OK before my head explodes, please," I wanted to beg her. After the
movie, I drove her home and gave her a quick kiss goodbye, as I had so many
years earlier when we played "spin the bottle."

Years later, actually more than a couple of decades later, when I got back in
touch with Linda she no longer spoke this way, thankfully. She did mention during this conversation a couple of things that made me laugh. First, she told me
that she remembered when I, way back in the summer of 1969 between my freshman and sophomore years of college, was out in front of our house on Keppen
kicking around a strange black and white ball and bouncing it off my head. Linda
said that was the first time she had ever seen a soccer ball or heard about the sport.
She mentioned how by the 1980s it had become such a popular sport that her
kids had played it while growing up, and it reminded her of me. She also told me
that I was the one who first turned her on to yogurt. I had forgotten until she said
this, but I had started eating yogurt in high school partially because I thought it
was exotic. Also, there was a TV commercial about people in some Russian village
in the Ural Mountains where they nearly all lived to be more than a hundred years
old, and it was implied that because they ate yogurt they lived that long. Back
then, I wanted to live to be a hundred too. Nowadays, I'm not so sure about
wanting to live to be a hundred, but I do still eat yogurt.

The next night I picked up Linda Boyne. No aggravating affectations from
her. She was so cute, so sweet, and I was so happy to be introducing her to Tony
and Bobbi. They were living downriver in Southgate. I picked up Linda over in
St. Clair Shores on the east side of Southeast Michigan and headed down I-94
toward the southwest right by the World's Largest Tire in Allen Park. Such a
beautiful sight for sore eyes, it was. This tire had been a ferris wheel at the 1964
New York World's Fair. In 1966, the twenty-four gondolas that had transported
people around in circles were removed and replaced by tread, then this eighty-
foot-tall tire was moved to Allen Park near the Uniroyal corporate building alongside the I-94 expressway. We picked up Tony and Bobbi at their apartment
complex and headed out to dinner. After dinner we headed back to their place for
drinks, and they gave us a tour of their apartment. My biggest memory is of their

living room and the abstract painting that they had above their sofa. "This paint-ing we bought at Sears," Tony said. "Yes," Bobbi added, "the colors just go per-fectly with our décor." Linda and I agreed, but I looked at this painting and said to myself, *"It is just a bunch of lines and colors. It has no meaning."* Yeah, OK (not "okaaay?" mind you) the colors did go with the sofa, the carpet, and the drapes, but so what? I also couldn't help thinking I wasn't ready for this kind of average American lifestyle. I did not want to get a normal nine-to-five job somewhere, live in the Detroit area, and buy a painting from Sears. I knew extending another year in the Peace Corps was the right decision for me. I still had no idea what I wanted to do when and if I ever grew up, but being an average, middle-class American was not in the cards for me—at least not right now. Yet, I looked over at Linda and couldn't help thinking, if I ever do want to settle down, I could see settling down with her. But????? Tony and Bobbi were still talking about their décor and why they got these curtains in the kitchen, etc. I could see they were excited, and I was happy for them, but I was missing Korea and my life there. We sat, drank, and talked for awhile with Tony and Bobbi. Then Linda and I headed back up northeast on I-94. I dropped off Linda at her parents' house, kissed her good-night, and I went home to my parents' home.

Three years later Billy Joel came out with his album *The Stranger*, and one of the songs on it always reminds me of Tony and Bobbi and their painting:

> They got an apartment with deep pile carpet
> And a couple of paintings from Sears
> ("Scenes From an Italian Restaurant" written and sung by Billy Joel)

The minute I heard that, I thought, *"Oh my God, he's describing Tony and Bobbi!"* (at least in that one part of the song).

Another college friend Otto Peach came up from Ohio on the last Saturday I was home. I had also contacted Kathy again, and we went on a double date with Kathy and her sister up to East Lansing. We hit some of the bars around Michi-gan State, which reminded me of my college days and some of the weekends I had spent up at MSU. We stayed overnight at Kathy's. The next morning, Otto and I headed back to Detroit, and then he left to return to his home.

The summer was about over. My last night home several relatives came over again to wish me well, and Linda Boyne came over to see me one last time. We had dated a couple of other times besides the wedding and the Saturday night with Tony and Bobbi. I was anxious to get back to Korea, but I was already dread-ing leaving Linda. This was why I had not really dated anyone my whole senior year in college. I had not wanted anyone pulling at my heartstrings. This last night in Detroit, around nine, when it was still light outside, Linda announced that she was going to leave and said goodbye to my aunts, uncles, and cousins who were visiting. I walked Linda out to her car, which was parked on the opposite side of the street. I suggested she stay a little longer, but she refused saying I should spend the rest of the evening together with my relatives. I kissed her a long, sweet kiss. I opened the car door, she got in, and I closed it for her. She began crying, and I stood there staring at her with tears in my eyes too. She had her window down, and I tried to lean in and kiss her again, but she pushed me away and said, "Please, go back in." I turned and walked a few steps and noticed the car was still not moving. I turned around and saw she was still crying. I started to walk back toward her. She repeated, "No, please go back in the house." Downhearted, downcast, and downright devastated, I walked back toward my parents' house. I got to the porch, and Linda was still sitting with her head down and obviously still sobbing. She looked over. I waved, and then she put the car in gear and slowly drove off. I dried my eyes as best I could, breathed in deeply, tried to put on a smile, and walked back into the house to face my family. Uncle Bob, my dad's older brother, said "Where have you been? What took so long?" I mumbled something to change the subject such as, "How about our Tigers, aren't they doing well?" Or, "Boy, it sure has been hot lately!"

The next morning, I packed up my bag, and my parents drove me back to Detroit's Metropolitan Airport (or DTW). In my youth, I always thought the DTW stood for DeTroit-Windsor, Canada, and I thought it was neat to be an international hub. Or, maybe it was for the French pronunciation of Detroit (De-TWa) which I also thought was cool. Only decades later did I realize DTW actually stood for DeTroit-Wayne County. Detroit and the airport are both in Wayne County, which is named, of course, after good ol' General "Mad" Anthony Wayne, who had served in the Revolutionary War and then later won the Battle of Fallen Timbers in northern Ohio against an Indian confederacy. I like DeTroit-Windsor better with my Canadian ancestry and global/international perspective, but it is what it is.

My Aunt Ruth also drove out to the airport with my cousins Cherie and Marcy, as well as our grandmother, Emma. This time grandma didn't tell me I had to marry a German gal. (I think maybe later when I actually married a Korean, she regretted this oversight.) As we were all at the gate waiting for the call for me to board, I remember walking over to the coffee shop at the airport with newly married Cherie and her sister Marcy, explaining to them about how the Koreans and Japanese pronounced coffee. In both Korean and Japanese, which are related Ural-Altaic languages, there is no "f" sound. But they both use the English word coffee for the hot, dark-brown beverage we all know and love. In Korea they replaced the "ff's" with a "p" sound. So they say "copee" which is funny because "co" can mean nose and "pee" means rain, so copee also means snot, mucus, or runny boogers. In Japanese they change the "ff's" to an "h" sound and they say "cohee." So I pontificated away on the different ways coffee is pronounced in East Asia on our way over to purchase said drink from the coffee shop near the gate. In those days it wasn't a Starbucks.

I was about to board a short flight to Chicago. There were no direct flights to Seoul from Detroit, but there were from Chicago. The call came to board the row where I was sitting, and I hugged and kissed my aunt, grandma, and cousins. Then I started to bid farewell to my parents when Tom Romeo walked up. Tom was a fellow Sigma Nu from Albion. He was a senior my sophomore year, and he was a suitemate with Matt and me in the frat house. He stopped, and I introduced him to my parents. Then he started asking questions, and I said, "Tom, how about we talk inside the plane after it gets off the ground?" "Sure," he replied, "I'll see you inside." I finished the long goodbyes with my parents and with a heavy heart slowly walked up the tunnel, looking back at my parents' sad faces until I turned a corner and could see them no longer. Little did I know it would be nearly three more years before I'd be back in Detroit and see them again.

Walking onto the plane I noticed Tom in First Class and waved at him as I went to my more plebeian seat further back in the plane. After settling in, I pulled out a notebook and began writing a letter to Linda. Our previous evening's parting, the tears in her eyes, the look on her face when I turned around halfway across the street and started to return to her, her waving me away, her obvious sobbing as she finally put the car in gear and drove off as I stood on my parents' porch watching in misery—all of these images were "rollin' cross my mind" ("Younger Girl," by John Sebastian as sung by The Lovin' Spoonful). When the plane leveled off and the captain announced that he was turning off the "FAS-TEN SEAT BELT" sign and that everyone was free to move about the cabin, I took a break from my letter writing. I walked up and talked with Tom. He was now a big shot lawyer like so many of my fellow Albion grads. Again I sort of felt like I was the only one who ever graduated from Albion who wasn't a doctor or a lawyer. Still I was happy, content but not proud—because I feel pride almost always comes before the fall and that to be proud is often to be smug and arrogant. I was not proud but instead pleased and honored to be a Peace Corps Volunteer. I thought it was an admirable vocation and one with a modicum of esteem. That's all I needed. Tom was working with a big law firm in Detroit and living in Bloomfield Hills, a very affluent suburb of Detroit in Oakland County. This county is the richest county in Michigan and one of the wealthiest counties in the country. I looked at him in his well-tailored suit and obviously expensive and highly polished wingtip shoes, and I knew again that this just wasn't for me, at least not for now. Being an average American, even an un-average wealthy upper echelon doctor or lawyer, still seemed too typically American to me. Though many lower- or middle-class folk might be willing to give their right arms to trade places with Tom or many of my other fellow Albion grads who were doctors or lawyers, I wasn't one of them. I was looking forward to the almost poverty-level (by American standards) lifestyle I was returning to in Korea. I was looking forward to the physical hardships of living in a cold climate without central heating, of having no running hot water and having to boil a pot full of water in order to wash my hair come autumn. Most of all I was looking forward to the happy, excited, and curious faces of a new class of first-year middle school boys and girls I would soon meet. So after Tom finished telling me of his career and good fortune, I quickly told him that I was headed back to Korea to do a third year of Peace Corps service, wished him well, and headed back to my seat. I began writing more in my letter to Linda. I wrote all about Tom and how I was just as glad I wasn't him.

Quickly we got to Chicago, and the plane landed. By the time I got off the plane Tom was long gone, and I headed to the international terminal to catch my flight to Korea. After a short wait we were boarded and heading up the runway at breakneck speed until the plane miraculously began lifting off the tarmac. It always amazes me that these heavy-as-hell devices actually achieve liftoff, but flying above the clouds we soon were. I continued writing to Linda in between each meal, snack, and movie. After six hours or so we were getting near to the Anchorage, Alaska, airport where all planes heading to Korea from the eastern part of the U.S. stopped and refueled in those days. Though Anchorage seems way out of the way to the north, it is shorter and faster to fly over near the top of the globe and then down to northeast Asia than it is to fly the southern route closer to the Equator and the wider part of the globe. The captain invited everyone to look out the window at a huge snow-covered mountain called Mt. Elias. I wrote in my letter to Linda that we were flying over Mt. Elias and that he was a "Big Boy." The Big Boy restaurant chain in Michigan was owned by the Elias brothers, so this would have been funny to Linda or any Michigander/Michiganian (both of these terms are used interchangeably by people living in the Great Lake State).

Off the plane in Anchorage I wandered around the small airport during the layover checking out the duty-free goods. I never bought anything at duty-free shops, but I always checked out the overpriced (to me) luxury brand products. There was a large stuffed polar bear in the waiting area that caught everyone's attention, and I was astonished by how huge these creatures were. Wouldn't want to run into one on a cold dark evening wandering around the tundra, but then why would one be wandering around in the dark on the tundra anyway?

This was my second layover in Anchorage, as there had been one on the way to Michigan a month and a half before. I might have guessed that I would return here for these one-hour or so layovers many more times in my life, but at this time probably not for I had learned to live each day one by one as a PCV, and I was still thinking more about Linda than about anything else.

On this flight to Anchorage I met a guy in the restroom line who told me he was going to teach in a remote community in northern Alaska. He explained to me how they were going to schlep him and all the supplies—food, toiletries, etc. that he would need for the whole school year—in a small plane up to his town and then dump him there for the winter. For a while I thought this sounded interesting. I sincerely considered doing this after my Peace Corps experience, but by the end of my third PC year I realized I would probably be lonely and go stir-crazy pretty quickly in such a remote location. I decided instead to stay in Korea and live in Seoul with its ten million residents—hard to be lonely there.

In the early 1990s, there was a period when I wrote several songs over the span of a few months. (This was after a two-decade hiatus from songwriting. I had written one song while in college.) One of them I wrote while remembering how I had considered spending a year teaching in the far north of Alaska. It's called "Anchor It Down" and the lyrics go like this:

Anchor It Down

Think I'll head up toward the northland to see the great frontier
Too late to be a cowboy, I'll go and follow reindeer.
Take a plane to Alaska, America's last hope
Head out toward the wilderness and see if I can cope.

(Chorus)
I'll anchor it down in Anchorage
And head for the northland.
I'll anchor it down in Anchorage and go as far as I can.

Train a team of sled dogs, mush across the snow
Drive 'em up a glacier pointed straight toward Nome.
Head above the tree line, camp out in a cave
Hope there ain't no avalanche to make that cave my grave.

 Repeat Chorus

Then I'll build an ice house, use some Elmer's glue
Probably catch myself a cold and come down with the flu.
If I find a walrus tusk, I'll carve some scrimshaw
Or trade it to a shaman if he'll tell me all.

 Repeat Chorus

And if I just can't make it I'll hitch a southbound train
Make just like a hobo and head for Bangor, Maine.

 Repeat Chorus

The Bangor, Maine, part is a nod to Roger Miller. ("King of The Road" by Roger Miller) Of course, if I couldn't make it, I would not have just been able to hitch a southbound train out of an isolated settlement while teaching in north Alaska, and that's why I decided against this plan of action that had seemed of interest for a while during my final year in Mukho.

An hour or so later my planemates and I were re-boarding for the second half of our flight to Korea. Back on board were more movies to watch and more meals and more snacks. Oh boy! I continued writing to Linda in between the movies, eating, and trips to the lavatory to get rid of all the coffee and other beverages consumed. I sometimes stood near one of the exit doors and did some stretches as inconspicuously as I could because my muscles cramped up from the inactivity if I didn't. Then I headed back to my seat and wrote more pages to Linda Boyne. By the time the plane got to Kimpo Airport in Seoul, I had filled a dozen standard-sized notebook pages front and back with my babbling, rambling, reminiscences, and longings for her.

I got off the plane on August 30, 1974, and went through customs with nothing to declare (but they opened my bag and searched through it anyway). I, of course, informed them that I was a Peace Corps Volunteer and was returning to Gangwon Province, Mukho Town where I was a middle school English teacher. That didn't seem to impress them.

From the airport I headed right downtown to the Gwanghwa-mun area and the Daeji Yeogwan where I checked into a room. After dumping my bag, I headed up to the Peace Corps office in the Korea Educational Association Building. I duly handed in my passport for safekeeping and then checked out the lounge to see who might be around. None of my buddies was around, but I ran into two guys, Phil and Don, the Eureka brothers. The three of us headed off for dinner and some beer before I headed back to the Daeji Yeogwan early and crashed for the night after again having been awake for a couple of days or so while traveling.

It was almost the beginning of the new school year, so I decided to head back to Mukho the next day. Seoul's first subway line had opened in the summer of 1974 on August 15, Korean Independence Day—the anniversary of the day the Japanese surrendered to the United States and our allies, freeing Korea from Japanese oppression. August 15 was also my father's birthday and I had been able to celebrate the day with him in Michigan. This was obviously my first chance to use this new subway line. It had stops at Gwanghwa-mun in downtown Seoul and at the Cheongnyangri Train Station. I left the Daeji Yeogwan, went out to near the statue of Yi, Sun-sin, and down the steps to the brand-spanking-new subway station. A trip by bus that would have taken an hour or more while bouncing along—usually standing up much of the way with the bus often stuck in traffic—now by subway train took only twenty minutes. What luxury! I got off the subway train, ran up the steps and then into Cheongnyangri Train Station, bought a ticket to Mukho, and caught the next regular train back to my town. Hallelujah!

The summer of '74 had been a whirlwind of fun and adventure for me. I had seen so many of my relatives and high school and college friends. I continued to write to many of them, but with staying two years longer in Korea after finishing my third year of Peace Corps, getting married to a Korean, coming back to the States in 1977, then heading off to grad school, followed by accepting a position with the Pearl S. Buck Foundation back in Korea again in 1979, and spending almost ten more years there, I lost touch with many of them. Some of the friends I saw in the summer of '74 I didn't see again for decades, and a few of them I have sadly never seen again.

CHAPTER 13

Fall Semester 1974:
The Silent Way and Shamanistic Heaven

After the nine-hour train ride back to Mukho from Seoul and some more writing to Linda, I de-trained and stood on the cement platform. I felt at home, sensed I belonged here, relished (or tartar sauced maybe) in the fish smell and returned back to my lodging room up the alley from the Mukho Theater. One of the first things I did was post my tome to Linda Boyne. But she already seemed miles and, in some ways, light years away. There was no way I could go back to Detroit and just settle down, certainly not at that time, and I couldn't imagine doing so a year from then either. I had changed too much. America had seemed almost like a foreign land to me while I was on vacation there. I knew I wouldn't miss the big box stores. They had grossed me out. I had stood in the cereal aisle at a grocery store at one point during the almost two months in Michigan, and I could not for the life of me fathom why we needed dozens of different kinds of breakfast cereal choices when rice, soup, vegetables, fish, and, of course, some kimchee would do just fine for breakfast. I thought about this as I walked to the Post Office to mail the oversized, overstuffed envelope that I needed to fit the billions and billions, as Carl Sagan used to say, of words (not stars) on those numerous pages to Linda. I had implied, though I hadn't come right out and said it, that I was in love, or at least deep like, with her, and a part of me thought that I was. But I was also looking forward to another year of teaching in Mukho, and I was glad to be back here in this smelly, ugly town that was covered with coal and cement dust—and that I also for some strange reason loved.

No time for illusions or delusions about Linda or nostalgia for that now-gone summer of romance. I knew she cared deeply for me, or at least I sincerely thought she did. If not, why that long sentimental goodbye? I continued thinking about Linda for months afterwards, and we corresponded for a year and a half longer until we both got engaged—her to a guy in Detroit and me to Kim, Mi-yun in Seoul.

Also, I had work to do. I had lesson planning to do for my special "Silent Way" class at the boys' middle school. As presented before, this method had the teacher saying each new word only once and then the students did all the talking afterwards. That was why it was called the "Silent Way," because the teacher was mostly silent. I had bought several pencils in the basic colors (red, green, blue, and yellow) while in the States and brought them back with me. As outlined before, Caleb Gattegno used colored rods to teach the "Silent Way." I could have bought long wooden rods, cut them up and painted them in primary colors while on home leave, but again I decided to use pencils. Talking about pencils was just as effective, and the students would be learning a meaningful and useful word rather than the word "rod," which we don't use much in everyday conversation unless we're talking about fishing. So I began lesson planning how I would use talking about different colored pencils in class while still fairly closely following the text-book. I was given special permission by the principal to use one class as my "guinea pig class," but because I would also still be teaching two days a week at Mukho Girls' Middle School, my experimental, guinea pig class would have one or two days each week in which my co-teacher, Mr. Hyun, Jong-jin, would teach alone and help them with any grammar questions they might have.

The first day of class, I walked into my experimental class and stood in front of these new and energetic students. I held up one pencil and said "pencil" one time and one time only. As I looked around I searched for an attentive student with a sparkle in his eyes among the fifty-some to choose from. There were many who fit this description. I pointed at one of them and then pointed at the pencil with an inquisitive look on my face. He said, "pencil" with perfect pronunciation. Then I pointed at one student after another while walking around the classroom until many in the class of fifty students had repeated this very key vocabulary word. I walked back to the front of the class, held up one at a time each color of pencil that I had and pointed at students to keep saying "pencil" so they would know all of the different colors were also just pencils. Then I held up the green pencil and said, "green pencil" one time and one time only. I pointed at one stu-dent and back at the pencil. He responded by saying "green pencil." From there we went through all the different colored pencils, and I tried to get every one of the students in the class to speak. The students seemed excited, interested, engaged, and they comprehended what they were saying.

After the first day of introducing the term "pencil" and the primary colors, I began teaching sentences built around these pencils and the different colors. I began by holding three or four different colored pencils in front of one student and saying, "Take a yellow pencil." The student grabbed the yellow pencil. Then I put a red pencil, a blue pencil, a green pencil, and a yellow pencil in front of him and motioned that he should ask the student next to him. "Take a yellow pencil," he perfectly intoned. Then I moved around the room, repeating this activity. Quickly one of the students improvised, "Take a red pencil." I had them in the palm of my hand (not the pencils, but the students). We moved into more than one color of pencil: "Take a red pencil and a blue pencil." Then I had them tell their classmates to take three or four pencils at a time and more than one of each of the colors, etc. Next I introduced the words "put it on the desk" as in, "Take a red pencil and put it on the desk." Then I worked up to the other different colors and more than one of each color and so on by introducing the word "them." I was in a groove.

It seemed to me that language teachers who did all the talking had students who not only couldn't speak, but also students who could only understand their teacher and probably no one else in that foreign language. In the "Silent Way" the students talked to each other. They were then forced to listen more attentively, and so they were able to understand many different people's intonations and idiosyncrasies in the foreign language.

Again I attempted to follow the patterns and grammar as they were introduced in their textbook, and yet because they needed only to know a very limited vocabulary they became very fluent in the sentence patterns and intonation of English. Where in the other classes only a handful of the students could actually speak, in this class every single student spoke very well with almost no noticeable accent, and they could all make quite long and complicated sentences.

After a few classes, I began also to work on their reading skills. I made a large poster with all the words we were using in class: pencil(s), yellow, red, blue, green, take, a, two, put, it, them, on, the, desk, and. I would then point to one word at a time to make a sentence. After finishing tapping out the sentence, I'd motion to a student who would then say the sentence. After doing that a few times, I'd have a student walk to the poster; I'd say a sentence and have the student point it out one word at a time. Then I'd have one student say a sentence while a different student pointed, or I'd give the student my pointer, encouraging him to make a sentence and then motion to another student to say that sentence. It got to the point where I could bang out sentences as fast as my hand could move, and still every student in the class could read and repeat these sentences pretty much every time.

When the first exam came, I was a little worried that maybe these students who spoke so well and so fluently might not do as well on the written exams, which were all about grammar with no oral component to test their speaking or listening skills. I needn't have worried. My experimental class students did as well as every other class in their grade and actually better than most of them. I was proving that Korean students could be taught in a way that would create excellent speakers of English and not just students who could translate and understand the grammar, without the ability to speak. Even most college graduates, who had studied English for ten years, could hardly articulate a simple sentence.

The problem, of course, was that even if my co-teacher, Mr. Hyun, had understood and replicated my method the next year after I was gone, during the following years of study after their first year of middle school, their spoken fluency would be lost due to disuse. Though I knew this to be true, I was proving my point and having a wonderful time doing it. Hopefully the students, even now forty-some years later, might still remember Mr. Ha, Doe-young and his modified "Silent Way" experiment and their ease of speaking in English for that all-too-short first year of middle school.

Otherwise, I continued as before with Mondays, Wednesdays, Fridays and half a day on Saturdays teaching at the boys' middle school and Tuesdays and Thursdays at the girls' school. I also had a new special class of the fifteen best male students whom I taught Mondays, Wednesdays, and Fridays from 5:00 to 6:00 pm after their regular school day and home room hour, as well as a similar class that I taught on Tuesdays and Thursdays of the fifteen best female students at Mukho Girls' Middle School.

I heard that there was a new volunteer, John Devereaux, joining our "prop set" on the east coast. He was a TESOL volunteer, but teaching at the college level. He was placed in Kangnung and was teaching at the Kangnung Technical School of Nursing where Glenn Vriesland's wife had taught back in 1973 before they married. I contacted John and invited him to come down to Mukho the next weekend.

There was another taekwondo instructor, besides Mr. Kim, Myung-ho, in town named Lee, Hong-il. He came up to me and introduced himself while I was having coffee at the Changmi (Rose) Tearoom one Sunday afternoon after one of my long hikes. I invited him to sit down. He was much younger than Mr. Chae, our instructor. After talking for a few minutes, Mr. Lee asked if I would be willing to go with him and some of his students the following Saturday afternoon out to Mangsang Beach to practice some taekwondo together and take pictures. I was wondering why he wanted to do this, but couldn't think of any important reason other than he might put up pictures in his *dojang* (gym) of this funny-looking American guy. Anyway, it sounded like fun. John Devereaux was coming down from Gangneung to hang out for the weekend, but I thought he wouldn't mind, so I said, "Sure, that would be good."

I met John at the train station the next Saturday when he arrived.

"Whew, how can you stand the smell?" he asked as he dismounted from the train.

Don and taekwondo instructor Mr. Lee practicing at Mangsang Beach near Mukho.

Mr. Lee (far left), Don, and John Devereaux with three of Mr. Lee's students at Mangsang Beach.

"That smell, it's like perfume," I answered.

"More like rotten fish."

"You'll grow to love it, just wait and see." As we walked downtown I told him about the beach trip. We stopped by my *yeogwan*, and I picked up my small bag with my taekwondo *dobok* (gym clothes) and my camera. John also had his camera. We headed down the main street to Mr. Lee's *dojang*. Mr. Lee and three of his students, two young men and one young lady, were waiting for us. After introductions, we went out and boarded the bus heading north.

About twenty minutes later we got out near the beach. We went behind rocks at the south end of Mangsang Beach and changed. We guys went behind one rock and the young lady Miss Huh behind another. I was the center of attention as I did different kicks, punches, and blocks back and forth with first Mr. Lee, then his male students Mr. Jun and Mr. Ko, and then lastly with Miss Huh. John and one or the other of Mr. Lee's students took pictures while Mr. Lee did the choreographing and directing. I fought back and forth on the sandy beach with one after the other until I had sparred with all four of them. Then we went up into the rocks, and again Mr. Lee choreographed different scenarios up, down, and around the rocks. By late afternoon we were finished, so we changed back into our street clothes and took some final pictures on the beach before jumping on a bus back to Mukho. A fun time was had by all.

As you can see in the photograph, John was a little shorter than I, had white-blond hair, and was balding already even though he was in his early twenties too. In addition he liked to wear round, horn-rimmed style sunglasses that looked similar to those worn by many elderly Korean men. I soon discovered that whenever he got onto crowded buses or the train, school-aged children would stand up and say, *"Halaboji, anjashipsheo"* (grandfather or honored elderly gentleman, please sit down). They thought he was an old man, and John would accept the proffered seat every time. It was quite amusing. Usually I'd be left standing.

Early in the semester, one Tuesday during my free period while I was sitting in the teachers' communal room at the girls' middle school, I was called to the principal's office. The third-year English teacher, Mr. Kim, Kil-su, came into the teachers' office and said in English, "Mr. Ha, master go." I'm thinking, *"OK, master go, maybe some of the teachers are playing paduk, the board game that in English we call by the Japanese name of 'go,' and maybe one of them is a master player."* Anyway I got up and followed him. He led me to the principal's office. *"Of course!"* I now realized that by "master" he meant the principal, which in British English is called the schoolmaster. In Korea, before Peace Corps Volunteers started teaching American-style English, the Koreans had learned British-style English because that is what the Japanese used when Korea was their colony. There were a lot of vestiges of the Japanese-style education in the Korean system, such as the school uniforms that looked like those in Japan and the school year being modeled on the Japanese system.

So I walked into the principal's office. A few months before in the spring, I had been called in because the principal, Mr. Pak, Tae-kun, who was the father of my friend and hiking partner from my first spring in Mukho, wanted to share his goat's milk with me. For some reason the school had a female goat. I drank a cup, and Principal Pak said, "How do you like it?" I decided to be honest and replied, "It's interesting, but I'm not really fond of it, maybe because I've never had any goat's milk before." (Also, it was warm.) He laughed and told me that it was a special treat and that he drank a cup every day.

As I walked in, I wondered what surprise he might have in store today. Mr. Kim didn't follow me into the office, and Principal Pak asked me to sit down. He then told me that to thank me for my diligence and dedication in teaching the first-year middle school girls, I was being invited to be one of the chaperones for the third-year girls' high school class trip to Gyeongju, the ancient capital of the Silla dynasty, which Charlie and I had visited during the winter break and where I had taken Muneaki. I told him I would very much like to go, but that I would have to ask permission from the principal of the boys' middle school because I would be missing a couple of days of classes there while on the trip. Principal Pak told me that he would call Principal Chai, Young-sun, at the boys' middle school and inform him of their offer. True to his word, when I asked to speak with Principal Chai the next day at the boys' middle school he had already heard from Principal Pak and told me that I was excused to be a chaperone for this excursion. I thought it was interesting that they would ask me, a twenty-three-year-old, single, foreign guy, to serve as a chaperone for nearly a hundred eighteen-year-old young ladies. It seemed a little like letting the fox into the hen house, but then it also showed the respect Koreans had for the teaching profession. I couldn't help thinking that if my daughter was an eighteen-year-old student and her school had picked a twenty-three-year-old foreign guy to be a chaperone, I'd be screaming to high heaven (or at least to low heaven). But evidently none of the parents of any of the young ladies complained at all.

A few days later we left for the three-day, two-night trip. There were three male high school teachers (two Mr. Kims and one Mr. Pak) and I who went as chaperones. I knew all three of them only from passing them in the playground, as the high school teachers' room was in a different building than our middle school teachers' room. We got on the train in Mukho and headed southwest on the five-hour ride to Yeongju, where Charlie lived. In Yeongju, we de-trained and then changed to another train heading due south for the nearly four-hour ride to Gyeongju. After sitting with the teachers for nearly nine hours straight, I had learned a lot about them, and they had learned a lot more about me than they had known before our excursion. From the Gyeongju train station we walked to the large *yeogwan* where we'd stay the next two nights. Before going into the *yeogwan*, Mr. Pak, Ki-duk, a math teacher who was the group leader, informed the girls where we would be heading for dinner and about the next day's activities. I, of course, roomed with the three teachers, while all the girls were packed like sardines into numerous other rooms.

The next morning we were all up before dawn to head to Seokguram to try to catch the morning sunlight hitting the head of the Buddha statue inside the grotto built into the east side of a mountain near Gyeongju. On a clear day, as the sun rises above the East Sea and clears the top of the mountains near the shoreline of the Sea of Japan to the east, the first beams of light come through the grotto entrance and strike the head of the beautifully carved granite Buddha, making it seem to glow. Unfortunately, as the year before when Charlie and I went there, the sky was cloudy on this morning.

**Mukho Girls' High School third-year students at Bulguk Temple—
Don is standing at the far right.**

Bunhwang-sa Pagoda with a few students in front.

We went back to the bus and down the mountain to Bulguk-sa (Bulguk Temple). This is one of the most famous Buddhist temples in Korea. As mentioned before, although the large stone foundation and beautiful stone stairway up to the temple entrance are from the Silla era, unfortunately, all of the wooden buildings are reproductions of the originals. The buildings had all been destroyed probably more than once during the several invasions of Korea over the centuries since the downfall of the Silla dynasty in 935 CE. After three or so hours at Bulguk-sa it was back to the bus and off to lunch. After lunch we went to Bunhwang-sa Pagoda, the three story high stone building that was once nine stories high until the Mongols during their invasion in the 1200s knocked off the top six stories. It was capped at three, and the other stories were never rebuilt. Then we went to Cheomseongdae Observatory, the oldest extant astronomical observatory in East Asia, to the famous Tumuli Park to see all the burial mounds of the Silla royal family, and finally to dinner.

Don with the other three chaperones on the Gyeongju trip.

I had been constipated since the day before, but after dinner things started rumbling in my tummy. When we got back to the *yeogwan*, I went into our room and dropped off my bag with my camera, book, notebook, and Korean-English dictionary that I always carried. I then hurried to the lavatory. I opened door after door and was horrified by the sight and smell. These were flush Korean-style toilets. They had the ceramic trough with a pull handle above that sends water through to wash the crap down. They were all broken or plugged up. The troughs were full of excrement, piled higher and deeper in every toilet. The smell was overwhelming, and I was gagging and nearly upchucking from the stench. I ran off and found the nearest tearoom I could. I quickly sat down, called over a tearoom lady, ordered a cup of coffee, asked where the *hwajangshil* (lavatory) was, and moved as quickly as I could in its direction without looking like I was running at breakneck speed. I got to the clean restroom, squatted, and exploded into the white and shiny porcelain trough. Ah, relief is just a dump away. I squatted there feeling sorry for all the poor students who had to use the facilities in the *yeogwan*.

The following day, we did a little more sightseeing and then returned to the train station for our trip back home. On the way back I ended up sitting with five students. We were on two booth-like benches with three of us on each side facing each other. I was in the middle on one bench with two young ladies on either side of me, and then three were sitting across from us. We talked for quite a while, and then the conversation lagged and I nodded off. When I woke up, the two young female students on each side of me had wrapped their arms around my arms and were sleeping with their heads resting on my shoulders. Again I couldn't help thinking that if these were my daughters sleeping snuggled up to a young,

A close-up photograph of some of the third-year high school girls on the Gyeongju trip.

single male teacher who was only five years older than they, I'd be concerned. Both of them were sweet, cute, curvy young ladies.

At Yeongju we again got off and switched to a train heading back to the northeast toward Mukho. I sat with the same five gals on this leg of the journey, and the same two snuggled up and used me as their pillow. It had been a fun trip other than the constipation then diarrhea and overall toilet experience. During the three days and two nights, I had talked with and gotten to know on a more personal level many of these high school girls. Before the trip I would recognize them around town, and I would know they were third-year high school girls by the length of their hair. While the boys kept their hair close cropped throughout middle and high school, the girls started in first-year middle school with their hair bobbed very short. In the back their hair ended a couple of inches above their collars, and they looked like someone had put a bowl upside down on their head and then cut any hair sticking down below the bowl. They let their hair grow, and each year it was longer until by high school they were braiding it in pigtails on either side of their heads. By third-year high school the braids were hanging down well below their shoulders. Just by looking at the length of their hair you could tell what year in school the girls were. Of course, walking around town and even on my jaunts far into the country, I was always running into middle and high school boys and girls whom I had taught over the past three years, and the students would greet me with smiles on their faces. The boys would salute and say, "*Myeol-gong!*" (destroy Communism). *Ban-gong* (anti-Communism) had not been good enough, and it was changed during my second year in Mukho to *myeol-gong*. Often the students would then add "Good afternoon, sir." The girls would usually just smile and bow. They did not have to say *ban-gong* or *myeol-gong*; I guess because they wouldn't be drafted into the army later. After this trip all the third-year high school girls started giving me a friendlier personal greeting rather than the slight bow I used to get before this trip and before getting to know them. This class trip was a wonderful experience for me.

This semester, there were two cute, young female teachers at the girls' middle school that I had my eyes on. One was a gym teacher who had first started teaching the previous year in September of 1973. She was a little husky with a muscular build, but curves in all the right places and a very cute face. Her name was Ou, Chong-suk, or as I called her in my imagination, Miss Ou. At school or anywhere in public, I called her Ou, *Seonsaeng-nim* (honorable teacher Ou). The other teacher, whom I instantly had my eyes on too, was a Korean language instructor who had just started this fall. She was taller than Miss Ou and thinner with a lovely, curvaceous body and an absolutely beautiful face. Her name was Yum, Jong-ran, or to me, Miss Yum. Miss Ou made me moan "oooouuu," every time I saw her, and Miss Yum made me say, "Oh, yum, yum." (This is true, their names really were Ou and Yum.) So I went out of my way to run into Miss Yum and Miss Ou as often as possible and chat with them. After a couple of months, they started hanging around together, both being young and newer teachers at the school, and they stated to me that they would both be interested in learning more English. They asked if I would be willing to teach them. I said, "Would I! Would I!" as the punch line in the old joke goes. (Oh, in case you don't know the joke: There was a woman with a harelip and a guy with a wooden eye, both of whom usually didn't attend the local dances because of their imperfections. One Saturday night they both decided to give the dance a try. When the guy with the wooden eye looked around and saw the young lady with the harelip, he said to himself, "I'll ask her to dance, she won't refuse me." So he walked up to her and said, "Excuse me, would you be interested in dancing with me?" She excitedly replied, "Would I! Would I!" and he angrily responded, "Harelip! Harelip!") But Miss Ou and Miss Yum didn't say, "Harelip! Harelip!" even though I had a hair lip (mustache) and beard at the time.

On Tuesday and Thursday nights, they would come to my room at 8:30 p.m. after I had finished taekwondo (which John Hudson and I, as you know, studied together from 7:00 to 8:00 p.m. every weeknight). They always came together because had they come individually, there might have been talk. I started with simple lessons and worked my way up to, among other techniques, "Situational Reinforcement" where we could work on three tenses all at once. I would say to Miss Yum, "Open the door." When she got up and was near the door, I'd say, "Stop. What are you going to do?" Miss Yum would answer, "I'm going to open the door." Then I'd ask Miss Ou, "What is she going to do?" She'd respond "She's going to open the door." Then I'd say, "Continue." As she began opening the door, I'd say again, "Stop. What are you doing?" Miss Yum would say, "I'm opening the door." I'd go through that exchange again with Miss Ou and then say to Miss Yum, "Continue." When she finished opening the door all the way, I'd ask, "What did you do?" Then we'd practice the past tense. After that I'd have them ask and answer the questions with me just doing the directing. After "open the door" we'd go through close the door, open a drawer, close a drawer, open a book, close a book, etc. I had visions of sugarplums dancing in my head as well as visions of me teaching the names of all the different pieces of clothing, including panties and bra, and then using "Situational Reinforcement" but in a different way. I would direct them to take off different pieces of clothing and go through all three tenses until…... Probably it was fortunate that I never got the nerve to follow through with my diabolical plan. But I still think it might have worked, don't you?

As you might imagine, one of the first things I did when I got back to Mukho after my vacation was to contact John Hudson and our taekwondo instructor Mr. Chae. Naturally, Mr. Chae was happy to see me back, and John and I were both thrilled to continue with our lessons. We had already memorized most of the set patterns or *hyongs*, and we had advanced from our starting white belt to yellow belt. Soon we were tested for our red belts. After getting our red belts there were only a couple of more *hyongs* to memorize before taking our black belt test. By mid-October we had completed all the black belt requirements, and we took and passed the test. We received our belts and official First Degree Black Belt Certificates on October 20, 1974. My certificate now hangs on the wall in our basement.

On the days when the students had their exams, I had mentioned to John the past spring that I just sat around all day in the teachers' office, reading the *Korea Herald*, doing lesson plans, and/or writing letters to friends and family back in the States. My co-teacher took charge of the testing. John had suggested we grab lunch together on these test days that came up once every couple of months. So when the first test day came up in the fall, I met John as usual at our favorite Chinese restaurant downtown right near the only main intersection in Mukho. We ate and talked. It's funny, I enjoyed being with John, and yet he and I were different enough that except for the one hour each evening that we had taekwondo classes Monday through Friday nights, I usually didn't see John much. Most weekends he went his way, and I went mine. These lunches became our one consistent exception.

One infrequent weekend exception was when Chris would call from Samcheok and invite John and me to visit the Catholic nuns at the Samcheok Clinic with him. Fairly soon after I had returned to Mukho, Chris invited us down to Samcheok, and we visited the nuns doing our usual routine of sharing the wonderful Irish-style food they cooked for dinner, playing the Hearts card game with a couple of them who enjoyed playing cards, and then staying there overnight in the basement rooms in the clinic underneath their convent. One of the Irish nuns had just returned from her home leave. They, of course, were in country many more years than us Peace Corps Volunteers before they were able to revisit their homeland. This nun, Sister Clarice, was very upset about a song that her nephews had been singing while she was home. Back in the early 1970s there was a Coca-Cola commercial with a catchy tune and the words were:

> I'd like to buy the world a Coke and keep it company
> It's the real thing.
> (To the tune of "I'd Like to Teach The World to Sing," songwriters Bill Backer, Roger Cook, Roger Greenaway, Roquel Davis, sung by "The Seekers.")

She told us her nephews sang:

> I'd like to join the IRA and get myself a gun,
> And line the British in a row and shoot them one by one.
> It's the real thing.

Sister Clarice was very upset and troubled by this rendition of the Coke commercial. I understood her being upset by these words, and yet I found them rather humorous even though I didn't then nor do I now condone violence or terrorism. But, as I often tell my history students at our local community college where I teach: "One person's terrorist is another's freedom fighter." I find it sad that children in Ireland then and around the world in many countries today are being brought up to hate. Still, at the time the words seemed humorous, and I've managed to remember these brutal lyrics all these years later. Of course, it helped that they were set to a catchy tune.

Not too long after our visit with the nuns, Chris contacted John and me again and told us about a retired American cement company engineer who was volunteering to help a small cement company in Samcheok expand their plant. He and his wife were living in Samcheok. I hadn't even known there was a cement company in Samcheok, but was only familiar with the Ssangyong plant near Bupyeong. This American couple in Samcheok invited the three of us for dinner the upcoming Saturday night.

Again John and I caught the bus to Samcheok. As we were bouncing along and both reading books, John stopped reading, said he was going to meditate, and asked me to not bother him for the next few minutes.

"Meditate? Can you teach me?" I inquired.

"No, I studied Transcendental Meditation back in New York, and you have to take the course."

"What do you mean you have to take the course? How can I take the course here? Just tell me the basics."

"No, we're not allowed. It's complicated, and you have to take the whole course."

"How complicated can it be? It's meditation. What, do you concentrate on the space between your eyes, or do you chant 'Om' to yourself? Give me a quick rundown."

"No, sorry, Don, but it's not that simple. You really have to take the whole Transcendental Meditation course. We're told not to try to teach anyone on our own."

"Sounds like the ol' Maharishi Yogi just wants to keep his money stream rolling in, if you ask me."

"You can think what you want, but how about letting me meditate?"

"OK, sure, have at it." I went back to reading my book, and John closed his eyes while sitting up straight. I still thought the ol' Maharishi was in it for the money, but maybe that's just cynical me being overly judgmental.

As usual Chris met us at the station and led us to near the cement factory where there was a rather western-looking house inhabited by Joe and Sally Monroe. They invited us in, and we sat down to talk before dinner. Joe had spent his career in the cement industry in the U.S. and had been involved with several plant expansions. After retiring, he volunteered with a group that matches retirees' experience with foreign firms in the developing world that need their expertise. This small cement manufacturer in Samcheok had asked for this organization's help, and they'd sent Joe Monroe. It turned out he and Sally were from Marshall, Michigan, which is not far from the town of Albion. Of course, I told them that I had graduated from Albion College.

"Do you know David Sturgis?" Mrs. Monroe asked.

"Know him? I sang in the choir at Albion, so I knew him very well," I responded. (Mr. Sturgis was a professor, chairman of the music department, and the choir director at Albion.) "How do you know him?" I asked.

"He's our nextdoor neighbor," Sally replied.

"Wow, what a small world, isn't it?"

"Sure is," Joe responded. We talked for a while about Michigan, and then they asked Chris and John questions about where they were from in the States and where they'd gone to college and whatnot. We had a lovely dinner with them and then left so that John and I could catch the last bus back to Mukho.

There was a new volunteer assigned to Kangnung Girls' Middle School named Pam Utica. I got in touch with her by mail and welcomed her as a new member of the East Coast "Prop Setter" Club. Pam had become friends with a missionary whose name was Ruth Standish. She invited John, Chris, and me to visit Kangnung and meet this American Methodist missionary who lived in Kangnung on the weekends, but taught during the week in the Department of Preventive Medicine and Public Health at Yonsei University in Seoul. Pam met us at the train station in midafternoon when we arrived, and we went by taxi to Ruth's house. We knocked on the metal gate, which was opened by a middle-aged Korean man. Inside the compound were two homes. Off to the left was a smaller one with a Korean woman and a young boy standing near the front door. Ruth came out from the larger one on the right, and we made our introductions. Ruth also introduced us to the Korean man, who was her driver, as well as his wife and son.

Ruth lived in the larger house to the right. She led us in and gave us a quick tour. She had several very beautiful Korean landscape paintings that she explained were by famous painters. She frequented Insa-dong in Seoul, the area renowned for antiques and traditional artworks. Having lived and worked in Korea since 1955, she had gotten to know many of the shop owners and some of the artists personally. I couldn't help thinking how lucky she was and how wonderful it would be to stay that long in Korea and know the country and its culture so well. I admired her for her great knowledge of Korean art.

We sat and talked and drank tea until dinner when Ruth served a wonderful Korean meal with many special center dishes. We ate our fill and then continued talking until late in the evening. She invited us to spend the night. She had enough *yos*, *ibols*, and *begaes* for all of us to spread out in her living room area.

There was also another new PCV, Bob Selfridge, teaching at the boys' middle school up in Sokcho near the border with North Korea and just north of Sorak National Park. I had first visited Sorak-san (Sorak Mountain) along with Mukho Middle School's Principal Yoo, Hyung-sul, on the third-year middle school boys' class trip back in the fall of 1972 and had been back several other times since then. Principal Yoo had contacted me two or three times since leaving Mukho to be the principal at Sokcho Boys' High School. Each time he invited me to stay at his house overnight on a Saturday. It was nice to have spent those evenings talking with him and his wife. Then on Sunday each time I had stayed, we had hiked in Sorak National Park before I headed back to Mukho. Principal Yoo contacted me again early in the fall of 1974. He had met and befriended Bob, who was teaching at the boys' middle school in Sokcho.

Principal Yoo and Don in Sorak National Park

Potato pancake snacks and makgeolli along the trail at Sorak National Park.

Principal Yoo invited me up again to stay overnight and to hike with him and Bob in the park.

The next weekend, after Saturday morning classes ended, I took the early afternoon train as usual on the hour-long trip up to Kangnung. Before the Korean War the train line continued north into what is now North Korea, but after the war the line from Kangnung north was not repaired. Consequently, I then grabbed a bus from Kangnung to Sokcho, which took another couple of hours. As we were leaving Kangnung, I noticed a road sign that stated we were leaving Gangneung. I thought, *"Gang-ne-ung? That sounds like the name of a horrible infection or some other serious malady."* The Korean government, I knew, was abandoning the traditional McCune-Reischauer system of Romanization in favor of their own new revised system. If this was an example of it, the new system was horrible. When Americans saw Kangnung and read it aloud, it would come out as two syllables and very close to the actual pronunciation in Korean. On the other hand, Gangneung (gang-ne-ung as I pronounced it) would be so far off when read by any foreigner that Koreans wouldn't be able to guess what they were saying. I couldn't wait to see other examples of this new system.

I arrived late in the afternoon and walked to Principal Yoo's home. Early the next morning Principal Yoo, Bob, and I took the bus into Sorak National Park and hiked one of the trails that ended at a beautiful waterfall. On the way back down we stopped at a vendor's tent along the trail and ate fried potato pancake-like snacks with *makgeolli* (rice wine) for lunch. Then we hiked back down the mountain. Principal Yoo and Bob headed back to Sokcho while I headed south and back to Mukho.

This was the only time I saw Bob and the last time, while in Peace Corps, that I saw Principal Yoo. I did, though, keep in touch with Mr. Yoo in the years after Peace Corps. In the early 1980s, while I was the Pearl S. Buck Foundation Director (PSBF) in Seoul, he was the principal of Chuncheon Girls' High School. He said this was an easier assignment, as high school girls caused fewer problems than high school boys. The PSBF dairy farm and training center in Ganwon-do (Gangwon Province) was down in Wonju, but upon occasion I had to go to Chuncheon, because it was the provincial capital, to meet with provincial officials in the Agriculture Department. On one occasion, I received a plaque of appreciation from the governor for the Pearl S. Buck Foundation's contributions to young farmers and dairy farming techniques in Gangwon Province. I still have the beautiful plaque. On the top in the middle is the Gangwon flag and then two dragons, one on either side. In Korean and English the plaque reads:

PLAQUE OF APPRECIATION
No. 524September 30, 1985
On behalf of the two million people of Kangwondo, I take
great pleasure in presenting this plaque of appreciation to:
Resident Director, Donald R. Haffner
Pearl S. Buck Foundation, Korea
For your great contribution not only to help young farmers in
the rural area to stand by themselves, but to do an extension
services (sic) of dairy farming techniques through the Pilot
Dairy Project established by an agreement between Kangwondo
and Pearl S. Buck Foundation, Korea.

Young Jin Kim
Governor
Kangwon Province
Republic of Korea

Before many of these trips, I would contact Principal Yoo and meet him for lunch in downtown Chuncheon. When he retired in the mid-1980s, he invited me to his retirement ceremony at Chuncheon Girls' High School. I met him before the ceremony, and I was surprised at how gaunt he looked compared to the last time I'd had lunch with him a few months earlier. He looked almost like a walking skeleton. It was all I could do to hide my shock. Then I sat in the audience listening to several speakers congratulating him and praising his many years of service to education in Gangwon Province and the Republic of Korea. Finally, he stood up and began to speak. He, of course, thanked all of the previous speakers and everyone who had helped him throughout his career. Then he said that he wanted to especially thank the former Peace Corps Volunteer, Mr. Donald Haffner, who had taught at Mukho Middle School when he was the principal there. Then he said, "Mr. Haffner is here today. He has come from Seoul to be here at my retirement celebration, and I want to thank him for attending." Tears began rolling down my cheeks the minute I heard him say Peace Corps, and though many people in the audience turned to look my way, I could not hide my tears or the emotions welling up inside of me. This kind man, who had treated me almost as if I were his son when I first got to Mukho, was now so frail, so fragile. This man, who gave his stamp of approval to my mustache and with whom I had spent so many wonderful hours discussing the latest news as it appeared in the *Korea Times* and the *Korea Herald* newspapers, was honoring me on his very special retirement day. I felt so humbled, so very privileged, and so darn lucky to have been sent to his school for my Peace Corps assignment.

A year after his retirement, Principal Yoo, Hyung-sul, passed away. I had sent the usual Christmas card to him, and his son wrote back to tell me that his father had left this world. He left it a much better place than he had found it, thanks to his dedication to studying English and his work in the field of education in his homeland. In the end, the love he made was far greater than the love he had taken. I could only hope that I too would someday leave this world after having made it a better place, even if my work only had a fraction of the impact I knew his had.

Charlie came to Mukho at the end of September during *Chuseok* (mid-autumn harvest festival). *Chuseok* occurs each year on the fifteenth day of the eighth month of the lunar calendar, which in 1974 occurred at the end of September. Charlie came on Saturday September 28, leaving Yeongju after he had finished his morning classes. Monday was *Chuseok,* and Tuesday October 1 every year is Armed Forces Day, which celebrates the day in 1950 when the Korean Armed Forces with a little help from the U.S. broke through the thirty-eighth parallel and stormed into North Korea. Of course, later they and the U.S. forces were sent packing back below the thirty-eighth parallel thanks mostly to the Chinese entering the war in a big way. At any rate, Charlie came for this long weekend, and I met him when he got off the train on Saturday afternoon.

"Wow, you gotta love that smell!" Charlie said while laughing.

"That's the wonderful smell of Mukho's drying fish," I answered.

"Interesting, sort of adds to the ambiance, doesn't it?"

"Yes, but in a few minutes, you won't even notice it anymore."

After dropping his stuff off at my *yeogwan*, we went to a tearoom for coffee and talked about our experiences back in the States over the summer. Charlie had visited Detroit because one of his Notre Dame buddies had moved there to work.

"Why didn't you call me?" I asked.

"Only had a couple of days and wanted to spend every minute with my old friend, and I knew we'd be back together here in Korea soon anyway," he replied.

"True enough," I said. Then I asked if he had seen the largest tire in the world along the I-94 expressway. He had. I then told Charlie the sad story of my youth.

"When I was in junior high school, my dad lost his job and my parents abandoned me in that big tire."

"Yeah, right."

"No, really." Then I told him how an opossum couple had adopted me as their son and raised me. Their names were Suzy and Sam. I explained how I had written a song titled "Opossum Suzy and Opossum Sam." But later a guy in Texas stole my idea, changed the opossums to muskrats and changed the title to "Muskrat Candlelight." Later, of course, Captain and Tennille had a huge hit with their cover of the song under the title "Muskrat Love." (Apologies to songwriter Willis Alan Ramsey and Captain & Tennille.)

"True story," I said. (Actually, I made it all up.)

"Yeah, right," Charlie said again as he chuckled.

Over the next three and a half days, I showed Charlie all the sights of Mukho: the harbor, the fish market, the racks of drying fish all over town, the boys' and the girls' middle schools, downtown (all two hundred yards of it), my favorite tearoom, the two theaters, and of course my digs at the Changshin Yeog-wan. Charlie's new hobby was playing guitar, and he had brought his guitar with him. He was into chords and strumming, not picking. We took several long hikes, and I took him along the shoreline both north and south, as well as west into the mountains. One of the days, we bought *kimpop* (sushi) lunchboxes, snacks, and juice drinks for lunch and walked west toward the stone Shaman towers on a hill a mile or so west of town. Charlie brought his guitar too. When we got to the top of the high hill (or small mountain) where these towers were, we sat down and ate lunch. While we were eating, low clouds settled in around us, and by the time we finished lunch it was as if we were sitting on top of a huge cloud. We could not see anything below us, as all was fog. Charlie began playing his guitar, and we sang songs as if we were in a Shamanistic Heaven with two twelve-feet-high stone towers somehow floating along with us on the clouds. "Om!"

On Tuesday Charlie left by train to head back to his town of Yeongju. October has many holidays in Korea, and two days later on October 3 the schools were closed for National Foundation Day. This day commemorates the day that Tangun founded Gojosean, the first Korean state, back in 2333 BCE. The story of Tangun is interesting. The story goes that God told a tiger and a bear that whichever one of them could stay for three months in a cave would be turned into a woman. Of course, the bear had an advantage being used to spending long periods dormant during hibernation. The tiger couldn't stand it and left the cave early. The bear stayed and was turned into a woman. The myth doesn't seem to say whether she was a gorgeous, drop-dead beauty or not, but either way through (evidently) immaculate conception, she became pregnant and bore a son named Tangun on the highest mountain in Korea, Baekdu-san (Baekdu Mountain). Kim, Il-sung, the first leader of North Korea, claimed to have led resistance against the Japanese from Baekdu-san. It is also claimed that his son Kim, Jong-il, who became the second ruler of North Korea and who fathered the present ruler Kim, Jong-un, was born on Baekdu-san. This is obviously a somewhat feeble attempt to tie the Kim family into Korea's "Foundation Myth." (Kim, Jong-il was actually born in the Soviet Union.) Tangun became the first king of Korea and later ascended into heaven from Mari-san (Mari Mountain) on Kanghwa Island near Seoul. There is a Tangun altar on Mari-san called Chamsongdan and years later while working with the Pearl S. Buck Foundation I remember hiking up to the top of Mari-san to see the altar one lovely summer day.

Just a few days after National Foundation Day there is one more Korean holiday in October—October 9 is Hangeul Day. *Hangeul* is the Korean phonetic alphabet. Easy to learn and more scientific than most other alphabets, this was a huge improvement over Chinese characters. Scholars were commissioned by King Sejong the Great (who reigned from 1418–1450) to create this alphabet, which was proclaimed in 1446. Unfortunately, though, after King Sejong died, the Confucian scholars persuaded the following king to discard it, and *Hangeul* didn't come into general use until the late 1800s when American missionaries revitalized it as a way to help them spread Christianity. It worked for them, as probably the majority of South Koreans today are Christian. *Hangeul* is now used throughout North and South Korea, though the South Koreans still use a few hundred Chinese characters along with this phonetic alphabet. Sort of, kind of defeats the purpose, but.....

I received a letter from Dan Holland, who was the Peace Corps TESOL (Teaching English to Speakers of Other Languages) Coordinator and who had been one of our trainers during the K-23 training program. I had written him about my schedule and using "The Silent Way" in one of my classes. He wrote back:

Dear Don,

Thanks for your up-to-the-minute schedule. I hope that everything is going well. It looks like you are having no trouble staying busy, especially with three special classes.

I'm glad that you are having some opportunities to use 'Silent Way' in some of your teaching. Charlie has a way of convincing people, doesn't he? He is quite enthusiastic about what has been happening in classes where he has used it. It is very encouraging to see people like you two who are so enthusiastic about teaching and willing to try other things that may improve teaching and learning.

I am sending along the handout that we developed on the Silent Way. I can't remember if you picked it up or not. A lot of people are using colored blocks instead of rods and some are having rods made at carpenters' shops and then painting them themselves. Please keep me posted on what you learn about Silent Way and how it works in your particular situations.

Take care and keep smiling,

An young (greetings, literally peace, written in *Hangeul*)

Dan

Later in October, in the middle of the week I got a phone call during my break hour. It was from Chris Sombra in Samcheok asking if I'd like to go with him on the next Sunday to climb a mountain he'd heard about that was about an hour train ride south of Bupyeong. John was heading out of town with the Mukho Health Center Director, so he wouldn't be joining us. This was supposed to be the best weekend to catch the autumn leaves changing color. I was game, so I told him I'd get on the morning train in Mukho while he'd get on in Bupyeong. After an hour train ride together, we got off at Togye high in the Taebaek Mountain range, bought snacks and drinks at a *gage*, and took a bus to where the trail started. It was a gorgeous fall day in Korea—one of those autumn days when the Koreans say, "The sky is high, and the horses are fat." We had a wonderful long hike up, ate our snacks at the top and looked off in the distance at the trees changing colors in all directions, and then meandered back down. We got back to Togye Train Station just in time to catch the evening train back north to our hometowns.

The nights were brisk, and the floor of my room was stoked up and hot. Koreans use an under-the-floor heating system called *ondol,* and interestingly enough the Romans used a similar system and called it *hypocaust.*

Used-up coal briquettes for heating homes.

In Korea during the 1970s most of the homes used cylindrical-shaped charcoal briquettes (*yeontan*) about eight inches high and six inches in diameter with several half inch holes drilled all the way through the cylinder.

Through a shaft outside each room these briquettes were inserted two at a time. The lower one burnt from the bottom up, turning white just like a burnt up barbecue charcoal briquette in our outdoor barbeque grills. After a few hours when the bottom one was totally burnt through, a large pair of tongs was pushed down into two of the half-inch-wide holes. The fingers of the tongs reached almost to the bottom of both briquettes and with a little pressure, both were pulled from the shaft. The lower, all-white thoroughly burnt briquette was knocked off, the upper one that was red hot was placed back into the shaft and a new black briquette was placed above it with the holes lined up with the lower one. The cover was then placed over the shaft, and the *ondol* floor would be hot for about eight more hours or so until another changing was necessary.

One Wednesday night, I went to sleep with the window of my room open as we had been told to always do during our Peace Corps training because if a crack happened to form in the cement floor, carbon monoxide gas could enter your room. The next morning I woke up with the most horrendous headache I have ever had in my life. I rarely get headaches. I often tell my wife, Carol, that I don't usually get headaches even though I tend to give them to others a lot. She usually smiles and agrees. So this terrible splitting headache was totally new to me. Still, I'm a trouper. I almost never miss work, no matter how sick or how bad I might feel. I got up and went through my usual routine except that I didn't study Chinese characters, which is how I had been starting each day since returning to Mukho after my summer in Detroit. By this point I knew a couple of hundred Chinese characters, and though this was not enough to read a Korean newspaper, I still felt a sense of accomplishment. I also didn't go to the taekwondo *dojang* to work out as I usually did. I slept a little later than usual, washed up, and went to the restaurant where I always ate. After a breakfast of rice, soup, kimchee, and other *banchan* (side dishes), I walked up to the girls' middle school. After teaching one or two classes, I apologized to my co-teacher, Mrs. Hwang, Sun-hui, and told her that I was too ill to continue teaching.

I returned to my room and fell asleep again. Many hours later, around 7:00 p.m., there was a knock at my door. Luckily, I had left my clothes on—I usually slept in my undershorts. I got up and opened the door to find all of my special class girls looking very concerned. I welcomed them in, rolled up my *yo* and *ibul*, and invited them all to sit down. After a few minutes, I brought out a deck of cards, and some of them played Hearts while the rest watched. After an hour or so they told me that they had to leave. As they got up, three of them passed out. Several said, "*Yeontan gasu,*" which is Korean for the gas from *yeontan* or, in other words, carbon monoxide. As soon as they said it, I thought, "*Oh, my God, you idiot, of course! Why didn't you figure that out?*" Not only had I not figured it out, but I had slept in the room for probably fourteen hours or more. If I hadn't left the window open, I'd have been dead. I carried one of the girls outside for fresh air, and the girls who were able to walk helped the other two. They told me I had to change rooms, and I assured them I would not spend another minute in that room. After the girls who had fainted recovered, they all left. I went right inside and talked to the lady who owned the *yeogwan*. She immediately helped me move my stuff to another room.

The next day, Friday, after class I asked my co-teacher at the boys' school, Mr. Hyun, to go with me to the Daehung Hasuk-jip (Daehung lodging house). The Daehung was a four-story modern lodging house that sat on the corner right in front of the Mukho Theater, and it had a hot water pipe *ondol* system. Although it was quite a bit more expensive than the Changshin Yeogwan where I had just gotten gassed, Mr. Hyun helped me work out a deal that wasn't too dear. I was just too scared of the possibility of being gassed again sometime during the coming winter, and so I thought it was worth the extra expenditure.

I told the *yeogwan* owner I was leaving, and after the morning classes on Saturday, I toted my stuff the fifty yards or so from the Changsin to the Daehung. My room was on the fourth floor, and my door opened out to the roof. On the other three floors there were eight rooms, four on each side with a hallway in between. On the fourth floor there were only four rooms, all opening to the roof. As you exited my room, in the right corner was the toilet room and in the left corner was the wash room (sink only). The wash room had cold water only. The boiler spread hot water through pipes that heated the floors of the rooms, but they hadn't bothered to extend a line into the wash room. From the edge of the roof in front of my room, I looked down on the Mukho Theater and the alley that wound its way toward the entrance to the Mukho Port.

Mukho Theater with the hand-painted scenes from a Bruce Lee movie showing that week

It was fun to stand near the edge of the roof and to look down at the front of Mukho Theater where every week with each new movie there would be a large hand-painted depiction of scenes from the latest flick. All the movie theaters in Korea had these hand-painted, bigger-than-life posters to advertise the latest film.

On some Saturdays, the students were offered discount tickets for the matinee showing of the current movie. Teachers could attend for free. I always thought it was to help ensure that all the students remained on their best behavior. I would often take advantage of the freebie offer. Theater goers in those days in Korea often ate dried cuttlefish during movies. Vendors with small carts would sell the treat outside the theaters. On the cart they would have a charcoal brazier stoked up, and the cuttlefish would be lightly grilled over the red-hot coals. I often purchased one before going in to see a movie. During the movie I would break off the arms one by one and chew them up. Then I would rip strips of the body about a quarter inch in width and slowly chew them up. Eating cuttlefish this way was like chewing on fish-flavored rubber bands. It took a long time to mash each piece to the point that it could actually be swallowed. By the end of the movie my jaw muscles would ache. If you like fish-flavored rubber bands, it was good eatin'.

The Sunday after moving in to the Daehung Hasuk, I took a long hike all the way past the girls' middle school around the large hill to the lovely sandy beach of Mangsang. I loved to hike there and walk along the sand, sometimes stopping and talking with the lonely Korean soldiers who had the small base in a hill near the south end of the beach. When I reached the main intersection of Mukho on the way back, I ran into Mr. Jang. He yelled over to me from the other side of the street, "Mr. Ha. Come with me, I'm headed to the port." "Good idea," I replied. He was good friends with the Port Master and often would invite me to visit along with him. We met his friend at the gate, and the friend took us aboard a Singaporean ship that was picking up cement. On the ship we met the captain, and he introduced us to a young man named Mr. Lee, Kuan-yew, who was from Singapore and spoke fluent English. Mr. Lee gave us a tour of the ship. He told me that he had gone to English-speaking schools his whole life, which explained why he spoke English so well. He asked me where I was from in the States. When I told him Detroit, Michigan, he told me that he had been to Detroit on a ship before. He then proceeded to tell me that the Great Lakes were more treacherous during storms than the oceans were. "How could that be?" I asked. "Because storms on the oceans usually blow in one direction, the pilot can position the ship to ride the waves quite easily. On the Great Lakes, when a storm churns up the waves, they can bounce off the shorelines and come at you from two or three directions at the same time. It sometimes makes it almost impossible to steer the ship." About a year after meeting Mr. Lee from Singapore, on the date of November 10, 1975, a ship named the Edmund Fitzgerald sank in Lake Superior near Whitefish Point, Michigan. Later, when Gordon Lightfoot wrote his song, "Wreck of the Edmund Fitzgerald," the first verse made a lot of sense to me having heard Mr. Lee's explanation of the wave action on the lakes:

> That good ship and true was a bone to be chewed
> When the gales of November came early.
> ("Wreck of the Edmund Fitzgerald" written, composed and performed by Gordon Lightfoot)

A couple of decades after my Peace Corps years, I went to a memorial service at the Mariner's Church in Detroit, which is also mentioned in the song. At the time of the sinking the minister there had rung the church bell twenty-nine times, one for each man lost on the ship. Gordon Lightfoot also attended this twenty-year memorial church service where a small bell was rung twenty-nine times, once each by twenty-nine different people, some of whom were relatives of the deceased seamen. It was a very moving and emotional church service. Also, it was neat to see Gordon Lightfoot, who was obviously moved by the service, too.

As we were leaving following the tour of the Singaporean ship, Mr. Lee said, "Tomorrow I have the day off." Then he asked, "May I visit your school and watch you teach?"

"Sure," I replied, "that would be great." I drew him a map of how to get to the school and told him to meet me at 8:00, as the first class started at 8:15 a.m.

"Are you sure you'll be able to follow the map?" I asked.

"If not, I'll just ask someone."

"There aren't that many people around who can speak English," I informed him.

"No problem. If they don't speak English I can write Mukho Middle School in Chinese characters, and they'll understand." That impressed me, as I hadn't thought of it before, but in China, Korea, and Japan, even when two people didn't understand each other's spoken language, they could always communicate using Chinese characters. Being pictographs, they had the same meaning across the different cultures and languages that used them. Using Chinese characters may be like trying to run a modern country with caveman drawings, as the British writer whose book I read in Japan had said, but they also had advantages over phonetic alphabets. I was finding that Chinese characters were almost impossible for me to learn with my slow mental capacities, but obviously they didn't slow down the East Asians.

Monday morning, Mr. Lee walked into the teachers' office, and I introduced him to all the other teachers who were there. It turned out that Mr. Lee, Kwan-sup, the English teacher who spoke using lots of GI slang, also spoke some Chinese. He and Mr. Lee from Singapore began talking with Mr. Lee, Kwan-sup translating into Korean for everyone's benefit. Mr. Lee, Kwan-sup was in his element. He loved to show off his English language skills, which often drove me nuts because of his insistence on using incorrect GI jargon, and now he had a captive audience as he showed off his Chinese language ability, too. After a few minutes, though, Mr. Cho, Hui-sam walked into the office. He too spoke Chinese because he had been born and raised in Manchuria. Mr. Cho had a large hook nose, and the other teachers jokingly called him Hawk-Nose. He would often comment on the size of his own nose too. I never saw another Korean with a nose that shape, and I often wondered if he might not have been part Russian. I never asked him, and he never mentioned any background other than Korean. If he were part Russian, it certainly wouldn't have been something to brag about with the Soviet Union being Communist and North Korea's ally.

When class started, Mr. Lee, Kuan-yew from Singapore tagged along with Mr. Hyun and me and watched us teach for a couple of hours. When my free hour came I told him I usually headed to the post office. He came along, and I showed him where I lived in case he might have more free time before his ship was completely filled with cement bags and had to leave. We parted; he returned to the harbor, while I headed to the post office, mailed some letters, bought some stamps, and then headed back to finish my day of teaching.

That evening after I'd finished practicing taekwondo, Mr. Lee came to my room and asked if I'd like to grab a couple of beers with him. I agreed, but he said he had to tell his girlfriend first. I'm thinking, *"Girlfriend? How did he find a girl-friend already?"* We walked up the alley in front of my place toward the harbor entrance, turned up another small side alley, and through an open metal gate into a typical Korean-style house. There were obviously several rooms all opening onto the wraparound stoop. As we walked in, one of my students from the boys' mid-dle school was sitting there. (It seemed that his mother owned or managed the place.) He stood up, saluted, and said, *"Myeolgong!"* (Destroy Communism!). I smiled and said, "Good evening." Several young ladies, looking rather sexy, were also sitting around. One of them came up to Mr. Lee and hugged him. He whis-pered something in her ear. She looked rather disappointed.

"Mr. Lee, are you sure you wouldn't rather stay with your girlfriend?"

"No, I'd like to talk with you some more," he replied.

"Yes, but she looks very upset."

"Oh, she will be fine. I told her I will come back later." I now understood how he had a girlfriend so quickly. Sometimes, even after nearly three years in Korea, I could still be very naive. He was a paying customer, of course. I was always amazed by the conservatism of the Korean people toward sex and nudity on one hand and the ubiquitous nature of prostitution on the other. There was the outright prosti-tution, which was encouraged by the government as a way to increase tourism and to pander to the American GIs. Supposedly all the prostitutes around the U.S. mil-itary bases carried government-issued inoculation cards. In addition, I had read arti-cles about how there were sex tours for horny Japanese men, who came across from their island nation on group tours, stayed in the expensive tourist hotels, and had dinners where each man had his own *gisaeng* girl. These girls hand-fed and enter-tained the men throughout the evening, and then for an added fee, rumor had it, they stayed the night. Supposedly nearly every morning of the week, if you stood behind some of the tourist hotels you'd see the ladies sneaking out the back entrances at dawn. In addition to outright prostitution, and as described before, supposedly many female employees in barber shops offered lewd services; tearoom girls, who would often deliver coffee in thermoses to men in hotels or offices, purportedly offered those same lewd services; and in addition there were the bar girls. As James Brown sang oh so well, "This is a Man's World," or at least Korea was a man's world back during my Peace Corps days. ("This is a Man's World," written by Betty Jean Newsome and James Brown, sung by James Brown.)

After Mr. Lee and I drank a couple of beers, we said our final goodbyes. He told me that his ship was loaded, and they'd be pulling out the next morning. I told him to look me up should he ever return, but I never saw him again.

I was back in touch with my college friend and fellow Residence Assistant, Fred Barbeau, and on October 15, 1974, a Tuesday, I wrote:

> Great to be back. Was pretty down in America. After two
> years away, I felt like a visitor and feel back home now. My
> life is beautiful. It revolves around school and taekwondo
> (a martial art).

I did feel culture shock in reverse back in the States, but had a blast visiting old buddies and especially dating Linda. Still, all that seemed far away and long ago already. I also mentioned to Fred that I was in touch with Greg Drummond, who had been

The "Dying Gaul."

on my corridor my junior year at Albion and whom I had traveled with to Washington, D.C. for one of the anti-Vietnam War demonstrations. I also mentioned hearing from David Wamplers, who had also been on my corridor in my junior year and was now in India studying the Tamil language. That's where I had wanted to go in the Peace Corps, and so I had a tinge of envy, but then I loved Korea and the Korean people so "all's well that ends well," as Shakespeare once said.

Fred sent me some photos of a statue that looked to be Roman or Greek, and the face on this bronze statue had an uncanny resemblance to mine. People always say that you have a double out there somewhere. Mine seems to have lived in ancient times. I used this picture

Don when he looked like the "Dying Gaul."

on my CD, *Haff Here, Haff There,* on the cover juxtaposed with a photo of me taken in Korea at one of the girls' middle and high school picnics. On the CD, I'm looking up at this statue staring down at me. I now know that this statue is entitled the "Dying Gaul" and the original is in a museum in Rome. (There is a copy of it at Jasmine Hill in Wetumpka, Alabama, and that's where Fred saw it and photographed it.) My son, Otto, a couple of years ago, saw a picture of this statue on the cover of a book called: *Spartacus: A New Edition,* by Howard Fast.

I wrote again to Fred on November 5, 1974:

I am changing. Purposely changing, striving to be better.
Each day is a good day! Each year seems better, yet I live
each day as it comes. Yesterday is nice to remember,
tomorrow is not as important as I used to think, and today
holds it all. I'm happy working hard, studying, pushing
myself hard, and loving it.

Interestingly, this seems to be the first paragraph in all my correspondence with Fred that didn't have the word "beautiful" in it at least once. (Maybe you noticed my overuse of that word in the quotes from my letters to Fred.) After this paragraph I talked about trying to study yoga on my own. I mentioned that I had several books about yoga and exercised, using them as a guide. Of course during our K-23 training we had studied yoga, and in Mukho during the first fall semester I had continued doing the postures I remembered from that training. I also tried to do the stretching exercise that the instructor in Daegu had said over time would extend my left leg and make it the same length as my right one. As discussed before, my legs are still off by about three-eighths of an inch, and I always have to have my slacks marked on both legs by tailors and each leg made a different length to take this into account. So those few months of stretching obviously were not enough. I don't think I managed to keep up the practice during the fall of 1974 for very long either. Now this last fall semester of my Peace Corps years drew to a close.

CHAPTER 14

Winter Vacation '74–'75: A Younger Girl

Winter break started the third week of December, and as usual we had a month and a half or so off. Charlie had suggested we head back to Haein-sa (Peaceful Sea Temple), which we had visited during our training program back in 1972, and spend Christmas Eve there. I agreed that it would be a great idea, so I headed down to Yeongju to meet him in his town. As usual he met me at the train station when I rolled in, and we went back to his boarding house.

The next morning, we got on the slow train to Daegu for the five-hour trip. It was a cold winter's day. There was snow on the barren rice fields. We found open seats, or actually benches, in one of the cars and sat down. We each pulled a book out of our bags, as per our usual, and began reading. After a half hour or so we noticed that it was getting colder and colder rather than warmer. We checked the adjacent cars, and they were the same. It seemed that the heaters on the train weren't working. My feet were getting cold, so I took my shoes off and sat cross-legged, taking turns tucking one foot and then the other underneath my thighs to warm them up. For the whole trip it just seemed to get colder until we were both nearly frozen by the time we reached Daegu.

We visited a nearby tearoom where we sat by the kerosene heater to warm up. Usually we found it too hot near the heaters and avoided them, but on this day it felt great. Once warm we headed to the bus station where we could get a bus going to Haein-sa.

By the time we reached Haein-sa it was late afternoon. We hiked through the snow to one of the outlying monasteries. One of the monks came out and met us, and we asked if we could stay in one of their rooms for two nights. It was December 23. He led us to a room and told us that dinner would be brought to us soon. Dinner came, and it was wonderful—all vegetarian with many roots, shoots, and leaves different from what you'd get in restaurants. The flavors were out of this world. Not only did I not miss meat while at Haein-sa, after we left I longed for this wonderful Buddhist vegetarian cuisine.

We sat and read all evening. I was reading *The Martyred,* by Richard E. Kim, the famous Korean-American author whose two most famous books are *The Martyred* and *Lost Names. Lost Names* is about his youth in North Korea during the Japanese occupation and about his father who was a Presbyterian minister.

His father was killed during the Korean War in Pyongyang by the North Korean Communists, which is part of the plot in *The Martyred*. Years later during the 1980s, while I was the Resident Director of the Pearl S. Buck Foundation's Korea Branch and living in Seoul, I was at a Royal Asiatic Society of Korea lecture given by Richard E. Kim. During the question and answer period after his talk, I mentioned that Jerzy Kosinski had visited my class in college. Mr. Kosinski said that he would not have been able to write his book, *The Painted Bird*, about his youth as a Jewish boy running away from the Nazis in his native language of Polish. But he told us that he could write about it in English because he felt more detached from the events. I asked Richard Kim if he found this to be true. Richard said that he had never thought about this until quite recently because he had lived in the U.S. since 1955 and had written all his books in English. At this time in the 1980s, back in Korea for a visit, one of the Korean newspapers had just asked him to write an article in Korean about his youth. He said that when he sat down and started to write, he burst into tears and was hardly able to finish the article. He stated that it was so much more vivid, real, personal, and emotional for him in his native Korean language.

Charlie and I would read books for hours on end. Sometimes, for a break, I'd pull out the latest Asian edition of *Newsweek* and read that for a while. Throughout my time in Peace Corps, when I wasn't teaching, lesson planning, hiking, or doing taekwondo, I was pretty much always reading.

The next morning, Christmas Eve, Charlie and I got up, washed up, ate another wonderful vegetarian meal, and then headed off to the main temple. We spent Christmas Eve day taking pictures at Haein-sa as well as hiking around the trails in the snow-covered mountains. By the time we returned to our room at dinnertime, our leather hiking boots were soaking wet. We sat on the stoop, took off our boots and socks, wrung out our socks, and took both the boots and the socks into the room. We laid them out over the hottest part of the *ondol* floor and hoped they'd dry out by morning.

Christmas morning 1974! The socks were dry, but our boots were still damp. We slipped them back on after breakfast anyway and wandered around Haein-sa again. Sitting on mats in the main temple meditating for a while was fun. Then in the early afternoon we headed back to Yeongju on Christmas Day (Wednesday, December 25, 1974).

Charlie, who was always more driven, more diligent, and even more enthusiastic about teaching than I, wanted to spend the rest of winter break in Yeongju lesson planning. I would have gone stir-crazy doing that, so on December 26 I headed up to Seoul by train from Yeongju alone.

In early October I had written to the Peace Corps office and asked for an increase in my living allowance. I was spending more each month for the non-lethal Daehung Hasuk with radiant hot water pipe heat instead of the coal briquette heat at the Changshin Yeogwan. In November, I received a letter back from the Director, Jon Kalkaska:

The "ladies" you addressed forwarded your letter to my desk. Sorry for the delay in responding to your request for a living allowance increase, but budgetary concerns have been very real recently. However, I can now approve your request for a 5,000 won increase effective with the December payment. This increase may deposited (sic) to your account a little late, but it will come.

Hope all is well, and that you are enjoying your extension year.

Consequently, after checking into the Daeji Yeogwan, I went up to the Peace Corps office and went right to the seventh floor. Although 5,000 won per month sounds like a lot of money, the value in dollars at that time was only about $10.00. Even so, I wanted to thank Jon for having given me the living allowance increase.

As I got off the elevator on the seventh floor, I noticed a new young lady who was serving as the receptionist answering the phone at the entrance to the office area. She was cute, and I stopped to greet her. I said something in Korean like, "How are you? I'm seeing you for the first time. My American name is Don, but my Korean name is Ha, Doe-young." She said, "Nice to meet you, my name is Kim, Hae-ju." When I heard her name was Hae-ju, knowing my love of songs, especially those from the 1960s and my admiration for the Beatles, I'm sure you can figure out which Beatles song came immediately to mind. Because Hae-ju sounded an awful lot like Hey Jude, the song I thought of was in fact "Hey Jude." I immediately began singing with my best operatic delivery:

Hae-ju, don't make it bad.
("Hey Jude," written by Paul McCartney, credited to John Lennon-Paul McCartney, performed by the Beatles)

Hae-ju smiled. I sat down in a chair off to the side of her desk, and it was then that I noticed she was wearing a black miniskirt (wearing a miniskirt was unusual for Koreans in those days) and a pair of light grey, snakeskin-like over-the-calf boots. We talked for a while, and then I wandered into the main office area while singing a different verse of "Hey Jude."

As I walked through the offices, I greeted all of the Korean employees, the Assistant Director, and the TESOL Coordinator. Mr. Song, the supervisor for Gyeonggi and Gangwon provinces, saw me and called out, "Hello, Mr. Ha, the best volunteer in Gangwon-do." I waved back and greeted him warmly. While still singing "Hey Jude," I nodded, bowed, and greeted the several ladies who worked in the financial office whose names I didn't know (which is why I had addressed my letter to "ladies" when asking for an increase in my monthly stipend).

I wandered toward the Peace Corps Director Jon Kalkaska's office to thank him for approving my living allowance increase. He was talking to a couple of other volunteers, Peter Walpole and Gordon Harsens, guys who I didn't really know but had seen around. Jon waved at me to come in. After talking for a few minutes, Jon invited the three of us to have dinner at his house that evening. I was excited to go as I had heard that he lived in a beautiful old *hanok* (traditional Korean-style) house just west of Kyungbok Palace. Jon, I had heard, had even let some ailing volunteers stay at his place. A couple of volunteers had been hospitalized in Severance Hospital for different illnesses and after leaving the hospital, while recuperating, they had stayed at Jon's house. All three of us agreed to go, and Jon drew us each a map of how to find his house. I left Jon's office so Peter and Gordon could finish their conversation with him. Jon bid me adieu and said, "See you at my place at 7:00." "Sounds great, I'll be there," I replied.

I returned to Miss Kim, Hae-ju's desk and flirted with her some more. Not wanting to get her in trouble I only stayed briefly and then went down to the sixth floor where the lending library and lounge were. I returned a few books that I had finished reading, picked out several others, put them in my bag and then went into the lounge. None of my good friends were around, and some of the volunteers who were there I recognized as among those who loved to complain about Korea and criticize the Korean people. So I left and hit the *mog* (bath house) for a thorough cleansing. I even paid for the service where a young man scraped your whole naked body with a course mitt-like gizmo that peeled off layers of dead skin. As the young boy (who is clothed, just so you all don't get the wrong impression) pushed down with all his might and pulled the scraping mitt towards him, I could see string-like globs of my skin rolling up. They looked like flesh-colored rubber bands. This was after I had already showered with soap and a wash cloth and had soaked for fifteen to twenty minutes or more in the hot tub. It is hard to believe there could be this much dirty, dead skin still on my body, but there was. Now I was all literally squeaky clean to visit Jon's house that evening.

I got to Jon's house at 7:00 p.m. and had run into Peter and Gordon on the way there. We wandered through the small alley-like paths toward Jon's house while talking about how we wouldn't want to live in "a world without love." Don't you agree? ("A World Without Love," written by Paul McCartney, credited to John Lennon-Paul McCartney, performed by Peter and Gordon)

Jon's house was gorgeous. We took our shoes off and went into the main front room. There was a seating arrangement with a sofa, a coffee table, and a couple of upholstered chairs in the middle. At the far end of the room was a wooden dining table and chairs. We all sat down on the comfy furniture and talked of trivial matters for a few minutes until Jon's Korean maid announced dinner was ready. It was a scrumptious Korean meal, after which we retreated into another seating area off to the side that was like a wide corridor into the back section of the house. It was all typical for a traditional Korean house with wide beams and flooring of highly-varnished, beautiful dark wood. On one long wall covered with this luxurious dark wood, there were four beautiful Korean paintings of mountain scenes. Around each of the paintings was a wide area of pink patterned silk. Jon said these panels were there when he moved in, so he picked up on the pink theme and added a pink patterned rug on top of the dark wood floor and other pink accents.

"Oh my gosh, this is such a beautiful room. Real men have pink accented sitting rooms," I said.

"Ha, ha," Jon laughed.

"Is it true that Kim, Jong-pil owns this house?" I inquired.

"Yes, he does. Luckily we've been able to get a long-term lease on it."

"It is a beautiful place," Peter added.

Kim, Jong-pil had earlier founded the Korean Central Intelligence Agency (KCIA) and was serving in the early 1970s as President Park, Chung-hee's Prime Minister. Of course, I've always thought that any CIA and/or "military intelligence" for that matter was a good example of an oxymoron, especially when one looks into how often they've been wrong. In addition, as also mentioned before, one of Korean history's most ironic incidents was when in 1979 President Park, Chung-hee was assassinated by his then KCIA director, Kim, Jae-kyu.

Jon had been a PCV in Thailand. Gordon started asking Jon about which country's women were prettier—Thailand's or Korea's. Jon basically said that he thought on average Thai women might be prettier, but that some outstanding Korean women were the prettiest of all. This made me think that I wanted to get to Thailand and make my own appraisal.

After being a Peace Corps Volunteer in Thailand, Jon had worked as a desk officer in the Peace Corps Washington, D.C. headquarters. He had been assigned to the Pacific Island desk. We started asking him questions about working for PC Washington and he mentioned that he got to take a trip to visit volunteers in various Pacific Island countries and territories. He mentioned that in one island group where there were PCVs, the female students actually attended school topless. My ears perked up at hearing this. Jon had visited one girls' high school where there was a male Peace Corps volunteer teaching. Jon walked in and sat at the back of the room while the male volunteer taught. The volunteer had gone native and wore a sarong-like wrap around his waist while the female students sat in rapt attention to his teaching. I listened to Jon's story, imagining myself teaching there and looking out at a room full of topless teenage girls. I told Jon that I didn't think I could have taught there without getting aroused. Peter and Gordon agreed. Jon said that he asked the volunteer if the toplessness didn't bother him, and the volunteer replied that after the first day he didn't even notice anymore.

After a while Jon got serious. I had hair down to my shoulders as well as a beard and mustache at that time. Jon looked at me and said, "You know, Don, you are the only PCV who has convinced me that your appearance—your long hair, beard, and mustache—does not interfere with your ability to perform your job. Somehow you have won over your school—or schools actually, both of them—and there are no problems." I made some weak acknowledgment and then Jon continued, "You do, though, make my job more difficult because other guys whose appearance is causing problems at their sites point at you and say, 'Look at Don.'" I thought about this and responded, "I certainly don't want anyone using me as an excuse, and actually I'm due for a change. Since my freshman year of college, every few months I've changed my appearance. I'd go from beard and mustache to goatee and mustache and then to just mustache, or I'd go from hair down to my shoulders to hair just barely over the top of my ears. I'll shave off my beard and cut my hair pretty short, and then no one can use me as an excuse." Jon told me that he'd appreciate it if I would do that.

After more small talk Peter, Gordon, and I left and headed back to our *yeogwans*. As I rolled out my *yo* and *ibul*, I noticed that there was a hole in the ceiling. The walls and ceilings of many rooms in Korea were covered with wallpaper, including this room. I didn't think anything of the hole and turned off the light and went to sleep. I have no idea how long I had been asleep before the pitter patter of little feet above the ceiling woke me up. As soon as I came to my senses, I knew what was making this noise—RATS! *"Cheeze it, the rats!"* I said to myself and cracked myself up at the same time. But I got up, turned on the lights, and heard the footsteps of at least one and maybe a couple of rats running away from near the hole. I had heard that sometimes the rats liked to eat the glue that held the ceiling paper onto the slats of wood. I also remembered one day sitting and talking to the owner of the Daeji Yeogwan when he saw a rat running around the small courtyard. He got a shovel and crushed the little varmint's head in. So I knew there were rats around. My heart began racing. There were also stories told by Peace Corps Volunteers, late at night when everyone was sufficiently drunk, about rats falling through holes just like this one and down onto slumbering volunteers. I lay back down, but left the light on. Sure enough, just after falling asleep again, I heard the little critters coming. I grabbed a shoe and lofted it at the ceiling near where the sound was coming from. The rat ran away. I went back to sleep only to repeat this shoe throwing every so often, or as Lionel Richie said oh so well, "All Night Long." ("All Night Long," written and performed by Lionel Richie.) The next morning, exhausted, I went and asked the owner if I could switch to another room.

Also the next morning for my one and only time in all the years I spent in Korea, I went to a Korean barber shop. I had been cutting my own hair and trimming my own beard ond/or mustache since I started college, but this was going to be major work. I walked in and asked for a shave of my beard only and a haircut. (It cost about "two bits"—only kidding!) A guy put a smock on me, and I told him to leave my hair a little long but to take off several inches (or actually the metric equivalent thereof). When he finished it was quite short. He also clipped off my beard with the electric hair clipper. Then a cute young lady came over and put scalding hot towels over my face that can only be described as a scorch and burn tactic. Then as I was sitting and silently weeping in agony, I could hear her slapping the straight razor against the strop, sharpening it up. When it got to the point where I stopped crying because the towel had cooled off a bit, she took it off and rubbed some hot cream lather on my face. She pulled out one of her hairs and cut the five-inch-long single hair lengthwise into two strands. The razor was that sharp. (Well maybe I just imagined this last demonstration of shaving prowess.) Then she began meticulously scraping my face with the razor. After finishing one side she went back and with her left hand's index finger and thumb, stretched the skin on my face as tight as she could and scraped it again with the razor. When she finished a cooling lotion was applied, but this didn't help. I looked in the mirror, and my face was beet red. I walked out and tried to touch my cheeks, but even the slightest touch caused immense pain. For three days I couldn't touch my face. I never went back to a barber shop in Korea ever again.

Following this indignity, I returned to the Peace Corps office and went right up to chat some more with Hae-ju. I strolled in after getting off the elevator in the hall again singing another verse of "Hey Jude."

She laughed again, and I sat down next to her. It was Friday and she asked, "Tomorrow do you have plans?" I thought, *"Oh, boy! My Pepé Le Pew-like French charms have already won her over."* "Why, no, no I don't," I replied. I had visions of myself out for the evening with Miss Kim, Hae-ju walking around Myeong-dong, she in her miniskirt and go-go boots and I with a big, wide grin on my face. Then she explained that she had met a British couple the day before, and they'd invited her to lunch with them on Saturday. They wanted her to take them to a traditional Korean restaurant. She wanted me to go with her and help answer their questions. I tried to not show my extreme disappointment and told her I'd be more than happy to assist.

I left her on the seventh floor and went back down to the sixth floor lounge where a couple of guys, whose names were Tom Tittabawassee and Jerry Mille-coquins, were hanging out. I hardly knew them, but they both had long hair. They looked pained when they saw me walk in.

"What happened to your hair and beard?" they cried out.

"I got tired of it all," I replied.

"Oh, man, we use you as an example when Jon Kalkaska gives us a hard time about our appearance," Tom said.

"Great! Don't use me as an excuse anymore. I proved that my hair and beard were no problem at all in my school or my town. Mr. Song, the Gangwon Province supervisor, came to my town, and he couldn't believe that no one was bothered at all by my appearance. Unless you can prove the same on your own, you should get your hair cut too," I told them.

"But we were following your example," Jerry interjected.

"Good, follow my new example."

"Don't follow leaders, and watch the parking meters," I sang to myself. ("Subterranean Homesick Blues," written and performed by Bob Dylan.) I walked out of the lounge and disappeared into the elevator heading down and away from the silliness.

Saturday morning, I met Miss Kim, Hae-ju in front of the Cosmos Department Store. Koreans pronounce cosmos *ko-su-mo-su* and department store is *baekwhajeom*, literally "one hundred shops place." So I met her in front of *Kosumosu Baekwhajeom* a few minutes before noon. The British couple arrived right at noon, and Miss Kim introduced me to Roger and Kathryn Cranbrook. They were tourists traveling on their winter break. We went to a large Korean-style restaurant that I had been to many times before very close to the Cosmos Department Store. I was glad that I was with Miss Kim, because Roger and Kathryn had a million questions; some of them neither Miss Kim nor I knew the answer to. But Miss Kim, with her limited English, would have been hard pressed to answer many of their inquires. Together we explained the whole menu to them, and finally we all ordered our food. I was starving because it took so long to explain everything. I was always hungry and always ate like a horse in those days.

The food came, and Kathryn and Roger immediately noticed that instead of the normal Korean white rice the rice bowls were filled with a hodgepodge of five grains. Instead of the usual beautiful glowing white of Korean rice, it was an ugly sandy-gray color. The Korean government in those days ordered restaurants to serve this five-grain garbage on Wednesdays and Saturdays to try to cut down on rice consumption and free up extra rice for export to Japan. The Japanese also loved the high quality of the glutinous Korean rice. Unlike Uncle Ben's rice, Korean rice has short fat grains and is very sticky, which makes it much easier to eat with chopsticks. In fact, cooked Korean rice makes for great glue. It actually beats Elmer's all to hell. Korean stamps didn't have the best glue on them in those days, and when a stamp wouldn't stick to an envelope, one grain of cooked rice mushed on the back of a stamp would affix it to an envelope and once dry it would hold for *man nyeon* (ten thousand years) or more. Besides restaurants, the students could not bring white rice for lunch, and teachers were charged with making sure they had no rice in their lunches on Wednesdays and Saturdays. Roger and Kathryn raved about this interesting blend of grains. They were separating individual grains out and naming each one. "Oh, look, there is barley," Roger said. "This is millet," exclaimed Kathryn. I, like the vast majority of Koreans, disliked this five-grain stuff and always would rather have had white rice. I'm sure the five-grain was more nutritious, but I was a rice snob after having lived in Korea for two and a half years now, and I wanted nothing to do with this ugly stuff.

After lunch we walked out and bid farewell to Roger and Kathryn. They thanked Miss Kim and me profusely for having met them for lunch and for having answered their myriad of questions. As they walked away I asked Miss Kim if she'd like to get a cup of coffee, and she agreed. We wandered into Myeongdong and went into my favorite tearoom/coffee shop. After sipping our coffee slowly and talking for an hour or so, I was still hoping to spend the evening with Kim, Hae-ju and "looking for a little romance, given half the chance," but... ("Lady in Red," written and performed by Chris DeBurgh.)

"I'm sorry, but I must leave," she said.

"Oh," I responded, "Really, must you go?"

"Yes, I must." I tried not to look too downhearted as we exited the tearoom, and I reluctantly bid her, "Au Revoir!" (Goodbye!) My French charms, obviously, had failed me this time.

I stayed a few more days in Seoul, often wandering off alone. One day I took a bus to Sajik Park west of Gwanghwa-mun. Sajik Park is just before Sajik Tunnel, which leads to Independence Gate. In Korean, Independence Gate is *"Tongnip-mun"* and was spelled this way in the McCune-Reischauer system. After getting off the bus, I noticed a new sign which read *Dogrib-moon* using the new government-sponsored revised romanization system. I cracked up. Out loud I said, "Dog Rib Moon, I love it." This was even better, and by that I mean worse, than Kangnung to *Gangneung*. I have registered my music with A.S.C.A.P. under the name of Dog Rib Moon Music in honor of this unique spelling of Tongnip-mun. (A few months later I noticed the sign was replaced with one reading Dongnim-mun.)

After laughing and making note of the "Dog-rib-moon" spelling for Independence Gate, I wandered into Sajik Park. There is a statue there of Yi, Yulgok, the great Yi Dynasty philosopher whose birthplace I had visited with the third-year students from Mukho Middle School during their class trip my first semester of teaching. There are also two square altars there, one each to the god of Earth and the god of Harvest, where every spring and fall the Yi Dynasty kings would come in ceremonial dress to offer sacrifices. These ceremonies took place here throughout the Chosun/Yi Dynasty period from its beginning in 1394 until 1897 when they were transferred to the Altar of Heaven located behind the Chosun Hotel.

Past the altars there was a traditional archery competition going on. The Korean bow is a composite bow made of wood, sinew, and horn and is much smaller and more arched/curved than western bows. I could not believe how far away the targets were. I'm guessing they were maybe a football field and a half (150 yards) from the shooting line. Nor could I believe the archers' accuracy from this great distance. In college I took bowling and archery one fall semester. We began with archery shooting outside with the standard, rather straight western bow. From about twenty yards away I barely hit the target half of the time while these Korean archers with their small bows and bamboo arrows were hitting targets that were so far away I thought they were in a different province. I stood fascinated and watched the competition for quite a while.

On another day after a snowfall I went with a couple of Peace Corps ladies, Wilma Peche and Betty Hiawatha, into Kyongbok Palace right behind the old Japanese capitol building. Kyongbok Palace was the royal residence after King Kojong and Queen Min moved there in 1872 from another palace east of Kyongbok. Queen Min was murdered here in her private quarters by Japanese thugs sent by the Japanese ambassador on October 8, 1895. I had learned about this in one of the Korean history books that I had read a few months earlier. As we were walking around inside the palace I was thinking about this and began telling the story to the ladies. Queen Min was anti-Japanese and pro-Russian and was seen by the Japanese as an obstacle to their expansion in Korea. Sword-carrying Japanese assassins scaled the palace walls, found the queen, and murdered her along with two other palace women. After they murdered Queen Min, they burned her body and spread her ashes around in the back (northern part) of the palace so there would be no grave. Wilma and Betty were duly horrified to hear of how terrible the Japanese had been at that time. A few months after Queen Min's murder, in 1896, the king and crown prince escaped the palace under the watchful eyes of the new Japanese-trained guards by dressing in women's clothing and heading out a side gate in enclosed sedan chairs. They headed to the Russian Legation (the Russian diplomatic office and residence) and lived there for several months while another smaller palace (which was near the Russian, British, and American legations) was being renovated. When finished, King Kojong and his son moved into this smaller palace, today called Deoksu Palace, feeling safer surrounded by these friendly pro-Korean independence ambassadors.

I had signed up to take the foreign service exam at the U. S. Embassy and was hoping that I would get hired by the State Department and spend the rest of my life in one exotic capital city or another working at U. S. Embassies and Consulates. Nick Mack had taken the exam a year earlier and had gone to work for the State Department, and even though I knew I was nowhere near as smart as Nick, I thought there might be a chance for me. The test took a couple of hours for the multiple-choice part, and then after a break we had to answer an essay question that was about the current events of the time. I thought I did fairly well, but we were told not to contact the embassy or the State Department and that they would get in contact with those chosen. In other words, "Don't call us, we'll call you." I checked my mail carefully for months, but to no avail. As weeks and months passed with no word, I began to realize that I'd need to make other plans for my future.

After a few more days in Seoul, I decided to head back home, as my funds were getting short. I couldn't afford to spend my whole vacation in Seoul, and so I took the new subway ("Oh, goody!") to Cheongnyangri and headed for Yeongju by train. When I got to Yeongju, Charlie told me that his former students Ko, Myung-shim and Chae, Sun-hui, who were now third-year middle school students, wanted to meet us. Ko, Myung-shim and I had become penpals. She wanted to practice her English, and so we had begun writing short letters back and forth. At some point she must have asked, and I must have told her that January 24 was my birthday.

Charlie and I met Miss Ko and Miss Chae at a Korean bakery, and they threw me a little surprise birthday party. I had forgotten that it was my birthday and didn't much care anyway, but it was a nice gesture. After visiting and staying a couple of nights with Charlie, I then boarded the train back to Mukho. I got back to working on lesson plans for the spring semester and reading some of the new books I'd brought back from Seoul.

Shortly after returning to Mukho, one afternoon I was sitting cross-legged on the floor—I think it was "25 or 6 to 4:00"—reading when there was a knock at the door. ("25 or 6 to 4," written by Robert Lamm, performed by Chicago) "Wait a minute," I said in Korean. I set down the book, got up, and opened the door. To my shock it was Ko, Myung-shim. I looked past her and around her, hoping there was someone else with her, but she seemed to be alone. "What are you doing here?" I asked. "Came to see you," was the response. I invited her in, and she plopped her bag down and made herself at home. It was late in the afternoon (remember 25 or 6 to 4:00?), so I asked if she was hungry. She was, and we went to the restaurant where I ate two meals every day on my monthly plan and paid for an extra meal for her. After dinner we returned to my room and talked a while, and then I started reading and so did she. (I had not told John Hudson I was back in town, and we hadn't started back doing taekwondo yet.) When it got to be time to go to sleep, I suggested I'd get an extra *yo, ibul,* and *begae* from the *hasuk-jip* owner. I came back and rolled out her bedding and mine right next to each other because the room wasn't big enough for much separation. We both took turns going out and washing up. She had put on pajama-like garments in the washroom and crawled under her *ibul.* I turned off the light, crawled under my *ibul,* and undressed under the cover to my underpants as I can't stand to sleep in any clothing other than u-trou. It was a clear night, and the moonlight came in through the small window illuminating Myung-shim's face. Her face was cute as hell. She was probably sixteen years old and had a now fairly fully matured, shapely body. I stared at her face and her puffy lips, which made her look like she was pouting. *"I can't believe she has come here by herself and with her parents' permission,"* I thought to myself. When I asked her earlier how she could come alone, she replied that she had told her parents that she was going to visit a teacher. Education was like a religion in Korea, especially learning English, but even so I was only a few years older, a foreigner, a male, single, and living alone in a tiny room. And she was a lovely, naïve, impressionable, shapely young lady. How her parents could just let her go without asking more questions was beyond me. I was also thinking of a line that had cracked me up in John Steinbeck's *Tortilla Flats,* which I had written down in my memorable quotes notebook a few weeks earlier: "It was not a safe thing to lead Joe into temptation, as he had no resistance to it at all." Luckily, I did have resistance to it. But even so, I was an adult male, and although she was physically a young lady, she was really still a child. I would never have been able to forgive myself if I had taken advantage of this situation. So, I rolled over and forced myself to go to sleep.

Myung-shim informed me that she had told her parents she would be gone for three nights and four days. I just didn't trust myself or want to take the chance of spending another night alone with her. Miss Ou, Chong-suk and Miss Yum, Jong-run had mentioned that they would return from their parents' homes back to Mukho a few days early and proposed that the three of us could maybe travel to Sorak National Park together for a couple of days. I suggested to Myung-shim that we go and visit a couple of other teachers to see if they still wanted to go to Sorak Mountain and that we could all go together. Miss Yum lived closer to my *hasuk* than Miss Ou did, and so we went to her rooming house first. I knocked on her door, and she answered. After introducing her to Myung-shim, I asked if she was still interested in going to Sorak Mountain. She said she was. "Do you think Ou Seonsaeng-nim would like to go with us, too?" I inquired. "Ou Seonsaeng-nim has not returned to Mukho yet." Miss Yum informed me.

So Miss Yum said she'd pack and meet us at the train station for the early afternoon northbound train. Myung-shim and I went back to my room and packed our bags. By late afternoon the three of us had arrived at Sorak National Park and procured a room in a small *yeogwan* inside the park and near the cable car that went up to a ridge where there are ruins of an ancient mountain fortress. We had dinner and returned to our room and played *hwatu*, a Korean card game. When it was time for bed we rolled out our *yos* and *ibuls*. I put mine near the door, while Miss Yum's was right next to mine and Myung-shim's was near the back wall of the room.

The first morning there when we woke and looked out our window it was snowing. Mt. Sorak is beautiful in the winter, and I was glad we had come and especially glad that Miss Yum was with us. After breakfast the snow ceased, and we hiked up one of the many mountain passes to Heundeul-bowi (Shaking Rock). Heundeul-bowi is an oval-shaped boulder about twelve feet by eight feet, which sits in a small depression on a stone outcropping. If two or more people push on one side of the rock it rolls forward a little and when you stop pushing, it rolls back, vibrates to and fro a few times, and then comes back to rest right where it started. After having lunch in the afternoon, we hiked up another valley and visited the beautiful waterfall at its end.

The next morning, we left on the bus back to Gangneung. Thankfully, this was Myung-shim's last day on the east coast, and she would be heading back to

Yeongju. The three of us got on the late morning Seoul-bound train leaving Gangneung. Miss Yum and I got off in Mukho while Myung-shim continued back to Yeongju. I was glad to be rid of her and the temptation of her cuteness. Miss Yum (who was also very cute) and I parted when I turned right up the side street toward my *hasuk* with the Mukho Theater right across from it. Miss Yum headed back to her room, and I didn't see her again until a few days later when the spring semester began. I just relaxed and did more hiking, lesson planning, and some reading for the last few days of winter vacation.

CHAPTER 15

Spring Semester 1975: By a Mountain Pool

Classes got back underway, and I continued with the same schedule as in the fall except that Mr. Hyun got transferred down to Bupyeong where Cho, Myung-hui, my lady friend who would contact me every few weeks, lived. He was teaching at Bupyeong Girls' Middle School. I now co-taught at Mukho Middle School with Mrs. Shim, Uhn-sook. The first day back at school during my free hour, I began talking with some of the other teachers who were also not teaching that hour. I told them of Myung-shim's visit and my surprise at her sudden appearance. They assured me that because she was visiting a teacher it was copacetic. *"Oh, my God!"* I thought. *"How naive can Koreans get? This is a recipe for disaster."* I couldn't help thinking of how this would be thought of in America. Imagine the parents of a six-teen-year-old girl in Detroit, when during Christmas break their daughter announces, "I'm taking the train to Chicago to visit a teacher, who is a friend of our school's Mr. So and So. They are both from Haiti (or France or Korea). Mr. So and So's friend is twenty-four years old, lives in a small studio apartment by himself, and he is single. Is that OK with you, Mom and Dad?"

I heard that again a new volunteer was joining our "prop set" on the east coast. Mark Mackinac was teaching at the boys' middle school in Bupyeong just south of Mukho where Mr. Hyun and, of course, Myung-hui both lived. I looked up Mark and visited him in his town. He had been working for IBM before he joined the Peace Corps, and he told me that IBM encouraged its employees to volunteer. When IBM employees joined the Peace Corps, they were given two years' unpaid leave, and their benefits accrued while serving. When he finished Peace Corps, Mark told me, he would be treated as if he had been working for IBM during those two years of Peace Corps service, and when he retired those two years would count toward his retirement benefits. I was impressed. We hit it off right away, and I enjoyed getting to know him. I suggested that the next Saturday he visit Mukho. Myung-hui had stopped by one afternoon a few days earlier to visit, and I had invited her to come on that same Saturday and bring her friend Shin, Kyung-ok. I told Mark about Myung-hui and Miss Shin and told him we could all hang out at my *hasuk*. He agreed.

The next Saturday he came to Mukho, and I met him at the train station. It was midafternoon, and we went back to my place. In the early evening Myung-hui and Miss Shin showed up and knocked on the door. They were hungry, but we couldn't go out to a restaurant together because this was my town, and I didn't want to be seen in the company of a young lady. So I took orders for Chinese food because Chinese restaurants in Korea always delivered. I went down to the office and borrowed the phone there to place an order. A while later the young delivery boy brought our meals. Chinese places always had boys or young men deliver the food, and they used those special large metal boxes described earlier to help keep the food warm. We ate our meal, and I had previously bought some of the new wine all the *gages* (small stores) now had and snacks to eat. One of my favorite snacks that I always bought was called *Sae-u-gang* (Shrimp Flavored Cracker). *Sae-u-gang* and McVities' cookies, and we were all happy. We talked and played the Korean *hwatu* card game all evening until before midnight Mark went and asked the owner for a room. Even though this place called itself a *hasuk-jip* (boarding house), it always had empty rooms and also served as a *yeogwan* (inn). Mark and Miss Shin left to go to their room.

Sunday afternoon after Myung-hui, Miss Shin, and Mark left, I went to take a *mog*. I sat down as usual on one of the small, six-inch high, plastic stools and using the low hot and cold spigots filled up a small plastic bowl, poured the water over me and then soaped up. There were also high spigots where you could take a regular standup shower, but I always liked to sit on a stool. I looked up and saw John Hudson and the Mukho Health Center Director, Mr. Kim, walking into the bathing area. All of us were, of course, buck naked. I waved and bowed slightly in greeting. Once finished rinsing off the soap, I stood up, walked over to the hot tub and slowly lowered my body in. A little later after taking showers, John and Mr. Kim also got into the hot tub, and we carried on a quiet conversation until I got out and went over to the much smaller cold water tub. After a couple of trips back and forth from the hot to the cold and cold to hot tubs, I walked back out into the dressing area and left before John and Mr. Kim came out.

On Monday after taekwondo John told me that Mr. Kim had noticed that I was a bit more endowed than John was. I laughed and said, "Probably not, maybe the angle of his view was just right or something." John laughed and suggested we get a cup of coffee at a tearoom, which we did. After our coffee came, he began to tell me that he had gone drinking Saturday night with Mr. Kim and a Mr. Song who was the policeman in charge of keeping tabs on the foreigners in town. Besides John, me, and two American priests who virtually never left the rectory in the Catholic church compound, there were also a couple of Japanese living in Mukho. Mr. Song had thanked John for being very fastidious about letting Mr. Kim know whenever he left town, where he was going, and when he'd be back. It seemed that one of Mr. Song's big tasks was to always know where we were, especially if we left Mukho and went anywhere else. Then he asked if John would talk to me because I never told anyone where I was going when I left town, and he had to nose around after I got back and piece it all together from conversations I had with the teachers or others in town.

"It would be nice if you'd tell your *hasuk-jip* owner before you leave town each time where you are going and when you'll be back. Then Mr. Song can easily do his job," John said.

"Screw him," I said, and then I told John the story of the cop who'd come to my room one night two years before, who might well have been this Mr. Song. John agreed that the cop two years ago had been rude.

"But Mr. Song is a nice guy, and he's just doing his job," John added.

"Maybe so," I injected, "but I don't really care for his job and don't feel any compulsion to make his work easier. Let him earn his damn pay."

"Don, why don't you just be nice?"

"I never claimed to be nice, so why start now?" I replied.

It's funny because years later in the 1980s when I worked for the Pearl S. Buck Foundation, I was very polite and kind to the policeman who was in charge of keeping track of the foreigners working for nonprofit organizations in Seoul. Mr. Ryu, Je-il, the director of PSBF's Korean Government program, had his desk right outside my office. The Korean government at that time gave the Pearl S. Buck Foundation the equivalent of over a quarter of a million dollars per year. This money was used to pay middle and high school tuition for all the Amerasians in Korea, and also all four hundred plus Amerasian children and adults received a monthly stipend out of these government funds. One day I walked out of my office and noticed that Mr. Ryu was talking to a well-dressed Korean man in a typical businessman's dark suit, white shirt, and tie. I stopped, and Mr. Ryu introduced me to Mr. Paik, Tae-hyun, who was a plain-clothed policeman whose responsibilities included keeping track of all the foreigners in Seoul doing social welfare work. I felt much more magnanimous by this point in my life, and I felt there was no reason to be rude. I had not encountered any rude policemen since that night in Mukho a decade before. So I invited him into my office and asked our bookkeeper to please bring us each a cup of coffee. Mr. Paik asked if I'd be leaving the country anytime soon, and I honestly answered his inquiry. I asked him about his education and work. He was a college graduate, spoke very good English, was a fourth degree black-belt in taekwondo, and had done military and police training in the U.S. on more than one occasion in both Texas and Georgia.

Every few weeks he'd stop by. I always sat and talked with him over coffee. On two or three occasions, he asked if I would proofread different things that he had written in English, which I did for him.

My supervisor from the Pearl S. Buck Foundation headquarters in Pennsylvania, Mrs. Jan Cavanaugh, along with another lady from the "home office," as I always called it, Mrs. Elizabeth Zeeland, came to visit Korea a couple of years or so after I first met Mr. Paik. They were flying back out on a Saturday morning, and my first wife and I went to the President Hotel, one of Seoul's excellent newer tourist hotels, to meet them. The President Hotel was located downtown, right across from Seoul City Hall. We had brunch at the hotel's restaurant with Jan and Elizabeth. After eating, they checked out and had their bags with them in the lobby, ready to leave for the airport. I was telling them to wait while I went to get the car when Mr. Paik walked up dressed in his usual dark business suit. After introducing him to Jan, Elizabeth, and my wife, I asked what brought him to the President Hotel on a Saturday morning. Mr. Paik told us that there was a foreign leader staying in the hotel and that he was part of the increased security for this dignitary. After talking for a few minutes more, I excused myself and explained to Mr. Paik that I was going to get the car in order to drive Mrs. Cavanaugh and Mrs. Zeeland to Kimpo Airport.

To my surprise, when I drove back up, Mr. Paik was still talking with the Pearl S. Buck Foundation ladies and my wife. They were now all standing in front of the hotel. He helped me put Jan's and Elizabeth's bags into the trunk of the car; we all thanked him and bid him our adieus. After dropping off Jan and Elizabeth at the airport and making sure they got through security, my wife, Mi-yun, told me that Mr. Paik had raved about me. He told them that I was the best foreign director of any nonprofit social welfare organization in Korea. He had talked about the amazing work that I was doing, how well thought of and respected I was by all of the Korean government officials in the Ministry of Health and Social Affairs as well as by the foreign community, and how lucky they were to have me as their director. I was blushing in embarrassment just hearing how much he had praised me. I was also very thankful that I hadn't been rude that first day when I met him. He had told me after I got to know him that the director before me at PSBF would not give him the time of day. I've found throughout my life that it pays to be polite and kind. It reminded me of the line Jan Cavanaugh once said to me and which I've since heard many times repeated, "You catch more flies with honey than you do with vinegar!"

Several of us east coast volunteers organized another trip to Sorak National Park. For me it was to see it one last time covered in snow before the end of my Peace Corps service. John, Chris, Mark, and I took the train up to Gangneung on a Saturday. Pam Utica met us at the station, and the five of us hurried to get the

Don sliding in the snow at Sorak National Park – "Peace Brothers and Sisters."

next bus to Sorak Mountain. We hiked through the snow up to the rock face with the zigzag metal stairway that led up to the crest of a sheer stone ridge. It was a hard climb, as there were places where the steps were covered with sheets of ice. Sometimes we were dragging ourselves—sliding up sheets of ice, grabbing the metal banister, and pulling our bodies up what was akin to a frozen waterfall. It was worth it when we got to the top on this sunny winter's day and saw the wonderful view of the city of Sokcho and the East Sea off in the distance with the sun glimmering on the snow and the water. I had never seen it this clear before. Before leaving on Sunday we walked up another one of the trails and spent much of the morning sliding down a steep snow-covered incline. I had on my nylon Sigma Nu jacket, and I ran and dove while flipping onto my back. The jacket was slippery, and I scooted headfirst down the slope until I turned sideways to roll and stop. The others joined in with me in this activity. What fun we had, but the weekend ended too quickly, and we had to head back to our respective towns.

On February 20, 1975, I wrote to Fred Barbeau for the last time while in the Peace Corps. In the last few paragraphs of the letter, I wrote:

> I don't know what the future holds but other than
> occasional inquires (sic) into alternatives I'm living
> each day as it's (sic) comes. I've always longed
> for this freedom from apprehension about the future.
> I'm closer than I've ever been. Also, I've come upon
> an inner contentment that I know will be with me no
> matter where I go or what I do. I've come to know
> myself better than ever before and – altho I will continue
> to strive for a perfection that this life probably won't
> bring – I'm happy with what I am.

I'm working on a new teaching idea, taekwondo (Korean
karate – I'm a black-belt), and writing a letter to the
president of the American Federation of Teachers about
an idea to improve racial relations in America's school (sic)
without massive busing.

America's racial problems are important and must be
improved. I'm convinced the multitude of races that
make up America will prove to be one of it's (sic) greatest
assets. Understanding is the key.

Strangely, I have no recollection of what the "idea to improve racial relations"
might have been, or if I ever actually wrote a letter to the American Federation of
Teachers' president. If it was tried, obviously, it didn't work anyway.

A rather strange letter came to me in early March:

DEPARTMENT OF THE ARMY HEADQUARTERS,
4TH UNITED STATES ARMY MISSILE COMMAND
APO SAN FRANCISCO 96208
    EAFM-A   10 MARCH 1975
    SUBJECT: Request for Information
    Mr. Donald Richard Hoffner (sic)
    5 Li, Balhan
    Myung Ju Gun
        Dear Mr. Hoffner (sic):

    1. The possibility exists that U.S. military forces could be tasked to
    provide assistance or to evacuate U.S. and third-country citizens residing
    in Kang Won Do in the event of military action, natural disaster, or
    similar situation. In order to be prepared to provide such assistance
    in a timely, responsive manner, it is necessary that this headquarters
    knows the names, addresses, sex, ages, and other pertinent information
    relative to such persons. We are asking your assistance to enable us
    to obtain complete, current, and reliable information.

    2. Inclosure one is a blank form which we ask you to fill out and return.
    The information will be held in the strictest confidence.

3. Inclosure two is believed to be a complete list of U.S. citizens and citizens of member nations of the United States Command living in Kang Won Do. Please review this list. If you happen to know of any other such persons not living in the household of someone on the list, please provide us with their name and address so we may contact them.

4. It is strongly emphasized that the fact that we are requesting this information is purely precautionary in nature and does not reflect a change in the military or political situation.

FOR THE COMMANDER:

And it was signed by a "Major, FA Adjutant." The list surprised me because there were fifty-seven names on it from six different countries: Australia, Canada, France, Japan, New Zealand, and the U.S. Forty-one were Americans. There were four each from Australia, Canada, and Japan. There were three from New Zealand and one from France. Glenn Vriesland, who had lived in Gangneung but got married and left in the summer of 1974, was still on the list, but Pam Utica was not on it. I filled out the form, corrected the spelling of my family name, added these two mistakes that I had noticed, and mailed it back. I couldn't help wondering why I had never received any correspondence from this missile command before.

It was a Saturday in early April when I went back up to Gangneung to visit John Devereaux. He'd invited me up for the spring festival at Gangneung Technical School of Nursing where he taught. John met me at the train station. We went to dinner and then headed over to the campus for the evening's activities. John introduced me to several of his young female students, and each one was cuter than the next.

"How can you not fall in love with all of them?" I inquired.

"It's hard, but my volunteering days probably wouldn't last long if I did."

"True enough!" I agreed. There was a bonfire and entertainment—singers and dancers. Some students were selling raffle tickets, and so I bought some to help whatever cause they were fundraising for. Later in the evening, we were still standing with several of John's cute students when the students who had been selling the raffle tickets started pulling tickets out of a bowl to pick the winners of different prizes. I pulled out my tickets, and sure enough the first ticket they pulled was one of mine. As the number was read and I realized it was one of my tickets, I panicked. First, I thought I'd give the ticket to one of John's young students standing with us, but then I was sure they would all push me up in front of the whole student body that was spread out in a big circle around the fire where the ticket plucking was going on. I did not want to be the center of attention, and all I could think of was that I might not understand what they were saying to me in Korean and would feel like a fool. I stuffed the ticket back in my pocket. The number was called a couple of more times, and then they announced they would pick another. When they did and called the new number, a student screamed and ran in to get her prize. Whew! The rest of the night passed without further mishap, and I returned home on Sunday after staying at John's place overnight.

I received a letter from Lyn Woodward, whom I had dated during our freshman year at Albion. She was one of many high school and college friends I was still corresponding with. Lyn was working for the National Geographic Society and was a caption writer for their book series. I envied her. How wonderful, I thought at the time (and still do), would it be to work for National Geographic! Lyn had run into my fellow K-23, Vicki Vermillac (Vicki from Vassar). Vicki was also living and working in Washington, D.C. at the time. The day they met, Vicki mentioned that she had been a Peace Corps Volunteer in Korea, and Lyn naturally asked if she happened to know me. "Know him?" she said. "We were in training together, and he sure looks great in a skimpy pair of tight, yellow nylon underpants." Lyn asked in the letter why it was that Vicki knew what I looked like in my nylon briefs. Although Lyn had probably gotten the whole lowdown from Vicki, I wrote back and explained how Vicki, Deric Gratiot, and another trainee had come into my room drunk, and Deric had ripped off my coverlet, exposing my nearly naked, well-ripped self.

Pam Utica invited both of the Johns now on the east coast, Chris, Mark, and me to Gangneung to have dinner and stay overnight once more with Ruth Standish, the missionary who lived in Kangnung. As I had the previous autumn, I spent a lot of time staring at each of Ruth's Korean landscape ink drawings and watercolors. I was fascinated by them and again thought how much I too would love to have such a collection some day. After another wonderful Korean dinner, the four of us sat talking into the evening until my illusions about Ruth were smashed. We got onto the subject of the Philippines. Ruth said some very derogatory things about the Filipino people, which shocked me, and I said something in their defense. Ruth said, "The Filipinos are stupid. They could have been Americans and instead picked independence, and look at the disaster the Philippines is now." Wow, I could not believe how ethnocentric and mean-spirited that comment was. Sure, the Philippines were a mess then with Marcos as president, but to call them stupid because they chose independence over possibly becoming an American state was unbelievable to me. When you look at the American occupation after the Spanish-American War and how brutally we put down their rebellion against American rule, how could anyone blame the Filippinos for still wanting their independence?

Ruth's attitude epitomized to me what I found to be a common trait, unfortunately, of a few of the missionaries I got to know during my years in Korea, especially later when I worked with the Pearl S. Buck Foundation and got to know so many of them. Don't get me wrong. Many of the finest, most empathetic, tolerant, and warmest people I've ever met in my life have been among the foreign missionaries in Korea. On the other hand, a few of the most narrow-minded, intolerant, egotistical, ethnocentric, xenophobic, and downright pig-headed people I've met have also been missionaries.

Another example, which also has to do with the Philippines, happened in 1982 when I worked for PSBF. I, along with my first wife and son, spent a week at the missionary beach at Daecheon. The southern half of this beautiful beach is owned by the foreign missionary community and is off-limits to non-members. There are dozens of small and a couple of not-so-small American-style cottages. We rented one cottage from the American missionary family who owned it. One day fellow Rotary Club member Horace Underwood of the prominent Underwood family invited me to attend the Thursday evening vesper service that was held outdoors at the far southern tip of the peninsula, which was actually a small Korean army base on this rock outcropping. The foreign missionaries were allowed to go past the base to a clearing high above the Yellow Sea that had an absolutely breathtaking view. I went by myself and sat down. After a hymn or two and some Bible readings, the Presbyterian minister announced that we were all in for a real treat. The college-aged son of one of the well-known American missionaries in Korea, Sam Woodhaven, was going to speak about his recent trip to the Philippines.

Sam stood up, walked to the lectern, and began speaking. It turned out he was part of a Christian basketball team that was chosen to tour the Philippines. He announced that they went to try to convert the Filipinos. All I could think of was that the Filipinos were already Christians—Catholics, but still Christians. Evidently, that was not good enough for those devout Protestants. The team went from town to town and played basketball games against local teams at whatever gym or court was available. Before the games, Sam explained, they passed out different books of the Bible—the Protestant Bible, I guess.

Another part of the story was about his father's expensive camera. He borrowed his dad's camera and took it with him even though his father, a minister, didn't think it was a good idea because it might be stolen. Sam promised his father he would never let it out of his sight. Of course, as we shall see, he did let it out of his sight.

One basketball arena/gym that they played in was fairly far outside of town. They found a *jeepney* (small jeep-like bus) driver to take them out to the gymnasium. They asked him to return to pick them up later after the game. As usual they passed out small pamphlets with one book of the New Testament in it to the adoring crowd. During the second half of the game the power went out. They had to cancel the game, fumbled their way into the locker room, got their clothes on, and went outside. The jeepney driver had said he would return after the game, but since it ended early, he wasn't there. They decided to walk back toward town. About five minutes down the road, Sam realized that he had left the bag with his father's precious camera in it back in the dressing room. The coach and his teammates urged him to turn around, and they would all walk with him back to the gym. "No," he said, "the Filipinos are all crooks. Someone certainly stole the camera by now and ran off with it." *"All crooks? How can this kid be so opinionated and rude?"* I thought. He showed no empathy whatsoever, not a word of compassion. He had no understanding that while this camera could easily be replaced by his wealthy father, to a Filipino it might have represented several months' salary. They all went back, and when they got to the gym, there was a Filipino man standing at the front entrance holding the bag. The man had found it and was keeping it for them until their return. He didn't steal it as Sam had predicted. "Thank God! I got the camera back. Otherwise, I would have had to listen to my father tell me, 'I told you so.'" Sam intoned. No words of apology for calling a whole ethnic group crooks even after having been proven wrong.

Then they walked again toward the town, as the jeepney driver still had not returned. After walking for a half hour or so, they saw the jeepney overturned in the field just off the road. They ran towards the vehicle. It had bullet holes all over it. The driver had been thrown out of the jeepney, and his bullet-ridden body was lying dead in the field. Sam didn't mention who might have shot the driver, but during the 1980s there were terrorist groups operating in the Philippines. Many were Islamist Moro tribesmen from the southernmost Philippine island of Mindanao, but there was also a Communist New People's Army in a long-running war with the Philippine government. Sam continued saying, "When we reached the body, we all got down on our knees and prayed." Oh, here I thought he would say that they prayed for this poor man, his soul, his family and friends. But, alas, I was grossly mistaken and just plain grossed out to the point of nausea. "We prayed to God and thanked Him that we were not in this jeepney when this happened," Sam said. I looked around me. Someone else must be shocked by this. Someone else must be grossed out. Someone else must want to scream at this spoiled-brat, pompous-assed, little Lord Fauntleroy the way I did. But, "Au contraire, mon ami!" (Quite the contrary, my friend!) They were all listening intently with looks of admiration. I was heartbroken and disgusted. I was sickened to my core. No wonder Pearl S. Buck once gave a talk to a missionary conference titled, "Is There a Case for Foreign Missions?" and basically said, "NO!" Pearl S. Buck felt far too many back in her day were nationalistic and racist or just plain petty and narrow-minded. It was still true in regards to some missionaries in the 1980s.

After returning to Seoul from the beach that summer, at our next KAVA (Korean Association of Voluntary Agencies) executive council meeting, where I was the chairman (even though I was about the only member who was not a priest, minister, nun, brother, pastor, or some other religious person), I mentioned about Sam Woodhaven to a couple of other members and told the above story. They knew Sam and said that he and his family lived in a walled-off missionary compound near Kimpo Airport in a very large home and were very isolated from Korea and the Korean people. "Is that how a missionary should live?" I asked. The missionaries on the KAVA executive council with me of course didn't think so.

One of them was from Australia and in the Salvation Army; her name was Margaret Hoare. Her rank was major, and so she was Major Hoare (pronounced just like whore) of the Salvation Army. When I first met her, I couldn't help but ask her if anyone ever kidded her about her family name, especially since she had the rank of major. She laughed and assured me that many had. "OK, then I won't," I said. "Thank you," she replied. I knew several Salvation Army members while in Korea, and I can unequivocally say that they were among the best of the best in their empathy for and commitment to the Korean people. Sam the Sham Woodhaven and his family? Not so much.

By late March, it was getting warmer, and I was already opening my window at night (not because I was worried about carbon monoxide, since my room had hot water pipe heating, but because I was too hot). I decided I wanted to move back into the cheaper *yeogwan* where I had lived before. There was a new lady owner at the Changshin Yeogwan, and so I wanted my co-teacher or another Korean teacher to go with me and help me negotiate a monthly fee. I decided that I would tell the new owner of the *yeogwan* that I did not want any heat whatsoever. I was sure this would be no problem, as it would cut down on the owner's expense with no *yeontan* (coal briquettes for heating) cost. There would also be less work because she would not need to switch out the used charcoal briquette and put in a new one every few hours. In addition, I knew this would mean I should get a lower charge per month.

I thought I'd ask Mr. Jong, Chul-chin, with whom I had lived my first few months in Mukho, to help me out. Friday night, after practicing taekwondo with John, I decided to visit Mr. Jong's house and ask for his assistance. I had not visited the home since I moved out. When I got to his house, I rang the door buzzer. The young girl, Soon-mi, whose relationship with Mr. Jong's mother I had never figured out and who was older and much taller now, opened the gate and greeted me. I asked to speak to Mr. Jong, but she said he no longer lived there. This surprised me, but I asked where he had moved to, and she gave me detailed directions to his new home. I thanked her and followed her directions—right at Mukho's only main street heading toward downtown and then left at a certain *gage*, up the alley so far, and there it was. I rang the gate bell and asked the young lady who answered the gate if Mr. Jong was home. She led me to his room. He slid open the door when he heard me coming, and I saw that he, his wife, and their little-pisser kid (remember that story?), now also older and taller, were living in a very small room that I guessed must have been rented. *"Mr. Jong must have had a disagreement with his mother over something,"* I thought to myself. *"Was it the motorcycle, or had he continued his overnight dalliances and been punished by his Mom?"* I never asked, and he never brought it up. I did ask if after school on Saturday he'd be willing to be my arbitrator with the new owner of the Chang-shin Yeogwan. He agreed, and we set a time to meet. He suggested that we meet for lunch at the Chinese restaurant near the main intersection of town along with a couple of other teachers before he and I would go to the *yeogwan*.

Mr. Jong, two other teachers from the girls' middle school, and I met at the Chinese restaurant. Besides meeting John Hudson there on test days, I had eaten there alone sometimes on Saturdays after classes had ended and after I had built up a hankering for gobs of food. I would often order the *tangsuyuk* (sweet and sour pork) portion that was supposed to be for sharing with other people in your party. Along with a huge bowl of rice, I'd eat the whole thing myself. The young waiter put the four of us into a small private room off to the side of the restaurant. Mr. Jong ordered the *tangsuyuk* and a chicken platter for our lunch. He asked if we three thought that was enough food. We all agreed that it was plenty. Then the young waiter blurted out, "No, it isn't enough; the American can eat the whole platter of *tangsuyuk* all by himself." I was so embarrassed, and I'm sure turned red as a tomato or at least as red as a Red Delicious apple. Mr. Jang quickly added another main dish over my denials that I could really eat as much as the kid had said, but unequivocally I really could and often did. We duly finished off all the food that was brought.

After lunch we parted company with the other two teachers, and Mr. Jong and I headed up to the corner in front of Mukho Theater where my *hasuk* room was, turned right, and headed to the end of the alley. The Changshin Yeogwan was the last building on the right next to the wall around the harbor. We walked in and met the owner. She took us back to the open seating area for guests at the back of the building. There we sat while Mr. Jong explained that I wanted to rent a room by the month until the end of the school semester and the other particulars, especially that I wanted no heat whatsoever. A young boy around four years old, who was obviously the owner's son, sat in her lap during much of the discussion. I sat looking around as they settled on a price, and I noticed that there were three different young ladies who wandered back and forth near where we were talking. I wondered if these young ladies were all the owner's daughters, as they didn't seem to be working but instead just wandering around. We came to an agreement on price. Then I told the owner that I would move in the following Saturday and left. As we were walking back toward my *hasuk* Mr. Jong told me that the young boy was half-Japanese. The owner had had an affair with a Japanese ship's captain. The ship docked upon occasion in Mukho, and the boy was the result of their liaison. Mr. Jong acted like this tainted the kid. I mentioned that I couldn't tell the difference between him and a full-Korean boy. Mr. Jong assured me that everyone knew in town and that her affair with the Japanese captain was also the reason she had enough money to buy the *yeogwan*. I thanked Mr. Jong and assured him that I truly appreciated his help. I didn't say it, but I was not thankful for the added information about the young boy.

The next Friday around 6:00 p.m., I was sitting in my room on the top floor of the Daehung Hasuk when a knock came at the door. I said, "Wait a minute," in Korean. A reply came back in Korean. When I opened the door, I was startled to see it was a PCV whom I had met before but didn't know well.

"You must be Mr. Ha," he said.

"Yes, I am," I responded.

"I'm Mr. Ha also," he informed me.

"Ha, ha," I said.

"Yes, we are like the brothers Ha," he suggested.

"Brothers Ha it is." After a few more Ha jokes, he told me his name was Ed Harper. "Harper is the name of a street in a suburb north of Detroit where my parents have a gift, jewelry, and greeting card store."

"Really?" he queried.

"Yes, what a coincidence," I said. "Oh, by the way, my name is Don Haffner," I added.

I asked Ed how he happened to be knocking at my door. "Oh, I was walking up the alley here toward the movie theater, when an *ajumoni* (middle-aged woman) came running out of the Daeyang Restaurant and said, 'You must be looking for Mr. Ha?'" Ed said he told her he was, as he knew I lived in Mukho, and that she must be talking about me. I laughed and told him that was the restaurant where I ate all my meals, and it must have been the owner, a very sweet lady, who informed him of my whereabouts. "What brought you to Mukho?" I inquired. Ed was a K-25, and they had trained during the winter of 1972 to 1973 as middle school instructors like us K-23s. I had first met him when I accompanied Miss Jang, Yong-sook, one of the Peace Corps secretaries, that time she and I went from Seoul to Chuncheon to deliver some papers to their training program. That was the trip where I had the upset stomach on the way back to Seoul, and it ended up being acute diarrhea. Ed also had extended for a year but switched from teaching English at the middle school level to teaching it at a university in Seoul. As his university was on break this week, he had gone up to Sorak National Park for a few days. While heading back toward Seoul, on a whim he got off at Mukho.

We talked until it was time for taekwondo. He went with me, and I introduced him to our instructor and to John Hudson, whom he had never actually met before. After taekwondo, Ed was hungry, so we hit a restaurant with John. Ed and I then headed back to my room. Ed asked if he could visit my school in the morning and watch a couple of classes, and then he was going to get on the late morning train heading back to Seoul.

The next morning we had breakfast and went to the boys' middle school where I introduced him to all my fellow teachers. He then sat and watched me teach during the first two class periods of my half-day of teaching on Saturdays. I had really enjoyed talking with Ed and was so glad he had stopped in at Mukho because he seemed like a great guy from the first greeting of "You must be Mr. Ha?" I walked him out to the gate of the schoolyard, and we parted company.

After the regular classes ended, I walked back downtown. I had no special class on Saturdays. When I got near the only intersection in town near my *hasuk*, I looked up and there was Ed walking toward me.

"I thought you were leaving on the morning train?" I asked.

"I was, but this is a neat town, and I enjoyed hanging out with you. I thought I'd stay with you another day and leave tomorrow, if that's OK. My classes start again Monday, but I'm all ready and don't need to do any lesson planning or anything anyway," he replied.

"Great, you can help me move."

Photograph of the Ssangyong Cement towers taken from the end of the breaker wall—Korean naval vessel was visiting that day.

Ed helped me pack up my stuff and cart it down the alley the fifty yards or so from the *hasuk* to the *yeogwan*. I got the key from the owner, and Ed and I dumped what we had carried over and went back for the remainder of my stuff. The only furniture I had was one small chest of drawers and a typical student's desk that was about fifteen inches high. There was no chair, obviously—you just sat cross-legged on the floor and did your writing or reading. Ed and I easily carried over the two pieces of furniture and my clothing. It didn't take long to finish.

I took Ed on a tour of Mukho, showing him the girls' middle and high schools up toward the north end of town and then over to the fish market and past the harbor where the fishing fleet was tied up in a jumble. Then we walked out to the end of the breaker wall for the fine view of the whole town of Mukho with the four huge Ssangyong Cement towers right in front of us in the main port area.

After dinner, we got some beers and snacks and returned to my room. First, one of the young ladies I had seen the previous Saturday walking around, then another, and then the final one wandered into my room. Miss Kim lived around the corner from my room. She was short and petite with a bubbly, vivacious personality. Miss Lee lived across the hall and back a few yards toward the seating area. She was tall for a Korean gal and a little stockier. She was also quieter and more shy than Miss Kim. The third one, Miss Pak, lived two doors down from me toward the back of the building on my side of the hallway. The room next to me, it turned out, was a storage room. Miss Pak was of medium height and build, a little quieter than Miss Kim, but not as reticent as Miss Lee was. They brought in glasses, and we gladly shared our beer and snacks with them.

After a while they took their leave. As Ed and I took turns hitting the head, which was on the other side of the building, we noticed that they were putting on makeup. It reminded me of Donovan's song "Lalena:"

Run your hand through your hair; paint your face with despair
That's your lot in life Lalena, can't blame ya, Lalena
("Lalena" written and performed by Donovan)

Again, it was my naiveté that had sprung up the previous Saturday. I had assumed
these young ladies were the owner's daughters, but it turned out they were part of
her meal ticket. They went off to work while Ed and I went out and got some
more beer. Ed toasted my choice of a bordello as a fine place to dwell, and we
both toasted my lovely corridor mates. Sunday he got up and caught the morning train back to Seoul.

I had decided that I would like to work on a Peace Corps training program
in the summer and extend my stay in Korea past the end of the semester. I wrote
to the Peace Corps Director, Jon Kalkaska, in mid-March with my request. He
wrote back on March 29, 1975:

> Dear Don,
>
> I appreciated your letter for several reasons. It is always good to hear
> from volunteers about their work, and I had been wondering how
> your experiments with the "Silent Way" and the new co-teaching
> approach were going. I agree with your analogy of "walking a tightrope"
> as it aptly depicts the extremely careful steps we must take to get across
> the chasm of cross-cultural misunderstanding; moreover, it is an
> expression I often use also! I am sharing your letter with Dan, for he
> should know of the progress you are making.
>
> I have already talked to Russ regarding your request to work on training.
> Such decisions are made by the training office, but I personally feel you
> would do a good job and will express my opinion for what it is worth. I
> could support you both for your interest in teaching and your involvement
> with the country and its people. Glad to know the appearance issue is
> behind us. Can't say I've ever been "afraid" of what volunteers think,
> for Peace Corps to me must permit a diversity of opinions as volunteers
> are diverse. But here again I get into the "tightrope walking" scene.
>
> We can easily take care of your passport next time you are in town. It
> just requires a letter and documentation from us. We do it so often, we
> even have a form letter.

Good to hear. Good luck with your efforts there.

Jon

I also got a letter from Dan Holland dated April 1, 1975. He wrote:

Dear Don,

Happy April Fool's Day! By the time you get this, the day will have passed. I hope that you made it through all with no catastrophes. I hope your approach with your co-teacher will offer some positive results. I think that you have tried something that can show the teacher something without feel (sic) that you are forcing something down her throat. I think this is especially important with something as "bizarre" to the Korean teachers as Silent Way is.

I would agree with you that much of what we have done in TESOL in Korea is "cosmetic work." I think that it has been that, though, because so much of what we have shown them is easily done by native speakers and enthusiastic Americans, but not so easily done by Korean teachers. That is one reason that we are working on the revision of *Methodology for Teachers*. We are trying to make the methodology as amenable as possible to Korean teachers. If we can do that, we have a better chance of giving them the tools that many of them so badly need.

I appreciate your interest in the training program. As Jon told you, the decision will be made by training staff in a few months, so it is difficult to say anything more than the fact that we need a lot of people who have the kinds of experience and successes in Korea like you have.

So much for now. Take care and enjoy your spring.

Anyong, (Bye)

Dan

I still kept in touch with my previous co-teacher, Mr. Hyun, Jong-jin, and he sometimes visited Mukho because he was dating the daughter of Dr. Kim who had his practice in Mukho. Dr. Kim's son, Kim, Chul-kuk, had been in my special class the previous year and had spoken the best English of any of the first-year middle school boys that year. Mr. Hyun and I had been invited to Dr. Kim's house for dinner one night during the previous school year. Mr. Hyun met Dr. Kim's daughter that night. She was a university student in Seoul, but she came home to Mukho during vacations and holiday weekends. By the time I left Mukho in the early summer of 1975, I was convinced that Mr. Hyun and Dr. Kim's daughter would get married at some time in the future.

While at Dr. Kims' house for dinner that one night, I looked through a brand-new, beautiful set of the *Encyclopaedia Britannica* that Dr. Kim had on his book shelves. I picked up the volume covering the letter "K" and opened it to the section on Korea. To my horror, parts of the article had been blackened out by a black magic marker. When I turned the page at an angle near the light I could still read it and noticed that where Park, Chung-hui had been called a "dictator" was one part that was blackened out as well as any other derogatory inferences. *"What a sacrilege!"* I thought. Of course, *Newsweek* magazine's Asian edition sold in Korea also often had sections blackened out (or in some cases even cut out completely) if an article about Korea said anything that President Park didn't like. The official government sensors were very efficient in their work.

On Sunday, April 6, 1975, Mr. Hyun and I made a plan to hike up to the Mureung Valley and to the beautiful Yongchu Waterfall. I met Mr. Hyun in Bupyeong, and we took the bus which headed past the large Ssangyong Cement plant and up the Mureung Valley toward Samhwa-sa (Samhwa Buddhist temple) and Yongchu Waterfall. During the ride Mr. Hyun told me that Myung-hui's younger sister was in his class. She had recently come up to him after class one day and told him that she knew her sister was having an affair with his American friend and fellow teacher, Mr. Ha. After a couple of years of our secret affair going on, I should not have been surprised that people in Mukho and Pupyeong knew, and yet I was shocked that her younger sister not only knew, but was so bold as to tell Mr. Hyun. This troubled and worried me. I did not want Myung-hui to be harmed by our relationship. Mr. Hyun and I got off the bus, began hiking, and rested as usual at Samhwa-sa before beginning the more difficult hike up to the waterfalls.

Although the weather was warm, there was still ice and snow covering the trail in some places. Yet we made good time and reached the lower of the two waterfalls near the top of the ridge about an hour after leaving the temple. We climbed up to the higher falls, which had the good-sized, very deep pool carved into the rock by the taller upper falls. There were about a dozen other picnickers talking, eating, and lying in the sun. After finishing our lunch, we noticed three

Girl who accidentally fell into the mountain pool.

young ladies, probably in their early twenties, who came into the area and begin taking pictures. I watched as they asked a young man to photograph all three of them with the waterfall in the background. The young man kept motioning for them to move back closer and closer to the water's edge. Suddenly, one of them slipped on some moss at the edge of the pool and fell into the water. She ended up near the middle of the pool about fifteen yards from the nearest side. I didn't know if she had fainted or what had happened because she neither moved nor spoke.

The other picnickers just stood there staring at the young lady, whose face was sticking out above the water. Not one of them moved, and I asked Mr. Hyun, "Can she swim?" He just kept looking toward her and didn't answer me. It was a stupid question on several levels. For one, she wasn't moving at all, and I knew that hardly any Koreans at that time knew how to swim. In addition, Mr. Hyun didn't know her, nor did I. Seeing no alternative, I kicked off my shoes, took off my jacket, and jumped into the ice cold pool. During previous summers, I had swum in this water, so I knew that even in July and August it was ice cold. The shock of jumping into this freezing water took my breath away. I gasped for air after coming up near her. Grabbing her left arm with my left hand and swimming sideways using my right arm and both legs, I propelled us forward. I was glad that she was unresponsive because I remember hearing that it can be difficult helping a drowning person who is hysterical. She was motionless, and I pulled her easily to the far side of the pool where I knew there was a small, underwater ledge that I could lift her onto and that would make it easier for her friends to pull her out. Her two friends and several other people were waiting at the edge when we got there. They got her out of the freezing cold water. Her friends covered her with their coats and a blanket they had been using to sit on and rushed her away.

Don pushing the young lady onto the underwater ledge.

I got out and began shaking incessantly. Several *adjumonies* called me and Mr. Hyun over to a fire they had just started. They helped me off with my clothes, except my underpants, and dried me off. Then they put blankets and coats over me to try to get me warmed up again. After wringing out my clothes, the women held my pants, shirt and socks over the fire while constantly adding more sticks of wood to keep the flames high.

The ladies talked continuously, asking me questions that I tried to answer while still shaking and through my loudly chattering teeth. Slowly I began to get feeling back in my fingers and toes. The women decided that even though my pants were nearly dry, Mr. Hyun should give me his, and he should wear my slightly damp ones. These women were very persuasive, and so we went behind a rock, I guess because Mr. Hyun was shy. (I was in my nylon brief underpants anyway, so I didn't need to go behind a rock.) We came out from behind the large boulder we had chosen to change behind, and the women were happy. Mr. Hyun and I decided to head back down the valley to the bus stop. As we walked neither of us said much. The trail was very rocky, so we needed to concentrate on our footing as we trekked along. I kept wondering what would have happened to the young lady who fell into the pool had I not been there.

When we got back to where the bus stop was, we felt hungry and started to head into one of the small restaurants there. Three young ladies approached us, and one of them began bowing in front of me and speaking. It was the young lady I had rescued. I could hardly understand a word she said because her language was so formal and honorific. I was conversant in the everyday level of speech, but not so much this high level that she was using. (Even though this is the level we had learned in training, I rarely used it once I got to Mukho.)

"What is she saying?" I asked Mr. Hyun in English.

"She is saying, 'Thank you!'" he replied. (That much I had already figured out.)

"You are welcome," I said back to her in Korean. They went off to catch the next bus, and we went into the restaurant.

That night before dozing off, I reviewed the events of the day at the mountain pool. Growing up I had often wondered what I might do in an emergency situation. I was pleased to have discovered that I had passed the audition. I had done the brave thing, even though I hesitated for a couple of seconds. I dove into that ice cold water and saved the drowning lady from an awful fate. Exhausted but contented, I quickly fell asleep.

The next morning, I went to school as usual, and all the teachers had already heard about what had happened by the Yongchu Waterfall. News travels at the speed of light in a small Korean town when it has to do with their Peace Corps Volunteer. All the teachers came over and shook my hand while all talking at the same time and carrying on about my exploit.

Later that day when I went to the post office, all the employees there had also heard what had happened the previous day near Bupyeong. I found myself shaking hands with all the male employees, while listening to them and all the female workers carrying on and asking questions. My fifteen minutes of fame lasted for a few days. It seemed everyone in Mukho had heard of my heroics, and in every shop I entered I was accosted by people wanting to shake my hand and praise me.

About a week later, after the novelty had worn off, I was heading back to school from the post office when an *adjumoni* grabbed my arm and guided me into her house. She took me into the family room and sat me down on the warmest place on the floor – the place for honored guests. While sitting there very uncomfortably with my rear end baking, I was wondering who this lady was and why in the world she had pulled me into her home. She brought out some cookies and coffee. Then she handed me a few pictures taken at the mountain pool the past Sunday. One photo was of the young lady in the water with only her face showing and another was of me pushing her onto the underwater ledge at the side of the pool. This was one of the women who had helped to warm me after I saved the young lady. This woman and the other women with her last Sunday, it turned out, were all from Mukho. She had photographed the event and made copies for me because, of course, they all knew I was Ha, Seonsaeng-nim (honorable teacher Mr. Ha) at Mukho Middle School. Those are the two pictures shown above. Whenever I look at them I wonder whatever happened to the young lady I rescued. I never asked her name, and after she thanked me in front of the restaurant, I never saw her again. I wonder if maybe she has told her grandchildren about the time she fell into that mountain pool near Bupyeong and how some American with a mustache jumped in and pulled her out of her dangerous predicament.

In the 1990s when I got on a roll with my songwriting, one of the tunes I created was about my Peace Corps days with references to the PRIST (PRe-Invitational Staging) in Denver, the K-23 Training Program, and saving this young lady's life.

Knew I Had to Leave

If you're homely and you're lonely
And nobody talks to you
Join the Peace Corps
Join the Peace Corps

Flew into Denver for something called the PRIST
They told us of Korea and all the things we'd miss
Knew I had to go there, knew I couldn't stay
So I joined the Peace Corps and I was on my way

Flight out from Frisco with the K-23s
Spent the time a drinkin', a lovely lady on my knees
Roommates in Tokyo at the airport hotel
Spoonful of lovin' got to know each other well

(Chorus)
Knew I had to leave, knew I couldn't stay
Knew I had to live outside the USA

Landed in Korea, there was red-haired Russ
He met us at the airport, waited by the bus
Took us down for training to a place called Daegu
We learned Korean language and English teaching methods too

Put me in a small town right beside the sea
For three years I taught English starting with ABC

Know my students loved me and I in turn loved them
Many are the times I dream of reliving those days again

Chorus

Picnic in the springtime by a mountain pool
Young lady drowning, I couldn't play the fool
So I dove right into that ice cold, frigid lake
To save that drowning lady from an awful fate

Chorus

Born in a rich land, shopping malls on every street
Everyone's got so much stuff, it's all the same to me
Must be a reason we're put upon this earth
Other than to count our coins as a measure of what we're worth

Chorus

If you're ugly and you're fugly and nobody talks to you
Join the Peace Corps today, today
Join the Peace Corps today!

Pam Utica invited me to come up and visit her in Gangneung, which I did the next Saturday. As usual she met me at the train station, and we went to a new music room coffee shop like they had in Seoul. It was a classical music coffee shop. You went in and ordered coffee, and then you could request whatever piece of music you'd like to hear. If it wasn't too busy, in a while your request would be played. As I always did in Seoul, I asked for the first movement of the Haffner Symphony by Mozart, great tune that it is! We stayed for much of the afternoon until we heard the Haffner. After that we went to a restaurant for dinner and then headed to Pam's place, which I had never visited before. On the way, as per Peace Corps volunteers' usual, we stopped at a *gage* and picked up some wine and snacks. As we went into her room, which was part of a larger house but could be entered from the courtyard without going into the owner's part of the house, we ran into the woman of the house. Pam introduced me to her, and then we went into Pam's room.

We began drinking, talking, and joking, but then Pam got serious. She began telling me that she and other female friends from her group had recently spent a weekend talking about how Peace Corps guys hardly gave Peace Corps gals the time of day. The guys were always running after Korean women and going out drinking with other male teachers to wine shops where there were always women employees there to serve the men's every beck and call. Women teachers, on the other hand, couldn't go out drinking because this was frowned upon. She told me that most of the female Peace Corps volunteers were very lonely and felt unloved. Pam also said that they were often very sexually frustrated because none of the guys wanted them. I assured her that I found her attractive, which I did. I wanted to tell her to stop talking, but she kept going, telling me that she and her friends had discussed this topic for hours. I leaned over and kissed her. Then I mumbled and fumbled, but we didn't tumble. We stopped.

"I'm sorry, I talked too much. It's entirely my fault," she said while sobbing.

"No, no, it's not," I said. "I'm sorry! I moved too fast. I should have let you finish talking."

"No, it's me," she said. By then we were both exhausted, and I suggested we turn the lights off and go to sleep.

The next morning I told Pam I needed to get back and do some lesson planning for Monday, and I left. Later in the week, I got a letter from Pam. She was all upset. It seemed the lady who owned her house assumed that we were now engaged because I had stayed overnight. The owner had Pam's life planned out. We'd get married, have two point four kids, live in an American home with a white picket fence, and be happy ever after. Pam was beside herself. I could never visit her again at her place, she told me. I wrote back and suggested she come down to Mukho some weekend. "No, the owner lady will know," she wrote back. "Who cares?" I replied, "We can pretend we're engaged, and later you can tell her we broke up." Pam wouldn't go along with that either, but we did continue to correspond by mail.

On another Saturday before regular lessons started, the students were all lining up by class in their usual military-like formations. Every once in awhile when the principal had an announcement or something he needed to tell the whole student body, the school would have these outdoor assemblies. These assemblies always reminded me of Principal Yoo because he said more than once that there was nothing more beautiful than the whole student body lined up on the playground by class, especially the first day of the school year when all the first-year students had new uniforms. By this time in the second semester even the first-year students' winter uniforms were not jet black anymore. They were graying. Many of the third-year students' uniforms were downright threadbare, and the pantlegs and coat sleeves were often fraying and way too short. (For some reason I never

Assembly of all Mukho's students at the girls' middle and high school playground.

took a picture of any of these assemblies at the boys' middle school, but I did take a picture at the Girls' Middle and High School of all the students in Mukho during the Education Week assembly one year—all the boys and the girls.)

During one of the morning line-ups, I was outside waiting for the students to finish organizing their lines, and being bored I took three coins out of my pocket. During high school and college sometimes at parties I would do a coin tossing trick to amaze and astound the audience that would gather. (I'm not sure when or where I learned to do this.) The trick was to line the three coins on the back of my right hand: one near the end of the middle finger, one near the base of the finger and the last one on the middle of the back of the hand. Then holding my right hand out, I would throw the coins into the air so that the one farthest away went highest, the middle one went second highest, and the one closest to me went the least high. I would grab each coin one at a time starting with the one closest to me. After grabbing the first one, I'd close my fist, sweep it up, and on the way down open my hand again, grab the middle coin, and then finally the one farthest away with the same kind of motion. I could grab each one separately one at a time without dropping the first or second one and before the third one hit the ground. Try it! Not so easy, is it? So I did this a few times before the students got lined up straight and the principal came out for his speech. During the breaks between classes that day and for a couple of days afterwards, I looked out of the teachers' office onto the playground and noticed many of the kids lining small stones and/or coins on the back of their right hands and tossing them up into the air trying to replicate my trick. Coins and rocks were flying all over the place, and I was worried that one or more of the students might get an eye poked out. Luckily no one got hurt, and after maybe a couple of days they all gave up.

This Saturday morning the principal came out and started talking. I was daydreaming when one of the other teachers said, "Mr. Ha, let's go." The students were filing out of the playground and down the road in front of the school toward Mukho's main street. I walked out with a couple of the other male teachers. We walked alongside the students who were marching in line out to the main street and toward downtown. Before we got to Mukho's only intersection near where I lived one of the teachers grabbed me and said, "Follow me." Two other teachers followed us too. It was 8:30 in the morning, but we headed right into a *makgeolli-jip* (wine house) serving the rice wine that looked like skim milk. The owner brought out the ubiquitous metal tea kettle-like serving apparatus and four small metal bowls, poured out a portion in each one, and the teacher who organized this little soiree-like event said, "Drink up!" And we did. A few bowls later one of the teachers ran back to the main street to see how much of our student body had passed by. He returned and said, "One more cup, then we must go." And that's what we did.

Joining back near the end of the parade, we followed the last of the students into Mukho's port area. Other than the schoolyards this was the only wide-open flat place in town. The girls' middle and high school students were also flowing in as well as the boys' high school students. The boys' high school was southwest of Mukho boys' middle school and the farthest of the schools away from downtown. As we went in people were passing out headbands that said, "*myeol-gong*" (destroy Communism) on them. I put mine on, as did all the students and teachers. Soon anti-Communist speeches started. I was listening, even though I only understood part of what they were saying. With the speakers almost screaming at the top of their lungs, their tone of voice, the enunciation and the vitriolic nature of the speaking, it was apparent that they didn't like Communism. John Hudson walked up to me.

"Fancy meeting you here," I said.

"Yeah, the whole town's here—or at least all the students and government workers, it seems. What the hell are you doing with that stupid bandana on your head?"

"Getting into the spirit," I replied.

"Let's go look at the two ships being loaded over at the dock," John said with an exasperated look on his face.

"Sure, let's go," I said.

We walked over and John took a picture of a couple of workers who were standing at the edge of the dock and looking down toward the water in between the ship and dock. Later, after getting the film developed, he showed his boss, who was also the owner of the house he lived in. When the Health Center Director, Mr. Kim (who had though me more well endowed than John), looked at the picture, he got angry. John told me that Mr. Kim thought the picture showed two guys taking a piss outdoors, and he assumed that John had taken the picture to show Americans how primitive the Koreans still were. John assured him that the guys were just looking to see how far the ship had descended into the water while being loaded.

The following Monday while sitting in the teachers' office at school, I read the *Sunday Korea Herald,* which had an article about the spontaneous anti-Communist rally that had taken place the day before in Mukho. I chuckled at that one. Spontaneous, my tuckus!

After finishing the newspaper, I was looking out the window and watching the gym teacher who had the students in his class lined up. (It was spring, and the male students had just started wearing their light blue short-sleeve shirt and pants uniforms.) Then the gym teacher had all the students take off their shirts. I thought this was strange, so I watched more intently as the gym teacher had each student hold out his right arm. I watched him spit on and then rub the right arm of each student. Then every now and then he'd make a big X with a felt pen on some of the students' chests.

"What is the gym teacher doing?" I asked my co-teacher, Mrs. Shim, Uhn-sook.

"He is checking to see which students need a bath."

"A bath?"

"Yes, some students are very poor, and all winter long they never go to the bathhouse because it is too expensive."

"So why is he putting an X on their chests?"

"He tells them that they'd better not come back tomorrow with the X still visible. This will force the parents to give them money to visit the bathhouse."

On Monday, April 28, 1975 (I know the exact date because it is printed in my yellow WHO card, which I still have), many of us were in Seoul for our gamma globulin inoculation and a T.B. test. I did the usual climbing up and down the stairs of the Korea Educational Association Building where the Peace Corps had its offices in order to get the gamma globulin to circulate and not stiffen up my left cheek and left upper thigh near where the needle had been jabbed in. After going from the seventh floor where the new Peace Corps doctor, Dr. Chu, Un-bong, had an office all the way down to the ground floor lobby and back up, I went into the PC lounge on the sixth floor. Sitting there was a gorgeous, buxom blonde whom I had seen around before but had never had the opportunity to meet and greet. Today was my lucky day. *"Hi there, gorgeous,"* I wanted to say, but only "Hi," in a much higher pitch than I wanted came out. She greeted me, and we started talking. She told me her name was Gail Baraga. After a few minutes she asked if I'd like to go to lunch with her to a place that had great *kimchi jjigae* (kimchi stew). I didn't really feel like *kimchi jjigae* all that much and would have rather gone to the old faux-hamburger place in Myeong-dong, but she was gorgeous, so I replied, "Would I, would I?" And she said, "Hare lip, hare lip!" Actually, we didn't say that, but instead I nodded and said, "Sure, let's go." We went to her favorite little restaurant near the Peace Corps office and had lunch. Gail needed to head back to her town by train and took off for the Cheongnyangri train station. Being a "prop setter," I had a flight out the next morning.

So I hopped on a bus over to Namdae-mun (The Great South Gate) Market. Namdae-mun Market was a huge area of shops along alleyways near the famous old city gate of Seoul, which is National Treasure number one. I wandered around, checking out the sights and sounds. People-watching was always fun in the markets. While the Myeong-dong shopping area was the place to go to see fashionable young women, Namdae-mun Market was full of common middle-aged people shopping for bargains. Many of the vendors would be calling out to the passersby holding up items for sale and loudly proclaiming the value, quality, and price of them.

After wandering around for a couple of hours, I decided to walk the mile or so back to Gwanghwa-mun. Heading north up Taepyeong-ro (Taepyeong Street), I suddenly noticed that rather than the usual busy traffic there were almost no vehicles on this main thoroughfare. Then my eyes started watering, and I heard yelling and screaming ahead. There was an elevated walkover for pedestrians close by, so I walked up the stairs and out to the middle of the walkway. Looking north I saw a large number of riot police in full riot gear with black padded uniforms, shields, and batons. Beyond them there were hundreds of young people throwing bricks and stones toward the police. Ahead of the police was a black armored van with heavy screening over the windows and with a turret-like thing on top that looked just like the Monitor's (the Union's ironclad ship in the civil war) cannon shooting tear gas canisters out in whichever direction was needed. The wind blowing north to south was carrying the tear gas my way. It was scary, but I watched mesmerized for a while. Then my eyes began burning too much, and I headed back toward Namdae-mun and then east to Myeong-dong where I ate dinner. Later I headed back to Gwanghwa-mun, and the rioters had either dispersed of their own accord or been driven away.

I had read about student demonstrations in Korea over the past nearly three years of Peace Corps service. They were demonstrating against President Park, Chung-hee and for democracy, but they were usually confined, more or less, to the areas in and around the major universities' campuses. This was the first time I had ever seen them downtown. Whenever the students did get off campus, the police would attack, and it would become more like a riot.

During my nearly ten years as the director of the Korean Branch of the Pearl S. Buck Foundation in the 1980s, I saw a couple of other student demonstrations and riots. One was in the spring of 1987 when I was escorting several Group Study Exchange Team Rotarians from Rotary District 519 in Sacramento, California. I still have the card of one of them who had the mighty fine first name of Don. Don Brodeur, an Attorney at Law specializing in tax and business law, was one of five District 519 Governor's Representatives visiting our District 365. I was on the Seoul Rotary Club's Program Committee, and since our PSBF vehicle was a seven-passenger KIA Bongo van at this time, I was asked to schlep them around on one of the days of their visit. We had toured a factory owned by one of our club's members in the morning where we also had lunch, and then we were driving across town to our next activity when we drove past the entrance to Yonsei University.

"Oh, boy," I said "the students are restless today."

"What do you mean?" asked Don.

"Look ahead."

"Wow, is it always like this?"

"Not always, but often and usually, like today, it is confined to the areas around the universities. We're coming up to the entrance of Yonsei University, the largest and most prestigious private university in Korea. It was founded by American missionaries."

Ahead we could see armored vans and hundreds of riot police just relaxing on the right side of the road. The Rotarians from California rolled down the windows of the PSBF van and had their cameras out. On the left side, as we got closer, was the main gate to Yonsei. Hundreds of students were just inside the gate with placards and signs calling for democracy. The visiting American Rotarians took numerous pictures on either side as we passed by.

Just a few months after escorting the Rotarians from California, I had my scariest encounter, up close and personal, with a student demonstration. In

January 1988, after nearly ten years of working for the Pearl S. Buck Foundation, I sent in my resignation. The reason I gave was that my first wife and I wanted to return to the U.S. and have our son Otto start the first grade in America. I felt it was getting to the point where, if I didn't leave soon, I would probably spend the rest of my working years in Korea. After fifteen years of living and working in the Land of the Morning Calm, I decided it was time to get back to the Land of the Free and the Home of the Brave. Knowing that PSBF would probably want to replace me with, as the Peace Corps used to say, a "host-country national" and that it would take some time to find a suitable person, I gave six month's advance warning. In January 1988, I announced that my family and I would leave at the end of July.

In late April, Glenn Rudyard, the Pearl S. Buck Foundation's Overseas Programs Director, visited Seoul to begin the search for my successor. After a day of visiting with the Republic of Korea's Ministry of Health and Social Welfare officials, I dropped Glenn off at the President Hotel near Seoul City Hall around 4:30 in the afternoon. For the evening I had made 7:00 p.m. reservations at the Korea House dinner theater for Glenn, my wife, Mi-yun, our son, Otto, and myself to eat dinner and watch the entertainment. Korea House featured an exquisite Korean dinner fit for a Yi Dynasty king and a fantastic traditional music and dance show every evening. When I dropped Glenn off I told him I'd come back and pick him up, but he insisted that he would just take a taxi the short mile or so to Korea House just off of Toegye-ro not too far from the south end of Myeong-dong.

I drove across the Han River to the southern part of Seoul where our apartment was located, freshened up, and then took Mi-yun and Otto with me back across the Hannamdae-gyo (Hannamdae Bridge) over the Han River and toward downtown Seoul. I turned left onto Toegye-ro, and I was shocked to see there was not a vehicle on the street. There were lots of indications of a struggle, though, including paving bricks from the sidewalks, which had been ripped up by the students and thrown at the police, and broken bottles. I drove slowly, swerving to miss the bricks and glass shards. It was about a mile until I'd reach the side street where Korea House was located, and not wanting to get a flat tire from the broken glass I turned left up a side street. Suddenly, I noticed that ahead of us the street was barricaded with students wearing bandanas standing atop the makeshift barricade. It looked like "Les Misérables." I inched forward, and the students pointed, indicating for me to turn right. I nodded and followed their directions. I had forgotten that Dongguk University's campus was here. The students had their whole campus cordoned off. I smiled and gave a fist pump signal with my right fist. I wanted them to know I was on their side, if only because I worried that one or more of them might be anti-American. Some students blamed the U.S. for Korea having been divided at the end of World War II. It would only take one angry student to toss a brick at our Bongo van, and who knows what might happen? I don't like or trust crowds; they can quickly turn into ugly mobs. Thankfully, they let us proceed.

When I finally got to Korea House just before 7:00 p.m. and drove through their large wooden gates similar to those at Gwanghwa-mun or Namdae-mun, I parked in their parking lot. As soon as we got out of the car, the tear gas overwhelmed us—but with much more force than it had in the spring of 1975 when I was walking north from Namdae-mun Market. We ran into Korea House, and because they had their air-conditioning on it was very pleasant inside. The only problem was that Glenn was not there. I walked back out to the edge of the parking lot and looked out between the wooden doors. Through my teary eyes I could see students throwing bricks and bottles toward the police line down on Toegye-ro. I cried my way back into the building. Then I started panicking with horrible thoughts running through my mind. *"What if Glenn is killed in the riot? How do I explain this to PSBF headquarters?"* After about ten minutes, which seemed like an eternity, I went back out to the gate. As I looked down toward the main street I could see a tall man walking toward me, and as he got close I could see it was Glenn. I have never been happier to see any boss of mine in my long working career. Glenn and I, both crying our eyes out due somewhat to emotion but mostly thanks to the tear gas, hugged in the joy of knowing we were both still alive on this planet.

"Where were you?" I asked.

"My taxi got to within about fifty yards of this side street, but it couldn't get any closer. The driver let me off, and I waited in a small store until the police pushed the students on past."

"You're kidding! That must have been quite a view."

"Ringside seats, actually, and very interesting other than wondering if I'd ever get out again."

"I'm sure glad you did; I was worried sick."

"All's well that ends well. Let's eat. I'm starved."

"Good idea." This conversation took place as we were crying together and walking into the front door of Korea House. Once inside the four of us were quickly seated. None of us was the worse for wear, and we had a wonderful dinner followed by the lovely show.

After the show ended I drove Glenn back to the President Hotel near Seoul City Hall. There was still no traffic on the roads. We let Glenn out and headed up Eulji-ro, another of Seoul's main downtown streets. Again, there was no traffic to be seen, but ahead was a large bonfire burning away in the center of the road. I turned right on Samil-ro toward Namsan. When nearly back to Toegye-ro, the street was blocked off by dozens of students who parted to let us drive by. Many of them were waving their towels and urging me to beep the car horn. I beeped it loud and clear, over and over, just wanting to get out of Dodge in one piece. Obviously, desperado law had taken over.

As I got to Toegye-ro the light turned yellow, I pushed the pedal down a little and went through the yellow light. There were no cars anywhere in sight anyway. Then I saw red lights reflecting in my rearview mirror—a cop. "*What now?*" I thought. I pulled over and rolled down the window. The cop came up and looked into the car, noticing my Korean wife in the front seat and Otto in the back. Every other time I'd been stopped by the police in Korea, I pretended to not speak Korean, and they just waved me on. Today I dropped the pretense and spoke in Korean.

"Why did you stop me?"

"You went through a red light."

"No, I didn't. It was yellow when I went through."

"Let me see your driver's license, please."

"Here you are," I said as I handed my license to him.

"Wait a minute, please," he said. He walked behind the car, and I watched him in my rearview mirror. I saw him write down my car license plate number, and then he copied information off my driver's license. He returned to my car, handed me back my license, and told me I was free to go. I imagine he later checked to see what I did in Korea and most likely whether or not I was a journalist. I also assumed that when they checked up on me Mr. Paik, Tae-hyun would have certainly vouched for me. After this last strange incident of the evening, I drove back to our apartment complex with no further abnormalities.

Returning to 1975 and the student demonstration in downtown Seoul, I "prop setted" it again back to the east coast the day after the demonstration. I went to see Mark Mackinac the following weekend down in Bupyeong after classes on Saturday. We decided to head over to the beach. Taking a shortcut from the train station, we zigzagged our way along the low-lying dikes between the rice paddies. The rice fields were located alongside a small river that ran into the sea just south of town. Mark marveled at how these small rice paddies seemed to float alongside the river as far as we could see and then sloped up the hillsides too. "Yes," I said professorily, "and that's why they say Korea wasn't built in a day." Mark cracked up. It was like he thought I was Bill Murray or something.

Typical rice fields in Korea—notice the lone farmer walking on the dikes between the fields.

Then he got serious as we neared the beach. He told me a story that troubled me. It turned out Miss Shin, Myung-hui's friend, was a nymphomaniac. She had pursued him and gotten him to sleep with her on several occasions. One night they went to a *yeogwan* just on the edge of town. Keep in mind Bupyeong is a much smaller town than Mukho. In the middle of the night, the *yeogwan* caught on fire. Miss Shin and Mark ran out from the room, and there were many townsfolk and some of his students who had come because of the commotion. After this, Mark said that things were very bad at his school, and he didn't think he could stay in Korea. I felt horrible. I was the one who had introduced him to this wild woman.

I suggested we go back to Mukho and he crash at my place to get him away from Bupyeong at least for a day. We had a nice dinner in downtown Mukho and were heading up the street toward the Mukho movie theater when a young lady with a lot of attitude walked up to us. She excitedly announced that she was Miss Shin's sister. She was talking very fast, and Mark asked me what she was saying. I translated. She said that her sister was pregnant with Mark's child. Mark assured me that was not possible. I couldn't understand how he was so sure, and Miss Shin's sister continued insisting that it was true. I kept looking around hoping no one was listening, as she was quite agitated and getting louder. I suggested to her that we go somewhere private to talk. She basically said there was nothing more to say and left. Mark looked much paler than usual. The two of us walked back to my room, and he told me he would leave Peace Corps and Korea.

"What will you do?"

"My job at IBM is waiting for me, so I'll just head home and return to work," he declared sadly.

"Well, you're lucky in that regard," I injected. He agreed. A few days later, he left the east coast and then Korea for good. To my knowledge, Miss Shin was never pregnant, but for Mark the damage had been done.

South Vietnam fell at the end of April 1975. What a shock! The United States Army's role in Vietnam had just ended in March 1973. Long before that, the United States had assisted the French in their fight against the Viet Minh from 1945 until 1954. Then the French withdrew, and the Geneva Accords divided Vietnam into a Communist state in the north and an anti-Communist state in the south. From 1954 on, the U.S. had military advisors in South Vietnam.

I couldn't help wondering, *"Why had the U.S. been so successful in South Korea and yet had seen such abject failure in South Vietnam?"* I've heard today's neo-conservatives say that if you justify the Korean War, you must justify the Vietnam War. They both seem very similar, don't they? In both cases, there was a northern, Communist, very aggressive and militaristic country invading the southern, anti-Communist, pro-American country. In both cases the north was militarily better prepared, more organized, and their soldiers seemed more determined. Also, in both cases the United States forcefully came in with a huge military force and stemmed the tide of northern, Communist expansion.

Why is South Korea today such a huge success story and South Vietnam non-existent? It seems to me now, although I'm not sure if I realized this in 1975, that there is one huge difference between South Korea and South Vietnam, and I sincerely believe this difference is the reason for our success in Korea and failure in Vietnam. In South Korea we were seen by nearly all the people as liberators. We had defeated the hated colonial power of Japan. We destroyed the Japanese military and took Japan's colonies away. August 15 (the day in 1945 that the Japanese surrendered to the United States and the other Allied powers) is celebrated as South Korea's Independence Day. After defeating the colonial power that was so hated by most of the Korean people, we gave South Korea its independence. We had "street cred" (credibility) among the Korean people. We were heroes! We were respected! That is why twenty-some years later people were still coming up to me, a lowly Peace Corps Volunteer, and thanking me as a representative of the United States of America, the very country that had saved them first from the horrible Japanese oppressors and then from those terribly brutal Communists. We were loved by the vast majority of the South Korean people in 1950 when the Korean War began.

What about in Vietnam? We had defeated the Japanese and even helped the Viet Minh in their struggle against Japanese imperialism, but then after the Second World War ended, we assisted the other and also hated imperialist power, France, in its attempt to reassert its dominion over Vietnam. We went quickly from being seen as liberators to being seen as oppressors by most of the people in Vietnam. When the French left in 1954 and Vietnam was divided in two, we were not seen as heroes by the peasants in the South as we were in Korea. We had not given South Vietnam its freedom after World War II as we had in South Korea. On the contrary, we had helped the French re-establish their imperial rule. Consequently, we were seen as being the same as the French, and we never had the "street cred" in South Vietnam that we had in South Korea. So in 1975, the people in South Vietnam did not defend their American-supported government, whereas earlier in South Korea the people had.

Meanwhile, back in Korea, also in April 1975, our taekwondo instructor, Mr. Chae, was trying to talk John and me into taking the second-degree black belt test before the end of the school semester and the end of John's two years of service. Neither of us felt that we had learned enough or progressed that much since we passed the first-degree black belt test the previous fall. We both promised Mr. Chae that we would continue practicing taekwondo back in the States, but that we really didn't feel ready for the second-degree test so soon. He probably saw it as a feather in his hat to have two American guys with black belts studying under him and maybe an even larger and more colorful feather if we both got our second-degree black belt certification. Thankfully, he relented, and we just coasted for the last couple of months.

He was having us spar more and more during our hour of study each evening five nights a week. As covered before, John and I were the only two students studying from 7:00 to 8:00 p.m., and so we would spar against each other. I often tried to use one of my favorite kicks, which I always called the "round-the-world kick." Starting in a fighting stance with one foot forward and the other back, you swing the back leg out and away from the body with the leg straight and then swing it hard toward the center or, in an actual fight, toward your opponent's head. There are two versions, though. In the other version, you bring the back leg inward crossing in front of the stationary leg and then bring it back toward the center aiming again at the opponent's head. I liked the first version and practiced it a lot, and every once in awhile in our sparring I'd use it against John. He often didn't see it coming. A couple of times I was a little overexuberant, and I smacked him upside the left side of his head with the inside of my incoming right foot. Once, I knocked John a little silly. Our instructor jumped up, led John over to a side bench, and had him sit out for a while. While John rested, Mr. Chae sparred with me.

Myung-hui stopped by the next Saturday night out of the blue, knocking on my door around 8:00 p.m. She hadn't visited in quite a while. I didn't say anything about Mark and Miss Shin, and neither did she. I went and got some wine and snacks as usual. Suddenly, there was a loud rap on my door. Myung-hui let out a squeal, and she drove her head into my shoulder, nearly knocking over my wine glass, as if she was trying to hide from whoever was at the door. I heard my corridor mate Miss Kim say, "Sorry, nothing really." We heard her footsteps as she ran off. I could feel the pounding of Myung-hui's heart like a jackhammer against my chest as she hugged me. She sat up, and her face was whiter than an Irish girl's in winter.

Sunday morning, Myung-hui got up fairly early and told me she had to leave. She opened my door and started to step out, but then she jumped back into the room with a frightened look on her face and said, "*Miguk saram* (American person)." "What?" I asked and looked out in the hall. Sure enough, standing in front of Miss Lee's room was an American whom I knew, Ken Kalamazoo. Ken was an ex-Peace Corps Volunteer from an earlier group than mine. I knew him, though not well. He had been a health volunteer like Chris Sombra and John Hudson. I walked out, and Ken and I began talking. Myung-hui snuck by us in the hallway and hid her face with her hands as she ran out. Ken explained that he had stopped off in Mukho as Ed Harper had done on his way back from Sorak Mountain knowing there were volunteers here. He had run into Chris and John on Mukho's main street. Then the three of them had met Miss Kim, Miss Lee, and Miss Pak, my corridor mates, in the alleyway near my place. After they had all settled in at a wine house, they sent Miss Kim to get me, but she found that I was indisposed. Ken told me that he and Miss Lee were off to take a tour of Mukho. I said, "Have fun" and returned to my *yo* for a little more beauty rest, which I always needed, and still do need.

It's kind of funny that even though I was living in a bordello, I never had any relations with any of the three young ladies on my corridor. I never made any advances, and neither did they. They knew that I had a girlfriend because they had seen Myung-hui once before. The ladies of the night in Korea did have a sort of code of chivalry, especially around the U.S. military facilities, which I heard about later when I taught on U.S. bases after Peace Corps. Many of the ladies were hoping to get a ticket to the U.S. through marriage, and they would leave alone a guy who was going steady, so to speak, with another gal. They did not want to hurt each other's chances of getting married to a GI. Either way, I was just friends with my hallway companions. They would often come in, plop down, and talk in my room. Several times I pulled out my camera and took photos of them. They would also often borrow my stuff, but they'd never return it. So after a couple of days, I'd have to remember to go knock on their doors and retrieve whatever it was they had borrowed. We were just friends, and that was it.

On another weekend in late May John asked if I'd like to head with him south to another beach he'd heard about located south of Samcheok. We headed south and got off at the place where John had been told there was a beautiful sandy beach. We hiked over, and sure enough there was a very nice beach that was totally void of human activity. It was a beautiful, warm, and sunny spring day. We rolled out our towels, and this time I had my Mark Spitz-like, American-flag Speedo bathing suit on under my blue jeans. I took off my shirt and jeans, rolled out a towel, and laid down. John took off all his clothes and sprawled out naked on his towel. "What the hell are you doing?" I asked. He explained to me that he had a bet with his college sweetheart, whom he'd kept in touch with during his two years of Peace Corps service, that he would come home with a completely tanned body—sans any tan lines.

I was still writing to Linda Boyne. But now, having lived another year in Korea after my summer of infatuation in 1974, I still had a gnawing desire to continue to live overseas, and I knew I wouldn't be heading home any time soon. I had no idea what I would do after Peace Corps, but by this time I had been told that I was chosen to be one of the TESOL instructors for the K-35 training program, which would start in late June. I was to leave Mukho in mid-June, a couple of weeks before the end of the school year, to work with the preparation group putting together lesson plans and scheduling the training sessions. As always during my youth, I was already looking ahead to the future and distancing myself mentally from Mukho and my Peace Corps middle school teaching experience. I was never nostalgic or all that emotional about leaving any educational institution or job at any time along the way up to this point in my life. I was always excited about the next adventure. Leaving Linda after the summer home leave was the only time I almost regretted my future plans, but even then, once I landed back in Korea, I was excitedly looking ahead to teaching using "The Silent Way" and getting back into my life here. Now that life in Mukho was almost over, I was looking forward to my next endeavor.

One of my last Sundays in Mukho I was invited again by Mr. Jong to visit Mukho's harbor. We went in and met his friend, the harbormaster, who took us on a small tugboat-like ship from the dock out to a freighter from Hong Kong that was sitting in the middle of the harbor halfway between the dock and the breaker wall. This freighter was larger than most that came into Mukho, and after getting half filled with bags of cement at the dock, it had to move out to deeper water. Otherwise, if loaded more, it would have gotten stuck near the dock. When we came up next to the freighter a gangplank was thrown down, and the harbormaster, Mr. Jong, and I crossed over it and onto the larger ship. We literally walked the plank and lived to tell about it. There was a strong wind that night, and even inside the harbor there was wave action going on. The Chinese captain came walking up to us and said right away, "No can do." The harbor-master replied, "Can do. OK. Number one." I realized that they were discussing whether or not to offload more cement bags from the smaller Korean craft or not. "No can do. Number ten. Hurt my ship," the Chinese captain of the freighter replied. "No hurt ship. Can do. OK. Number one." the harbormaster repeated. This went on for a while. Of course, "number one" meant good while "number ten" meant bad in Konglish (Korean-English). There were a lot of number ones and number tens being thrown back and forth, but as long as no one was throwing number two around it was kosher. Finally, the Chinese captain relented. The Korean men started to schlep cement bags onto the freighter, and then the Chinese merchant mariners tossed them down into the hold where they were caught by other seamen down there and stacked. I thought, *"Well this is going to be a long night because obviously the Chinese captain can't speak English, and we're stuck here until the offloading is done."* That's when the captain turned toward me and asked in English, "Would you like to come with me down to the galley? We can have something to drink and some snacks." I agreed, and Mr. Jong and I followed him into the cabin area of the ship. It turned out he spoke excellent English! That crazy simplified Pidgin English was the international language of harbors throughout Asia when the people involved spoke different languages. We sat for a couple of hours drinking, snacking, and talking with the captain. I was trans-lating the captain's life history into Korean for Mr. Jong's benefit, as his spoken English couldn't keep up.

Students from my special class and three other teachers from the girls' middle school at a farewell outing to Mangsan Beach.

The Saturday of my last full weekend in Mukho, three other teachers from the girls' middle school and I took my fifteen special class students to Mangsan Beach for a farewell outing.

The very next day, my last Sunday in Mukho, Myung-hui stopped by my room in the early afternoon. She, of course, knew that I'd be leaving the next weekend.

"Jal ga" (go well), she said.

"Would it be OK if I write to you?" I asked in Korean.

"Yes, that would be fine," she replied.

I had never written to Myung-hui from Mukho, nor had I ever called her on the telephone or visited her family's home. She once told me approximately where she lived. Supposedly, when standing in front of the Bupyeong Train Station you could see her parents' house. A couple times when I visited Bupyeong to see Mark Mackinac or Mr. Hyun, Jong-jin, I stood in front of the train station and looked in the direction specified, but I never could discern which gate led into the court-yard of her family's home. Myung-hui and I kept in touch for a few months after I left Mukho.

I had a hard time believing this was the last week of my volunteering on the east coast of Korea. I had given away all my possessions, which were not all that many to start with, and could put almost all my clothes and everything I owned in a backpack that I had purchased from the Kolon store the last time I was in Seoul. What little didn't fit in the backpack I put in a small duffel bag. I had given my chest of drawers and low desk to one of the teachers at the boys' middle school. I had also donated my small portable tape recorder to the music teacher at the boys' middle school. I sold the rather large tripod that I had bought for my camera when in Japan the second time to a local camera shop. I just didn't want to carry the darn thing. It felt good to be able to pick up and carry everything I owned. There are times these days when I almost wish I could still do that, but those days and the freedom implied by that kind of lack of crap are long since gone. That ship done sailed a long time ago!

On my last Wednesday, I was walking down the main street of town when I saw ahead of me two white guys heading my way. One was about my height but stockier, and the other was thin but quite a bit taller than I. When they got close, one of them said, "Hello, you must be Don," with a German accent. I assured them that indeed I was Don. "How do you know my name?" I asked them. It turns out they were German tourists who had run into Ken Kalamazoo on the Shimonoseki to Busan ferry a couple of days before. They'd befriended Ken and told him that they wanted to visit a typical Korean town, off the beaten path and far away from tourist areas. Ken told them that they must go to Mukho in Gangwon Province. That was the best town in all of Korea to visit, he informed them, and they believed him. I assume he told them to look for me—he evidently hadn't told them John Hudson's name—because I lived in a more interesting place than John did. There was no easy way to get from Busan to Mukho in those days, so I inquired as to what route they had taken. They traveled all the way along the coast from Busan to Pohang and then up to Mukho a total of about 250 miles or so by bus. Most of the way they traveled over two-lane dirt roads on local buses that stopped at every nook and cranny along the way. "How many hours did it take?" I asked them. "Ten hours or so," was their response. I had never taken that route and never wanted to. These German guys were obviously intrepid travelers.

They reminded me of my distant cousin who was related to my great-grand-mother Haffner. I often wonder if my wanderlust, such as it is, didn't come from my great-grandmother Haffner's side of the family. Her maiden name was Martha Knust, and she married my great-grandfather, Robert August Haffner, in Germany. They had three daughters and one son (Lena, Mina, Frieda, and Otto, my grandfather) in Germany before immigrating to the U.S. in 1892 and settling in Detroit.

Martha's cousin, Willy Schwiegershausen, the son of her mother's sister, spent nearly five years of thrilling adventure on a bicycle trip across six continents from 1899 to 1904. Willy and two companions were sent on a round-the-world bicycle trip by a German publication. They were promised 25,000 marks for their diaries and photographs of the expedition. The itinerary was mapped out by the publication and took them through some of the roughest countries and away from civilization where no bicycle had ever been seen before. They had to get a signature and seal from an official, often the ruler, in every place they passed en route. In Mexico President Diaz wrote: "I give my cordial welcome to the most daring traveler I know."

Willy, who spoke five languages, and his two companions began their trip in 1899 in Germany. Early in the journey one of his companions became ill and returned home, the other was killed by Bedouins in the Arabian Desert, and Willy completed the rest of the trip alone.

When the trip was nearly over, Willy said in a Sunday, June 19, 1904 *New York Times* article, of which I have a copy:

> Today I have completed the task on which I set out four
> years and eleven months ago: To girdle the globe and cross
> the six continents on a bicycle. Besides this record I have
> accomplished the longest journey ever made on land. I am
> satisfied when I look back, but there is not money enough
> in the world to hire me to repeat it.

Asked by the same *New York Times* reporter if he had any fear during the trip, Willy replied:

> I have never known the feeling of fear in my life. No,
> not fear, but a wonderfully romantic feeling of grandeur,
> liberty and sublimity came over me in those lonely Oriental
> nights – a feeling too grand to be described.

Can't say that I haven't known fear in my life, but I do agree with Willy about the "romantic feeling of grandeur, liberty and sublimity" that he felt "in those lonely Oriental nights." I too felt and still feel that way about my Peace Corps days and nights in Korea. Memories of my three years in the Peace Corps still give me "a feeling too grand to be described," even though I have attempted to do so in these pages.

According to our family legend, as told to me by my Aunt Ruth, Willy visited Detroit and stayed at my great-grandparents' house in 1904. My grandfather, Otto, was twelve years old at the time. I grew up hearing stories of Cousin Willy's bicycle ride around the world. In the 1920s Otto's oldest sister, my great-aunt Lena, spent six months visiting our relatives in Germany. Great-aunt Lena told my Aunt Ruth that she had visited Willy's home while in Germany and that he lived in a large mansion with a beautiful water fountain in the entrance hall.

Before I found the above-mentioned *New York Times* article, all of this about Cousin Willy's trip had seemed like a typical family exaggeration to me. It seemed similar to the story that the Detroit Haffners were direct descendents of the Burgermeister Sigmund Haffner of Salzburg for whom the Haffner Serenade and Symphony had been written by Mozart. Through research that I did back in the 1980s, I found that good ol' Sigmund Haffner of Salzburg had no sons. In addition, our family is from Prussia near the Baltic Sea, which is nowhere near Salzburg. Also evidently not true was my maternal grandmother Hazel Hannenberg's story that her grandmother was Native American. This was disproved by the National Geographic's Geno20 DNA test, which I had done a few years ago. No Native American ancestry appeared in my DNA. So, I also assumed and envisioned that young Willy had actually ridden his tricycle around the block once, but after many retellings, family lore had it that he was a world traveler who had circumnavigated the globe on two wheels. Consequently, a few years ago I decided to check the Detroit newspapers from 1904 just to see if there were any articles about my fine cousin Willy Schwiegershausen. Unfortunately, none of the Detroit newspapers was indexed that far back, but a librarian at the Detroit Public Library informed me that the *New York Times* newspaper was. She checked for me and found that there was in fact a full-page article in the June 19, 1904, Sunday edition of the *New York Times* about Willy. She made a copy of this article complete with photographs from his journey. It turns out that, as the *New York Times* reporter so well stated, after "many hairbreadth escapes," Cousin Willy really did ride a bicycle around the world. So as far as family lore goes and to paraphrase Mr. Loaf, "One out of three ain't bad!" ("Two Out of Three Ain't Bad," written by Jim Steinman, sung by Meat Loaf)

As for the two German tourists who reminded me of Willy, the short one was named Benny Schoenherr, and the tall one Bjorn Groesbeck. They told me they were going to travel around all of Asia and that they had left Germany several weeks earlier. First, they'd traveled to Moscow. After a week or so visiting the sights in and around Moscow, they then took the Trans-Siberian Railroad's five-day and five-night-long journey across to the city of Vladivostok. From Vladivostok they went by freighter to Sapporo, Japan on the northernmost Japanese island of Hokkaido. After a couple of more weeks they had made their way down to Shimonoseki at the southernmost tip of Honshu, Japan's largest island. It was on the Shimonoseki to Pusan, Korea ferry that they had met Ken Kalamazoo.

"Have you found a place to stay?" I asked.

"Yes, we're at the Gangwon Hotel," they said. This was Mukho's only tourist hotel down near the entrance to the harbor.

"Do you guys want to meet later this evening?" I inquired.

"Yes, we'd enjoy meeting with you tonight," Benny said.

"Great, how about I'll go to the Gangwon Hotel tonight around 8:30 after my taekwondo practice?"

"Good, we'll see you then," they said.

That night I went to their room after taekwondo. I had invited John, but he had something else to do. Bjorn, Benny, and I sat with the door of their room open and talked for a while. They told me that they had met a Soviet General on the Trans-Siberian Railroad and had drunk vodka with him. Both Benny and Bjorn had been in the German army, and they compared military forces and equipment with this Russian general. After he got drunk, the general told them that he wished the Soviet army had German equipment. He told them the German equipment, especially their tanks, was much better than the Russian equipment, and in fact the German equipment was the best in the world.

As we were talking a couple of young mid-twenties Korean gals who were also staying in the hotel sauntered in. They were Miss Choi and Miss Lee. Miss Choi was solid and on the stocky side; in fact, she reminded me of the gym teacher at the girls' middle school (Miss Ou), while Miss Lee was slimmer. They sat and talked for a while and then we invited them to go to Mukho's only beer hall with us. Bjorn excused himself and said he had to go see his girlfriend. *"That didn't take long,"* I thought. He left first, and then Benny and I headed out, following the gals. As we walked out of the hotel's front door there were two other gals who walked up to us. They had met Benny and Bjorn earlier in the afternoon and wanted to go have a drink with them. The other two gals from the hotel waited a discreet distance ahead, which was common Korean etiquette. I told the new young ladies that we unfortunately had plans tonight. They asked, "Maybe tomorrow?" I asked Benny, and he said sure, so I translated the information to them and they wandered off. We met up with the first pair of gals and headed off to drink and dance. I ended up with the stockier of the two gals, and Benny got the slim one. We drank, danced some, and talked with me translating, although the gals both knew some English. As the midnight curfew hour drew near, I suggested we head back to the hotel. We went back to Benny's room, and I excused myself because I wanted to get up early and do my usual taekwondo workout at the *dojang* the next morning.

The next afternoon, I ran into Benny and on my way to the post office during my free hour. Benny told me that Bjorn came barging in drunk in the middle of the night and was so noisy that he woke up everyone in the hotel. These Germans obviously were pretty wild. I was glad I left before curfew and went back to my room. Even with only a couple days left in Mukho, I did not want to leave with the reputation of having been a wild partier during my last days as a Peace Corps Volunteer.

I told Benny that I was going to be busy the next couple of evenings with teachers from the two middle schools where I taught, so I wouldn't be spending the next two evenings with them. I had, though, invited them to come on Saturday along with Chris and John to go up to Gyeongpodae Beach just north of Gangneung. We were meeting Pam at the train station, and then all of us would head off to the beach to celebrate my last Saturday night on the east coast as a Peace Corps Volunteer and a "prop setter." I told Benny when he and Bjorn should meet us at the train station, and I headed back to school.

Later in the afternoon on Thursday, I had my last classes at Mukho Girls' Middle School and my last emotional special class there. These girls were cute as can be. They were the same students who had visited me the day I had been so sick from the carbon monoxide poisoning. Later that evening, I met some of the girls' school teachers for drinks after taekwondo.

On Friday I had my last special class at Mukho Middle School with the fifteen boys in my class, my last taekwondo lesson and a last *sul-jip* (wine house) visit with teachers from the boys' school. This whole week got more and more emotional as it went along. The "fare thee wells" got harder and harder to get through, but even so I was also very excited to be going to work on the K-35 training program, and I was mentally half gone already.

Saturday morning, I got up and had all my possessions packed in my backpack and small duffel bag. My "outsa" (Peace Corps slang and opposite of *insa* "greeting") or farewell speech was written with the help of my co-teacher, Mrs. Shim, and I was ready for my last day of classes. When I got to school the students were already lining up for the last assembly I'd ever see at Mukho Middle School. I went into the teachers' office and started saying goodbye to everyone, as I had told them I needed to catch the early afternoon train. As mentioned, the goodbyes had really been going on for days, but now the urgency was there.

Principal Chai, Young-sun came into the teachers' office. Instead of having a morning meeting, he presented me with a very handsome *Hanbok* (Men's traditional clothing), a gold pin with Mukho Middle School's symbol on it, and the latest school yearbook. The note that was attached to the yearbook said:

> We present album for you!
> Thank you for your kindness and God bless you forever!
>   By Muk Ho Middle School
>   Principal Chai Young Sun

Then we all went out onto the school grounds, and Principal Chai announced that this was going to be Ha, Doe-young Seonsaeng-nim's (honorable teacher's) last day and that Ha Seonsaeng-nim was going to say a few words of farewell. Unfortunately, I didn't keep a written version of my speech, but what I remember saying sounded something like this:

> Honored people, please listen to the words that I am about to say. I want to thank everyone at Mukho Middle School, all the faculty, staff, and students for welcoming me three years ago and for having been so kind to me for these past three years. I have taught every one of you students standing on the field today during these past three years. It has been my honor to have been your teacher. I hope that you will long remember me, as I know I will remember all of you for the rest of my life. I will also remember Mukho Middle School, the town of Mukho, Kangwon Province, and Korea all my life.

Here's where I started to get serious and a little political. I continued:

> I want to also say that education is more than just memorization.

This was political because that is what all of Korean education really was, just rote memorization, and we PCV's were supposed to be trying to change that, but change doesn't come easy. I now heard Principal Chai say behind me, "Time is up." He didn't want me to continue because he, I'm sure, was a little concerned where I might take this speech now. But I didn't stop:

> Education is about learning to think. I hope that my presence here has helped you all to also learn to think for yourselves beyond just memorizing things.

"Time up, Ha, Seonsaeng." Principal Chai reiterated, dropping the "nim" (more honorific) part.

> So, I leave today with a heavy heart. But, again, I thank you so much for your having welcomed me and your kindness to me for these last three years. I know that I will always remember these years as among the best years of my life. Thank you so much.

I bowed and walked away. The principal ran up to the microphone and looked relieved that I was finally finished. He began making other announcements.

I taught my last classes, headed back to my *yeogwan* one last time to get my bags, said goodbye to my corridor mates Miss Kim, Miss Pak, and Miss Lee, and headed off to continue the rest of my life.

I met Chris, John, Benny, and Bjorn at the train station, and we all headed up to Gangneung. Pam met us at the Gangneung train station, and we caught the bus for the short trip to the beach. Gyeongpodae is the provincial park that I first visited in the fall of 1972 when I went on the third-year boys' middle school class trip. There is a beautiful pavilion that was built during the Yi dynasty located between Gyeongpo Lake, which is really a lagoon, and the East Sea (Sea of Japan). The beach itself on the East Sea shore is beautiful. Gyeongpo Pavilion is famous for people supposedly being able to see five moons there: the moon in the sky and four reflections—one in the lake, one in the sea, one in your drinking glass, and one in your lover's eyes. (I think they should say seven moons. I'd add one in your lover's drinking glass, and unless your lover is a Cyclops, one each reflected in both of your lover's eyes.) I had visited Gyeongpodae several times over the past three years, including a couple of times with Myung-hui, but there was no full moon those nights. Now, I was visiting with Pam, and I was thinking she and I should come back at night, if there was a full moon, and test my theory of seven moons, but then those other four guys were cramping my style.

We found a *yeogwan,* which had a large room suitable for all six of us to sleep in one room, and then we stood out on the back porch of our room, which was right on the beach. What a beautiful view! I started practicing my taekwondo punches against the banister along the back of the porch. I was punching hard but trying to stop just as I touched the top board to hone my control skills. Bjorn walked up and punched the board, and it went flying out into the sand. "What the hell?" I yelled. Bjorn said, "Sorry, but I thought you were punching it hard." "No, I was practicing my control," I explained. Bjorn jumped down and got the board and we both did our best to reattach it.

We all decided to go swimming. It was still the weekend before June 15, and even though the temperature was very warm, there were hardly any people on the beach. We all ran out, us guys all in our swimsuits and Pam in her jeans and a T-shirt. After a few minutes John announced he was stripping to his birthday suit and explained his bet with his college honey back in the States. The German guys joined right in. They all ran into the cold water and then came out playing Frisbee on the beach. I looked at Chris and said again, but with less volume and emotion then before, "What the hell!" Chris and I both stripped and ran off into the water. I came out and noticed Pam looking pained, while sitting off and away from where we all had thrown our towels and bathing suits. I ran up and put on my swimsuit, as well as my jeans and T-shirt. Then I went over and sat next to Pam.

"Are you OK?" I asked.

"No, I'm not OK. You guys are only here for the weekend, and then you're all leaving, but this is near my town, and I'll continue living here. If everyone at school hears that I was at the beach with a bunch of nude guys, I'll be embarrassed to say the least." She was almost crying.

"You're right," I agreed. "Let's go for a walk."

"OK!"

We walked up the beach and got away from those "wild and crazy guys" (from *Saturday Night Live*). I was extremely sorry that I had joined in, but it was too late now. I was complicit in the crime. We walked far away from the other guys, way down the beach. While walking I started thinking about Bill Comb and how angry I had been at him for acting the way he did in "MY" town when he started yelling at the tearoom lady that he wanted a full cup of coffee. I was sorry to have been involved in something similar here near Pam's town. *"Was I any better than Bill?"* I wondered to myself.

When we returned I saw a policeman walking up to Chris, Benny, and Bjorn who were standing near our towels and who thankfully now had their bathing suits back on. Pam headed back to the *yeogwan*, while I walked up to the guys just as the policeman did. I felt sorry for the poor policeman. With obviously very limited English, he started talking, "In America, no panty can do. In Korea, no panty no can do." Chris and I said, "Oh, yes, we understand." The policeman continued talking. I looked over to see that John was still in the shallow water but crouching down so that his lower body was hidden in the water. Obviously, he was still naked. I snuck away. Discreetly I picked up John's bathing suit off his towel, kicked off my shoes, rolled up my pant legs and walked out into the East Sea to where he was. Without drawing any attention to us or letting the police-man see what I was doing I dropped John's suit in front of him and said, "Here put this back on. The poor policeman is explaining that we shouldn't be running around naked." By the time we walked back to the group the policeman, having performed his duty to the best of his ability (poor guy), walked away and left us. "Anyone up for dinner?" I suggested.

Later when we got ready to sleep, I had Pam sleep on the end of the room near the door with me next to her and the other four guys on the other side of me. I felt like I needed to protect her or at least be close to comfort her. I'm not sure that she noticed or cared.

The next day, Sunday, after spending the morning on the beach, we all took the bus back to Gangneung together. At the bus station, I shook hands and bade farewell to all the guys. John and Chris I had known for two years since they were first assigned to the east coast. Both of them were about to finish their Peace Corps experience and leave Korea. Bjorn and Benny I had known for less than a week, and that was probably long enough. The four guys got into a taxi and headed back to the train station to catch the late afternoon train heading south. Pam I had known now for a year. After I hugged her and wished her the best for the remaining year of her Peace Corps service, she walked back toward the room she rented near Gangneung Girls' Middle School. I grabbed a taxi to the airport for my late afternoon small-prop-plane flight to Seoul, my last act as a trendy east coast "prop setter"!

CHAPTER 16

K-35 Training: Seeing You Makes My Heart Soar Like an Eagle!

Monday morning, I walked into the Peace Corps office for the first planning session. I knew all of the Americans at the table, but several of the Korean language instructors I didn't know. Everyone around the table introduced themselves. After our introductory morning meeting, we split into two groups to begin planning. The TESOL (Teaching English to Speakers of Other Languages) group went into one room, and the Korean language group went into another.

Near the end of the week in Seoul, the TESOL group visited a prestigious middle school. I had been chosen to teach a dialogue to a first-year boys' class. My teaching was going to be videotaped by the very same camera and recorder that Peace Corps had acquired during our K-23 training program. It's the one that Nick Mack had dropped trou in front of while they were first testing the equipment. I wondered, *"Do they still have Nick's keister on film?"* We went to the school, and the first thing that caught my attention was that there were kerosene heaters in every classroom. In Mukho not even one classroom in any of the schools had heaters. Here every classroom did. I asked some of the students if the heaters were actually turned on during the cold months of the year, and they assured me that they were. Miss Cheon, Myung-sook, also a TESOL instructor with the training program, served as my co-teacher. We taught the same dialogue that I had taught in my first semester in Mukho where Mr. B said, "I don't know," and I had shrugged my shoulders, causing a hilarious outburst when the students replicated my movement. This time I did it with no shrugging, although maybe I should have shrugged. That might have made the film more interesting, except these were some of Korea's best and brightest kids, and they may not have reacted the way my Mukho students had. The dialogue went like this:

> Mr. A: What time is it?
> Mr. B: I don't know!
> Mr. A: Oh, there is a clock.
> Mr. B: Yes, it is 3:30.
> Mr. A: I am late. I must go.
> Mr. B: I will see you tomorrow.

So I wrote on the blackboard all the Mr. As and Bs and then lines for each one of the words, a clock in the space where Mr. A says "clock," and one or two key words to give the students clues. First I modeled the dialogue, acting as both A and B. I had them practice the sentences by repeating after me, and then I did Mr. A while the whole class did Mr. B in unison and vice versa. Finally I had different students be Mr. A and Mr. B individually. All this was captured on videotape and was later shown to the K-35s during one of their TESOL sessions. (The photograph on the back cover of this book is a still photo taken by one of the other trainers that day.)

After a week in Seoul, we all relocated to Cheongju, the capital of Chungcheongbuk-do, the same Chungcheongbuk-do that some of the gals in our training group had sung about during our K-23 talent show. It was the one province on the peninsula with no curfew because it was landlocked. Peace Corps had leased the Daelimjang Yeogwan there to use as an official training site for Korea. The whole *yeogwan* was used for classrooms, meeting rooms, offices, and a PC lounge. The staff and volunteers stayed elsewhere and ate elsewhere, unlike our K-23 training program in which we all trained, ate, and slept in the Daegu New Grand Hotel. Joe Macomb, another of the TESOL instructors, Gail Baraga, whom I had eaten *kimchi jjigae* with a few weeks before while in Seoul for inoculations, and I rented two rooms next to each other in a *yeogwan* north of the training center. Joe and I roomed together while Gail had a single room to herself.

We had another week of planning in Cheongju before the K-35s arrived. This week we finished preparing our lesson plans for the first few weeks of TESOL (Teaching English to Speakers of Other Languages) instruction and laying out the semester's syllabus. In addition to TESOL, another part of our duties was to set up cross-cultural experiences for the new trainees. The Peace Corps driver who was assigned to the training program, Mr. Pak, Yong-hwa, was a fourth-degree black belt in taekwondo. He and I visited a local taekwondo *dojang* and set it up so that the K-35s would be able to learn this Korean martial art each afternoon Monday through Friday from 5:30 to 6:30 p.m. The *dojang* started their evening classes at 7:00 p.m., so we were borrowing their facilities during their downtime. Of course, Peace Corps paid a fee for the space, which was negotiated by Mr. Pak. Mr. Pak agreed to be the instructor with me as his assistant instructor.

Two more TESOL instructors showed up during this week. The first was Ed Harper, who had appeared at my *hasuk* earlier in the spring, the weekend that I had moved back into the bordello, I mean *yeogwan*. The second was Bill Tuscolo, a good friend of Ed's. Bill and Ed were K-25s and had both started their

Peace Corps service in the winter of 1972–73. They had also both extended for another year as I had. Instead of extending in their middle schools, though, they both extended as higher education volunteers at two different universities in Seoul. Their universities had just ended their semesters, and they came down to Cheongju after giving their final exams and turning in the students' grades. They would go back to Seoul in the fall to finish their last semesters as PCVs.

D Day arrived! (De day dat the new volunteers landed in Korea, that is.) Several of us went to Kimpo Airport and met them as several of our instructors had met us K-23s three years earlier. I still had my hair quite short compared to my usual length of the past three years and would have been approved even by President Park, but I still had my mustache. I came to Seoul without having shaved it off and figured if anyone told me to shave I would. No one did so. As the K-35s came out of the customs clearance area, one of them, Jim Mullett, walked directly up to me.

"Why do you have a mustache?"

"Why? Did Peace Corps make you shave before coming over?"

"Yes, but now I wonder why?" he declared.

"I shaved before I came to Korea, too."

"Yeah," he said, "so why do you have a mustache now?"

"Well, I grew my mustache after I had been at my site for a few months during the first winter break. I was lucky because my principal supported me. On the first day of class after the break, he announced to all the teachers, 'Don't Americans look good in mustaches?' Other volunteers have not been so lucky, and having facial hair caused them problems. You'll have to play it by ear, or by your nose, when you get to your school. If my mustache had been a problem I would have shaved it back off right away." I'm not sure I convinced him, but he said, "Oh, OK." There were thirty-nine K-35s, and after meeting them at Kimpo Airport we all bussed down to Cheongju together.

When we got to the training site in Cheongju, each new volunteer was given a welcome packet. In addition, they were all given instructions on how to spot *yeogwans*, approximately how much the charge should be, and how to procure a room. They were told to head south of the training center, as most of the *yeogwans* were that way. The rooms rented by Gail, Joe, and me were on the outskirts of town in the opposite direction. Classes started the next day.

The first Friday night, July 4, we had a party on the roof of the training center with food, drinks, and a boom box playing loud music. All thirty-nine trainees, as well as the twenty-four training staff members, had a rowdy evening on the roof of the three-story building. There was one guest that evening, Miss

Shim, Hae-kyung, who had been a Korean language instructor on previous Peace Corps programs and who was about to leave to attend grad school in the States. Because I don't like mingling, I talked and danced with her most of the evening.

Quickly I fell into a nightly routine of co-teaching taekwondo with Mr. Pak, having dinner with some of those who studied taekwondo, and then heading off to *sul-jips* (bars) around the Daerimjang for drinking. Someone along the way came up with the paraphrasing of a line from the movie "Little Big Man." In the movie Dustin Hoffman plays an American who is raised by the Cheyenne Indians and moves back and forth between the White world and that of the Indians. Whenever he returns to the Cheyenne, he is welcomed by the Chief, his adopted father, who is always seated and says with no emotion whatsoever, "To see you again makes my heart soar like a hawk," while crossing his right arm against his chest and then slowly straightening this arm out in front of him. One of the K-35s one day, when another trainee came walking into a bar, said, "Seeing you makes my heart soar like an eagle," while making the aforementioned arm movement. We all laughed like crazy. From that day on whenever any trainee or staff member wandered into a bar where we were drinking, one or more of us would make the arm gesture and say with absolutely no emotion, "Seeing you makes my heart soar like an eagle." Then we'd all laugh again. Being drunk probably helped make it funnier.

That reminded me of one of my favorite lines from that movie. I brought it up the first time "Seeing you makes my heart soar like an eagle" was used—just after the laughter died down, that is. The Cheyenne, in the movie at least, called themselves the "human beings." Once when the Chief was talking to Dustin Hoffman's character, Jack Crabb, the Chief stated, "There is an endless supply of white men. There has always been a limited number of human beings." "Truer words were never spoken," I added. Everyone laughed, and we all returned to drinking. I wished that I was part Native American. I've always admired their close relationship with animals and the natural world.

The next weekend, Gail Baraga invited Joe Macomb and me to come up to Seoul with her on Saturday. She still co-rented an upstairs flat in Seoul with another Peace Corps gal, and they were having a party on Saturday night. So on Saturday night Gail, Joe, and I, along with Gail's roommate Sally McNichols, Sally's Korean boyfriend Kim, Kyung-ho, and three other PCV guys named David Woodmere, Steven Elmwood, and Graham Olivet, showed up for the party. We all pitched in funds and got Chinese take-out delivered for dinner and bought beer, wine, and snacks, such as Sae-u-gang and McVities Digestives, for the evening's delight. As night fell we were drinking, snacking, singing, and talking up a storm.

I made sure that I was ensconced next to Gail. As it got later and later, I was yawning up a storm, and Gail suggested I lay my head on her lap. At one point Kyung-ho had his shirt off. He was pretty well ripped, maybe not quite as well as I was, mind you, but like half a six-pack's worth. He had fairly large pecks like mine, and he was bouncing one peck up and down on one side, and then he'd bounce the other one up and down on the other side to everyone's amazement. Since I was comfy with my head in Gail's lap, I didn't feel like moving. Even so, I was thinking with a little practice I could do that, but then I was too tired to try. Eventually, as it got to be past midnight, after curfew began, and no one would be able to leave until morning, someone suggested it was time to go to sleep. Gail and Sally only had four sets of *yos, ibols,* and *begaes.* They laid them out on the floor. Kyung-ho and Sally plopped down together on the *yo* near the front window. Gail had to double up with someone, and she motioned for me to lay down with her on the *yo* next to them. Joe and Graham ended up together next to us on the other side, while David and Steven slept on the *yo* farthest from the front window. With only a couple of feet of empty space left between each of the *yos,* these were tight quarters. It would have been especially tricky when a late-night bathroom break was needed because the bathroom was on the first floor down a dark and rickety back stairway. So Gail and Sally actually had a chamber pot in the far back corner of the room.

Joe was quite inebriated and started complaining about why he had to sleep with a guy. He was hilarious. He also began telling his life story, and when he mentioned he was from Iowa, I asked, "What city are you from?"

"I'm from Davenport."

"Oh, we should call you Joe Davenport." Then we all started repeating, "Hey, Joe Davenport."

"Yeah, what do you want?" Joe asked.

"Hey, Davenport! Have you got a chair?" I interjected.

"No chair, just an ottoman." Everyone was laughing uproariously, and this went on for a while until we all ran out of gas and everyone crashed.

The next day Joe took off saying that he would see us that evening in Cheongju. David, Steven, and Graham also left when Joe did. Gail and I spent the morning and much of the afternoon with Kyung-ho and Sally. Late in the afternoon, the two of us caught the bus back to Cheongju. On the trip down Gail asked, "Did you know Karen Gibraltar?" "Sure, she was in my training group," I replied. Then she told me that Kyung-ho had been the reason that Karen Gibraltar left Korea. I had heard the gist of the story before: Karen Gibraltar was dating some Korean guy, had been dumped, had a breakdown, or so the rumor went, and shortly thereafter went back to the States. At the very least, she had left Korea long before finishing her two years of Peace Corps service and under somewhat mysterious circumstances. It seems that Karen and Kyung-ho, who at the time had been a Peace Corps training program Korean language instructor, started dating. Then Kyung-ho dumped Karen Gibraltar for Sally, after which Karen had issues.

I grew quiet and thought about this revelation for quite a while. I remembered the K-23s' first night outside the U.S. in Tokyo when Carrie Anne Tawas came up and said that Karen Gibraltar wanted to room with her, but Carrie Anne didn't want to room with her as she thought Karen was a little crazy. That's when I jokingly suggested that Carrie Anne and I room together. I had gotten to know Karen Gibraltar a little better during our training when several of us had taken that trip to Guryongpo one weekend. She seemed nice to me. It had seemed like she was chasing after Charlie for a while during training, but Charlie made it clear that he only wanted to be friends with her. I now felt sad and sorry for her. In addition, I felt some animosity towards Kyung-ho who had rubbed me the wrong way from the moment I first met him and shook hands with him twenty-four hours earlier. Even though I try not to let first impressions prejudice me, in this case I had the feeling my first impression was correct. When we arrived in Cheongju, Gail and I returned to the *yeogwan* north of the Daelimjang (training center). Joe had returned a couple hours earlier and was reading in our room. Gail dumped her bag in her room, and I dumped my bag next to Joe's, and we went out to dinner. Joe had already eaten but came along anyway.

I continued going out drinking every single night with the other staff members and trainees. I had never done this before in my life. In college I had often gone months or at least weeks without drinking, if for no other reason than I couldn't afford it, and I didn't turn twenty-one (the drinking age in Michigan at the time) until halfway through my senior year of college. In Mukho I had always ducked out of school quickly at the end of my special class in order to avoid running into any of the other male teachers who might want to take me out drinking. Part of the reason I agreed to start taking taekwondo with John Hudson was that it was a good excuse not to drink. Again, I often had gone weeks without drinking in Mukho too. Now I was falling into a life of debauchery. There was too much free time, too little to do, and it was too easy to just wander into one *sul-jip* after another every night. Most nights I'd get back to our *yeogwan* at midnight or so (remember, there was no curfew in Cheongju) very inebriated.

The weekend after Gail and Sally's party, the training program sponsored another party on the roof of the training center. Again, there were food, drinks, and a boom box playing loud music. I had a couple of drinks, watched the dancing, talked for a while, and then went down to take a leak. After "emptying my dragon," I sat in the lounge area and started reading the latest *Newsweek* magazine. After a few minutes, in walked Helen Sandusky. Helen was an interesting gal. She was pretty and shapely, so I had noticed her since the beginning of training, but she seemed distant, even standoffish. I had noticed that she always said, "Thank you, no," instead of "No, thank you," which struck me as interesting—odd, but interesting. I had never really talked to her before this, but she plopped down and asked me why I wasn't up at the party.

"I'm pretty much partied out," I said, "and you?"

"Me too, I guess," she responded.

"Where are you from in the States?"

"Upstate New York. You?"

"Detroit—Motown." We talked for a while, and then she excused herself saying she was tired and heading back to her *yeogwan*. "See ya," I said. I stayed and continued reading, but I never went back upstairs. I just didn't feel like partying.

In fact, I was getting tired of this lifestyle and working on this training program. I almost missed the loneliness of my first year in Mukho and those early Peace Corps days. I was feeling exhausted, and many times when I wasn't leading a TESOL class I'd sneak off and take a nap during the day. In addition, we were supposed to write up or type up an extensive lesson plan for each hour we taught. At first I was gung ho and diligently typed up elaborate step-by-step instructions on special training forms. After a while, though, I quit typing up these lesson plans—partially because I was hung over all the time, but also because I began to wonder why I bothered. It seemed to me that it was a waste of my time. We had file cabinets filled with file after file of past training groups' lesson plans, and I never looked at any of them. Not only did I never look at any of them, but I never saw anyone else look at them either. I'm a firm believer in efficient time management. I'm also a firm believer in not getting bogged down with meaningless busy work. Of course, Peace Corps is a government organization, and government organizations love paperwork, usually in triplicate, but I decided it was totally ludicrous to fill out these forms. I quit bothering and figured if anyone ever called me on it, I'd type out a bunch quickly and hand them in. No one ever noticed the difference, which to me proved they were superfluous.

Also, I was getting tired of the close quarters and tension. One day Don Kalamo, the training director, came into our TESOL office when Ed and I were lesson planning, and he made a big deal about how one of the male Korean language teachers was upset. The teacher had come into the lounge area, and the trainees who were sitting on the floor or lying around had not properly greeted him or risen to their feet and bowed. I thought the language teacher was a bit off base. The trainees were going through six to eight hours of training every day. They were immersed in Korean language, cross-cultural training, and TESOL training. I felt they needed to be given at least a little slack. But here we had an example of the typical Korean male-chauvinist, Confucian, very conservative attitude. I wanted to say to Don that maybe he should explain to the language teachers that the lounge is like a little piece of America where the trainees are relaxing American-style, but I didn't. Ed and I both told him we'd talk to the trainees, but I didn't bother.

One night after taekwondo, Mr. Pak invited Ed Harper, who was studying taekwondo with us, Paul Batavia and Art Adrian, a couple of the K-35s who were also studying taekwondo, and me out to dinner with him. We were all game, but maybe we shouldn't have been. It was the dog days of summer, those extremely humid summer days in Korea. We followed Mr. Pak until he found the special place he was looking for. We went in and up a rickety stairway to an open-air rooftop. A waitress came, and Mr. Pak ordered *boshin-tang* (dog soup) for all five of us. Either Ed or I translated for Paul and Art what we were about to eat. They asked if we had ever had it before, and we said no, then together Ed and I, the Ha brothers, said "We hear it tastes like chicken. Ha,ha!" The dog stew came, and it tasted like chicken. Although none of us relished the thought of what we were eating, we just tried not to think about it. We all grinned, thought happy thoughts, and ate while watching Mr. Pak just savoring every mouthful.

Gail, who was also finishing her Peace Corps Service at the end of the K-35 training, had mentioned several times that she was going to travel to Thailand before heading back to the States.

"Don, why don't you come with me to Thailand?"

"No, I think I'd like to stay in Korea and teach English, make some more money, and then travel after that."

"But you could still come back to Korea after Thailand and start teaching. It'd be fun to travel with you."

"Sure that would be fun, but I don't know. Let me think about it." Of course I was thinking that if the women in Thailand were as beautiful as Jon Kalkaska had said, I wouldn't want to be traveling there with a woman. I'd rather head down there with another guy or alone.

One guy in the K-35 training group, Tim Leelanau, had been a Peace Corps Volunteer in Ethiopia. After a few months in Ethiopia, he had to leave because there was a Soviet-backed military coup and the country had become too dangerous for PCVs to stay. The whole country's program was ended, and he was offered an assignment in Korea. He talked about how he'd had his own small house at the edge of his town and had a young lady who served as his maid and cook. I'm not sure if there were other services offered, but either way he missed his life in Ethiopia. He was also a little loopy. He would walk around with bare feet outside even though we repeatedly told him that this was CIS (Culturally InSensitive), as Koreans never go outside barefoot. He would walk around, and the local residents would stare, but he didn't seem to notice. He also walked around in Bermuda shorts, which we told him was also CIS. In addition, his Korean seemed to be the worst of all the trainees. Instead of saying *An-yong-ha-say-o* (hello), he said *an-dan-ie-say-o*, which in Korean means absolutely nothing. I joked that he spoke Korean with an Ethiopian accent. He just didn't seem to fit in at all.

Oddly enough, my family has a small Ethiopian connection. My father stood up in the wedding of Howard Wilson. Howard and my father had sung together in their Lutheran church choir during their school days. Howard went off to college in Minnesota and later became a Lutheran pastor. Just before graduating from college he got engaged and asked my father to stand up in his wedding. I still have a picture of the wedding party, and among the five men who served as groomsmen, one is a thin and rather short African man. My father always told me growing up that this man was Emperor Haile Selassie's nephew. Fast-forward to the early 2000s when I was working on my master's degree in history at Oakland University (OU), and my African history professor was—you guessed it—an Ethiopian. I mentioned that my father had been in a wedding with Haile Selassie's nephew, and my professor asked to see the picture. Upon seeing it he agreed that the man in the picture looked Ethiopian.

"What is his name?" he asked me.

"I don't know."

"Can you find out?"

"I think I might be able to; give me a few days."

My father had already passed away, and so had Howard, but thanks to Howard having been a professor at a Lutheran university, I contacted the university and was able to get in touch with his wife, Marti. She told me that Haile Selassie's nephew had gone to college with her and that his name was Taifasu Selassie. When I told my OU professor he checked into it and found out that Taifasu had been the Minister of Transportation in the fall of 1974 when the military deposed and imprisoned Haile Selassie. During or shortly after the coup, Taifasu had been murdered by the military. After this very coup, Peace Corps pulled all of its volunteers out of Ethiopia, and Tim Leelanau was given the opportunity to join the K-35 training group. Past-emperor Haile Selassie died a year after the coup while under house arrest, and many believe he too was assassinated. Rastafarians still grieve.

Back in Korea, the time came for the practice teaching part of the K-35 training. During my K-23 training program, I had gone with a small group to Gwangju, and that was when I got dysentery. The K-35s were split into three groups and I, along with several other trainers, accompanied the group that went to Daejeon, about forty kilometers south of Cheongju. Ed, Bill, Joe, and Gail went with one of the other two groups. I helped escort twelve K-35s to Daejeon where they did practice teaching at a school during the day. In the late afternoons we went swimming in a lovely pool that the city had built alongside the river that ran through the town. This was the first time I had ever been in a swimming pool in Korea.

A couple of days after starting the practice teaching, I was asked to take three of the volunteers who needed to visit a doctor to a nearby U.S. Army base. As with the K-23 training when I spent a week in the hospital at the U.S. Army base in Daegu, whenever a U.S. military facility was near they treated volunteers with medical problems. In Cheongju I had also taken sick K-35s to a medical clinic, but it was a clinic run by foreign Roman Catholic nuns like the one in Samcheok where we East Coast volunteers visited for dinner and card playing. We took a taxi out to an American missile base near Daejeon, and I escorted the ill volunteers to the base clinic.

While they were being seen by the doctor, I wandered around the base. With my mustache, fairly long hair (compared to the GIs), and civilian clothes, I stuck out like a sore thumb and was stopped several times by soldiers.

"Hey, man, what are you doing in Korea?"

"I'm a Peace Corps Volunteer teaching English here."

"You mean you weren't forced to come here?"

"No, not at all, I came because I wanted to."

"Are you shittin' me?" they'd ask. This same conversation went on several times with several different soldiers. They just couldn't believe that anyone would come to Korea of their own free will. Many soldiers hated being in Korea, and their favorite question to each other was, "Are you getting short?" which meant, "Is your time in Korea about up yet?" They would answer while looking at their watch something like, "Yeah, three weeks, three days, six hours, and about twenty-five minutes."

At the end of the practice teaching week, three of the K-35 guys, Jack Muskegon, Ginger Cheboygan (whom we called "Hat" simply because he wore a hat all the time), Eric Niles, and I headed over to Daejeon Beach, which is on the Yellow Sea and about 100 kilometers from Daejeon City, for some much-deserved R&R over the weekend. (This is the same beach with the missionary compound that I talked about earlier where I stayed one week while working for the Pearl S. Buck Foundation in the early 1980s.) We kicked back and sat on the beautiful beach there drinking Budweiser beer. There must have been a U.S. military facility nearby, as there were several *ajumonies* (middle-aged women) wandering up and down the beach with ice coolers full of cans of Bud. Funny how the black market in Korea selling American PX and commissary (U.S. military department stores and grocery markets) goods gave employment to so many Korean people back in those days.

Don in his American Flag Speedo at Daejeon Beach.

We also hung out with a couple of Australian guys we met on the beach. One of them made a funny comment that I've remembered all these years and repeat upon occasion to the students in my history classes at our local community college.

"You know, we're the lucky ones compared to you Americans," one Australian said.

"Oh, yeah, why is that?" I asked.

"Because we got the prisoners while you got the Puritans. The prisoners knew how to have fun while the Puritans—not so much."

"True enough," I said, and we all guffawed. On Sunday Jack, Ginger, Eric and I returned to Cheongju together.

The K-35s had all been warned to be careful when returning to Cheongju after the practice teaching, as there were several towns in Korea with names similar to Cheongju. Monday morning came and Tim Leelanau, the trainee who spoke Korean with an Ethiopian accent, didn't appear for the morning classes. Finally on Wednesday, a call came from the Peace Corps office in Seoul letting Don Kalamo know that Tim had ended up in Jeonju, Jeollabuk-do (North Jeolla Province). Local police found him wandering around the town, picked him up, and called the Peace Corps office in Seoul. Peace Corps asked them to put him on a bus to Cheongju, Chungchunbuk-do, which they did. Tim showed up Wednesday afternoon.

We had an emergency staff meeting and voted to terminate Tim's training. He was sent up to Seoul where he demanded to be allowed to visit the Peace Corps Headquarters in Washington, D.C. to argue for his reinstatement. A few weeks later, the Peace Corps Korea Director, Jon Kalkaska, told me that Tim had met with the Peace Corps psychologist in Washington, D.C. The shrink told Jon that we had done Tim a big favor by sending him back to the States because he had some major psychological issues he needed to deal with. Had he stayed in Korea, Jon was told, Tim's mental problems would most likely have become more serious. This was supposedly the first time a trainee had ever been sent home from a training program since the trainings started in Korea beginning with our K-23 group. Many of his fellow K-35s were up in arms in solidarity with him after we sent him home. They obviously had more group spirit than us K-23s had demonstrated. Many of them were angry at all of us staff members for a few days or even a week or two. They got over it, but it was awkward for a while. Back in the winter of 1972, the staff of the K-25 group had wanted to terminate Bill Comb and send him back to the States, but my letter had helped him talk his way into being allowed to stay. Later, of course, I was sorry I had written in his favor, and I think Bill, Peace Corps Korea, and the Republic of South Korea probably would have been better off had he been sent back too. Obviously, I had been one of those who voted to send Tim packing.

Don drinking coffee with Bill Tuscola and Ed Harper.

Over the course of the training program I was spending more and more time with Bill Tuscola and Ed Harper. They both spoke Korean much better than I did, which was par for the course, and both had a great appreciation for Korean culture. Ed later told me that they also enjoyed my company because of my very positive attitude toward Korea, her people, and her culture. I enjoyed being with them for the same reason.

Bill was an amazing artist, and he'd sit sometimes doing pencil drawings. In a tearoom or restaurant his pictures would often get "oohs and ahhhhs" from the waitresses. He would also do calligraphy, writing beautiful Chinese characters. When I drew Chinese characters, it looked like some elementary school kid trying his hand, but Bill's were works of art. Korean men sitting around in tearooms would often notice his work and compliment him on his level of accomplishment. It was always fun to be with Bill.

Ed was fun to be around too. He had a great sense of humor, and his timing was impeccable. Wait a minute, here it comes, and then "Bam!" the punch line. In addition, you never knew if he was making stuff up or if these funny things that he said happened to him had really happened.

One joke he told was that one afternoon he had walked into class at the university where he taught in Seoul, and there was only one student, a female, sitting in the classroom. He asked her where all the students were, and she answered, "They all went to see the crass erection (class election)."

A second joke he told on another night was that the past winter when he had gone home on his leave after his first two years of service, he and his family went to a Chinese restaurant. His father said to the young Chinese man who was their waiter, "What is your specialty?" The waiter didn't understand, and Ed's father did what most Americans do when someone whose first language isn't English doesn't understand—he spoke louder. "WHAT IS YOUR SPECIALTY? SPECIALTY!" "Oh, yes, specialty," the waiter responded and left the room. He returned a few minutes later with a tray and on it was a teapot and several tea bowls. The waiter proclaimed, "Special Tea!"

One night at the end of the K-35 training when we were all in Seoul and sitting at a bar, Ed walked in and swore he was followed by a Korean man who was trying to "English conversation" with him.

"Hello, may I English conversation with you?" the man asked. Ed walked faster, but the man followed.

"Hello! I am sorry to meet you," the man exclaimed.

"Yes, I am sorry to meet you, too," Ed replied.

"Are you an American?"

"No, I'm a Russian."

"Oh, you must be pushing my leg," the eager English conversationer replied to Ed. We all cracked up as we always did at Ed's jokes. Ever since hearing this last line in Ed's joke, like so many others from our Peace Corps days it has become one of my favorite go-to lines, "Oh, you must be pushing my leg!"

On still another occasion Ed started with the same scenario, a guy was following him trying to English conversation, but the man began with, "Hello, you must be Peace Craps?" This is a line that I also use all the time when I'm around fellow Returned Peace Corps Volunteers. When I see them I say, "Hello, you must be Peace Craps?"

Whenever any of us volunteers rode on public transport, we were often accosted by people who wanted to practice their English, especially in Seoul. In the capital learning English was like a religion. Consequently, we always read something when traveling on buses and subways. Even when standing I'd hook my wrist through one of the rings hanging from the ceiling of buses and subway cars and read while bouncing up and down. Also, I tried never to make eye contact with anyone, unless I saw a cute young lady, of course. If you made eye contact, especially with men, they often would try to begin English conversationing with you. "Always read and make no eye contact." That was the Peace Corps mantra.

When we did make eye contact and reluctantly did get into a conversation, it almost always seemed like the same ten questions would be asked. We often joked that we should print up cards with those ten answers written on them so that we could just hand one to each conversationer and walk away.

---

1. Yes, I'm an American.
2. No, I am not a soldier.
3. I teach English at a middle school.
4. No, I am not married.
5. I am twenty-four years old.

TURN OVER

Of course, not only English learning but education in general was like a religion to most Koreans. I believe that a lot of the drive for education in Korea comes from Confucianism. Many foreigners in the late 1800s and early 1900s said that Korea was more Confucian than China was, and this carried over into the late twentieth century and even into the twenty-first century. It is manifested in this tremendous love for and drive for education. It showed up in how all families pushed their children to study hard. It did not, though, always extend to the provincial-level English teachers. As noted before, many of the local English teachers in Mukho often skipped my evening English classes when I had them. On the other hand, after Peace Corps, when I taught English in the evening adult education program at the Hankuk University of Foreign Studies, the adult students' dedication and determination were incredible. The semester lasted for six months. We had classes five nights a week for three hours each night from 6:30 to 9:30 p.m. At the end of each semester that I taught, it amazed me how many of the adult students, all middle-aged men, all with full-time jobs five and a half days a week, probably all with wives and children, got perfect attendance certificates. I find it hard to imagine adult Americans studying five nights a week for three hours each night in a six-month-long program learning a foreign language and never missing any classes. That was the level of drive to learn English in much of Korea among middle-level management types. Learning English usually meant that they would be rewarded with a promotion. Without good English skills, they were much less likely to advance in their chosen career field.

As the hot, muggy summer dragged on in Cheongju, my downward spiral of overdrinking and partying had reached rock bottom. Also, by this point in time, I was getting even more tired of the training program and tired of Peace Corps in general. What I had loved most about my three years of Peace Corps experience before this training program was the individuality of it all. My experience was just that—"MY" experience. I carved out my own way without any help or interference from the Peace Corps office and bureaucracy in Seoul. There was far too much help and interference involved in the training program for my blood. Also, I thought there were too many chiefs and not enough Indians. There were thirty-nine trainees and twenty-four training staff members. How many trainers does it take to screw in a light bulb? There just wasn't enough work for the nine TESOL trainers we had. Most days we only did TESOL instruction in the afternoon, and often eight out of the nine of us just sat around. I was bored and looking forward to getting out on my own. Even with my extra activity of helping to teach taekwondo every weekday evening, there just wasn't enough to do on a daily basis and far too much free time. I needed more structure in my life. I got it in spades shortly after leaving Peace Corps when I started teaching at two different places around Seoul with seven hours of instruction a day and several hours of commuting on mass transit between my abode and the two jobs. By the end of the K-35 training, I was also looking forward to being an individual totally on my own. As with the end of high school and college it was all about the future for me— no looking back. I was chomping at the bit to be on my own, free of Peace

Corps and its bureaucratic nonsense. I wanted to run my own life. In addition, I could see that being around all these Americans during the training program had had a debilitating effect on me. I needed to be alone again. I needed to figure out what I really wanted to do with the rest of my life. *"Is there life after Peace Corps?"* I wondered, but I knew I had to get away from this training program lifestyle in order to find out.

On a weekend near the end of training, Ed invited me and three or four of the K-35s to go with him to his original Peace Corps site of Nonsan. Nonsan is in Chungcheongnam-do (South Chungcheong Province) and is about 80 kilometers away from Cheongju. We got to Nonsan and met Mr. Kim, Ki-young, Ed's former co-teacher. He was a trip. Like Mr. Lee in Mukho, Mr. Kim had served with the American forces during his military service as a KATUSA (Korean Augmentation To the United States Army). He put "gotta" into almost every sentence he constructed in English. He said things like, "We gotta cross that bridge. Then we gotta follow that trail over there." By the end of the day, we were all about to "gotta" go crazy. He reminded me of my high school neighbor Linda with her "OK?" fixation.

The highlight of the trip was a visit to Kwahchok-sa (Kwahchok Buddhist Temple) and its famous standing Buddha, carved from stone around the year 1000 CE. The Unjin-miruk (Standing Stone Future Buddha) is about six meters high and looks like the "cone heads" from the Saturday Night Live skit with a mortarboard hat atop it and with large hands crossed over its chest. It was raining the whole day, and we were running in and out from under the eaves of the temple buildings. At one point we were on top of a hill under a pavilion watching the rain when Mr. Kim announced, "Rain gotta stop, we gotta go." On cue and as if it had been a pronouncement from the "Buddha of Fractured English" the rain stopped. Then the sun came out, brightened our path and enlightened our way.

On our last Friday in Cheongju, we planned a presentation to the owner of the taekwondo *dojang* where Mr. Park, Yong-hwa and I had taught this martial art for most of the weeknights during the past three months. We all pitched in funds to purchase a large wall clock with a plaque stating that this was from the K-35 Peace Corps Training group. I had to do the presentation and give a speech, which made me quite nervous, and I asked Ed to help me write it because I knew his Korean was much better than mine. He was most gracious and helped me elevate my language to the proper level of formality. The presentation went as planned, and a group commemorative photo was taken.

Group photo of K-35 taekwondo class.

In early September during the last week of training, the K-35s were sent out on their site visits to spend three or four days with a volunteer at his/her town and school. Schools had already started their fall semester, and the K-35s were given instructions on how to get to their assigned PCV's town.

At the end of the K-35 training, we all went up to Seoul for the K-35 formal swearing-in ceremony. After the ceremony, they dispersed with their principals and co-teachers to begin their Peace Corps assignments. Bill, Ed, Gail, Joe, all the other trainers, and I had done the best we could to train the K-35s well and give them the language, cross-cultural, and TESOL skills they would need to have a successful and satisfactory PC experience.

Even with spending many weekends in spring semester with other "East Coast prop set" volunteers and with all the carousing done during the K-35 training program, I still managed to keep up my book reading campaign. One of the most interesting books I read was *The Living Reed,* by Pearl S. Buck. This novel follows four generations of an aristocratic Korean family from 1881 to 1945. The only other book by Pearl S. Buck that I had read before this was, of course, *The Good Earth.* (Pearl S. Buck won the Pulitzer Prize in 1932 for *The Good Earth,* and in 1938 she won the Nobel Prize in Literature for the body of her work up to that point in her career. She was the first American woman to win the Nobel Prize in Literature.) Another interesting book that I read during this period was *Written in the Stars: The Story of Suki,* by Erna Ingeborg Moen. When I began working for the Pearl S. Buck Foundation in 1979, I learned that Erna Ingeborg Moen was the wife of the first Resident Director of PSBF's Korea Branch.

After the K-35s were sworn in and left Seoul, I began filling out my separation from Peace Corps paperwork. I asked for my settling-back-into-the-U.S. allowance, which had been set aside monthly by PC during my more than three years of service, to be given to me in Korea rather than sent to my U.S. home address. In addition, I asked for a check in place of the plane ticket to my home of record. I had to do the three poops to check for any parasites, as I had done before going home the previous summer on home leave, as well as the parting physical exam by the Peace Corps doctor.

During my last full week as a volunteer, on Tuesday, September 30, I got my last inoculations paid for by the U.S. Government—one last gamma globulin, after which I ran up and down the stairs one final time at the Korea Educational Association Building as per the usual; one last cholera vaccine; and a smallpox revaccination all given by Dr. Chu, Un-bong.

Ed, Bill, Joe, and I met with Gail one last time at a bar in Myeong-dong just before she left for Thailand. She suggested again that maybe I'd like to accompany her, but I told her I was about to start teaching GIs at U.S. military facilities north of Seoul and was looking forward to getting started.

The last Sunday before ending my volunteer service, Ed, Bill, three or four other volunteers, and I met on the campus of Sogang University, where Bill taught, to play football. Sogang University is a Catholic university in Seoul near both Yonsei University and Ewha Womans University. (This is the official spelling of the university.) We had been playing for quite a while when an American priest sauntered by. He stopped and talked to us for a few minutes, and as he turned to continue on his way he said, "Have a nice day." All of us gave some comment in return, and I said what had become one of my stock replies when someone was leaving.

"Be good!"

"What else can he be, he's a priest?" Ed and Bill said.

"Yes, I guess that's true," I replied. Everyone chuckled, and we went on with our game.

During my PSBF years in the 1980s, I got to know the former priest, Ken Killoren, who had founded Sogang University. Ken was one of the kindest, gentlest, and most interesting men I have ever had the pleasure of meeting in my life.

He was a young Jesuit priest when he was sent to Korea after the Korean War in 1955. The Society of Jesus, whose members are known as Jesuits, sent him to Seoul with $100,000 at his disposal and orders to purchase land and start a Catholic institution of higher learning. Ken told me that there were days when he'd walk out of his lodging place and see poor children begging on the streets, and he wanted to take all of the money out of the bank and give it to these poor children. But then he told himself over and over that if he built the university, in the long run it would help far more people and be of much greater assistance to the Republic of Korea. He bought the land, had the first building built, and opened the school in 1960. He was also the first president of the university.

When I met him in the mid-1980s, he had just become the director of International Human Assistance Programs (IHAP), an American nonprofit which, among other things, had a program to help adult Amerasians (mixed-heritage individuals fathered and abandoned by Americans in Asia) while the Pearl S. Buck Foundation mostly helped the preschool and school-aged Amerasian children. After Ken told me about founding Sogang University, one of the first questions I asked him was about the large square, not round, chimney on campus which had a stairway that wrapped around it and went all the way up to the top.

"Why is there a stairway around the chimney?" I asked.

"Because I thought if it ever needed to have repair work done on it, the stairway would make it easier."

"I suppose that makes sense."

"That and the chimney just looked so desolate all by itself," he told me.

"Well, we Peace Corps Volunteers called it the stairway to heaven." Ken got a kick out of that.

After a few years as the president of Sogang, Ken left the priesthood and later back in the States married a Korean lady who had graduated a few years earlier from Sogang. They returned to Korea, and she ended up being more famous than he was as she set up a company with its office in the Chosun Hotel to assist businessmen with any administrative work they needed and/or to organize meetings, conferences, or get-togethers of any kind.

I asked Ken once if he ever wondered where he might be had he stayed in the priesthood. He told me that he knew right where he would have been, and that was in the Vatican City. He had been informed that he would have been posted to the Vatican for the rest of his career after leaving Sogang. He decided that wasn't how he wanted to spend the rest of his life, and so he left the priesthood.

In the mid-1980s at Sogang University they had large photographs of all the past presidents on the wall of the main campus building, except for Ken's. As he told me about this, I could see he was hurt, and I could feel his pain. Ken, who had founded Sogang and who had served as its first president, was not acknowledged at all evidently because he had left the priesthood. This seemed very petty to me. Sure, he had left the priesthood, but he still deserved recognition for a job well done. I have since heard that his picture was finally hung on the wall of the main campus building, and I was pleased to hear this.

Ken and I were both members of the Seoul Rotary Club. The Seoul Rotary Club was founded in 1927 as the first Rotary Club in Korea. It is the oldest club in Korea and the only English-language club. When Ken and I were members there were more than a dozen different nationalities represented even though the majority of members were Korean. Ken and I often sat together at the meetings and at parties. In addition, we were both members of the Korean Association of Voluntary Agencies (KAVA). KAVA was made up of members from all the foreign religious and secular nonprofit social welfare agencies in Korea. I was the Chairman of KAVA during the years Ken was the Director of IHAP and at that time Ken served as the KAVA newsletter editor. Even after he stepped down from being director of IHAP, Ken continued to be the editor for the KAVA newsletter. Several times I visited him at his home on the back part of the campus of Yonsei University. He and his wife rented one of the many homes on the campus, which were mostly used by faculty. (Ken's home or one near his was where Horace and Dick Underwood's mother, who'd graduated from Albion College, was murdered in 1949 by Communist terrorists.) I'd drop off everything for inclusion in the newsletter on one day, and then when he finished organizing it, I'd swing back by to pick up the finished product. Ken always invited me in, and we'd drink a beer and talk. I relished these afternoons talking with him. On one of the visits he showed me portrait pictures taken of him, his wife, and their two lovely high school-aged daughters. He had two eight-by-ten photographs of all four of them together; one was surrounded by an oval mat, and the other one by a rectangular mat. He handed both of them to me and asked which one I liked better. I looked at them both, and the photographs looked very similar, so I glanced back and forth checking each person's head, eye, and hand positions. I looked up at Ken quizzically.

"Ken? They are both the same," I stated.

"I've asked many people which one they liked better, and they all picked one or the other. You are the first one to realize the pictures are the same," he said while laughing.

"Trying to trick me, eh? It is funny because I'll bet most people concentrate on the differently shaped mats and are actually telling you which shape mat, oval or rectangle, that they liked best."

"Yes, but you're pretty sharp to have ignored that and noticed it's the same photo."

We finished our football game on Sogang University's campus on this, my last full day as a Peace Corps Volunteer, and headed off to a restaurant for dinner. The next morning, I walked into the Peace Corps office up to the seventh floor to finish my withdrawal from the Corps. I sang to the tune of the U.S. Marine Corps Hymn:

> From the halls of Ouagadougou
> To the shores of the Yellow Sea
> We will serve to make the world better
> On all the continents and seas
> (Marine Corps lyrics author unknown, music composed by Jacques
> Offenbach from the opera "Genevieve de Brabant.")

As stated earlier, I knew I needed to get away from hanging around and drinking with Peace Corps volunteers every night. I needed to clear my head and reset my moral compass, which had gotten stuck in the wrong direction. It took some time, and I did some backsliding, but again as Nat King Cole sang, I intended to "straighten up and fly right." ("Straighten Up And Fly Right," written by Nat King Cole and Irving Mills, performed by the Nat King Cole Trio.) Past Peace Corps Korea Director Jim Wixom had done so, and so would I. I knew also that I would now be an independent human being, no longer under the wing of Uncle Sam. I would no longer be like a soldier, "Government Issued." Now, if I got sick, it would be up to me and my own resources. If I had any problems of any kind, it would be my problem and not Peace Corps' or the United States Government's problem. But I also didn't have to follow any of their rules anymore, not that I always did anyway. Nor would I have to fill out any more of their damn forms.

I did fill out all the appropriate separation from Peace Corps papers in triplicate and signed on all the dotted lines. Being a government agency, there were lots of dotted lines to sign. I crossed all the "i's" and dotted all the "t's"—or however that saying goes. I regained control of my own passport. I was no longer under U.S. Government control and protection. I was my own man. As I walked out of the Peace Corps office and towards the elevator to take me down to street level and out to the always crowded and exciting streets of Seoul, I began singing The Who's song, "I'm Free:"

I'm free, I am free
And freedom tastes of reality.
("I'm Free," written by Pete Townshend, performed by The Who.)

The elevator door opened, and I stepped in, still not knowing what I wanted to do when I grew up. What I did know was that I had already achieved the main goal that I had set for myself when I was just a young downriver Detroit kid growing up in Allen Park, Michigan. I had lived in an exotic foreign country. I had learned a foreign language and had intimately studied another culture. More than that, I had volunteered to help my country and the world by doing my small part to make our planet a better place to live. I knew that, though the world had not changed all that much, there had been a huge change within me. There had been an inextricable change in me. I could never go back to being just an Allen Parker, a Detroiter, just a Michigander, or even just an American. I was now a global villager. Like Diogenes, the ancient Greek philosopher, and Socrates both said, "I am a citizen of the world." That was the way I now felt. In addition, I knew again that this day too—the end of my Peace Corps service—was the first day of the rest of my life.

After Peace Corps and Later Trips to Korea

Warts and all, that was me! In my defense, I was so young then, only twenty-one when I entered Peace Corps and only twenty-four when I left. At twenty-four, I was still a little, or maybe even a lot, wet behind the ears, and I still had no idea what I wanted to do with the rest of my life—or as I often said then and still say now upon occasion, "When I grow up." I knew I didn't want to go back to Detroit or the U.S. yet. I had no marketable skills in the States. If I had listened to my father and gotten a teaching certificate, I could have gone back to Detroit and taught high school history. But I had no desire to do that anyway. Sometimes I now think I should have gone right to grad school and gotten a master's degree in history. Then I could have gotten a job at a community college and taught history as I am doing now. Or I could have continued and gotten a PhD in history and taught at a community college or university. But I don't think I would have been happy spending decades teaching. Also, I still had not learned as much about Korea as I wanted to know. Another problem was that even after Albion and three years of Peace Corps, I still didn't have enough confidence in myself to go to grad school. I really didn't think I was smart enough. It's funny looking back now with my three master's degrees and remembering how I thought I wasn't capable of post-graduate study. *"Confidence, man. You needed to get up your confidence!"*

So I did the easy thing. I stayed in Korea because there I had a marketable skill, thanks to Peace Corps. I could "Teach English to Speakers of Other Languages" (TESOL). First, I got a job teaching in the mornings on U.S. Army bases. My employer was the University of Hawaii Programs in Korea. The paychecks actually came from the University of Hawaii. I started teaching ESL (English as a Second Language) to mostly Puerto Rican, but also some Korean-born, U.S. soldiers who had immigrated to the U.S. and then joined the army. In our army these Koreans could get their U.S. citizenship faster, have a steady paying job, make a lot of extra cash on the black market in Korea, improve their English language ability, possibly learn a skill, and in addition, according to many of them, the U.S. Army basic training was a piece of cake compared to the Korean military training that they had all been through before immigrating to America. My favorite part about teaching classes with Koreans and Puerto Ricans together was to teach dialogues and have one Korean student speak part A and a Puerto Rican student speak part B or vice versa. The Puerto Rican students spoke English as they did Spanish—very fast. They spoke a mile a minute, and the Koreans couldn't follow. My Korean students got mad and said, "Slow down, you speak too fast." Then the Korean did his part and spoke very, very slowly, carefully enunciating every word and often stopping to contemplate the next word. The Puerto Rican student would get anxious and say, "Hurry up! Speak faster, you talk too slow. Let's go." I would sit there laughing and say, "OK, let's be patient with each other." Again, my goal was to force them to listen to each other and learn how to understand English spoken by people who didn't speak it the way they did. Listening skills are so very important in language learning.

Later I got into teaching GED (General Educational Development) test preparation classes to GIs who didn't have a high school diploma. In the 1970s the economy was doing well in the U.S., and the army couldn't get enough high school grad recruits. So they let them in without a high school diploma, but if they didn't pass the GED tests before their initial two-year stint was up, they were drummed out. I taught English grammar, reading skills, and mathematics using individualized methods.

Over the two years that I stayed in Korea after Peace Corps, I taught at several different U.S. Army bases north of Seoul in the two corridors heading from Seoul toward North Korea. On the western corridor (Munsan to Panmunjom) I taught off and on at Camp Howse, or as Ed Harper called it "Camp Howitzer" and Camp East Edwards. In 1976 when the North Korean guards at Panmunjom murdered two American captains who were supervising a South Korean team of workers trimming a tree, some of my East Edwards students were among those who marched in full military gear into the DMZ and into the Truce Village (even though this was against the truce provisions) in order to cut down the tree that was at the center of this tragic event. While this was going on, classes were suspended, and it was the only time in all my years spent in Korea that I was actually worried that a war might break out. On the eastern corridor (Ouijungbu to Dongducheon) I taught sometimes at Camp Red Cloud, at Camp Casey, or at Camp East Casey. Every ten weeks I would finish at one base and then usually start the next week at another.

Shortly after I started teaching for the University of Hawaii programs, I ran into Byron Redford, whom I had visited during our K-23 training for practice teaching. He asked if I wanted to take over his afternoon freshman English class and his evening Adult Education Program position, both at the Hankuk University of Foreign Studies (Waedae) in Seoul. I did.

It wasn't too long after this that I saw Kim, Mi-yun, who later became my first wife, "across a crowded room." I was sitting in the Maeum Gwa Maeum (Heart to Heart) coffee shop in Myeong-dong one Saturday evening when she caught my eye. It was very crowded that evening, and as always at crowded coffee shops or tearooms the tearoom ladies would seat people wherever there was an empty seat. Often you'd sit with people you didn't know. The man sitting next to Mi-yun got up and left, so I knew that she wasn't on a date with him. I quickly ran over and sat next to her, striking up a conversation immediately after sitting down. Somehow I "knew I'd see her again and again." ("Some Enchanted Evening," written by Oscar Hammerstein II, composed by Richard Rogers.)

I was living in Huam-dong just outside the gate of Camp Coiner where the University of Hawaii office was located. This was the same area of Seoul where Gail and Sally had rented their place. Camp Coiner was attached to the north side of Yongsan, the U.S. 8th Army and United Nations Headquarters in Seoul. Every day I left the little upper flat I lived in before 6:00 am. I taught from 8:00 a.m. to noon at one of the army bases. During the first fall semester I taught a one-hour regular class twice a week at the Hankuk University of Foreign Studies (Waedae) in mid-afternoon and from 6:30 to 9:30 p.m. Mondays through Fridays in Waedae's Adult Education Program. Even after the fall semester when I stopped teaching the regular university class, I was teaching seven hours each day, and I spent from five to six hours each day on public transportation including taxis, city buses, inter-city buses, and the subway. This was the opposite of my schedule with the K-35 training program. I enjoyed being this busy as opposed to being bored while working as a Peace Corps trainer. Besides I was young then, and I could handle this enormously busy schedule.

Another reason that I didn't go to grad school right after Peace Corps was that I had very little money. At the end of Peace Corps, I had about $5,000 with the readjustment allowance and the value of return airfare to the U.S., but I still owed $3,000 in student loans, which had been deferred during my volunteer service. So after Peace Corps my net worth, had I returned to the U.S., might have been around a thousand dollars in total. I had no car and no other tangible assets. It was hardly enough to easily fund grad school, and I still didn't have much confidence in my intellectual abilities anyway.

* * * * *

If you read all the chapters in this book and didn't just skip to the postscript, you know that music has always been an important part of my life. My father often walked around singing, and I've always done the same. When I hear Frank Sinatra I think of my father because he always spoke of Sinatra's great enunciation and delivery. So many other artists and their songs remind me of old friends. Johnny Horton and especially his song "The Battle of New Orleans" remind me of my old friend, Joe Kercheval. Joe had a copy of the *Johnny Horton Makes History* album, and we played the heck out of it. Another song that I sing every Christmas also reminds me of Joe. The song is titled "Ol' Fatso" with the great refrain "Don't care who you are Ol' Fatso, get those reindeer off the roof." ("Ol' Fatso," sung by Augie Rios.) Joe had this song on a forty-five rpm record, and we'd play it over and over every Christmas season. Many early Beatles songs also remind me of Joe and our bike hikes up to the Sears store on the corner of South-field and Dix to buy the newest Beatles albums when they first came out. The Moody Blues' "Days of Future Passed" reminds me of another high school friend, Willy Bender. In the summer of 1969, between our freshman and sophomore years, Willy came over just after I returned home for summer vacation from Albion. He was all excited about a new album he wanted to share. Willy was attending Henry Ford Community College in Dearborn, Michigan. In one of Willy's classes the professor had them listen to and discuss "Days of Future Passed." Fender-Bender, as we called Willy, and I sat and listened to this album several times. He was right to have been excited about this seminal work, and after listening to it with him I ran right out and bought a copy of my own. Simon and Garfunkel's "Bridge Over Troubled Water" album reminds me of Sara Swift, Kathy Pinckney, and John Sebewaing and the Simon and Garfunkel concert at Detroit's Cobo Hall that we attended together. *The Richard Harris Love Album,* with songs written mostly by Jimmy Webb, reminds me of my sophomore year roommate Matt Engadine and also Sara Swift. Matt and I often played this album when I had Sara and he had his girlfriend visiting in our room. After Sara broke up with me, I often walked around campus singing the song "Didn't We" with its poignant lyrics:

> This time we almost sang our song in tune
> Didn't we, girl?
> ("Didn't We," written by Jimmy L. Webb, performed by Richard Harris.)

Donovan songs bring back memories of Kathy Pinckney and the Donovan concert we attended together at Eastern Michigan University during our senior year of college. In addition, I especially remember Kathy when I listen to the double album of Donovan's children's songs, *HMS Donovan,* that she gave to me. John

Sebastian songs remind me of Otto Peach because we attended the Sebastian concert in Kresge Gymnasium at Albion College together in 1972. John Denver's music reminds me of Charlie Sarnia because near the end of our Peace Corps volunteering days, Charlie became a huge John Denver fan and played cassettes of Denver's songs over and over. Lastly, whenever I hear any of the songs from George Harrison's *All Things Must Pass* album, I'm reminded of Linda Boyne and that beautiful summer of romance in 1974. She borrowed this album from me a couple of weeks before I left to return to Korea for my third and final year of volunteering. She told me that she would listen to it a few times and return it to my parents, which she did after I had gone back to Mukho. I still have this album in my collection as well as all of the others mentioned above. Once in a while I will pull one of these out, play it, and remember the days of my youth and those friends of old. Memories CAN be beautiful!

*　*　*　*　*　*

After a couple of years of teaching at the Hankuk University of Foreign Studies and at U.S. Army bases, I finally returned to Detroit. I had gotten married to Mi-yun a little over a year after finishing Peace Corps. When my Grandmother Emma passed away in the spring of 1977, I came home by myself for the funeral. My Aunt Ruth, who owned the house that Grandma Emma and my step-grandfather Lyman had been living in, told me that Mi-yun and I could stay there rent-free for as long as we liked. Lyman was moving out to Stockton, California, to be with his daughter. This seemed too good to pass up, so Mi-yun and I moved to East Detroit, Michigan, in the fall of 1977, and I worked again as a manager of a United Shirt Distributors store while looking for "an executive position, but no matter how smooth I talked they wouldn't listen." ("Workin' At the Car Wash Blues," written and performed by Jim Croce.) I thought maybe I would get hired by General Motors to manage their Korea operations since I spoke Korean. If not GM, then certainly some other U.S. multinational company with operations in Korea would want to hire me. As that pipe dream faded, I decided to go to grad school, as I saw no other way to get back overseas, and that's what I desired more than anything. I still wasn't so sure I could handle grad school-level work, but I applied to the School for International Training (SIT) in Brattleboro, Vermont. Other Peace Corps buddies I knew had gone there, including Ed Harper, and I thought, *"What the heck? I'll give it that ol' high school try."* One of the most appealing parts of the SIT degree program was that it consisted of only six months of studying on campus. I was accepted, I went, I saw, I conquered, and the rest is history or rather my story. I earned a Master's in International Administration (MIA) degree geared toward working with nonprofit social welfare organizations from this fine institution of higher learning, the School for International Training.

Right out of SIT I was hired by the Pearl S. Buck Foundation (PSBF) to be the Resident Director of their Korea Branch. I couldn't have wished for a more perfect job. PSBF assisted fatherless Amerasian children. We were helping those often destitute children who had been abandoned by their U.S. military fathers and who were being raised by their Korean mothers or other family members. I was a civil rights advocate. I was semi-famous with my name and photo often appearing in Korean and even some American publications. On our bookshelf today is a large binder labeled "Don's Fifteen Minutes of Fame" filled with many of those articles and photos from my PSBF days as well as a second smaller one labeled "Don's Fifteen Minutes of Fame, Volume II" with more recent accolades. In all of the articles, my favorite quote is from an article entitled "Are You Racist?" which appeared in the "Here and There" column of the *Korea Herald* newspaper on Wednesday July 27, 1988. It was written by Simon Warner, a British journalist who was a *Korea Herald* reporter. He wrote:

> Racism is a curse, a blight on humanity, an invisible enemy within the citadels of our hearts; it is also one of the few things that is invidious and potent enough to enrage the mild-mannered Donald R. Haffner.
> There is an iron fist inside his velvet glove, a hardness beneath the soft exterior.

When he interviewed me for the article, I talked to him about how it bothered me when Americans came to Korea and made statements like, "Korea is the most racist country in the world."I couldn't help thinking, *"Ach, mein GOTT in himmel!"* (Oh! My GOD in heaven!). I would argue that Koreans were doing very well in coping with a phenomenon they had never known in their history until the middle of the twentieth century, i.e. children fathered by non-Asians. Among other things I would ask these pompous Americans, "How long was it before we in the U.S. allowed Black Americans to play professional baseball?" I would then explain that in the 1980s there was already a first-generation Amerasian playing professional baseball in Korea. That usually quieted down the room. I spent nine and a half years as the Pearl S. Buck Foundation's Resident Director in Korea from 1979 to 1988 and left after having helped more than five hundred Amerasians immigrate to the U.S. starting when the U.S. Congress passed the Amerasian Immigration Bill in 1982. (Many other wonderful people and organizations were also involved in assisting in this very gratifying aspect of my work.) By 1988, most of the Amerasians who wanted to immigrate to the U.S. had already left. I felt that I had to an extent worked myself out of a job, and after helping to find a Korean gentleman to replace me, I returned to the U.S. In fact, I left just a few days after the Simon Warner article appeared in the *Korea Herald.*

During the almost ten years that I served as the PSBF/Korea Branch Director, my family and I came back to the States four times. Every time I would spend a week at PSBF's headquarters near Perkasie, Pennsylvania (my wife and son would then meet me in Detroit). The headquarters was located at Green Hills Farm, Pearl S. Buck's home, which was, and still is, a National Historic Monument. I always toured her home at least once each time I visited. I had read a couple of dozen or more of Pearl's books, and I was pretty much the "in-house specialist" on her writings and her life. Various things in her home and on the grounds reminded me of passages or events in her writings or even the titles of her books. In Pearl's study was a framed work of calligraphy on the wall with four Chinese characters, which translate as, "All under heaven are one family." In Korean the four characters are pronounced, *"Chun Ha Il Ga."* One of Pearl's books is titled *All Under Heaven.* A few years after leaving Korea, I wrote a song by that title. I have not recorded this song yet, but the lyrics go as follows:

All Under Heaven

> Black, yellow, brown, red and white
> There's no reason for us to fight
> No color's wrong no color's right
> All equal in God's sight
>
> (First Chorus)
> All under heaven are one family
> That's what she said to me
> See God's design from the first
> Intermarry and give birth
> To lovely children so brave and free
> All under heaven are one family

Yellow, brown, red, white and black
It's just a matter of fact
Makes no difference where you're at
What matters is how we act

Brown, red, white, black and yellow
It all depends on where they settled
No color's bad all are mellow
Like shades of flowers in a meadow

> (Second Chorus)
> All under heaven are one family
> Drink a toast to harmony
> No problem with what color your face
> There's no such thing as race
> We're all part of the human kind
> The only problem is in small minds

Red, white, black, yellow and brown
People walking on this ground
None are lost all are found
Let's all join hands in the round

White, black, yellow, brown and red
Have you heard a word I've said
When we die we're all dead
The answer's in all our heads

> (Repeat First Chorus)

Black, yellow, brown, red and white
There's no reason for us to fight....

During the last four years that I worked for PSBF, I studied for an MS in Education from the University of Southern California's U.S. military program on the Yongsan Base. I finished in the spring of 1988 just before I left Korea. After leaving PSBF, my family and I settled in Boston, Massachusetts, where I was hired as an Associate Dean at Middlesex Community College (MCC). I thought

I was set for life, but then instead it led to the most horrible period I've had the displeasure of living through.

This period began with my being laid off from my job at MCC in the summer of 1989 as Massachusetts went through a recession, and state funding for their community college system was cut drastically. Then, after moving back to Detroit in 1990, I became estranged from my first wife. She left Detroit in the late summer of 1990 and took our son with her to Los Angeles. After a year of separation from Otto in the late summer of 1991, I flew out to LA to save him. He was unhappy and wanted to be with me. His mother and I were still married at the time, and no divorce papers had been filed as yet. I knew that she was working at night and leaving him in their apartment alone. I flew out to LA, and after dark I went to the apartment and asked him if he wanted to come back to Detroit with me, which he did. I left a note for his mother, scooped him up, and brought him home. Upon returning to Detroit I immediately filed for divorce and got custody of him. The story of my rescuing him is portrayed in my song "Remember When."

Remember When

Driving down the road in Michigan
Hoping, praying, and wishing again
Wonder if I'll ever see my son and when
Driving down the road in Michigan

V.J. Day when she went away
Didn't have a single word to say
Took our son and went out to L.A.
Know she'll have the devil to pay

Hear my son's not doing well
Living in that California hell
Wish that I could just ring a bell
And bring him back to Michigan

(Chorus)
Remember when we were family
Lots of time then for revelry
You know I miss our camaraderie
Back when we were family

Leaves are changing, the trees on fire
In my heart there's a burning desire
Guess the pain won't get no higher
Till I'm roasting on my funeral pyre

Christmas season the time of joy
All I know is I miss my boy
He wants to come here for some Christmas cheer
She says maybe some time next year

Winds are howling, screaming by
Snows drifting real high
Spring is coming but I don't know why
Michigan winters they make me cry

> (Chorus)
> You remember when we were family
> We had time then for revelry
> I know you miss our camaraderie
> Wish that you were here with me

After a year I had to regain
My poor son's life back again
Got on that big jet airplane
Flew across our fruited plains

Knocked on the door and my son said, "Who's there?"
I said, "It's Daddy and I am here."
The door opened and we fell into tears
"Son, we'll make up for this long lost year."

He said, "Wait, we'll let mother know."
I said, "No, now we've got to go.
We don't want to see her put on a show
You know her temper will surely blow."

(Chorus)
Now that we are family
We'll have time again for revelry
Glad we've got our camaraderie
Now that you're back here with me

Driving down the road in Michigan
No more hoping and wishing again
Now my son and I together we can
Love every minute in Michigan

For most of the 1990s, I worked in retail management and taught ESL (English as a Second Language) to foreigners working in the Detroit area. Off and on over the decades since leaving Peace Corps, I have often taught ESL to keep up my TESOL (Teaching English to Speakers of Other Languages) skills. On my days off during the week I also worked as a substitute teacher at two local Lutheran high schools.

At one point in the early to mid-1990s, I got a call from an American non-profit social welfare agency doing food donation work in North Korea. They had gotten my name from Peace Corps, and they wanted to know if I was interested in going to North Korea for six months to work on their food distribution program to help feed the starving population in this Communist self-proclaimed paradise. I told the person on the phone that I was a single parent raising my middle school-aged son and couldn't go to North Korea. Even if I hadn't had Otto to think about, going to North Korea was not on my bucket list, and I probably would not have been interested anyway.

During this decade, I subscribed to the *Chronicle of Higher Education* and often applied for positions that looked interesting in their want ad section. One that I applied for in the spring of 1996, which looked very interesting to me, was with the Fulbright Commission in Korea. They were looking for a Director of Testing to oversee the ESL and GRE testing. I got a call from the Executive Director of the Fulbright Korea Branch, Dr. Jim Manistique. He told me that they were very interested in interviewing me. He mentioned there was some travel involved with the position, and I let him know right away that this would be a problem for me as I was a single parent with a teenaged son. He said they'd still like me to visit Korea for an interview. I asked Otto how he felt about maybe returning to Korea, and he was all for it. But this threw my parents into a tizzy. The last thing they wanted was for me, their only child, and Otto, their only grandchild, to take off overseas again. My Uncle Bob called me the night before I left for the interview and tried to get me to agree that I wouldn't take the job even if they ended up offering it to me. "Go for the interview," he said, "and enjoy the trip, but tell them you're not interested in the job." I assured him that there was only a slim chance that they'd offer me the job anyway as it entailed travel in-country, and I couldn't leave Otto alone.

I flew to Korea on September 22, 1996, and I was shocked by how much bigger Seoul had gotten since 1988 when I left after almost ten years with PSBF. The Seoul subway, which had opened its first line on August 15, 1974, was by 1988 already a huge system. (It is now, in 2016, the world's longest subway system by length and the second largest by number of stations after New York City's system.) I stayed for three nights and two full days at the Ambassador Hotel, which was an older hotel probably built in the 1960s and located at the south end of Myeong-dong, Seoul's famous shopping area. The first day I met Dr. Manistique and the other staff members, including Mrs. Paik, Mun-ja, their treasurer/bookkeeper. Before walking into her office, Dr. Manistique mentioned that she had previously worked for the Peace Corps. As we entered, Mrs. Paik looked up from her desk and said, "Aren't you the volunteer who used to sing all the time?" I laughed and said, "Yes, that would be me!" She had last seen me in 1975, and this was twenty-one years later, but she remembered me as the "always singing volunteer."

The job of Testing Director entailed visiting Gwangju, Daegu, and Busan and going to the USIS (United States Information Service) offices in each of these cities to monitor ESL and GRE testing there for a few days each month. I again informed Dr. Manistique that I probably could not do this because of my son.

All three nights that I was there I wandered around Myeong-dong, the big shopping area in downtown Seoul. One thing that caught my attention immediately was that there were blond-haired, blue-eyed youth (possibly they were blind—remember that story?) selling trinkets and things on the sidewalks. I listened to them speaking to each other and discovered that they were Russians. There were no Russians in South Korea during my Peace Corps days, but since the fall of the Soviet Union, with Vladivostok so close and Korea having such a vibrant economy, young Russians came to Seoul to hang out and try to make some money.

One reason that I was very happy to get away from America in the fall of 1996 was to escape from the ubiquitous song "Macarena." I couldn't stand that song. On the plane over to Korea I was thinking how nice it would be to not hear this song for a couple of days. Then the first night walking around Myeongdong it seemed that in every other store when the doors were opened by customers, the song "Macarena" came blaring out. Unfortunately, like Walt Disney said, "It's a small world"—sometimes too small for my liking! But then, who asked me anyway?

By the end of the second and last full day in Korea, Dr. Manistique said that they had also interviewed another Returned Peace Corps Volunteer (RPCV) who had likewise served in Korea. Jim told me that we were so similar in background and even personality that he had asked one of the other American Fulbright staff members if he saw any difference between the two of us. That staff member had answered, "Yes, Don wears suspenders." The other returned PCV was married with three kids and had no problem with the travel aspects of the position, as his wife was able to take care of the children. So they offered him the position. Dr. Manistique never told me the name of the other RPCV, I never asked, and I never bothered to try to find out later who he was. I returned home a little disappointed but also relieved.

In January of 1998, I finally found a job working for a nonprofit organization again when I was hired by Recording for the Blind & Dyslexic (RFB&D) as their Studio Director in charge of recording production for the Michigan Unit on Rochester Road in Troy, Michigan, a northern suburb of Detroit. We recorded textbooks for use by students who were blind or dyslexic. Again, I had a job that I fell in love with, I took pleasure in, and that gave me a sense of dignity and satisfaction while performing my duties. Even more importantly, I met my lovely wife, Carol, at RFB&D, as she was a volunteer reader there.

Carol and I started dating in the fall of 1998. She is a librarian, and in March of 2000 she invited me to attend a library conference in Washington, D.C. with her. As covered earlier, during my years of working with the Pearl S. Buck Foundation (PSBF) in Korea, I helped hundreds of Amerasians to immigrate to the United States. More than two dozen adult Amerasians with their families had immigrated to the Washington, D.C. area thanks to the help of the Organization of Korean American Women (OKAW) of Washington, D.C. I contacted the president of the club and asked if she could tell the Amerasians living in the greater D.C. area that I would like to meet with them. She set up a dinner meeting at a Korean restaurant near Alexandria, Virginia. Five Amerasians, their spouses, and the president of OKAW met Carol and me for dinner. We spoke mostly in Korean. I was happy to hear that they all had jobs and were doing well with their transition to life in America. The most gratifying part of my work with PSBF had been seeing the joy on the faces of the adult Amerasians when they were approved by the Immigration and Naturalization Service, and then even more so

Don and his wife Carol—to the left of him in back—and several Amerasians who live in the Washington, D.C. area.

when I would sometimes be with them at Seoul's Kimpo Airport when they were getting on their flights to immigrate to the United States. Most of the adult Amerasians were married to Korean, not fellow Amerasian, spouses and most had children of their own who were known as second-generation Amerasians. It was wonderful to meet several of them at this restaurant more than ten years after helping them leave Korea. I was filled with joy and a feeling of complete contentment. In the end, I believe I will feel that I gave more love than I took from this world in large part thanks to my work with helping Korean Amerasians.

During the years I worked for RFB&D (1998–2009), I was also an active board member and vice president of our Southeast Michigan (SEMI) Returned Peace Corps Volunteer group. Our President, Jeff Jackson, who had been a PCV in the Philippines, and his wife, Nati, had gone in 2000 to the Habitat for Humanity build in the Philippines. When they came back, they told me they would be going in 2001 to the next international build, which would be in Korea. "Don't you want to go?" they asked, and of course I did. So in August 2001, Jeff, Nati, and I flew together to the new and amazing Incheon Airport. Again I was shocked, first at how amazing this new airport was, and second at the amount of new construction between it and Seoul. There were six Habitat building sites: Paju, Taebaek, Asan, Daegu, Gunsan, and Jinju. We were assigned to the largest site at Asan with nineteen buildings running up the side of a hill and with four housing units in each of the buildings. Each building's rough walls and roof were already constructed, and we would be doing the finishing work.

The first night in Asan there was an opening ceremony in the brand-new auditorium of Hoseo University. Jeff and I went to the opening ceremony. We moved right up to the front row as if we owned the place and ended up sitting about twelve seats away from President Jimmy Carter and former First Lady Rosalynn.

For the week-long build we worked on building twelve. The first day we did drywall installation on the first floor, right side unit. Jeff and I, along with another guy from Michigan, David Trumbull, worked as one team with Nati supporting us. In another room of our apartment another team was also doing drywall. They were a team of four Koreans from Hoseo University. One man was a professor, and the other three were students—two guys and one gal. As we were working in our room, I listened to the conversation going on in Korean in the other room. Every little while, I'd start laughing. Jeff and David would look quizzically at me, and I'd translate some of what was being said by the Hoseo team members. I cracked up because the young female student was smarter than the two male students and the male professor put together. She ended up taking over their team because after not listening to her sage advice a couple of times they found that they had miscut the drywall. The three guys gave up the reins of control to her.

The next day Jeff, David, and I moved outdoors and were taught how to do the aluminum framing of all the doors and windows in the two-story structure. Again Jeff, David, and I worked as a team while the Korean students, their professor, and other students who had been working in the other three apartments were busy installing the aluminum siding.

Midway through the week there was to be a talent show, and I had volunteered to be one of the performers. I had a CD with the music to the song that I had written a couple of years earlier for my then girlfriend and now wife, Carol. She was born on Christmas Day, and the song I wrote for her is called "Christmas Carol"—clever, right? Its lyrics are:

Christmas Carol

When I see you there by the Christmas tree
With your dark eyes and hair, so glad you're close to me
Thank my lucky stars that you came my way
Cuz I thought you'd leave, never ever thought you'd stay

(Chorus)
Christmas Carol, Christmas Carol
Don't ever go away

With a little kiss, found the love I'd missed
Melt away the winter chill, oh I know you will
And though Christmas comes only once a year
Now that you're next to me every day I'll hear

Christmas carols, Christmas carols
Don't ever fade away

Christmas Carol, Christmas Carol
Don't ever go away

When the talent show day came, we returned to the state-of-the art Hoseo University auditorium. Preparations were still going on inside the auditorium, and there were several hundred of us volunteers standing outside in the summer heat and humidity waiting for them to open the doors. One young American lady, Diana Van Dyke, who had eaten dinner with several of us outside the hotel the night before and consequently knew I spoke Korean, asked if I could explain to the people manning the doors that she had to use the bathroom. I said, "Sure, follow me." We walked up to the door together, and the man inside opened it a crack. I explained that this nice lady needed to use the toilet, and he let us both in. I figured I'd use the men's room while I was inside in the nice air-conditioned building and sauntered up to the urinal. A minute later and before I had finished, two tall—at least taller than five-foot-eight me—young American guys in black suits with sunglasses on and ear plugs in one ear, walked up to the two urinals situated on either side of me. Outside we had all been talking and wondering if Jimmy and Rosalynn Carter would be in the audience, as they had been doing some traveling to the other build sites, but now I had the answer. These guys were obviously President Carter's Secret Service guys. I finished peeing and went to wash my hands before the young men finished. Then I went out into the lobby and told Diana that the Prez and Rosalynn were going to be attending. We stood by the windows and didn't go back outside, figuring until someone told us to leave we'd enjoy the cool temperature. As we looked out at all the other roasting volunteers, many were looking at us, and we could read their lips saying, "How'd you get in?"

When they finally opened the doors and let everyone else in, I went down to the front on the left side of the theater. There I met one of the coordinators and gave him my CD with the instrumental version of my song for them to play. He informed me that I would be the first performer. I sat down and relaxed. Soon it started. A Korean guy and gal who were both TV personalities were the announcers. They called me up and asked me in English if I liked Korea. I told them that I did and that when I was younger I had lived in Korea for fifteen years. They translated this into Korean. Then they asked if I could speak Korean, and I answered in Korean that I could speak a little. Then in Korean they said, "Oh, are you going to sing a Korean song?"

"No," I answered, "I'm going to sing a song I wrote in English."

"Do you know any Korean songs?"

"Yes, my favorite Korean song is *Newt-ki Jun-ae* (Before It's Too Late)."

"Can you sing it for us?"

Don singing in a talent show.

"Sure!" I started singing. Later Jeff Jackson told me that many of the Koreans around him in the audience were singing along with me and clapping in time. But I had only gotten a couple of lines into it when I think the announcers must have gotten word from the producer to cut it short. They jumped in and said, "Thank you. Now what song are you going to sing for the contest?" I told them it was a song I wrote for my girlfriend called "Christmas Carol" because her name is Carol and she was born on Christmas Day. I sang, and behind me at the back of the stage was a screen about twelve feet by twelve feet with my face projected live while I was singing the song. When I first sent in the form saying I would volunteer to perform in their talent show, long before leaving for Korea, I had it in my mind that I'd be on a little wooden makeshift stage with a few people listening. Instead I was on this large high-tech stage, with the large projection screen behind me, stage fog machines going in front of me, and probably a thousand people in the audience, including Jimmy and Rosalynn Carter, and sitting next to them, Corazon Aquino, the past president of the Philippines. I was sure glad I went first. After I finished I could just sit and enjoy the other performers. First prize was given to a Filipino group who did a song and dance with audience participation. Even though I didn't win I enjoyed performing, and a good time was had by all.

At the end of the week on Friday, the finishing work was all done. Jimmy and Rosalynn Carter, along with the head of Habitat for Humanity, came and gave a Bible to each of the four families who would be living in the building we finished. Then the owners were each given the keys to their new homes. The unit that we had worked in the first day was for a family of three—father, mother, and young son. The father and mother had been working alongside us during the week, and we had gotten to know them well. The father seemed very stoic until he was given the key. Then he broke down in tears. So did I; it was very moving.

That night, they had entertainment for us. Jeff, David, Nati, and I were standing near the stage before the show began, and a beautiful young Korean lady started talking to us. Her name was Lee, Tae-won, and she was going to sing as part of the evening's show. She mentioned that she had played the part of Queen Min, the queen who had been murdered by the Japanese at the end of the Yi dynasty, in a musical production titled *Queen Min*. I later saw that she was performing this role in London. But the first thing that caught my attention was her name. Itaewon is the famous shopping area for foreigners in Seoul near the U.S. Army headquarters of Yongsan. Her name is almost the same as the shopping area. I had to ask if anyone ever mentioned that her name sounded like Itaewon, the shopping area in Seoul. She laughed and said, "Yes, people often mention that." We all took a few pictures with her. Later she sang, and she had a most lovely voice to go along with her gorgeous looks. This was a beautiful ending to a wonderful though somewhat physically demanding week.

Jeff, Nati, and I stayed a few extra days. The first night back in Seoul, I had dinner with nine former staff members who had worked with me during the 1980s at the Pearl S. Buck Foundation. It was a lovely reunion with them. The day after that, Sunday, I visited my former father-in-law who was in the hospital, his wife, two of my ex-brothers-in-law, and a couple of ex-nephews. One of the nephews had graduated from the Hankuk University of Foreign Studies where I used to teach. It was a very emotional meeting, and I still had and even now have strong feelings for all of them. The older of the two brothers-in-law suggested that since my ex-wife, his sister, and I were both still not married that they were hoping maybe we'd get back together. I gently deflated that helium balloon and told him that I had a very serious relationship with a woman in Detroit. I still love my former in-laws. They are wonderful people, and they are still part of Otto's family even though Mi-yun and I are divorced.

The next day, I grabbed a highway bus to Mukho, my former Peace Corps town. Its name has changed to Donghae-shi (East Sea City). Even when I lived there the people thought that Mukho should be a city, as it had a population of more than 50,000 people and supposedly that was the cutoff between town and city. During the last few months I lived in Mukho, they had begun tearing up the beach south of Mukho where the Bupyeong Airport used to sit. The government had announced that they were building a new and larger seaport there. After it was finished Mukho and Bupyeong were combined as one municipality and renamed Donghae-shi.

Modern Mukho Middle School in 2001.

Mukho's smaller and much more orderly fishing fleet in 2001. (Compare with the earlier photo of Mukho's fishing fleet.)

I got off the bus and walked around thinking someone would recognize me, a crowd would gather, and I would be carried around on the shoulders of some of my former students. No one recognized me. I went to Mukho Middle School; it still carries its original name. The students were on break, but I talked to some young people who were playing on the playground. "I used to teach here," I told them in Korean. They looked rather disinterested and seemed to be thinking, *"Who cares?"* All of the buildings that I had worked in were gone, and they had brand-spanking-new, very modern school buildings. I liked the old ones better, and I reminded myself of the Peace Corps Volunteer who thought that the Koreans should keep living in thatched roof houses because they were quaint. *"Bring the quaint old school buildings back,"* I wanted to yell.

I walked over to Mukho's port; it is still called Port of Mukho. It had a far smaller number of fishing vessels, and instead of it looking like bumper cars with them all jammed in confusingly, they were in two very tidy rows. *"My God, they've ruined my town,"* I thought to myself.

I found a small hotel right where the Mukho Theater used to be. The theater had burned down long ago, I was told. The Daehung Hasuk and the Chang shin Yeogwan were also gone. I ate dinner, went to sleep early, and returned back to Seoul the next day with a sad and heavy heart, but with lots of fond memories of the "good ol' days."

Finally, my last visit to Korea (until the next time) was in 2011. The Korean government had already been staging U.S. Peace Corps Volunteers' Revisits to Korea for two or three years. Other than the airfare over, the Korean government covered all the costs for a weeklong revisit back to Korea. There were two revisits each year: one in the summer and another in the fall. Each time before, I had held off thinking, *"Maybe next year."* I probably would have held off again in 2011 except that I got an email from Ed Harper saying that he and Bill Tuscola were going in July of 2011 and that there were still a few spaces left. Ed suggested, "Don, why don't you sign up?" With fond remembrances of our times together back in our volunteering days, I talked it over with Carol. We decided there was no time like the present and signed up. Carol was excited to see the Land of the Morning Calm that I talk about all the time. I also couldn't wait for her to see it and to spend time again with Ed and Bill. In addition, Steve (who was typing on the airplane in 1972) Marquette from our K-23 training group was also going.

Ed told us he'd fly up from his hometown in the south, and he'd have a short layover in Detroit where he'd get on the direct flight from Detroit to Seoul. Carol and I made sure that we were on the same flight from Detroit with seats next to Ed, so we'd have the fourteen-hour trip to talk with him.

We landed at the Incheon Airport on Saturday, July 9, one day short of the thirty-ninth anniversary of the day we K-23s landed at Kimpo Airport to begin our Peace Corps training. Ed, Carol, and I got our bags and then went out to the bus stop for the downtown Seoul bus. There were a couple of cute young Chinese ladies looking at the bus route sign, and Ed asked them where they were going. "Downtown Seoul. Is this the right bus?" they asked. We assured them it was.

As we got into the city I was telling Carol all about our surroundings. Ed was sitting in the seat in front of us, and the two Chinese gals were in the seat just in front of Ed. We passed Yonsei University, and I was telling Carol all about how it was founded by American missionaries and so forth. At the next stop near Ehwa University, still the largest women's university in the world and where I had spilled milk all over the table in their cafeteria way back in 1972, Ed told the Chinese gals that this was where they wanted to get off. I watched them exit the bus and get their bags from the storage compartment underneath.

"Why are they getting off here?" I asked Ed.

"Oh, they were told that there are a lot of cheap hotels around Gwanghwa-mun."

"But this isn't Gwanghwa-mun. This is the Ehwa University stop. Gwanghwa-mun is the next stop."

"Oh no, we gotta tell them," he said as the bus pulled away.

"Wow, they're not going to trust Americans anymore," I said, and we laughed.

"Gee, I hope they figure out where they are and how to get to Gwanghwa-mun." Ed replied. Two stops later, we got off at Insa-dong, which is a popular shopping area that used to be full of antique shops, but now has a mixture of many shops and restaurants.

Our hotel, the Somerset Palace, was nearby. As we walked along, we saw several elderly men who were sitting in a small pocket park-like area. They were singing an old Korean folk song, which Ed and I both remembered—at least we remembered the chorus part. We both walked up and started singing with them. They stood up, and we all finished the song together. After our raucous finish we talked to them for a while.

Then we walked to the hotel for check-in. Our apartment-style room had a bedroom, living room area, kitchenette, bathroom, and even a washer and dryer. From our window we looked out onto the grounds of Kyungbok Palace, where Queen Min was murdered, and just beyond it the "Blue House" where Korea's president lives.

Monday's activities included a visit to the Ministry of Foreign Affairs and Trade, a visit to the brand-new Samsung Library at Yonsei University, and later in the afternoon a visit to the U.S. Ambassador's residence known as the Habib House, named after Philip C. Habib who was the ambassador from 1971 to 1974 and who insisted that when they built this new ambassador's home it retain the strictly Korean style of the original. The Habib House is a beautiful *hanok*-style structure, which looks like a palace building or a Buddhist temple. The ambassador in 2011 was Kathy Stephens, who was a trainee in the K-35 Peace Corps Training Program. She went on to serve her two years of Peace Corps, took the Foreign Service Exam, but unlike me she was contacted and became a Foreign Service Officer in the State Department. During some of my Pearl S. Buck Foundation years, she was serving in Korea, and I would upon occasion run into her in the elevator on my way to the second floor visa section. I remember one afternoon getting on the elevator on the second floor and running into Kathy and an American priest I knew well. I greeted both of them, and the priest who had been visiting with Kathy asked how I knew her. Kathy and I explained our Peace Corps connection. When we got out of the elevator in the lobby, Kathy shook the priest's hand, said some parting words to the two of us, and got back into the elevator. As we walked out the priest said, "Kathy is a brilliant person, and she is doing an excellent job." I told him, "I know, she's incredible."

When we RPCV's (Returned Peace Corps Volunteers) assembled in the living and dining room area of the Habib House, Kathy walked in. I went right up to her and said, "Hi, Kathy. I'm Don Haffner." Since I was now bald and a couple of decades older, I didn't expect she'd know who I was right off the bat without hearing my name. She actually looked exactly the same as when I was running into her in the 1980s at the embassy. We talked a bit, and I handed her a copy of my CD, *Haff Here, Haff There.* She thanked me, and after Carol took a couple of pictures of me with Kathy, I stepped aside so that others could speak with her. I was telling a couple of the other RPCVs how I had taught Kathy taekwondo back in 1975 when one of the embassy staff in attendance overheard and told me I might be in the taekwondo group photo on the wall near the front door. Carol and I wandered over, and sure enough there I was. In fact, I'm standing right behind Kathy in the photo along with about twenty other K-35s and several Korean women who had done a taekwondo exhibition at the *dojang* the day the picture was taken. Ed was in the picture too, as he had also taken instruction from Mr. Park and me, so I called over to Ed to make sure he didn't miss the photo. (It is the same photo that appears earlier.)

The highlight of the week for me was Tuesday. Before leaving home for Korea, we were asked if there were any individuals from our Peace Corps days we would like to see again. I sent back that I would love to see my second-to-last co-teacher at the boys' middle school, Mr. Hyun, Jong-jin. They were able to find him because he still worked for the school system in Gangwon Province as the Principal of Chuncheon High School. Chuncheon is the capital of Gangwon-do, and Chuncheon High School is the premier boys' high school in the province. A van picked Carol and me up at 8:30 a.m. in front of the Somerset Palace. Besides the driver there were two other Koreans who accompanied us—a cameraman who documented the day's activities and our guide, Mrs. Hong, Hye-Jeong. In addition, a fellow RPCV, George Manistee, who had been a volunteer in a school near Chuncheon also tagged along. Now with an expressway connection between Seoul and Chuncheon the trip only took a couple of hours rather than the four hours it used to take.

When we arrived Mr. Hyun was waiting at the front gate under an umbrella because it was raining. After more than three decades, it was wonderful to see him. We went into the school and entered his office where we met the Vice Principal and some other teachers. We sat for coffee, and Mr. Hyun gave me a present of a beautiful lacquered papier maché box that his wife had made. Interestingly enough, even though when we were co-teachers back in Mukho we spoke to each other in English most of the time, Mr. Hyun spoke only in Korean throughout our visit. One of the first things that he said to me was, "Do you remember Dr. Kim?" I answered, "Yes, I do. Did you marry his daughter?" He laughed and informed me that indeed he had as I had predicted back in 1975. He also told me that he had entered the Korean Army shortly after I finished Peace Corps. This is when we lost contact with each other. He had stayed in the military for ten years finishing with the rank of Captain.

I presented him with a copy of my CD *Haff Here, Haff There* and a large coffee table book that the Returned Peace Corps Volunteer/Friends of Korea group in the U.S. had published in 2009 titled *Through Our Eyes: Peace Corps In Korea, 1966–1981*. In it are a couple of pictures that I had taken in Mukho and the story of Mr. Hyun's and my visit to Yongchu Waterfall when the young lady fell into the mountain pool and I jumped in to save her.

After coffee in his office, we went to visit the English class of an American teacher who worked at Chuncheon High School. She was not a volunteer but a paid instructor. Peace Corps, of course, left Korea in 1981 because Korea was already a developed country by then. On our way to the class Mr. Hyun asked me a question.

"Do you remember when you saved the lady who fell into the pool?"

"Yes," I replied, "In fact, the story is in the book I just gave you."

"I look forward to reading it," he responded.

In the classroom, we met the teacher, Mary Amherstburg. The young male students had made what my wife called "cootie catchers." They are made by folding a piece of paper with hidden words and numbers within it. After picking a square and looking at the number, the cootie catcher is opened and closed up and down and side to side until the number is reached. Inside these cootie catchers were written different occupations. When they stopped the students had to read the occupation they finished on. "Oh, I'll be a firefighter," one student said. When the class ended, Mary came along with Mr. Hyun, the vice principal, George, Carol, Mrs. Hong, and our cameraman as we exited the school. We all visited their school library in a separate building after I told Mr. Hyun that Carol is a librarian.

Then we went off to lunch. We went to a lovely old wooden cabin-like structure, which housed a restaurant with excellent Korean food. Mr. Hyun ordered a bottle of *soju* (Korean liquor), and he, George, and I polished it off while eating a huge spread of food. Then Mr. Hyun suggested that his vice principal and Ms. Amherstburg head back for afternoon classes while he would stay with the rest of us, and we'd have another bottle of *soju*. They left and Mr. Hyun, George, and I drank some more. Carol found the *soju* too strong for her taste, but she loved the food.

Don and Mr. Hyun drinking *soju*.

After talking and drinking the early afternoon away, it was time to leave. We all used the restrooms. Carol and Mrs. Hong went to the Women's WC while Mr. Hyun, George and I went to the Men's. (The men's and women's toilets are not together in the same room anymore.) Also, Carol used a squat toilet for the first time. She did not come out screaming or crying as Patty Olivet had in Gwangju during our K-23 training program. But, of course, I had forewarned her of such a possibility. At the door, Mr. Hyun started tearing up, and I started tearing up too. We hugged each other. He said something in Korean to Mrs. Hong, which I didn't catch; we bowed to each other while shaking hands. Carol, George, Mrs. Hong, and I then ran out into the rain toward our van.

In the van, Mrs. Hong asked if I had understood what Mr. Hyun had said. I told her I hadn't. She told me that he had said, *"Man-gam-ie kyo-cha-handa!"* She explained that in English it means: "There are ten thousand feelings welling up inside of me." I teared up again as she told me this. In Korean the word *man*, ten thousand, is used to mean forever or uncountable. A fountain pen is called a *man-yun-pil* (ten thousand year writing implement). Instead of victory, Koreans yell *man-sei* (ten thousand years). Also, *man* is a basic unit for numbering. *Ship-man* (ten, ten thousands) is in English one hundred thousand, *paik-man* (one hundred, ten thousands) is one million and *chun-man* (one thousand, ten thousands) is ten million. So the meaning of his phrase is much deeper and more meaningful than the English translation provides. In our youth, Mr. Hyun and I had spent many hours together in the classroom and had spent many hours hiking around Mukho together on weekends, swimming during the non-swimming season, and saving a young lady's life. I too had ten thousand feelings and memories welling up in my heart and mind of the most wonderful years of my life. Almost as much as I love America, I also love Korea and the Korean people and especially certain special ones like my favorite co-teacher and now Chuncheon High School's Principal Hyun, Jong-jin and former Mukho Middle School's Principal Yoo, Hyung-sul.

After explaining Mr. Hyun's heartfelt expression, Mrs. Hong began telling us that her high school-aged son wasn't doing as well in English as she wanted and that she was very concerned that he was not studying hard enough. She asked if I would be willing to talk to him on the phone and encourage him to study harder. Of course, I agreed. She called him right up and handed the cell phone to me after explaining who I was. I greeted him in English. Then, also in English, I told him that learning English well was very important. "English is the language of the world," I said. I explained to him that in every country English is the language of travel and business. It is necessary to know English for every job, so no matter what he wanted to do after finishing his schooling English would be needed. He thanked me for my sage advice. Then I gave the phone back to Mrs. Hong, and she thanked me profusely for my encouraging words to her son.

The rest of the week flew by. At last, after thirty-nine years since first landing in Korea for Peace Corps Training, including almost fifteen years of living in Korea and with three visits to Korea since those years ended, Carol and I visited Panmunjom, the truce village in the DMZ (demilitarized zone), with our revisit group. Even though virtually every foreign tourist who visits Korea goes there, I had never seen Panmunjom before. It is a surreal place, but I wasn't overly impressed, and I still think going to visit Ewha Womans University at the end of our training instead of going to the DMZ was the right move. I just wish I hadn't been such a klutz in the cafeteria there. (Remember the spilled milk? No use crying over it now, though.)

Other activities during our revisit included seeing a fun comedy stage production called *Nanta,* attending a wonderful *gayageum* (Korean sitar-like instrument) performance, and having Korean traditional experiences with Korean Youth Volunteers. With them we toured a palace, which had not been open to the public during the years I had lived in Korea. I was paired with a cute middle school girl as my tour guide. At one point in the tour, she pointed to a tree.

"That tree was given a royal title by the king. There is one other tree in Korea that was also given a title, but I don't know where it is."

"Oh, it's in Songnisan National Park," I told her.

"Really!"

"Yes, the story is that when the king came near the tree, it raised its branches so the king could easily pass by. Afterwards the king gave the tree a royal title."

"I think you know more about Korean history than I do," said my young guide.

"No, I just happen to have visited Songnisan years ago, and I was impressed by that story," I replied.

Every night we had wonderful dinners including a reception at the swanky Lotte Hotel hosted by the Ministry of Foreign Affairs and Trade at which I sang a cappella (or is that archipelago) "Yesterday" by the Beatles and *"Newtki Junae"* (Before It's Too Late), my go-to Korean bar drinking song, which was originally sung by Kim, Chu-ja. I sang it in Korean first and then again with an English version (not a direct translation) that I came up with many years ago. My English version follows:

Before It's Too Late

Before it's too late, 'fore it's too late
Come on back here now to me

In my mind I know just what I would say to you
I would give my soul and possessions to you

But if you go, my heart will ache, my soul will break
My life will quickly fade

The last night of the revisit, we went to the Seoul Yacht Club on Yoiedo just behind the National Assembly Building, home of the legislative branch of the South Korean government. During our Peace Corps days, we would have never guessed that there would be a Seoul Yacht Club, and yet there we were for dinner. It was a wonderful meal, including a darling salad with the dressing served in half of a small bird's eggshell, and for the main course, sirloin steak with BBQ sauce, tomato sauce marinade, and endive *kimchi*—a far cry from the simple fare we had all eaten every day during our Peace Corps service. The musical entertainment for the farewell dinner was a trio of musicians including: on Piano—Park, Kyoung-hoon, on Cello—Kang, Chan-wook, and on *Saenghwang* (the only chord musical instrument among the traditional Korean wind instruments)—Kim, Hyo-young. After the dinner and entertainment, we wrote messages on a yard-wide "dream lantern" with strings attached to a holder with a candle in it. I wrote "Peaceful Korean Unification" on ours. Each table had one. Then we went out and held them up, lit the candles, and let go of them. They flew off right over

Entertainment at the Peace Corps Korea Revisit dinner in 2011 at the Seoul Marina Club House.

the National Assembly Building. I said, "I can see tomorrow's headlines, 'Peace Corps Volunteers start National Assembly Building on Fire with Flaming Dream Lanterns.'" It was a beautiful ending to a wonderful week filled with camaraderie, memories, and love. If I had a dollar for every time we were thanked throughout the week by Koreans for helping their nation develop into the modern, capitalist, democratic, wealthy trading nation that it is today, as the Bare Naked Ladies said oh so well, "I'd be rich." ("If I Had a Million Dollars," written by Steven Page and Ed Robertson, performed by Barenaked Ladies.)

Obviously, I love singing, and one of the songs I break into upon occasion while going about my daily activities is "My Way" made famous by Frank Sinatra, who as my father often said, enunciated and projected oh so well. When I get to the lines:

> Regrets, I've had a few
> But then again too few to mention
> ("My Way," written by Paul Anka, performed by Frank Sinatra.)

I can't help remembering that I've had enough to mention, and I have mentioned some of them within these pages. But by now it's all "water under the dam,' or is it "water over the bridge?"

My first marriage, which ended in 1991, is a regret—except, of course, for the wonderful part when we had a son. I probably married the first time for all the wrong reasons, but my second wife and I married for all the right reasons. As mentioned earlier, we met in 1998 at Recording for the Blind and Dyslexic where I worked from 1998 until the Michigan studio closed in 2009.

Carol was a volunteer reader at RFB&D from 1996 to 2009. As I mentioned in the dedication to this book, love is lovelier the second time around. This second time it was true love, and Carol and I are true soulmates. It was worth the long wait through most of the 1990s when I was busy raising Otto and when I didn't date at all till I met the love of my life, Carol.

In our late middle age, or in my case closer to old age, we are the sum total of the decisions we made throughout our lives. Thankfully, I learned from the mistakes I made while young. But even when young the two most important decisions of my youth—attending Albion College and joining the Peace Corps—were perfect for me. Going to Albion showed me that even though I wasn't the sharpest knife in the drawer, I could compete. I learned that, if nothing else, my personality and my wits would pull me through even the toughest times. Still the best decision of my life and the most important one was deciding to join the Peace Corps. I would not be who I am today if I had not made that decision. My life would have been very different. I would probably have ended up stuck in an uninteresting job in Detroit. I would also probably have been miserable and always had an empty place in my heart where my memories of Korea now dwell. My wanderlust certainly would have been unfulfilled. But instead I've had an interesting and exciting life. I feel an inimitable contentment. In addition, my life has given me something, hopefully interesting, to write about in my late middle to slightly old age, and you are nearly finished reading about it now.

But where did my wanderlust come from? Was it from reading or at least looking at the pictures of many *National Geographic* magazines as a kid? Or was I born with a gene that caused it? Was it nature or nurture? Maybe I got a gene from my great-grandmother Haffner's side of the family like her good ol' cousin, Willy Schwiegershausen, who rode his bicycle around the world.

Now I've come full circle as Willy did. I used to say while living in Korea that "I'm from Detroit, and Detroit is a nice place to be *from*." I'd tell people that Detroit was one of the most segregated metropolitan areas in the country. With the city of Detroit at that time mostly black but many, even most, of the suburbs lilly-white, it was also possibly the most racist city in the U.S. I was born in Deaconess Hospital on Jefferson Avenue in Detroit, Michigan, and then my parents moved out to the lilly-white, downriver suburb of Allen Park as so many white people did in those days. Yet, as explained before, I don't think of myself as an Allen Parker, a Detroiter, a Michigander, a United Statesian (I made this term up) or a North American only, but as a "citizen of the world"—and what a wonderful world it is. Here in the summer of 2016 I sit at my desk in Beverly Hills, unfortunately not the one in California (only kidding), but the suburb of Detroit.

I'm filled with wonder at the chimerical nature of this world. As I often tell my students at our local community college where I teach, truth is stranger and funnier than fiction. Detroit, with a population more than eighty percent black, has a white mayor while America elected a black president, Barrack Obama, twice (once in 2008 and again in 2012). South Korea, with its male-chauvinist, Confucian ways, elected a woman to be president in 2013 and it is the first Northeast Asian country to have a female leader. Gotta love this strange, weird, bizarre, exceptional world we live in, don't ya?

In the evening of my life, the autumn heading into winter, I can't help wondering, what if? I've read many biographies over the years, and I've noticed that often great men had overbearing mothers, mothers who pushed them, pressured them into succeeding. My mother was surprised I had done as well as I did in college. I can't help thinking that if my mother and/or my father had pushed me more and had had more confidence in me then maybe I would have been President of the United States or Secretary-General of the United Nations, but then again, maybe not. Even with having had to push myself, I've had a successful life all in all, so far. With my personality, I probably wouldn't have done well if pushed anyway. My contrary nature would have caused me to go the opposite way. I've made some mistakes along the way and tried to learn from them. These mistakes later helped me to make some of the good choices that I've made through the years, especially, like I just mentioned a few pages ago, getting married for a second time for the right reasons. I also made the great choice of going to grad school in Brattleboro, Vermont, at the School for International Training (SIT). After SIT, I decided, thankfully, to accept the job offer from the Pearl S. Buck Foundation (PSBF), rather than an offer from a leading American defense contractor to teach English to Saudi airmen in Jeddah, Saudi Arabia. Even though the PSBF job paid way less than half of the salary offered by the defense contractor, I thought then and think now that money is less important than job satisfaction—not to mention following your moral compass and values.

At any rate, I consider myself to have been very lucky, especially that day a manila envelope came to my college dorm mail slot from Peace Corps asking if I'd be interested in volunteering in Korea. That truly was the first day of the rest of my life!

That's All, Folks!

Glossary

ajumoni: aunt (friendly form of address to women)

angyeong: eyeglasses

anju: food consumed with alcohol

ashidashipi: as you know

baekwajeom: department store

banchan: side dish

bangong: anti-Communism

begae: pillow, usually like a bean-bag

bogunso: health center

bokjaphaeyo: complicated

boricha: barley tea

boshintang: dog soup

bulgogi: marinated beef

chegae: thick soup

chibujang: branch manager/resident director (nim at the end makes it honorific)

CIS: Culturally InSensitive

dabang: tea room, café

dakgalbi: marinated chicken with bones

DMZ: DeMilitarized Zone

dobok: taekwondo clothing

dojang: taekwondo gym

eomeoni: mother

EMU: Eastern Michigan University

ESL: English as a Second Language

gage: small convenience store

gaijin: foreigner (Japanese)

gamsahamnida: thank you

gayageum: Korean sitar-like instrument

gimpop: sushi

gisaeng: traditional female entertainers (geisha in Japanese)

gwonseub: custom

gyojang-nim: principal with hororific "nim" ending

halmeoni: grandmother

hanbok: traditional Korean clothing

hangeul: Korean alphabet

hanok (jip): traditional Korean-style house

hasuk (jip): boarding house

hwajangshil: lavatory

hwatu: Korean card game

ibul: coverlet

insa: greeting

JAL: Japan Air Lines

jip: house

jjigae: stew

KAVA: Korea Association of Voluntary Agencies

kimchi: spicy pickled cabbage

maekju: beer

makgeolli: milky colored alcoholic beverage

man nyeon: ten thousand years

miguk: America

miguk saram: American

mipalgun: American 8th Army

mog: Peace Corps contraction for mog-yok-tang

mogyoktang: bath house

myeolchi: anchovies

myeolgong: destroy communism

nim: honorific suffix used with job titles

nun: snow, eye

OKAW: Organization of Korean American Women

ondol: under the floor radiant heating system

PCV: Peace Corps Volunteer

poshidashipi: as you can see

ppangjip: bakery

PRIST: PRe-Invitational Staging

RFB&D: Recording For the Blind & Dyslexic

RPCV: Returned Peace Corps Volunteer

PSBF: Pearl S. Buck Foundation

RA: Resident Assistant

ryokan: traditional inn (Japanese)

saenghwang: traditional wind instrument

saram: person

sarang   : love

SEMI: SouthEast MIchigan RPCV

seonsaeng-nim: honorific for teacher with "nim" ending to make it even more honorific sikdang: restaurant

SIT: School for International Training

soju: clear distilled beverage

suljip: bar

takgujang: ping-pong parlor

TESOL: Teaching English to Speakers of Other Languages

uri: our

USD: United Shirt Distributors

yangban: aristocrat

yeogwan: inn

yeontan: cylindrical coal briquettes for heating

yo: quilted mattress

ZPG: Zero Population Growth

About the Author

Don Haffner for most of his life has worked for non-profit organizations and in the field of education. Among the positions he has held over the years, he has worked as the Resident Director of the Pearl S. Buck Foundation's Korea Branch, Studio Director of Recording for the Blind and Dyslexic's Michigan Unit, and Associate Dean of the Open Campus of Middlesex Community College in Massachusetts.

Don has three graduate degrees: Master of Arts in International Administration from the School for International Training in Vermont, Master of Science in Education from the University of Southern California, and Master of Arts in History from Oakland University in Michigan.

His career in education began when he joined the Peace Corps fresh out of college. Don served in the Republic of Korea as a middle school English teacher from 1972 through 1975.

Presently, Don Haffner works as an Adjunct Professor of History at Oakland Community College in Royal Oak, Michigan.

CPSIA information can be obtained
at www.ICGtesting.com
Printed in the USA
FFOW01n0301240517
35867FF